Canadian
Industrial Relations

CANADIAN INDUSTRIAL RELATIONS

Eleventh Edition

FRANK KEHOE, B.A., M.B.A.

MAURICE ARCHER, B.Sc. (Econ.), M.A.

CENTURY LABOUR PUBLICATIONS
Oakville, Ontario
Tel: (905) 844-1183   Fax: (905) 844-5030

ELEVENTH EDITION

Copyright © 2005 Frank Kehoe and Maurice Archer
All rights reserved — no part of this book may be
reproduced in any form without permission in writing
from the publisher. First edition, 1980

Canadian Cataloguing in Publication Data

Kehoe, Frank, date
   Canadian Industrial Relations

11th ed.
Includes index
ISBN 0-9690739-6-8

1. Industrial Relations — Canada

2. Labour Relations — Canada

3. Labour — Law and Legislation

4. Trade unions — Canada

5. Archer, Maurice, Date, II.   Title

Printed and bound in Canada

About the Book ...

Canadian Industrial Relations is an up-to-date Canadian textbook that describes clearly and succinctly the various components of the Canadian industrial relations scene, notably the framework used, the parties involved, the laws that apply, the negotiation and administration of collective agreements in both the private and public sectors, and the search for "industrial harmony" through participative management and employee involvement.

As well as descriptive and analytical material, the book contains twenty-five case studies, an actual collective agreement, and three collective bargaining simulations. Based on realistic situations, with current bargaining statistics and other relevant information included, the simulations are suitable for resolution by students who are called upon to act as company and union negotiating teams engaged in a series of collective bargaining sessions. The book also contains a glossary of industrial relations terms and a summary of Ontario's Labour Relations Act, 1995.

About the Authors ...

Frank Kehoe obtained both a B.A. and a Master's Degree in Business Administration from the University of Toronto. His business career has centred on the Industrial Relations area including senior management positions with several major Canadian companies and consulting activities with numerous other organizations including smaller companies. This experience includes extensive activity in the negotiation of collective agreements and arbitration of disputes under collective agreements. He lectured at McMaster University Business School before joining Ryerson University as Professor of Labour Relations.

Maurice Archer received his B.Sc. (Econ.) from the London School of Economics and his M.A. in Economics from Yale University. He is a well-known author of Canadian business and economics texts, and worked in banking and real estate before joining the Ryerson Business Faculty as Professor of Business Management.

Figure 1.1 — A Schematic Presentation of the Canadian Industrial Relations System

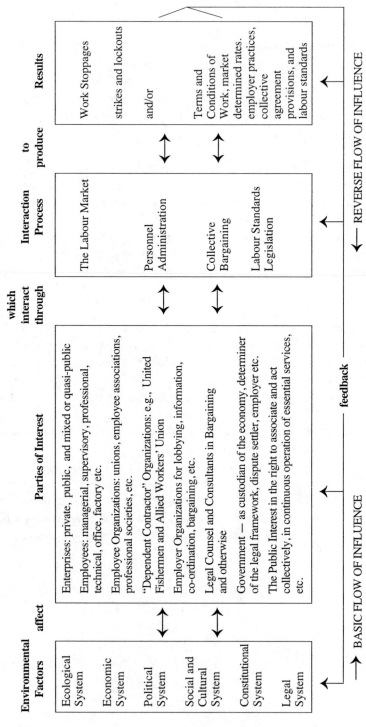

Source: *Canadian Industrial Relations*, The Report of the Task Force on Labour Relations, Ottawa: Queen's Printer, 1969, p.10.

PREFACE

The material in this book is organized in accordance with the model of Canada's industrial relations system shown in Figure 1.1. Thus, in Part A, we look at the basic framework for industrial relations, or, put in another way, the setting for the collective bargaining process, with its occasional labour-management battles and other dramas. It involves an examination of many factors: the economic, social and political circumstances that underlie our North American type of employer-employee interaction; the constitution that divides legislative power in labour matters between our federal and provincial governments; the statutes that govern our labour relations and the history of their development in Canada; and the concept of "protection of the public interest".

In Part B, we look at the parties involved in industrial relations: the labour unions and other employee representatives, their nature, history and philosophy; the employers and their associations, policies and practices; and the so-called third parties: (a) our governments which get involved in conciliation and other attempts to promote harmonious employer-employee relations and (b) the public which often bears the inconvenience and even hardship that prolonged strikes or lockouts often cause, particularly by public sector employees such as teachers, fire-fighters, postal workers, and air traffic controllers.

In Part C, we describe how a trade union recruits new members and how it becomes certified as the bargaining agent for a firm's employees. We also examine the certification procedure itself and give an example of an actual certification application. We then consider how, although unusual, a union may lose its bargaining rights. Finally, we consider the "unfair practices", forbidden by law, that a union or employer may engage in at various stages of the collective bargaining process.

In Part D, we consider how a collective agreement (the basic document that governs employer-employee relations in a unionized business firm or other organization) is negotiated and what it contains, including the provisions of union security. We also consider what can happen if negotiations fail and how an outside conciliator is often brought in to help the parties reach agreement. Finally, we discuss the different types of strikes and other labour actions that can occur and the action of an employer in locking out its employees.

In Part E, we examine the nature and purpose of a grievance procedure and how an outside arbitrator is used to resolve disputes arising out of the collective agreement. We then discuss the key issues of discipline and seniority that are often the subject of labour-management disputes in the day-to-day interpretation of a collective agreement.

In Part F, we look at industrial relations in the public sector and the changes that have been made in recent years— notably, the extension of the right to strike to many public service employees.

In Part G, entitled *The Way Ahead*, we describe some of the attempts that have been made to improve industrial relations in Canada. In Chapter 21, the concept of "industrial harmony" is explained. In Chapter 22, the experience of some companies with industrial harmony is reviewed. And, finally, in Chapter 23, the focus is on participative management and employee involvement at Ford of Canada.

In Part H, entitled *Collective Bargaining Simulations*, we provide: three simulations, a costing exercise, and a collective agreement. The first two simulations and the costing exercise are contained in Chapter 24. With the simulations, students can be formed into management and union teams and asked to resolve the differences between them as the basis for a new Collective Agreement. The third simulation, *Consolidated Electrical Products*, contained in Chapter 25, is more sophisticated, requiring greater effort on the part of union and management negotiating teams to reach a new agreement. With these simulations, handled as suggested, students should get the feel of actual contract negotiations. The agreement that is being renegotiated, in the case of Consolidated Electrical Products, is set out in Chapter 26.

In Part I, we include twenty case studies covering different aspects of the industrial relations process.

In Part J, we relate five true stories from the industrial relations world. The first three involve negotiations for a new collective agreement. The other two focus upon employee involvement and participation.

In Part K, we provide a glossary of industrial relations terms.

Finally, in Part L, we include a summary of Ontario's Labour Relations Act, 1995 — the labour relations statute now in force in Ontario.

Summary of Contents

Table of Contents

PART B: LABOUR, EMPLOYERS, GOVERNMENT, AND THE PUBLIC

PART E: ADMINISTERING THE COLLECTIVE AGREEMENT

PART H: COLLECTIVE BARGAINING
SIMULATIONS

PART I: CASE STUDIES

Unfair Practices

Union Certification

Arbitration Cases

PART J: TRUE STORIES

Negotiations for a Collective Agreement

Employee Involvement and Participation

Developed and Implemented — Accident Level Improved on Plant
Comparison Basis, from 31 out of 33 to Second Best

CHAPTER 1: CANADA'S SYSTEM OF INDUSTRIAL RELATIONS

This book is about the theory and practice of industrial relations in Canada. Our first step therefore is to define exactly what we mean by the term "industrial relations" and its relationship to other related terms such as labour relations, union-management relations, collective bargaining, and labour economics.

1.1 INDUSTRIAL RELATIONS DEFINED

According to most writers and practitioners, industrial relations is a broad term that covers all forms of interaction between employers and employees. Therefore all the other terms mentioned above describe specific aspects of this whole system of employer-employee interaction. They are in effect subsystems of the industrial relations system. Also, logically, personnel management (or administration) and organizational behaviour, although usually treated as separate areas of study, can be considered as an integral part of industrial relations.

The term "industrial relations system" refers to the institutional framework within which employer-employee interaction takes place. Thus, according to the Woods Task Force on Labour Relations in Canada, the industrial relations system is:

> "the complex of market and institutional arrangements, private and public, which society permits, encourages or establishes to handle superior-subordinate relationships growing out of employment and related activities."[1]

1.2 FRAMEWORK FOR ANALYSIS

A great deal of effort has already been expended by various people in setting out in conceptual form a basic framework for the analysis of industrial relations.

---

[1] *Canadian Industrial Relations*. The Report of the Task Force on Labour Relations. Queen's Printer, Ottawa, 1969, p. 9.

Dunlop Model

In the United States, John Dunlop presented in the 1950s what is now considered to be a classic model involving four basic elements.[2] These four elements, according to Dunlop, are as follows:

1. *The actors* — These are the three key parties which Dunlop called the "actors", involved in industrial relations:

    a) employees, their organizations, and their spokespersons;

    b) employers, their organizations, and their spokespersons; and

    c) government agencies and specialized private agencies concerned with employer-employee relationships.

2. *The environment* — These are environmental factors such as production technology, size of the market, and the relative prestige and power of the employers and labour unions.

3. *Ideology held* — This is the ideology held by each of the "actors". Unless these ideologies are compatible between the partners and between each party and the general public, no industrial relations stability is possible.

4. *The Web of Rules* — These are the rules and regulations that govern the economy and the work place and the parties within them.

Craig Model

Later, in Canada, Professor Alton Craig developed a schematic model of the Canadian industrial relations system that was subsequently used, in adapted form, by the Woods Task Force.[3] This schematic model is set out in Figure 1.1. It states, in its simplest version, that environmental factors (such as the legal system) affect the various interested parties (such as employers and labour unions) who then interact (through, for example, collective bargaining) to produce results (such as a strike or a collective agreement). The model also shows that there is a basic flow of influence in one direction and a reverse flow in the other. For example, labour unions are affected by existing laws but also help determine new legislation and repeal of the old.

Four Basic Elements

The four basic elements that can be identified in this industrial relations

---

[2] *John T. Dunlop, Industrial Relations Systems*, Rinehart and Winston, New York, 1958.
[3] *Alton W. J. Craig, A Model for the Analysis of Industrial Relations Systems*, a paper presented at the annual meeting of the Canadian Political Science Associations on June 7, 1967.

model are as follows:

1. The **ENVIRONMENT**

a) *Ecological System*
— What is the physical environment, including technology used in the work place?

b) *Economic System*
— How is work organized? What is the factory population? What is the level of unemployment? How is income distributed? Are employees' real earnings substantial? Are workers becoming worse off in time of inflation?

c) *Political System*
— Are workers permitted to form trade unions? Are unions recognized as bargaining agents for workers? Are employers required by law to bargain in good faith with the unions? On whose side is the government?

d) *Social System*
— Is there deep-rooted animosity between labour and management? Does class warfare exist on the factory floor? Do employees willingly accept orders? Do they resent authority?

e) *Cultural System*
— Are trade unions part of the tradition of the people? Are workers willing to join unions? Are workers naturally loyal and disciplined?

f) *Constitutional System*
— Who has legislative jurisdiction over labour matters? What is the jurisdiction of the federal and provincial governments?

g) *Legal System*
— What rights and duties does the Common Law place upon employer and employee? What statutory laws govern labour-management relations, working conditions, wage rates, holidays, occupational health and safety, etc.?

2. The **PARTICIPANTS**

a) *Employees and their organizations*
— labour unions
— staff associations
— Labour Councils
— Labour Federations

— Canadian Labour Congress and CNTU
— Professional Societies

b) *Employers and their organizations*
— domestic and multinational corporations
— industry associations
— government enterprises, departments

c) *The Federal and Provincial Governments*
— Labour Relations Boards
— Arbitration Commissions
— Conciliators and mediators
— Ministers of Labour
— Departments of Labour

d) *The Public*
— Consumers' Association of Canada
— newspapers
— irate citizens

3. The INTERACTION PROCESS

a) *Demand for different types of labour*
— rates of industry growth
— rates of mechanization and automation
— capital per worker
— foreign product competition

b) *Supply of labour*
— age, size, and rate of growth of population
— education, skills, experience
— female participation rate
— immigration
— restrictions on entry into a trade or profession
— unemployment benefits

c) *Wage rates*
— supply and demand
— minimum wage rates
— fringe benefits

d) *Collective bargaining*
— union vs. employer
— Labour Relations Act

e) *Personnel management*
— management's policy towards the employees

— Theory X and Theory Y
— Theory Z

f) *Labour legislation*
— Labour Relations Act
— Employment Standards Act
— Occupational Health and Safety Act
— Other statutes

4. The RESULTS

a) *Collective agreement*
— terms of employment
— better wages, etc.

b) *Strikes and lockouts*

c) *Sabotage, go-slow, etc.*

d) *Closing down of plants*

e) *Government intervention.*

1.3 LABOUR RELATIONS

This is the term most commonly used to describe the interaction that takes place between employee organizations (notably labour unions) on the one hand and employer organizations on the other. The main focus is on the relationship between the employer and its employees within a particular firm or establishment. The term covers negotiations for a collective agreement to govern the terms of employment of the labour force, and the application and interpretation of the agreement on a day-to-day basis, once it has come into force. Many small problems that arise in the work place are quickly settled at the foreperson or supervisor level. Others, as explained later, may require the use of the grievance procedure as set out in the collective agreement and even the use of an outside arbitrator to settle the dispute. The term, Labour Relations, is also often used as the name for the department in a large firm that has specialist responsibility for the firm's labour-management relations.

The term "union-management relations" is sometimes used instead of labour relations to describe basically the same thing. However, not all employees are represented by unions. Some employee associations are not certified as collective bargaining agents under the federal or provincial Labour Relations Act concerned and, in other cases, no employee association exists. So, strictly speaking, the term "union-management relations" has a narrower scope than the term "labour relations".

1.4 COLLECTIVE BARGAINING

This is the process whereby employees together, rather than singly, negotiate the terms of their employment with their employer. An employee, acting alone, has very little power to secure better terms of employment. However, all or most employees in a firm, acting together or "collectively", have tremendous power to do so. This collective power has been exerted through trade unions (or labour unions) that have emerged as the official representatives, or "bargaining agents" for the workers in various trades and industries. It has been strengthened by labour legislation that requires an employer to recognize and negotiate "in good faith" with the union certified as the bargaining agent for its employees. And it has been reinforced by practices such as the requirement of union membership as a prerequisite for employment.

Another ingredient of the collective bargaining process is the signing, by the company and the trade union, of a collective agreement that sets out in writing the terms of employment for a specified period (usually one, two, or three years) for the union's members. Both parties are required by law to adhere faithfully to the agreement, which includes a provision for settlement of any disputes by arbitration rather than by resort to strikes, lockouts, or other means.

In summary, the collective bargaining process involves:

1. collective rather than individual negotiations by employees with an employer;
2. compulsory recognition by the employer of the union certified as the bargaining agent for the employees;
3. the statutory requirement of "bargaining in good faith" by employer and union;
4. signing by both parties of a written collective agreement setting out the terms of employment of the employees for a stipulated period of time;
5. prohibition of strikes and lockouts during the life of the collective agreement, and
6. compulsory inclusion in the agreement of a requirement for arbitration of outstanding grievances.

1.5 LABOUR ECONOMICS

This is the study of the demand for, and supply of, different types of workers and the resulting wage and employment levels. On the demand side, it involves a consideration of the sales prospects of a firm and industry and the resulting need for employees, the productivity of various types of employees, the type of production technology used, and the relative costs of capital and labour. On the supply side, it involves consideration of the size and nature of the labour force, education, skills, and experience, immigration, hours of work, minimum wage levels, participation of women in the labour force, restrictions on entry into a trade or profession, and so on.

In this book (Chapter 2), we discuss only briefly the economic factors involved in labour-management relations. Nevertheless, we should recognize that the whole topic of labour economics is very important — as it deals with the economic background behind all employer-employee interaction. And this economic background is something that participants in the industrial relations process cannot afford to ignore. If an industry is dying in the face of foreign competition, no amount of labour union action can raise wages and/or increase employment for its members. At many Canadian universities, labour economics is taught as a separate course.

1.6 PERSONNEL MANAGEMENT

This term refers to the way in which a firm's managers, at all the various levels, treat the firm's personnel, or "human resources". It involves the following main areas: recruitment and placement; induction, training, and follow-up; motivation; merit rating and employee evaluation; labour relations; employee services; employee health and safety; and employee records and statistics.

The labour relations area covers such activities as: improving employee morale; the handling, on behalf of management, of collective agreement negotiations; the handling of employee complaints and grievances; the formation and administration of joint management-labour committees; and the development and enforcement of personnel policies involving discipline, discharges, layoffs, promotions, transfers, etc.

Personnel management, it should be emphasized, involves all employees in a firm — not just blue-collar, or plant employees and not just union members. Basically, it is a line function rather than a staff one although there may well be, in the larger firm, a personnel department to assist in this function. In other words, every line manager is involved in managing people. It is not just the concern of a few personnel specialists.

In terms of the industrial relations framework, personnel management is the practical translation of the point of view of one key party (the employer) towards another key party (the employee) in terms of the work place and what the employee is supposed to be doing in it.

1.7 ORGANIZATIONAL BEHAVIOUR

This is the term used to describe the systematic study of a person's behaviour when he or she is employed in a business firm, government department, or other organization. It involves a study of the roles played by individuals in the organization and the relationship of individuals to each other. It attempts to explain how and why people in business firms and other organizations, private or public, act as they do — singly and in groups. It looks at the needs of both managers and non-managers. It enables a person to understand better the problems actually encountered in managing and working with people and the alternative solutions available when confronted by a human relations problem within an organization.

The scope of organizational behaviour includes such topics as: the needs people seek to achieve in their work; the formal and informal organization of the work place; motivation and job satisfaction; styles of leadership; group dynamics; the work environment; delegation of authority; the overcoming of resistance to change; the creation of a harmonious climate for employer-employee relations; principles of good supervision; overcoming communications barriers; job enrichment; and discrimination in the work place.

From the above description, it can be seen that the study of organizational behaviour can shed considerable light on the problems that occur in the work place: why some firms have a much more harmonious employer-employee relationship than others; and how a more harmonious relationship can be developed, often with an improvement in labour productivity. Although a specialized area of study, organizational behaviour is an important part of Canada's industrial relations framework. In many cases, it is the key to better industrial relations.

1.8 WORKPLACE INFORMATION DIRECTORATE

Human Resources Development Canada (HRDC), through its Workplace Information Directorate, is a source of current information about industrial relations and collective bargaining in Canada.

WID has three key publications:

1. **Wage Settlement Bulletin** — this is a monthly publication containing the most up-to-date information on, and analysis of, major wage developments in collective bargaining in Canada.
2. **Collective Bargaining Bulletin** — this is also a monthly publication but which contains information about recently-signed major collective agreements in Canada.
3. **Workplace Gazette** — this is a quarterly publication that provides information and analysis about wage adjustments, collective agreement provisions, innovative workplace practices, work stoppages, upcoming key negotiations and other related topics. Each issue groups the information under the following main headings: wages and work

environment, case studies, articles, Canadian labour laws, and HRDC Departmental Library.

The WID also makes its resources available to negotiators, researchers, economists, consultants, journalists, teachers, etc.

REVIEW QUESTIONS

1. What is meant by the term "industrial relations"?

2. Explain and discuss the Dunlop model of an industrial relations system.

3. What elements are included in the Craig model of the industrial relations system in Canada? What elements, if any, are omitted?

4. Distinguish between labour relations and union-management relations.

5. What are the basic ingredients of collective bargaining? Why do most employees favour such a system? What are the arguments against it?

6. What factors determine the demand for and supply of the following types of labour in Canada: (a) auto workers; (b) medical doctors; (c) accountants; and (d) computer programmers?

7. Explain, with examples, how changes in the demand for and supply of particular types of labour, affect wage and salary rates.

8. What, typically, is the job of the labour relations, or industrial relations department of a large manufacturing firm?

9. "The study of organizational behaviour is the key to better industrial relations in most large firms." Explain and discuss with reference to a particular private firm or public organization.

10. What are the various possible sources of current information about industrial relations and collective bargaining in Canada?

CHAPTER 2: THE POLITICAL, ECONOMIC, AND SOCIAL SETTING

There are many different factors — political, economic, and social — that affect industrial relations in Canada. In this chapter, we look at each broad group in turn.

2.1 POLITICAL FACTORS

Collective Bargaining Rights

In some countries, trade unions are illegal and a person trying to organize or become a member of one is likely to be arrested and put in jail. In other countries, trade unions operate under government control and do not represent the real interests of their members. In the Western democracies, trade unions now enjoy an established place and workers are free to bargain collectively with employers within a legal framework carefully designed to protect the interests of both employer and employee. Of course, the right of employees to establish a trade union and bargain collectively with their employer has not always existed, even in the so-called liberal Western democracies. Only in this century has it come about. In nineteenth-century England, for example, the "Tolpuddle Martyrs", the agricultural labourers who tried to band their fellow workers together to fight for better wages, were charged with criminal conspiracy and, on conviction, were deported to Australia.

Personal Freedoms

Today, in Canada, and in other Western democracies, a variety of personal freedoms have come to be recognized as fundamental human rights. These include freedom of the person, freedom of speech, freedom of religion, freedom of assembly, freedom from discrimination, freedom of the press, freedom of political action, freedom from economic exploitation, the right to own property, freedom to enter into contracts, and the right to receive a minimum standard of living. These fundamental human rights have sometimes been set down on paper, often in a constitutional document or other Act of Parliament. In Canada, this is the Charter of Rights and Freedoms passed by the Federal Parliament in 1980. Of course, the maintenance of these freedoms requires a system of courts and judges that operates independently of government. It also requires the right to vote at periodic elections to change peacefully a government that might start to restrict these fundamental human rights or that proves otherwise undesirable.

Market Freedoms

One of the fundamental rights that we have mentioned is that of owning property. Without it, we would not have private firms acting as employers. As in many communist or socialist countries, the sole employer would be the state. In some countries, as in Canada, state-owned enterprises operate side by side with private ones and their employees are still allowed to bargain collectively. However, in a country in which little or no private enterprise is permitted, the temptation is for the state (which owns all or most property on behalf of its citizens) to deny to its employees the right to bargain collectively — even though they may be dissatisfied with their pay, fringe benefits, or conditions of work.

Although, in Canada, private firms are the rule rather than the exception, they are of course restricted by Parliament in many ways. "Market freedoms" are not usually permitted priority over "social freedoms". Thus there are, for example, minimum wage laws, employment standards acts, pollution control legislation, and human rights codes.

The CLC and the NDP

The trade union movement in Canada has looked upon both the conservative and the liberal parties as right-wing forces, dedicated to preserving the "status quo". That is why the Canadian Labour Congress (CLC) has for many years supported the NDP, a party that offers a more radical and nationalist solution to Canada's social and economic problems. However, unlike the situation in some countries, the CLC does not advocate the overthrow of the present political, economic and social system. It merely wishes to reform it.

Quebec Labour Separatism

In Quebec, some leaders of the trade union movement have adopted a much more radical approach, advocating the reform of the present political system and its replacement by a more left-wing one. This difference in political objective between trade union leaders in Quebec and those in other provinces has made co-operation difficult. Even more of an obstacle to co-operation between Quebec trade unionists and those from the rest of Canada is the more deep-seated language difference, and the ethnic and political differences between French Canadians ("maitres chez nous") and other Canadians. This labour "separatism" has already led to Quebec breakaways from national and international unions. One of the most publicized examples of conflict caused by language differences was in the Canadian Air Traffic Control Association (CATCA), as a result of the attempt to introduce bilingual air traffic service in Quebec. Quebec trade unions have also joined their own provincial labour association, called in English the Confederation of National Trade Unions (CNTU), rather than the Canadian Labour Congress to which most other unions belong.

2.2 ECONOMIC FACTORS

There are many different economic factors, involving the demand for and supply of different types of labour, that affect industrial relations.

Demand for Labour

On the demand side, we look first at the individual firm, the individual industry, and then at industry in general. In the public sector, the demand for labour also has an impact on labour relations. But this varies between different types of public employees, federal, provincial, or municipal, and with their location within Canada.

The Individual Firm

The more successful a firm is in the marketplace, the better it will be able to provide good economic benefits to its employees. Of course, economic success for a firm is a combination of circumstances: favourable external factors (such as new markets), management expertise (for example, ability to take advantage of such markets and to take advantage of new production technology), and worker effort (for example, ability and willingness to produce a good-quality product at reasonable cost). Nevertheless, even in an industry that is enjoying mixed market success, individual firms can prosper depending on the managers and workers involved. And the greater the degree of management-labour harmony, the more likely it is, that this will come about.

The Individual Industry

Is it a growing or declining industry in Canada? Word-processing equipment is an example of the former; textiles an example of the latter. But again, as pointed out in the previous section, there are individual firms that can run against the tide. For example, firms which cannot succeed in producing and marketing word-processing equipment; and textile firms that are succeeding in specialty lines when much of the industry is able to stay alive thanks only to quota restrictions on foreign imports. But, obviously, it is much easier to succeed (and for workers to share in the benefits) in a thriving industry than in a dying one.

Elasticity of Demand. What is the demand for the product of the industry as a whole? Is it price-elastic? In other words, can a difference in price compared with competitive products (often foreign imports) cause consumers to switch rapidly to the cheaper product? Or is there a loyal market for the Canadian product? Do consumers prefer to buy, for example, North American cars rather than Japanese ones whatever the difference in cost? What would happen if there were an interruption in the Canadian supply as the result of a strike? Would consumers switch permanently to other sources of supply? If so, employers may be less willing to risk a strike. Does the industry enjoy a monopoly in the supply of the product? In other words, is it the only supplier — as, for example, the telephone service?

Seasonal Variations in Demand. Another factor affecting labour relations is whether demand for the product is relatively stable or whether it fluctuates from month to month or from year to year. In the first case, seasonal factors may affect demand — for example, an increased demand for TV sets in the Fall and an increased demand for sports clothing in the Summer. Most firms try to ensure steady production by stockpiling finished goods in the slow season to the extent that financing costs allow or by selecting a product-mix that dovetails products with different seasonal demands. However, this can be done only to a limited extent. From the labour relations point of view, management is particularly vulnerable to union demands at the time of year when demand for the product is high and management needs extra output to fill sales orders. Similarly, in the case of industries such as agriculture, where production is concentrated at a particular time of year, management is less able during this critical period to withstand union demands.

Cyclical Variations in Demand. It is a well-known fact that the North American economy is subject to cyclical variations in the overall level of demand for goods and services. Also, the governments of the United States and Canada, despite all their Keynesian "pump-priming" activities, have not been very successful in evening out such economic variations. It is also a well-known economic fact that industries producing capital goods and raw materials for them (for example, machine tools and the steel for their production) are subject to even more acute cyclical variations. This is because of the "accelerator" effect of changes in demand for consumer goods that cause even greater changes in the demand for the equipment that produces them. This means that labour relations in such industries operate in a much more uncertain economic climate than industries with a relatively stable demand — for example, medical services and pharmaceutical products. This uncertainty means much greater emphasis in contract negotiations on job security, lay-off pay, supplementary unemployment benefits, early retirement, pensions, and so on.

Foreign Competition. In North America, to make matters worse, the economic insecurity just mentioned has been heightened in recent years by the emergence of Japan, Hong Kong, Taiwan, South Korea, Singapore, Malaysia and other South-east Asian countries as low-cost suppliers of good-quality consumer goods such as cameras, watches and cars, of capital goods such as ships, and of basic manufactured raw materials such as steel and chemicals. Already, for many years, the Canadian consumer-goods manufacturing sector has been wilting from the effect of cheaper and often better-made foreign goods. South-east Asian manufacturers now have not only the benefit of lower-wage costs but also of advanced technology, heavy capital investment, and apparently better labour-management relations.

Labour Cost. How important is the labour cost as a percentage of the total cost of making and marketing the product? The smaller the percentage, the easier it is for labour to obtain pay increases — as the final cost of the product will be affected less. Alternatively, the greater the labour cost as a percentage of the total cost, the larger will be the impact of a pay raise on the final cost of the product and, therefore, on its marketability. Also, of course, the greater will be management resistance to union demands for extra pay. An example of a low-percentage labour cost industry is electricity generation and supply. An example of a high-percentage labour cost industry, at least for the present, is textiles.

New Technology. Another important economic factor affecting labour relations within an industry is the state of technology used and the pace at which it is changing. In particular, there is the question: how easy is it for management to substitute machines for workers? If labour is a unique input in the manufacturing process, then it is in a much stronger position to improve its share of the firm's revenue than if it can be replaced by machines. In the nineteenth century, there were many instances of workers rebelling against the introduction of machines. One notable example was the Luddite riots in England when workers smashed textile machinery. However, examples also exist today — for example, the fight against the introduction of computerized type-setting equipment in many newspaper plants in the nineteen-seventies. Another example is today's gradual replacement of "live tellers" in the banking industry by automatic ones — a trend hastened by various bank mergers.

In principle, labour unions in Canada favour the introduction of new technology. Without it, Canadian manufacturers and other industries will inevitably become less and less competitive, particularly against foreign goods both at home and abroad. And if an industry cannot sell its goods, it cannot afford to provide employment for Canadians, let alone pay higher wages. In practice, unions try to negotiate safeguards for their members, including job termination allowances and retraining grants for workers who are displaced.

With the advent of relatively cheap electronic micro-processors, which allow machines to be re-instructed quickly and cheaply as to what to do, many jobs in both plant and office will disappear in the coming years. Only if industries are growing rapidly will they be able to retrain and reassign the displaced workers. As the new machines fall in relative price compared with the workers whose jobs they can replace (for example, the spot-welding robots in the automobile plants or the word-processing machines in the business office) the pace of substitution will rapidly increase. Also in industries where labour unions are not yet active or only just becoming so, unionization with resultant improvements in workers' pay and working conditions can mean that mechanization and automation will rapidly become more attractive to employers. As a result, not only may jobs be eliminated but the degree of service to the public may also be curtailed. A prime example in the public sector is the post office, where automated processing of mail has already been introduced. One of the most critical aspects of labour relations in many industries in the coming years will be the introduction of computer technology, as the micro-processor promises (or threatens, depending on the point of view) a new industrial revolution comparable in economic and social impact to that of the nineteenth century.

Given the state of the technology in a particular industry, another consideration from the viewpoint of labour relations is the ability of management to keep the plants operating in the event of a union strike. The easier it is to do so, the less potent is the strike weapon.

The type of technology employed in an industry will also affect bargaining issues — for example, wash-up time in the mining industry. It will also affect management's ability to introduce piece-work or other motivational systems.

Industry in General

If the economy is in a state of recession or depression, labour unions cannot be so ambitious in their aspirations. If management cannot afford to pay higher wages because it cannot sell the goods produced, the union will only be putting some of its members out of work by insisting on receiving more. Conversely, in time of economic boom, employers can afford to be generous and unions, aware of this, can negotiate from strength — knowing that employers, with full order books, will hesitate to risk a prolonged strike.

Regional Differences. The difference in wage rates and living standards from one part of the country to another also affects industrial relations in Canada. These differences are the inevitable result of the fact that different areas have different endowments of natural resources, labour, and public and private capital. Moreover, many regions are too isolated and small in themselves to provide a substantial local market, and, for one reason or another, are unable to sell effectively abroad or to other parts of Canada. Nevertheless, union members in, for example, the Maritime provinces naturally resent being paid less for the same work than, say, workers in Alberta.

U.S. Ownership. Many manufacturing, mining, oil and other resource firms in Canada are foreign-owned, mainly by U.S. multinational corporations. Consequently, the head office of the parent company, usually in the United States, may have a great deal to say when its Canadian employees are being unionized or when a collective agreement is being negotiated. The resultant settlement sometimes resembles strongly in its content and character, agreements made south of the border.

International Unions. Many union members in Canada belong to international unions with their head office in the United States. Not only are the head office personnel and the total union membership predominantly American, so also is the union organization structure. These unions bargain with employers for improved pay and fringe benefits for their members in both U.S. and Canadian plants. One important result of this has been a gradual movement towards wage parity among employees both north and south of the border. This has meant higher wages for Canadian members to catch up with their American counterparts. At the same time, it has reduced the incentive for the U.S. multinational corporations to place work north of the border and has helped prevent "unfair competition" by lower-paid Canadian workers.

Economic Dependence on the U.S. Economically, Canada is heavily dependent on the United States. In terms of dollar value, over 85 per cent of our exports are sold to that country and about 75 per cent of our imports are purchased from it. Particularly important in trade with the United States are machinery and equipment, automotive products, and industrial goods and materials, trade in which has rapidly increased since the various Canada–U.S. free trade agreements culminating in the North American Free Trade Agrement (NAFTA) which came into force on January 1, 1994. This means that the labour movement cannot afford to push wages and fringe benefits of its members much higher than those of their American counterparts. Also, the labour movement cannot afford to be too hostile to the many U.S. multi-nationals operating in this country or to the United States itself. Any blockade on Canadian exports to the United States would have a disastrous effect on Canadian income and employment. This economic dependence also means that the economic welfare of Canadian labour union members depends as much on U.S. economic policy as it does on Canadian. Any economic recession in the United States is quickly felt in Canada. As part of the same mixed free enterprise system, industries in this country are subject to the same cyclical fluctuations in demand for their products, and union members to the same economic insecurity, as their U.S. counterparts. In the Communist world, by contrast, steady work is usually guaranteed but at much lower real wages and not always in the career of one's choice.

The Public Sector

Economic factors also have an important impact on public sector employees.

Federal Employees. One of the benefits of employment in the federal public service or in the many crown corporations and commissions that abound has long been job security. Today, however, pay and fringe benefits, particularly pensions that are adjusted with the rise in the cost of living, make the economic benefits of working for the federal government perhaps more attractive for many public employees, particularly in the lower levels, than working for the private sector. Economically, the right to strike that was given to many types of federal civil servants in the nineteen-sixties enabled the various public employee unions to catch up if not surpass the wages that could be earned in private employment.

The demand for the services of public sector employees shows little signs of abating. Although at election time, promises are made of cutbacks in public sector employment, the political party that is elected seems to change its mind quite quickly. Over the years, public sector employment has grown by leaps and bounds as new government departments and so on have been established. Unlike the private sector, there is little or no competition to be faced and cyclical changes in demand for government services are non-existent. Also, because many of the services provided (for example, mail delivery and medical care) are essential to the public, the effect of a strike is soon felt. As a result, there is considerable pressure exerted on the government of the day to bring such a strike to a rapid halt, even at the expense of a hefty increase in the governmental payroll. Unlike the private employer who, if driven too far, must inevitably go bankrupt, the federal government is blessed (from the viewpoint of the public employee unions) with a seemingly bottomless purse. If there is not enough money currently available, all the government needs to do is to increase its taxes or borrow some more. And to avoid the loss of voter support, particularly near election time, the government is prone to do just that. If it refuses to grant the increases demanded, it loses the sympathy of the union members. And if its "intransigence" brings about a strike, with all its inconvenience to the public, it loses their support as well. So in reality the government is in a "no-win" situation. But of course expensive wage settlements in the public sector are soon imitated by expensive wage settlements in the private sector. And before long the inflationary fires are burning again. But to the public, the relationship between public sector settlements and the rise in the general cost of living is usually obscure. Certainly one that tends to be ignored at election time. Also, generous increases in the pay and other benefits of federal and provincial politicians do little to help restrain public sector union demands.

Provincial Employees. Employment in the provincial public sector, particularly of publicly-subsidized employees in such institutions as hospitals and educational establishments rapidly expanded in the nineteen-seventies. This was caused partly by the federal government which, to implement its goals of a nationwide system of free medical care and universal access to post-secondary education, offered to match provincial spending in these areas. Also, the provincial governments have undertaken a number of projects, which although worthwhile in themselves, have increased the demand for qualified people.

In recent years, many provincial governments have found themselves faced with large operating deficits and have attempted to cut back on provincial spending. This new "penny-pinching" attitude has meant that many provincial sector employees have in recent years been given wage increases that have not even matched the rise in the cost of living. And this has meant increasing friction between the rank-and-file employees and the managements of these public sector institutions — for example, between nurses and hospitals.

In many cases, the public sector employees are denied the right to strike because of the essential nature of their services. However, this can lead to illegal walkouts and growing dissatisfaction and poorer service on the job. If the provincial governments continue to be faced with tight budgets, partly the result of a general economic recession and falling tax revenue, this source of conflict will remain. The situation of public sector employees is discussed more fully in Chapter 20.

Municipal Employees. At the local level, the provision of basic community services such as education, bus transit, parks and recreation, police, fire protection, electricity, water supply, sewage disposal and garbage pickup, is the responsibility of the municipal government. To provide these services, most municipalities employ large numbers of people, most of whom are represented by labour unions. Unless prevented by statute, these unions do not hesitate to call a strike if they believe their members are being treated unfairly. Prominent in the public eye are the elementary and secondary school teachers. Although much of the money to pay municipal employees comes from the provincial government, a sizeable portion comes from local home and business owners. And any substantial increase in rates of pay and associated benefits is widely publicized and often adversely received. As a result, most of the public employees have to take a militant attitude merely to ensure that rates of pay keep up with inflation. Certainly, the days of the underpaid, under-privileged local school teacher, police officer, or firefighter are now but a distant memory, due in a large part to the emergence of the public-sector employee unions.

Supply of Labour

From the labour relations point of view, there has been a steady growth in the Canadian population as a whole. Thus there has been no undue pressure on the labour supply side (as, for example, from unrestricted immigration) that would impair labour's bargaining position. There has, however, been a continuing movement of the population from the East of Canada to the West. Also there have, at various times, been surpluses of certain types of labour such as teachers and nurses; and shortages of others, particularly the skilled trades such as tool and diemakers. Government licensing programs have also slowed down the increase in the supply of certain types of skilled and semi-professional persons.

One factor, not so far mentioned, affecting the supply of labour in Canada, is what is called the "labour force participation rate". This is the percentage of the civilian population, excluding members of the Armed Forces, who are members of the civilian labour force. This percentage has been steadily rising as more and more women, for economic and career reasons, enter and re-enter the work force than was traditionally the case.

When unemployment is high, the larger numbers of persons looking for work makes it more difficult for labour unions to succeed in negotiating better pay and improved conditions of work for their members. In recent years, Canada has experienced relatively high annual *rates of unemployment* (the number of unemployed as a percentage of the civilian labour force). The reasons for this have been touched upon previously, and include foreign competition, particularly in manufactured goods; labour-saving technology; a higher labour force participation rate; and lack of the required skills.

Of course, the rates of unemployment vary geographically. The highest rates have been in the Atlantic provinces and Quebec and the lowest in the prairie provinces. Hence the Westward flow of the population, seeking jobs. For various reasons, unemployment rates were highest among the young.

Of those employed, the vast majority is in the non-agricultural sector of the economy. Of the persons employed in non-agricultural establishments, most were in the various service industries.

2.3 SOCIAL FACTORS

Quebec

Over the years, the French Canadians in Quebec have been making a determined effort to preserve their culture, including the use of the French language. Because their number is so large compared with other minority groups such as the Ukrainians, Poles, Germans, Italians, Hungarians, Chinese, and so on, and because they were, like the British, one of Canada's two founding races, they have been relatively successful in standing apart from the rest of Canada. This attitude, reflected politically, has inevitably carried over into the industrial relations scene, with Quebec labour officials taking a different, usually more radical stand, on many labour issues.

Immigration

Since World War II, the entry into Canada of many immigrants from all over the world, often fiercely independent and extremely anxious for work, has made it more difficult for many unions to gain higher pay and other improvements for their members. In some industries (for example, house building), non-union labour is still the order of the day.

REVIEW QUESTIONS

1. What fundamental human rights do we take for granted in Canada?

2. In accordance with the democratic spirit, should every union have the right to strike?

3. "Trade unions are unnecessary in a communist state". Discuss.

4. In Canada, market freedoms are not usually permitted priority over social freedoms. Explain and discuss.

5. What political role do trade unions play in Canada?

6. To what extent do ethnic differences affect the trade union movement in Canada?

7. "The welfare of the employee depends ultimately on the economic success of his or her employer." What factors determine such economic success? How can the employee help ensure such success? How can he /she be sure to benefit from it?

8. "Unions prosper in both growing and declining industries." Which industries in Canada are growing? Which are declining? Discuss the statement.

9. How can "elasticity of demand" for an industry's product affect the action of (a) employers, and (b) labour unions?

10. How can seasonal variations in demand for a product affect collective bargaining?

11. How do cyclical variations in demand for a product affect industrial relations in any particular industry?

12. What has been the effect of foreign competition in manufactured goods on the welfare of Canadian workers?

13. How does labour cost as a percentage of the final cost of a product affect collective bargaining? What are examples of low-labour-cost and high-labour- cost industries in Canada?

14. How can technological innovation affect union members? What should be the attitude towards it of (a) management, and (b) the union?

15. How is the advent of the cheap electronic microprocessor affecting industry? Will it really mean a "new industrial revolution"? If so, what are the long-term implications?

16. How does the state of the economy in general affect collective

bargaining?

17. How do regional differences affect industrial relations in Canada?

18. How does the high degree of U.S. ownership of Canadian industry affect Canadian trade union members?

19. "International unions make good sense for Canadian workers." Discuss.

20. Canada's economic dependence on the U.S. places severe restrictions on the Canadian labour movement. Explain.

21. "The economic factors that apply to employment in private industry do not apply to employment in the public sector." Explain and discuss.

22. What policy should the federal government adopt when negotiating for pay, etc. with the public service unions?

23. Should public sector employees have the right to strike?

24. How is Canada's population growing? What has been happening to births, deaths, and immigration?

25. What is the size of Canada's labour force? How fast is it growing? What factors will affect its future growth?

26. Explain the term: "labour force participation rate". Why has the rate increased in recent years? What problem can this create?

27. How is Canada's population distributed among the various regions? How has the distribution pattern been changing? What are the reasons for such change?

28. What is meant by the "unemployment rate"? How has the rate changed in recent years? Why?

29. How does the unemployment rate vary in Canada from region to region? Why? What changes are occurring?

30. What can be done to reduce unemployment rates in Canada? Do unions share any of the blame for high rates of unemployment?

31. How is the labour force in Canada distributed among different kinds of industries?

32. How do the participation and unemployment rates vary between different age groups? Why is this? What significance does it have?

33. How has immigration affected the Canadian labour movement since World War II?

CHAPTER 3: THE CONSTITUTIONAL AND LEGAL ENVIRONMENT

3.1 LABOUR JURISDICTION IN CANADA

Canada's political constitution is set out mainly in the Constitution Act, 1867. This Act, passed by the British Parliament in that year, created the Dominion of Canada and divided the legislative powers in the new state between the federal Parliament on the one hand and the provincial legislatures on the other. The Act was originally called the British North America Act, 1867.

Amongst the powers assigned to the provinces was the right to pass laws concerning "property and civil rights". This has been interpreted to give the provinces jurisdiction over labour matters such as hours of work, minimum wages, and minimum age of employment. However, the federal government is empowered to pass labour laws with regard to industries specifically under its jurisdiction. These include: navigation, shipping, interprovincial railways, canals, telegraphs, steamship lines and ferries, airports, air transportation, radio stations, and works declared by Parliament to be for the general advantage of Canada or of two or more provinces. It also has jurisdiction over workers employed under federal government work contracts and on works partly financed by federal government funds. The federal Parliament can also pass laws concerning matters surrendered to it by the Provincial legislatures such as unemployment assistance and old age pensions.

3.2 THE CONSPIRACY DOCTRINE

The system of English Common Law which Canada inherited from Britain had been fashioned partly to protect the interests of the English land-owning, employer class. Consequently, any attempt by workers in agriculture or in the various skilled trades to join together to negotiate with an employer was considered to be "in restraint of trade" and a criminal act, falling under the doctrine of criminal conspiracy. Thus, anyone attempting to form a trade union could be imprisoned, fined, or both. This situation continued to exist in Britain until 1871 when the British Parliament, after continued worker pressure, passed legislation which no longer made the mere combining of workers to increase wages or to reduce working hours a conspiracy in violation of the common law. However, in Canada in 1872, a Toronto printers' strike for a 54-hour work week was followed by the arrest and conviction on criminal charges of the strike leaders. Soon thereafter, the federal government, responding to great public indignation, passed the Trade Union Act of 1872 that, like the British Act of the previous year, made combinations of workers no longer a criminal offence. At the same time, another statute, the Criminal Law Amendment Act, was passed, imposing penalties for violence or intimidation during organizing campaigns and strikes. To placate employers, the Act stated that a union-management contract was not legally enforceable.

3.3 INDUSTRIAL DISPUTES LEGISLATION

By the end of the nineteenth century, several provinces had passed legislation designed to help resolve disputes between employers and employees. In 1900 the Federal Parliament followed suit, passing a Conciliation Act which gave to the Minister of Labour the authority to appoint conciliation officers or conciliation boards to help settle industrial disputes.

In 1903, after a long strike by C.P.R. trackmen, the Federal Parliament passed a Railway Labour Disputes Act which authorized the appointment of a three-person conciliation board to handle disputes. The employer and the union would each choose one nominee, and the two nominees would then choose a chairperson. The board would then investigate the dispute and try to bring about an agreement between the two parties. If this failed, resort could be made to an arbitration board. However, since such a board could make only non-binding recommendations, its influence was limited. Also, the Act did nothing to forbid strikes and lockouts.

In 1906, the Federal Parliament passed a Conciliation and Labour Act that included the best features of both the 1900 Conciliation Act and the 1903 Railway Labour Disputes Act. However, the legislation was still unsatisfactory and, following a rash of strikes, was replaced in 1907 by the Industrial Disputes Investigation Act. This Act was considered a great improvement over its predecessors and served as the model for similar Provincial Acts.

Industrial Disputes Investigation Act

This Act, which applied to disputes involving employers of ten or more persons engaged in mining, transportation, communication, and public utility operations, made provision for a three-person Board of Conciliation and Investigation with powers similar to those in the 1903 Railway Labour Disputes Act. However, extremely important, it also required that any strike or lockout be postponed and that wages and other conditions of work remain unchanged while the dispute was being investigated. Should the Board fail to bring the parties to a voluntary agreement, it was required to make recommendations as to what should or should not be done by them. The Act provided for voluntary extension of its scope to any industrial dispute not coming within the groups subject to compulsion. Unfortunately, the Act gave no protection to employees who wished to join a union nor did it require an employer to bargain with the union that its employees may have formed or joined. As a result, organized labour became increasingly critical of the Act.

Toronto Electric Commissioners v. Snider

The Industrial Disputes Investigation Act, although passed by the Federal Parliament rather than by the Provincial legislatures, provided for its application to any industrial dispute. However, in 1925 the legality of the Act was challenged in court in the case of *Toronto Electric Commissioners v. Snider*. The Judicial Committee of the Privy Council of England, to whom the appeal went, agreed that the Federal Parliament had exceeded its jurisdictional rights. This was because Section 92 of the Constitution Act specifically assigns the matter of civil rights of employers and employees to the provinces. Consequently, the Judicial Committee declared the Act unconstitutional. Thereupon, Canada's Federal Parliament quickly amended the Industrial Disputes Investigation Act so that it would apply only to disputes within its own jurisdiction — for example, Crown corporations, railways, and longshoring.

Provincial Acts

The amendment to the Federal IDI Act also provided for the Act's applicability to employees normally outside federal jurisdiction, so long as the provincial legislature gave its approval. Subsequently, between 1925 and 1932, all the provinces except Prince Edward Island passed enabling Acts. Later, Alberta and British Columbia replaced such enabling legislation with their own provincial Acts similar to the Federal one. As a result, despite the Snider decision, a new national labour relations policy emerged in Canada.

3.4 THE WAGNER ACT

In the United States, the severe economic depression that began in 1929 eventually led to the election of a Democratic President, Franklin D. Roosevelt, whose much more sympathetic attitude towards organized labour was summed up in the phrase, the *New Deal*. This attitude resulted in the passage through Congress in 1935 of a new National Labour Relations Act, known for short as the Wagner Act, that affirmed workers' rights to organize unions of their choice and to be free from employer interference or control in doing so. Also, under the Act, employers were required to negotiate conditions of work with the appropriate unions. The act listed five management practices considered to be unfair to labour:

a) interference with an employee's right to join a union,

b) domination of a labour union,

c) discrimination against an employee for engaging in union activities,

d) dismissal or otherwise penalizing an employee for filing charges under the Act, and

e) refusal to bargain with the union representing the employees.

A National Labour Relations Board, established under the Act, was required to investigate any complaints of unfair labour practices by management, to prosecute the companies and persons involved, and to hold and supervise elections to determine which union it should certify as the official bargaining agent of the employees in each particular bargaining unit. The Act also provided for a Federal Mediation and Conciliation Service (FMCS) which would supply mediation services on request. There was no mention in the Act of possible unfair labour practices by unions. As a result the unions had very much a free hand in recruiting new members. In 1947, however, the Act was amended to permit unions also to be prosecuted for unfair labour practices.

In the United States, in the nineteen-thirties, the American Federation of Labour and the new, but rapidly growing Congress of Industrial Organizations found the Wagner Act, with its principle of compulsory recognition of unions and compulsory bargaining with them, to be of tremendous help in their efforts to increase union membership. This was particularly so after the Act was upheld by the U.S. Supreme Court in 1937. Not surprisingly, therefore, the many trade unions in Canada affiliated with these organizations soon started to press for similar legislation in this country. One result was the preparation by the Trades and Labour Congress of a draft bill for such an Act that the provincial governments were then urged to adopt. This pressure by organized labour eventually resulted in the enactment by many provincial legislatures in the second half of the nineteen-thirties, of Wagner-type labour relations statutes, some of which were based on the TLC's draft bill. However, the lack of any machinery of enforcement effectively removed the teeth from these statutes.

3.5 WAR-TIME DEVELOPMENTS

With the outbreak of World War II, the federal government, armed with its powers under the War Measures Act of 1914, temporarily re-established its supremacy in labour relations matters. Thus in 1939, just after the war began, the federal government, by means of an Order in Council, extended the coverage of the federal Industrial Disputes Investigation Act to all industries involved with the war effort. This included all the basic industries such as fishing, farming, lumber, mining, and most of the manufacturing ones as well. Later, in 1940, the federal government began to reveal its intentions for a new, comprehensive Canadian labour relations policy which in some ways closely resembled the Wagner Act. However, a novel feature, not in the Wagner Act, was settlement machinery to which disputes arising during a collective agreement or at renewal could be referred.

During the war, stronger provincial labour relations legislation began to appear on the statute books. Especially important was the Ontario Collective Bargaining Act of 1943. While purporting to deal with the problems of rights of association and negotiation, this Act went beyond the pre-war laws of other provinces by providing machinery for administration and enforcement. With its passage, Ontario labour legislation was brought more or less into line with that of the United States. However, many workers in Ontario were still subject to the federal IDI Act, as extended in wartime.

In 1944, Ottawa suspended the IDI Act, replacing it with new labour relations regulations (Order in Council PC 1003). This whole new policy, talked about since 1940, combined the IDI Act disputes-investigation principle, including the delay on strikes and lockouts, with the Wagner Act principles of compulsory recognition and bargaining. Ontario, in agreement with the new policy, repealed its statute, thereby letting industrial disputes in Ontario come under the jurisdiction of the new federal regulations. Because of the national emergency, the coverage of the new Canadian labour relations policy was very broad, extending well beyond the normal scope of federal labour relations jurisdiction. It included: (a) industries of a national or inter-provincial character ordinarily within federal jurisdiction, including Crown corporations handling or manufacturing war supplies; (b) war industries as described in the regulations, or later added by Order in Council; and (c) all other industries within a province where such province by appropriate legislation brought such industries within the scope of the regulations. The regulations themselves contained the following main features:

a) the right of employees to form and join unions;

b) protection against unfair labour practices which, if allowed to continue, would result in discouraging the exercise of the previous rights;

c) a system of defining bargaining units and certifying bargaining representatives;

d) compulsory collective bargaining;

e) compulsory postponement of strikes and lockouts, coupled with compulsory two-stage conciliation;

f) the right to resort to strikes and lockouts after compulsory conciliation procedures had been completed.

During World War II, wage increases were severely restricted. Initially, by a 1940 Order-in-Council, wage increases were permitted up to 5 per cent a year over a base wage related to the years 1926 to 1939. Also cost-of-living bonuses were allowed. However, in 1941, another Order-in-Council was issued that prohibited wages increases except as authorized by a specially established National War Labour Board that was empowered to investigate wages and working conditions in whichever industries it saw fit and to make recommendations for any changes. In 1943, another Order-in-Council was issued that authorized a wage increase only in exceptional circumstances — namely, where the present wage level was grossly inadequate. Also, during the war, labour unions and workers in general were asked, in the name of the war effort specifically, and the public interest generally, to refrain from strike action. As a result, strikes were few and far between.

3.6 THE POST-WAR PERIOD

With the end of the war, all the pent-up employee dissatisfactions burst forth. After all the war-time sacrifices, workers now wanted better pay and improved working conditions. During the war, they had seen most employers benefit greatly from the war-time demand for vehicles, ships, aircraft, ammunition, food, clothing, and so on. And this economic prosperity, to the surprise of some leading economists who predicted the same severe economic depression that followed World War I, showed no signs of abating in the post-war period — thanks to heavy consumer demand in North America and the various U.S. and Canadian foreign aid programs, particularly for Western Europe. As a result, the unions confronted employers with large catch-up pay demands and, in the face of employer resistance, called their members out on strike in many different parts of Canada.

Gradually, following this period of industrial turmoil, employers and employees made their peace. However, the labour unrest forced the federal and provincial governments to look again at the legal framework for settling such disputes. Already, towards the end of the war, the federal authorities had, at the suggestion of the provinces, prepared the draft of a federal labour relations bill. This draft was then discussed with the provinces and, after amendments, was passed by the federal Parliament in 1948. The new Act, the *Industrial Relations and Disputes Act*, replaced the previous war-time regulations. Like the war-time regulations, the new Act included the Wagner Act's basic principles of compulsory union recognition and bargaining and the IDI Act's principle of compulsory conciliation. However, unlike the war-time regulations, the coverage of the new federal Act was restricted to industries normally within federal jurisdiction.

At about the same time, most of the provinces in Canada passed new labour relations statutes of their own, incorporating in varying degree the system of industrial relations that had developed during the war-time period.

3.7 PROVINCIAL LABOUR RELATIONS ACTS

All provinces now have Labour Relations Acts designed to promote harmonious relations between employers and employees and to facilitate the settlement of industrial disputes. One basic provision of these statutes is the requirement that an employer must bargain in good faith with the labour union that has been certified by the provincial Labour Relations Board as the bargaining agent for its employees. Another basic provision, in most provinces, is the requirement of compulsory conciliation in negotiations for a collective agreement. This means that before a strike or lockout may legally take place, the conciliation procedure set out in the particular provincial statute must be followed.

The provincial Labour Relations statutes also require the compulsory arbitration of any alleged violation of the collective agreement between the employer and the union, if the matter cannot be resolved by the grievance procedure set out in the Agreement. A strike or lockout is illegal while the collective agreement is in force. However, illegal or "wildcat" strikes do sometimes occur, with or without the tacit support of the union.

In Ontario, the Labour Relations Act, 1995 (or LRA), states the following as its purposes:

1. To facilitate collective bargaining between employers and trade unions that are the freely-designated representatives of the employees.

2. To recognize the importance of work place parties adapting to change.

3. To promote flexibility, productivity and employee involvement in the work place.

4. To encourage communication between employers and employees in the

work place.

5. To recognize the importance of economic growth as the foundation for mutually beneficial relations amongst employers, employees and trade unions.

6. To encourage co-operative participation of employers and trade unions in
resolving work place issues.

7. To promote the expeditious resolution of work place disputes.

3.8 PROVINCIAL PUBLIC SECTOR EMPLOYEES

In most provinces, provincial government employees are denied the right to
strike because of the harm that could be caused to the general public. Instead,
differences between the employer and the union involved must be settled by
arbitration. In Ontario, however, this is not the case. In Ontario, labour
relations in the Ontario Public Service and Crown agencies are governed by
the Crown Employees Collective Bargaining Act (CECBA). The Crown
agencies involved include the Workers' Compensation Board, Ontario
Housing Corporation, Metro Toronto Correction Centre, Metro Toronto
Housing Authority, GO Transit, Niagara Parks Commission, Liquor Control
and Licensing Boards of Ontario and some ambulance services.

The CECBA, when it came into force in 1972, established a Grievance
Settlement Board as an arbitration panel to settle disputes involving unionized
Crown employees. In 1994, the Public Service and Labour Relations Statute
Act (Bill 117) extended the labour legislation changes in Bill 40 (the labour
relations statute which took effect on January 1, 1993) to the Ontario Public
Service. The changes involved included: the extension of access to collective
bargaining to about 9,000 OPS employees; giving the right to strike to OPS
employees and about 100,000 Crown employees, while protecting the public's
access to essential services; expansion of the scope of bargaining to negotiate
any work place issue; and a reform of the Grievance Settlement Board.

In 1995, the new provincial government included in the Labour Relations
Act, 1995, various amendments to the Crown Employees Collective
Bargaining Act. These included:

• exemption of the Crown from successor rights for work that is no longer
performed by the public service;

• elimination of bargaining rights: for lawyers and architects employed in the
public service; employees whose work includes significant time raising or
borrowing money; strategic policy advisers who give advice on employ-
ment-related legislation or on matters of financial policy to cabinet, cabinet

committees, ministers or deputy ministers; and employees in the Office of the Premier and cabinet office.

• a reduction in the authority of the Grievance Settlement Board to make its power consistent with that of the Ontario Labour Relations Board and to give greater control over dispute resolution to the parties involved.

Other types of public sector employees such as hospital workers, teachers, police officers, and firefighters, are governed by special Acts. Because of the essential nature of their work, they are not usually given the right to strike — only the right to arbitration.

3.9 CANADA LABOUR CODE

At the federal level, labour relations have been governed, since 1970, by Part 5 of the Canada Labour Code.

The Labour Code applies to all employees in:

a) air transport, aircraft and airports;

b) radio and television broadcasting;

c) banks;

d) Federal Crown Corporations (e.g., the St. Lawrence Seaway Authority);

e) all extra-provincial shipping and services connected thereto (such as long-shoring and stevedoring);

f) works or undertakings connecting one province with another or with another country, such as rail, bus, or truck services, ferries, tunnels, bridges, canals, pipelines, telegraph, telephone and cable systems; and

g) defined operations or specific works that have been declared to be for the general advantage of Canada or of two or more provinces, such as flour, feed and seed cleaning mills, feed warehouses, grain elevators and uranium mining and processing.

The Code recognizes the right of employees to organize and bargain collectively through trade unions. However, both employers and employees are required to bargain in good faith and to include in their collective agreement a provision for the arbitration of disputes. The Code prohibits unfair labour practices (such as discrimination and coercion) by employers and employees, and provides for government conciliation officers or boards to help mediate differences between the two parties in negotiations. The administration of Part Five of the Code is the responsibility of the Federal Minister of Labour. Part of his/her authority — for example, the provisions covering the certification of bargaining agents — has been delegated to the Canada Labour Relations Board.

3.10 PUBLIC SERVICE STAFF RELATIONS ACT

This Act, passed in 1967, gave to federal government employees the right to bargain collectively with the government as represented by the Treasury Board, about wages, hours of work, and other conditions of employment. The certified bargaining agent for each particular group of employees is given a choice, early in negotiations for a new collective agreement, as to how any outstanding issues should be resolved. One alternative is to use the services of a conciliation board which, if unsuccessful, could be followed after a specified time period by the right to strike. The other alternative is to use compulsory arbitration, legally binding on both parties, without the right to strike. More details are provided in Chapter 20.

3.11 PROTECTION OF THE PUBLIC INTEREST

Perhaps the most important factor that has helped shape the legal system governing labour relations in Canada has been the desire, on the part of the government of the day, to "protect the public interest". Ostensibly, this concept means protecting the general public from the hardships that arise when essential public services such as the supply of water or electricity are cut off. In itself, this is a justifiable political and social concern. That is why many jurisdictions deny the right to strike to various types of public employees such as police officers and firefighters. Over the years, however, the right to strike has been extended to more and more public employees — not because the services provided are less essential than they were previously but because of the relentless pressure of the unions and employees concerned to improve their bargaining powers and the desire for political popularity of the legislators involved.

Public or semi-public employees denied the right to strike are usually permitted to resolve their differences with their employers (e.g. hospital boards) by resort to arbitration. However, this has often meant awards that are unsatisfactory to the employees concerned. As a result, the concept of protection of the public interest is seen by many public employees today as a government stratagem for holding down pay raises in the public sector rather than a genuine concern for the public at large.

The concept of protection of the public interest is also occasionally used by the government as a justification for intervening in a protracted labour-management dispute in the private sector that, because of the effect of a strike or lock-out, is causing public hardship. Sometimes, the employer or union involved may even call upon the government to step in and impose a settlement, again ostensibly on grounds of protecting the public interest. In fact, the real reason may be that the party concerned has got itself into a corner from which there is no escape other than by outright acceptance of the other party's terms.

The various provincial Labour Relations statutes reflect government concern to protect the public from hardships caused by management-labour disputes in the private sector. Thus these statutes forbid strikes or lockouts during the life of a collective agreement and require the use of a government conciliation officer after the expiry of a contract before a strike or lockout may take place.

3.12 INTERNATIONAL LABOUR ORGANIZATION

The ILO is a United Nations agency that monitors U.N.-approved labour standards around the world — labour standards that have been ratified by the Canadian government. Although the ILO has no power to overrule federal or provincial labour standards in Canada, it does exert a moral and ethical influence upon the governments involved. In November 2001, B.C. labour unions representing nurses, teachers, and school support workers, filed a formal complaint to the ILO that recent provincial legislation had imposed a collective agreement on nurses and declared education an "essential service", thereby removing the teachers' right to strike.

REVIEW QUESTIONS

1. Who has the right, under Canada's constitution, to pass laws governing labour relations?

2. Explain what is meant by the "conspiracy doctrine". What was its effect? Is it still applicable?

3. How, at the beginning of this century, did the Canadian government try to help resolve disputes between employers and employees?

4. Explain the significance of the case of Toronto Electric Commissioners vs. Snider.

5. What are the key principles of the Wagner Act? How did the Act affect unions in the U.S.? What was its significance for Canada?

6. What was so different about Ontario's Collective Bargaining Act

of 1943 compared with previous labour relations statutes?

7. What basic labour relations principles were embodied in the federal labour relations regulations (Order in Council PC 1003) proclaimed in 1944?

8. What happened in the labour relations field in the early post World War II years? Why?

9. What are some of the key features of the provincial Labour Relations Acts?

10. How are labour disputes settled in the provincial public sector? What statutes apply?

11. What are the basic provisions of Part 5 of the Canada Labour Code? To whom do they apply?

12. What collective bargaining rights, if any, do federal government employees have? Are they permitted to strike?

13. What is the Public Service Staff Relations Act? What is one of its key features?

14. "The desire to protect the public interest has been the most important factor affecting federal labour relations policy in the nineteen seventies and eighties." Discuss.

15. "Compulsory arbitration for public service employees has been a convenient device for holding down the wages of these workers." Discuss.

16. Explain the nature and purpose of the ILO. Why would a Canadian labour union file complaints with such an international body?

CHAPTER 4: LABOUR ORGANIZATIONS IN CANADA

4.1 LABOUR UNION DEFINED

The term *labour organization* is a broad term that includes not only various types of labour unions and other employee associations, but also various regional and central labour bodies. In this chapter, we look first at the labour unions and then at the various central labour bodies such as the CLC.

A *labour union* (also called a *trade union*) is an association of workers, practising a similar trade or employed in the same company or industry. Its basic purpose is to improve the economic welfare, including pay and job security, of its members through collective, rather than individual, bargaining of wage rates, hours of work, and other conditions of employment, with employers.

In Ontario's LRA, as one provincial example, a *trade union* is defined as "an organization of employees formed for purposes that include the regulation of relations between employees and employers and includes a provincial, national, or international trade union, a certified council of trade unions and a designated or certified employee bargaining agency".

Many labour unions use the term "union" in their official title, but many others use terms such as association, brotherhood, federation, or alliance, and in two instances (the American Guild of Variety Artists and the Newspaper Guild) the term "guild".

In the various Labour Relations Acts or Labour Codes, depending on the province, the term "trade union" is used. In fact, the terms "trade union" and "labour union" are often used interchangeably. However, the term *trade union* is more commonly used with reference to a group of workers possessing a certain type of industrial skill or "trade", whereas the term "labour union" is more commonly used with reference to a group of unskilled and/or semi-skilled workers employed in a particular industry. Throughout this book, we mainly use the term labour union.

There are, in addition to the labour unions referred to above, many *employee associations*. These are associations of employees in a particular firm or industry that have not been certified, under the terms of a Labour Relations statute, as the bargaining agent for those employees. Although without legal status, these unofficial or "quasi labour unions" are nevertheless recognized by the employer as the spokesperson for its employees — bargaining on their behalf or at least presenting their complaints to the employer. However, the legal status of any collective bargaining outside provincial or federal labour legislation tends to be uncertain.

In its broadest sense, a *labour union* may be considered to be any type of labour organization, whether formally or informally recognized by the employer, that represents the interests of the employees in that particular plant, store, office, or industry.

4.2 WHY WORKERS JOIN UNIONS

Each employee has his or her own personal reasons for joining a labour union. Some employees flock to join, many others need to be cajoled, and some resolutely oppose union membership.

Reasons for Joining a Labour Union

For many employees, one good reason for joining a union is that a group of employees, acting collectively, can usually negotiate much better terms of employment than if each employee negotiates alone. Thus membership in a union offers the very real chance of better pay and fringe benefits and other working conditions. Also, the most effective method of enforcing the employees' viewpoint, the use of the strike weapon, demands common action by all or most employees. Otherwise the strike is ineffective in halting or hampering the employer's operations.

A second reason for union membership is that in many business firms and other organizations in which a union has been officially certified as the bargaining agent for the employees, and in which a collective agreement is in force, membership in the union is compulsory for most employees, usually after a probationary employment period. Unofficially, there is also pressure to join from fellow-workers who already belong to the union.

A third reason for joining is that membership in a union increases an employee's sense of economic security. Employees no longer feel weak and alone in their dealings with management. They can no longer be dismissed at the employer's whim. There is a grievance procedure set out in the collective agreement to handle disputes and there are union officials to help ensure that the union member gets fair treatment. Also, the employee now belongs to an organization whose representatives are not only very well informed but can also talk and bargain as competently as management. The inclusion in the collective agreement, at union instigation, of *seniority* (or length of service with the firm) as the major criterion in lay-offs, when work shortages occur, also helps increase an employee's sense of economic security.

A fourth reason for joining a union is that human beings, as "social animals", enjoy membership in a group. They feel the need to belong. And the union offers the rank-and-file worker the companionship of people of similar background and outlook, and similar economic and social goals. This membership bond exists not only in the work place and on the picket line, but also in the union hall, where social activities are organized for members and their families.

Reasons for Not Joining a Labour Union

As the statistics show, not every worker belongs to a union, even if the option is available. Some plants are "non-union". One reason is that the employees believe they are economically better off without a union. Management may currently offer wages and fringe benefits that are equal to or better than those in comparable unionized plants. Also, management may have a more progressive or enlightened approach in its treatment of rank-and-file employees (e.g. as in some of the new auto plants in North America). Another reason may be a negative one — management uses various forms of economic and psychological pressure on its employees to keep them from voting for a union. Instead, the employer may encourage a "token" form of employee association that represents the views of the employer more than those of the employees.

4.3 TYPES OF LABOUR UNIONS

Labour unions can be divided into various types according to (a) type of worker, (b) geographical scope, and (c) Congress affiliation.

Type of Worker

Historically, unions have been divided into two basic types according to type of worker eligible for membership.

Craft Union. This is a labour organization representing workers practising the same craft or "trade". Examples are the International Association of Firefighters, the Air Line Pilots Association International, and the Playwrights Union of Canada. Today, however, some craft unions represent all the workers in a plant, not just those with a particular skill or "craft".

Industrial Union. This is a labour organization whose members usually, but not always, include most of the workers eligible for union membership in a particular company or industry, irrespective of the type of work performed. Examples are the National Union of Public and General Employees and the Communications, Energy and Paperworkers Union of Canada.

General Union. Although the traditional distinction is between craft unions and industrial unions, some unions might be more accurately described as *general unions*. This is because their membership is not confined to one type of skilled occupation or to one type of industry. The International Brotherhood of Teamsters' is considered to be an example of this type of labour union.

Geographical Scope

Unions can also be distinguished from each other according to their geographical scope. Table 4.1 shows the number of national, international, and other unions in Canada over a number of years.

National Unions. These are labour unions which charter branches in Canada only and have their head office in this country. Examples of national unions are the Canadian Union of Public Employees, the Canadian Paperworkers Union, and the Canadian Union of Operating Engineers and General Workers. Many of the unions included under the heading of national are really provincial in scope — for example, the Alberta Union of Provincial Employees and the Ontario Secondary School Teachers' Federation.

Table 4.1 — *Number of Unions in Canada, by Type, Selected Years, 1978 to 2004*

Year	National	International	Other	Total
1978	88	121	321	530
1990	234	61	721	1,016
1992	235	62	648	945
1997	233	51	727	1,011
2000	224	47	737	1,008
2001	219	47	720	986
2004	218	46	599	863
		%		
1978	16.6	22.8	60.6	100.0
1990	23.0	6.0	71.0	100.0
1992	24.9	6.5	68.6	100.0
1997	23.0	5.0	71.9	100.0
2000	22.2	4.7	73.1	100.0
2001	22.2	4.8	73.0	100.0
2004	25.3	5.3	69.4	100.0

Source: Human Resources Development Canada, *Workplace Information Directorate*

Table 4.2 — *Number of Union Members, by Type of Union, Selected Years,*
1978 to 2004

Year	National	International	Other	Total
		(000)		
1978	1,553	1,638	87	3,278
1990	2,563	1,283	184	4,030
1992	2,660	1,253	176	4,089
1997	2,663	1,217	195	4,075
2000	2,651	1,198	209	4,058
2001	2,694	1,212	204	4,110
2004	1,960	1,160	2	3,121
		%		
1978	47.4	50.0	2.6	100.00
1990	63.6	31.8	4.6	100.00
1992	65.1	30.6	4.3	100.00
1997	65.4	29.9	4.8	100.00
2000	65.3	29.5	5.2	100.00
2001	65.5	29.5	5.0	100.00
2004	62.8	37.2	0.0	100.00

Source: Human Resources Development Canada, *Workplace Information Directorate*

Note: "Other" includes directly chartered unions and independent local organizations.

International Unions. These are labour unions which charter "locals", or branches, in both the United States and Canada. However, because of their predominantly U.S. membership, such unions have their head office in the U.S. Until recently, Canadian membership in such unions has been declining (see Table 4.2). This is because Canadian branches of international unions have been breaking away from the parent unions and forming their own Canadian unions — for example, the National Automobile, Aerospace, Transportation and General Workers Union of Canada, which was formed from breakaway locals of the International Auto Workers' Union. An example of a prominent international union is the United Mine Workers of America, with head office in Washington, D.C.

Local Organizations. There are two types of labour organizations that are purely local in geographical scope. First, there are *directly chartered local unions*. These are local labour unions which have been organized by and have received their *charter* (or official document of establishment) directly from the Canadian Labour Congress, the major central organization for national trade unions in Canada. Such local unions are not part of a national or international union. Membership in directly chartered local unions is usually relatively small. The second type of local labour organization is the *independent local organization*. This is a local not formally connected or affiliated with any other labour organization. Membership in such unions is also usually quite small.

Congress Affiliation

A third way of distinguishing between labour unions is according to affiliation with one or other central labour organization (see Table 4.3). These central organizations are as follows:

Table 4.3 — *Union Membership, by Type of Union and Affiliation, 2004*

Type and Affiliation	Number of unions	Number of locals	Union Membership Number	Per cent
International Unions	46	3,141	1,180,230	27.7
AFL — CIO/CLC	40	3,095	1,160,480	27.2
AFL — CIO only	3	34	17,630	0.4
Unaffiliated unions	3	12	2,120	0.1
National Unions	218	13,126	2,873,450	67.4
CLC	65	7,631	1,960,530	46.0
CSN	10	2,457	278,170	6.5
CEQ	15	421	126,060	3.0
CCU	6	25	8,940	0.2
CSD	4	100	11,550	0.3
Unaffiliated unions	118	2,492	488,200	11.4
Directly Chartered Unions	315	–	51,830	1.2
CSD	309	–	55,000	1.2
CLC	6	–	1,830	0.0
Independent Local Organizations	284	–	155,800	3.7
Total	863	16,267	4,261,000	100.0

Source: Human Resources Development Canada, *Workplace Information Directorate*

CLC — Canadian Labour Congress

CSN — Confédération des Syndicats Nationaux (In English, — Confederation of National Trade Unions, or CNTU)

CSD — Centrale des syndicats démocratiques

CCU — Confederation of Canadian Unions

AFL-CIO — American Federation of Labour and Congress of Industrial Organizations.

The CLC, described later in this chapter, is the central labour organization in Canada, with the largest number of affiliated union members. The next largest is the CSN, prominent in Quebec. Union membership by congress affiliation is shown in Table 4.4.

Table 4.4 — *Union Membership, by Congress Affiliation, 2004*

Congress Affiliation	Union Membership	
	Number	Per cent
CLC	3,121,010	73.2
CLC only	1,960,530	46.0
AFL — CIO/CLC	1,160,480	27.2
CSN	278,170	6.5
AFL — CIO only	17,630	0.4
CEQ	126,060	3.0
CSD	63,070	1.5
CCU	8,940	0.2
Unaffiliated International Unions	2,120	0.1
Unaffiliated National Unions	488,200	11.4
Independent Local Organizations	155,800	3.7
Total	4,261,000	100.0

Source: Human Resources Development Canada, *Workplace Information Directorate*

4.4 UNION MEMBERSHIP IN CANADA

For many years, the number of persons belonging to labour unions has gradually increased in Canada. However, as a percentage of the civilian labour force and of total non-agricultural paid workers, union membership is still quite low (see Tables 4.5 and 4.6).

Table 4.5 — *Union Membership and the Civilian Labour Force in Canada,*
1985-2004

	Union membership (000s)	Civilian labour force (000s)	Union membership as a percentage of civilian labour force
1985	3,666	12,953	28.3
1986	3,730	13,123	28.4
1987	3,782	13,378	28.3
1988	3,841	13,512	28.4
1989	3,944	13,779	28.6
1990	4,031	14,047	28.7
1991	4,068	14,241	28.6
1992	4,089	14,330	28.5
1993	4,071	14,362	28.3
1994	4,078	14,505	28.1
1995	4,003	14,627	27.4
1996	4,033	14,750	27.3
1997	4,074	14,900	27.3
1998	3,938	15,153	26.0
1999	4,010	15,418	26.0
2000	4,058	15,721	25.8
2001	4,110	15,999	25.7
2002	4,174	16,242	25.7
2003	4,178	16,690	25.0
2004	4,261	14,881	28.6

Source: Human Resources Development Canada, *Workplace Information Directorate*

Table 4.6 — *Union Membership and Non-agricultural Paid Workers in Canada,*
1985-2004

	Union membership (000s)	Non-agricultural paid workers (000s)	Union membership as a percentage of non-agricultural paid workers
1985	3,666	10,060	36.4
1986	3,730	10,375	36.0
1987	3,782	10,744	35.2
1988	3,841	10,963	35.0
1989	3,944	11,340	34.8
1990	4,031	11,598	34.8
1991	4,068	11,679	34.8
1992	4,089	11,414	35.8
1993	4,071	11,303	36.0
1994	4,078	11,310	36.1
1995	4,003	11,526	34.7
1996	4,033	11,764	34.3
1997	4,074	11,802	34.5
1998	3,938	12,031	32.7
1999	4,010	12,295	32.6
2000	4,058	12,707	31.9
2001	4,111	13,146	31.3
2002	4,174	13,414	31.1
2003	4,178	13,737	30.4
2004	4,261	14,035	30.4

Source: Human Resources Development Canada, *Workplace Information Directorate*

Canadianization of Union Membership

Nowadays (see Table 4.2) about 63% of union members belong to Canadian labour unions and only 37% belong to international unions. This is a complete reversal of the situation in 1962, for example, when only 23% of union members belonged to Canadian labour unions.

Canadian nationalists have long objected to the high degree of U.S. investment in Canada and to the great amount of U.S. influence in the Canadian labour movement. They claim that policies developed in the U.S.-based international unions are sometimes more concerned with problems peculiar to the United States than to Canada. Some also believe that Canadian members of international unions pay substantially more in union dues to U.S. head offices of such unions than they get back in expertise and other services and in financial benefits. However, others have argued that Canadian workers benefit more, in job security, strike support, etc. by belonging to a large international union, with larger combined financial assets, better labour expertise, and political influence.

In response, some international unions have set up separate Canadian units to take better account of the political, economic and social differences of Canadian life. Nevertheless, there has been a steady erosion over the last thirty years of Canadian membership in the international unions. Greater attention by the international unions to Canadian concerns has failed to prevent some Canadian branches of international unions from breaking away to set up their own Canadian unions. The most notable example of this secession from international unions was the breakaway of the Canadian locals of the United Auto Workers (UAW) to form the Canadian Auto Workers (CAW).

Women in Unions

The proportion of women in the unionized work force in Canada has increased drastically in recent years. This increase is due largely to the unionization of the public and quasi-public sectors. This growth in the proportion of women means that the concerns of women will demand greater support and attention in the labour union movement. Women who have in many instances become the prime wage earner for their families are concerned with their ability to manage their households, maintain relationships with their children, and cope with the stresses of their dual careers, one inside and one outside the home.

An immediate concern is the length of the work week and the scheduling of those hours of work. Maternity leave and maternity financial benefits have already become a major bargaining issue and concern with the problem of day care for the children of working mothers is bound to increase.

Women are taking on more leadership roles in the work force, although still proportionately less than the ratio of women to men in the labour movement. Nevertheless, central and provincial labour organizations have increased the number of women vice-presidents and in 1986 Shirley Carr became the first female president of the CLC, after a long union career in the public sector, as a member of the Canadian Union of Public Employees.

Largest Unions

The thirty-two largest labour unions in Canada, in terms of Canadian membership are shown in Table 4.7.

One interesting point to note is that the two largest labour unions are made up of government employees. Another labour union of government employees, the Public Service Alliance, is sixth. The United Steelworkers, which was, for many years, the largest union in Canada, has now dropped to fifth.

Degree of Union Membership

Not all industries have the same degree of union membership. Thus, there is very little unionization so far among workers in agriculture, trade, finance, insurance, real estate, and service industries generally. However, this picture has been changing in recent years with nurses, teachers, and bank clerks joining the ranks of organized labour. In some industries — for example, railways, transportation equipment, leather, and paper and allied industries — the degree of unionization is extremely high.

Persons Excluded from Coverage

The federal and provincial labour relations acts do not apply to all employees. This means that an employer has no legal obligation to recognize or bargain collectively with unions representing such persons. In Ontario, persons not covered by the Labour Relations Act, 1995, include domestic workers employed in private homes; persons employed in agriculture, hunting or trapping; persons employed in horticulture (other than employees of a municipality or persons employed in silviculture) whose employer's primary business is agriculture or horticulture; provincial judges; and persons employed as a labour mediator or labour conciliator. Members of the architectural, dental, land surveying, legal or medical professions entitled to practise in Ontario and employed in a professional capacity are not considered to be employees covered by the Act. Nor are persons who, in the opinion of the Labour Relations Board, exercise managerial functions or are employed in a confidential capacity in matters relating to labour relations. Members of the police force, full-time firefighters, teachers, college employees, and provincial government employees, are groups covered by their own collective bargaining legislation. Contrary to Ontario's LRA (see page 84), the Supreme Court of Canada, in December 2001, in an 8 to 1 ruling, stated that agricultural workers have a constitutional right to unionize without fear of reprisals.

Table 4.7 — Unions in Canada with Largest Membership, 2004

Labour union	Membership (000)
1. Canadian Union of Public Employees	535
2. National Union of Public and General Employees	337
3. National Automobile, Aerospace, Transportation and General Workers Union of Canada	260
4. United Food and Commercial Workers International Union	188
5. United Steelworkers of America	180
6. Public Service Alliance of Canada	153
7. Communications, Energy and Paperworkers Union of Canada	150
8. International Brotherhood of Teamsters	110
9. Fédération de la santé et des services sociaux	101
10. Labourers' International Union of North America	85
11. Service Employees International Union	84
12. Fédération des syndicats de l'enseignement	81
13. Elementary Teachers' Federation of Ontario	65
14. International Brotherhood of Electrical Workers	55
15. Industrial Wood and Allied Workers of Canada	55
16. Canadian Union of Postal Workers	54
17. Ontario Secondary School Teachers' Federation	53
18. United Brotherhood of Carpenters and Joiners of America	52
19. Ontario Nurses' Association	48
20. Professional Institute of the Public Service of Canada	48
21. British Columbia Teachers' Federation	50
22. Fédération des infirmières et infirmiers du Québec	50
23. Syndicat de la fonction publique du Québec	43
24. Fédération des employées et employés de services publics inc.	42
25. United Association of Journeymen and Apprentices of the Plumbing and Pipe Fitting Industry of the United States and Canada	41
26. International Association of Machinists and Aerospace Workers	39
27. International Union of Operating Engineers	36
28. Fédération du commerce inc.	35
29. Ontario English Catholic Teachers' Association	35
30. Office and Professional Employees International Union	35
31. Alberta Teachers' Association	32
32. Hotel Employees and Restaurant Employees International Union	30

Source: Human Resources Development Canada, *Workplace Information Directorate*

4.5 LABOUR UNION ORGANIZATION

A labour union has a *central* (or *"national"*) *office*, with various departments, and a number of branches, geographically dispersed, called *union locals*.

Union Central Office

The central office of a labour union has a variety of responsibilities. First, it must decide policy for the union as a whole in such matters as collective bargaining, jurisdictional disputes, new branches, enrolment of new members, union dues, etc. Second, it must operate the union harmoniously as well as efficiently, maintaining contact with branches and assisting the union locals as the need arises. Third, it must administer the union's finances in an orderly and responsible fashion. And fourth, it must maintain contact with outside bodies such as the CLC, NDP, Labour Federations, etc., participating in various conferences and other meetings to decide on a common labour movement policy on matters of social, economic, and political concern.

The union central office and its staff should have considerable knowledge and experience which should be of assistance to the group that is organizing, in a variety of ways. It can help them to organize and, if it is appropriate, set up a union local. When the time is appropriate, it can assist them to apply for certification and guide them through the certification process. After the union becomes certified, the "national" can provide assistance to them in regard to the negotiation of an agreement with the employer.

As desired and as appropriate, the central office can assist in subsequent negotiations.

Very often, during the life of the agreement, the central office will provide assistance in the processing of grievances with the employer. Also, because of its knowledge and experience, it will almost certainly assist in the presentation of arbitration cases.

Again, during the life of the labour agreement, problems will probably arise between the union local and the employer. Where resolution of the matter can be assisted by central office representatives, due to their greater experience and the credibility that this experience gives them with the employer, their assistance can be called upon.

The national, because of its size and its financial resources, can provide services, as required, to its various locals in regard to such specialized areas as legal assistance, financial analysis for purpose of negotiations, and perhaps public relations, etc.

Also, the "national" can, and often does, provide and co-ordinate assistance to the local during a strike.

The Union Local

The basic unit of a labour union, formed in a particular plant or locality, is known as the *local*. In the case of an industrial union, a local may consist of either the employees of several small firms in a given area or the employees of one large firm. In the case of a craft union, the membership usually consists of persons practising a common skill — for example, bricklaying — in a given area.

The *internal organization* of a typical local will vary considerably from one union to another. One example is shown in Figure 4.1.

The union local has its own constitution, draws up its own bylaws governing the conduct of its officers and members, and has authority for such matters as: obtaining new members, handling grievances, collective bargaining, and recreational activities. Power is usually exercised by an executive committee, comprising the president, vice-president, and business agent. Part of this authority is delegated to the various other committees: the organizing and membership committee (which is responsible for recruiting new members); the bargaining committee that looks after negotiations for a new collective agreement: the grievance committee (which is concerned with the processing of grievances with the employer); the recreation committee (which looks after dances, parties, excursions, and so on); and the education committee (which provides information about union aims and activities to members and others). Having a constitution is a necessary step for a union local since in Ontario, for example, the Labour Relations Act requires a union to have a constitution before the provincial Labour Relations Board will consider the union's application for certification as bargaining agent.

In the plant itself, other union officials, called *shop stewards*, (or *zone representatives*, etc.), look after the grievances submitted to them by union members. The senior steward for a particular area or division is known as the *chief steward*.

In the smaller locals, all the various positions are held on a voluntary part-time basis by union members working at their regular jobs. These persons are elected by the members of the local, for periods ranging from several months to several years. Only in the larger locals is there a full-time *business agent* whose salary is paid either by the local itself or by the national or international office. The part-time officials are reimbursed by the local for time taken from work for union business. If there is a business agent, he or she will handle much of the work of the union, helping in the enrollment of new members and in the representation of the union in grievance matters and in contract negotiations.

The powers of the local can vary considerably according to the labour union of which it is a part.

Figure 4.1 *Example of the Organization of a Union Local*

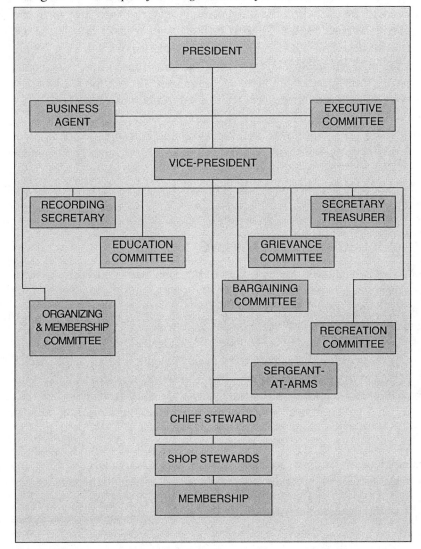

Decentralized Character of Unions

Unlike their counterparts in other parts of the world, most labour unions in Canada and the U.S. are highly decentralized. In other words, most of the action takes place at the local level rather than at the national level. It is the union local, close to the place of employment, where the new members are enlisted, where the employers send the union dues that are deducted from the worker's pay, where meetings are held to discuss the problems encountered

by members at their work, where social activities are organized, where grievances are discussed, where the strike committees are formed, and where the
president and other local officers as well as shop stewards are elected. Of
course, the degree of autonomy that a union local enjoys will vary greatly
from union to union. Nevertheless, compared with those in other countries,
unions in North America are highly decentralized — with the local unions,
to say nothing of the independently chartered local unions, enjoying a great
deal of autonomy. Only in certain circumstances has the national or international union the right to interfere in local affairs. This high degree of local
autonomy or decentralization is sometimes described as "grass- roots unionism". In some other countries, by contrast, the unions may not even have
plant-level local organizations. All union matters are administered from the
central office.

4.6 COLLECTIVE BARGAINING

Collective bargaining is the term used to describe the negotiations that take
place between a labour union, collectively representing the employees of a
plant or industry, and the employer or employers' association in drawing up a
mutually acceptable labour-management agreement.

In line with the decentralized nature of Canadian and U.S. labour unions,
most of the collective bargaining takes place at the local level. In the case of
some large companies, the various locals will use a company-wide bargaining committee to negotiate certain company-wide issues, leaving local issues
to be bargained on a local basis. Such a settlement might result in what is
commonly called a company-wide "master agreement" with local supplements. In other words, each local union usually negotiates with the company
that employs its members. In other countries such as Germany and Sweden,
collective bargaining is conducted at the national level by representatives of
all the unions and employers in a particular industry and the agreement is
binding nation-wide.

4.7 LABOUR COUNCILS

In Canada, the locals of many labour unions are affiliated with a Labour
Council established by charter of the Canadian Labour Congress for their
particular city or district — for example, the Toronto and District Labour
Council (C.L.C.). The delegates from the various locals elect the Council's
officers, who are responsible for furthering the interests of the labour union
movement at the community level — for example, by lobbying municipal

governments or by organizing strike aid. These district councils are some-times called *joint boards* or *conference boards*.

In industries organized along craft lines (such as painting and decorating), unions or union locals in a particular area may form a special council to co-ordinate members' activities and resolve jurisdictional problems. Such a council is sometimes called an *Allied Trades Federation*.

4.8 LABOUR FEDERATIONS

Most provinces have a Federation of Labour, chartered by the Canadian Labour Congress, which acts as the central organization for the labour union movement in the province. The Federation holds annual conventions where delegates from the affiliated locals vote on policy matters and elect officers. The purpose of the Federation is to represent labour's interest at the provin-cial level, particularly in the establishment or amendment of labour legisla-tion by the provincial government — for example, lobbying for guaranteed severance pay for workers whose employers declare bankruptcy.

4.9 CANADIAN LABOUR CONGRESS

The major central organization for labour unions in Canada is the *Canadian Labour Congress*, with headquarters in Ottawa and regional offices in most of the provinces. Most international, national and local unions, and all labour councils and federations are directly affiliated with the C.L.C. and send dele-gates to its biennial conventions.

Purpose

The purpose of the C.L.C. is primarily a political one: to act as the common spokesperson, particularly in Ottawa, for organized labour throughout Canada. It is also active in helping to settle *jurisdictional disputes* among the affiliated unions. These are disputes in which two or more unions claim the right to be certified as the bargaining agent for the same group of employees — employees who may or may not already be represented by a union. It also endeavours to ensure the observance of its Code of Ethical Practices. Another important function is to represent Canadian organized labour in international labour organizations such as the International Confederation of Free Trade Unions and the Commonwealth Trade Union. It also represents Canadian labour at international labour conferences.

The CLC also has a political role — it tries to influence federal and provincial government policies and the administration of existing labour and other relevant legislation by an ongoing program of communication. When new government or administration practices are being considered, the CLC tries to influence the outcome by such means as general and informal communication, formal presentations to government bodies or groups whose function it is to investigate a particular matter and make recommendations for action.

The CLC also tries to provide information and communicate its point of view through press releases and other representations to the written media, as well as to radio and television stations.

In Canada, labour relations is primarily within the jurisdiction of the provinces, so the CLC has provincial federations in order to exert political influence at the provincial level.

Jurisdictional Matters

The CLC consists of a number of different unions each with its own labour jurisdiction. This jurisdiction is as it was when the CLC was founded on May 1, 1956 or as subsequently granted or amended by the CLC. However, circumstances change — for example, companies merge, technological methods change, and new areas of union activity or interest emerge. Also, different labour unions may have different viewpoints and opinions as to their duty, opportunity and ability (a) to provide appropriate representation and support to employees in process of unionization and (b) to undertake activities to support and maintain the welfare of existing union members. The CLC attempts to resolve such interjurisdictional disputes.

Ethics

The CLC is also responsible for enforcing the Code of Ethical Practices contained in its constitution. The Code provides for, amongst other things, the right of union members to have honest elections, to run for office, and to receive fair treatment in the application of union rules. The CLC is also responsible for prohibiting corrupt practices.

If one of its member unions breaks the rules, the CLC must try to persuade the offending union to change its behaviour. If the offending union persists, the CLC may vote, at its regular convention, to expel the union from its organization.

4.10 THE CLC AND THE CANADIANIZATION OF INTERNATIONAL UNIONS IN CANADA

The CLC has long been concerned with the Canadianization of the Canadian branches of international unions. Thus, at its 1974 Convention, the CLC reaffirmed and expanded the standards of self-government that it had previously established for the affiliated Canadian divisions of international unions.

These standards provide for the election of Canadian officers by Canadian union members, the determination of policies dealing with national matters by elected Canadian officers and members, and the requirement that only Canadian elected representatives have the authority to speak for the union concerned in Canada. As regards affiliation to an international union organization, the Canadian division should be affiliated separately to ensure proper Canadian representation. Also, the international union must take the necessary action to ensure that the Canadian union membership is not prevented by constitutional requirements or policy decisions from taking part in the social, cultural, economic, and political life of Canada.

4.11 POLITICAL ROLE OF LABOUR UNIONS

Labour unions through their various provincial and national labour organizations, can exert pressure in municipal, provincial, and federal politics by offering support to political parties willing to help promote union aims. Labour unions also make direct representations to the provincial and federal governments on matters of urgent importance such as a high rate of unemployment or the need for price or profit controls. The labour movement, as a whole, usually through the CLC, provides financial and other support to the New Democratic Party, or NDP.

Political Conservatism

A characteristic of Canadian and U.S. labour unions is their basic acceptance of the political and economic systems of their countries. Their emphasis, therefore, is not on radical political and economic change but on the economic welfare of their members. Only in recent years have Canadian labour unions become more active politically, with increased financial and other support to the New Democratic Party. And this party, although occupying the left-wing of the political spectrum in Canada, is not a radical political movement of the Marxist-Leninist type. It is certainly not dedicated to the overthrow of the Canadian political system and the predominantly private enterprise system that exists in this country.

The increasing number of Canadian labour unions has had its effect on the political scene. Canadian unions tend to be more politically oriented than U.S. unions and Canadian autonomy for many former Canadian branches of U.S.-based international unions has given the new Canadian unions more opportunity to debate particularly Canadian social issues such as health insurance plans, pensions, unemployment insurance, and political support for the New Democratic Party (NDP). However, Canadian autonomy has, conversely, lessened the ability of Canadian union members to influence government policy in the United States which could ultimately have an adverse effect on job opportunities in Canada.

4.12 ECONOMIC GOALS OF LABOUR UNIONS

The primary goal of the labour unions active in Canada is to secure from employers greater economic benefits for their members. This includes better pay and fringe benefits as well as greater job security and improvements in working conditions, including occupational health and safety. This union philosophy, with its emphasis on economic rather than political goals, is sometimes called "business unionism". However, so far as most Canadian and U.S. union leaders are concerned, North American style democracy and the private enterprise system, despite their faults, have provided union members in this continent with one of the highest material standards of living in the world.

4.13 LABOUR DAY

Every September 5, trade unionists in Canada and the U.S. undertake a labour solidarity march in their local communities. Originally started in the 1880s, to press the demand for a shorter working week, the annual march helps make the public more aware of the important role that trade unions still play in our modern industrial society.

REVIEW QUESTIONS

1. How would you define a labour union or trade union? Is there any difference between the meaning of these terms?

2. Distinguish between a trade union and an employee association.

3. Why do people join labour unions? Why do they sometimes refuse to join?

4. Distinguish between craft unions and industrial unions.

5. Distinguish between international and national unions.

6. What are the two basic types of local labour organizations?

7. Explain the following abbreviations: CLC, CSN, CSD, CCU, AFL-CIO.

8. How substantial is union membership in Canada? Is membership increasing as a percentage of the labour force?

9. To what extent is union membership Canadianized?

10. What effect can increasing female participation have on the Canadian labour movement?

11. Which are the largest trade unions, by membership, in Canada? What type of unions are they?

12. Why are some industries more heavily unionized than others?

13. In which industries has union membership been rapidly growing in recent times? Why?

14. Which persons are excluded from coverage under the federal and provincial labour relations acts?

15. Explain the possible role of a union central office, or "national".

16. How is the union local typically organized? What is the local's role?

17. What is the role of the shop steward? How is he or she selected? What qualifications does he or she need?

18. What is a union "business agent"? What does he or she do?

19. Explain the nature purpose and relationship of labour councils, labour federations and the Canadian Labour Congress.

20. One of the functions of the CLC is to help settle "jurisdictional disputes" among affiliated unions. Explain.

21. Why are North American labour unions said to be highly decentralized? What are the possible reasons for this? What are its benefits for union members?

22. Compare the local collective bargaining that takes place in North America with the system in West Germany and Sweden.

23. What is the CLC's attitude towards Canadianization of the labour movement in Canada?

24. North American labour unions are said to be guided by a philosophy of "business unionism". Explain and discuss.

CHAPTER 5: THE CANADIAN LABOUR MOVEMENT — HISTORY AND PHILOSOPHY

5.1 NINETEENTH CENTURY ORIGINS

Historically, the Canadian labour movement can trace its origins to the early nineteenth century when several small local unions were formed among skilled workers to fight particular issues. Thus, for example, printers were organized in Quebec City in 1827 and in Montreal and Hamilton in 1833. In Toronto, the York Printers were organized in 1832. However, most of the early efforts to form unions were of relatively short duration. One exception was the Toronto Typographical Union which was established in 1844 and has existed ever since. An unsympathetic government, employer opposition, worker apathy, and a still predominantly rural society all helped check the growth of unions in Canada. Also, extremely important, under the common law inherited from Britain and based on precedent (or prior court decisions), persons organizing a union or calling a strike might well be charged with the criminal offence of "conspiracy to restrain trade" and, on being found guilty, subject to imprisonment and heavy fines. Only towards the end of the nineteenth century was legislation passed by the Canadian Parliament to help prevent this. And only towards the end of the century did government leaders, federal and provincial, start to give mild approval to the concept of trade unions and the collective bargaining process.

Unfortunately, during this long period of union growth, there was a great deal of dissension among the various unions — based largely on two basic ideological conflicts: the first, between craft unions and industrial unions, on grounds of membership eligibility; and the second, between national and international unions, on grounds of nationalism. Nevertheless, with growing economic prosperity, linked in part to the introduction of tariff protection in 1879, and the building of the Canadian Pacific Railway in the years 1881 to 1885, more and more workers joined labour unions. In fact railway unions just followed the railroad westward. In Nova Scotia, in 1879, the coal miners formed the first coal miners' union in North America. This union, the Provincial Workmen's Association, was later broadened to include many different types of workers as well as coal miners — for example, iron workers, steel workers, railway men, tramway men, glass blowers, boot and shoe workers, and retail clerks — a classic example of a "general union".

External Influences

Immigrants to Canada, during the nineteenth century, included many persons who had been active in labour unions in the British Isles. As a result, several British unions established locals or branches in Canada. Thus, for example, the Amalgamated Society of Engineers set up its first local in Canada in 1850 and three more in 1851. Also, a number of immigrants already familiar with the concept of trade unions, helped establish Canadian unions without any official assistance. Examples of the establishment of such purely Canadian local unions were the shipbuilders at Quebec City and Victoria in 1862, and a variety of trades in Quebec in 1865, including bakers, tailors, bricklayers, stonecutters, wharf-porters, longshoremen, and bookbinders.

Although British immigrants were and still are very active in the Canadian labour movement, the closeness of the United States has made the American unions the predominant external influence on organized labour in Canada. The first union to come to Canada was the Iron Moulders in 1861 followed by, for example, the Locomotive Engineers in 1864; the National Typographical Society, and the Cigarmakers in 1865; the Knights of St. Crispin (shoemakers) in 1867; the Railway Conductors in 1868; and the Coopers in 1869.

Trades Councils

Initially, the various trade unions were solely preoccupied with their own affairs. However, in 1871, five craft unions joined to form the Toronto Trades Assembly. And by 1873, Trades Councils, uniting various local unions, were active in Ottawa and Hamilton. In that same year, on the initiative of the Toronto Trades Assembly, a convention of trade unions was held in Toronto, attended by delegates from 31 locals of 14 unions located in Ontario. Letters of approval were also received from typographical unions in Quebec City and Montreal. At this convention, it was decided to establish a central national labour organization, to be called the Canadian Labour Union. Meetings of the C.L.U. were then held in each of the years from 1874 to 1877. However, the serious economic depression that afflicted Canada beginning in 1878 caused the meetings to come to a halt.

In 1881, after the depression, the Toronto Trades Assembly was replaced by the Toronto Trades and Labour Council. Other labour councils were formed in London, Montreal, Ottawa, Brantford, Hamilton, Vancouver, and Victoria during the 1880s. Nationally, a convention of labour unions, organized by the Toronto Council in 1883, established a new central labour organization, which later came to be known as The Trades and Labour Congress.

5.2 NATIONAL VERSUS INTERNATIONAL UNIONS

Initially, the unions formed in Canada were purely Canadian ones with no outside links. However, in the 1860s, some of the craft unions such as printers and moulders, began to establish fraternal, and later formal, links with similar U.S. unions. The incentives to do so were several: the greater opportunity for a Canadian union member with a union card to find work in the U.S., should he decide to move South; the greater psychological strength derived from membership in a larger organization of similar craftsmen; and greater financial strength. The American union that "took in" a Canadian branch came to be called an International Union. These international unions, exclusively of the craft type, were joined together in the U.S. in a central organization called the American Federation of Labour, or AFL for short.

The international unions gradually became stronger in Canada so that in 1902, for example, under pressure from the AFL, the Trades and Labour Congress, Canada's central labour body, even amended its constitution to the effect that it would not recognize a national union if an international union existed in that same jurisdiction. Furthermore, at this same convention, the TLC elected John Flett, a paid officer of an international union, as its new president. It also refused to seat delegates from the Montreal Federated Trades Council, a purely Canadian body.

In Quebec, unions of French-speaking workers, completely independent from the international unions, were formed with the active encouragement of the Catholic Church.

5.3 THE WINNIPEG GENERAL STRIKE

On May 15, 1919, a variety of unions went on strike in Winnipeg because of the refusal of Winnipeg employers to negotiate with a newly established metal trades council. The metal trades workers, who earned from $12 to $15 a week, were incensed by the fact that, because of inflation, the purchasing power of their wages had fallen drastically while employers had benefited from high profits throughout the war. The strikers' demands included: (a) recognition of the metal trades council, (b) an 8-hour day and a maximum 44-hour week, (c) double rate of pay for overtime work and 1-hour premium pay for night-shift work, and (d) a pay rate of 85 cents per hour for skilled workers and 25 cents per hour for apprentices.

Sympathy with the metal workers was widespread, fuelled in large part by general dissatisfaction with Canada's social and economic system, particularly the high rates of inflation and unemployment, the latter being aggravated by soldiers returning from the First World War. Workers who went on strike to support the metal workers' demands were from both the private and public sectors, including postal workers and the police. The strikers effectively halted all production, construction, transportation, and communications in Winnipeg and the surrounding areas and succeeded in closing the hotels, banks, and other main buildings. A Central Strike Committee comprising 287 delegates (three from each of 94 union locals and five from the TLC) administered the strike.

The Canadian Prime Minister, Robert Borden, arguing that public servants had no right to strike, sent the RCMP to Winnipeg, followed by a battalion of soldiers and two Lewis machine guns. The federal government then ordered all postal workers back to work. Likewise, the provincial government ordered back all telephone workers, and the municipal government all police and firemen. However, the postal workers and police refused to return and most were dismissed.

The principal leaders of the strike were then arrested on June 17 and held in jail for 72 hours. That same day, in front of the Winnipeg Town Hall, a large crowd assembled only to have the Riot Act read to them by the mayor and to become involved in a confrontation with 50 mounted RCMP and "special" police, that ended with two persons being killed and 30 injured. The Canadian government then placed the city under military rule and many arrests were made. On June 26, the strike effectively broken, people returned to work. Many were locked out, blacklisted, dismissed or otherwise discriminated against.

5.4 THE DEPRESSION YEARS

In the fall of 1929, the stock market collapsed, to be followed by the worst economic depression in history. By 1932, at the bottom of the "Great Depression", about one-third of the labour force in Canada and the United States was unemployed. Even for those fortunate enough to have jobs, conditions were bad. Hours of work were long, wages were low, and wage cutting was rampant.

Workers Unity League

The increasing mass misery gave impetus to a new group — the *Workers Unity League*, founded in 1930. Included in it were unions like the Amalgamated Mine Workers of Nova Scotia, the Mine Workers Industrial Union, and a number of Textile, Furniture and Rubber locals in Ontario.

The WUL never became a major force in Canadian trade union life but it was important at that time. In 1932, its membership was reported to be 40,000. It was active in organizing the non-union workers and in helping to conduct strikes. In fact, in 1934 it claimed leadership in 90% of the strikes that had been fought. Its constituent unions were all national and industrial, in line with its support of the principle of Canadian as compared with international (or U.S. dominated) industrial unions. When its membership is combined with that of the Canadian and Catholic Confederation of Labour and all Canadian Congress of Labour, it shows that by the middle 1930s about half the total trade union membership in Canada was grouped in national unions.

Major Strikes

Bitter strikes were fought in those early depression years. For example, in September 1931, at Estevan, Saskatchewan, 500 coal miners, who were members of the Mine Workers Union of Canada (WUL), went on strike, when the mine owners refused to negotiate. The miners demanded an eight-hour day, a minimum of $5.40 per day for underground work, and union recognition. Present in Estevan were 47 RCMP constables armed with rifles, revolvers, and machine guns. As the strikers passed by the town hall, the RCMP and local police opened fire. Three miners were killed, between 12 and 18 wounded, and almost 50 arrested. Across Canada, trade union sympathy was stirred, resulting in resolutions and protest demonstrations. Following this show of support, the Estevan strike was soon settled. The terms included recognition of the union district committee, an 8-hour day for contract work, and the miners' right to appoint their own checkmen — in sum, a partial victory for the union.

Another major strike was that of the Stratford Furniture Workers, in Ontario in 1933. The authorities sent in troops, tanks, and machine guns. The strikers countered with mass picketing. The outcome was a partial victory for the strikers: wage increases ranging from 10 to 25%, a 45-hour week, and recognition of the shop committee. The strike was led by the WUL but it won assistance from locals of other unions and received express support from the Trades and Labour Congress.

The U.S. Experience

In the United States, 1932 was a presidential election year. Franklin D. Roosevelt, who campaigned on the program of a "New Deal", was elected president. In his campaign, he gave clear evidence of his sympathy for the labourers and pledged assistance for the "forgotten men at the bottom of the economic pyramid".

In March 1932, labour had received some encouragement from the passage of the Norris-LaGuardia Act (The Federal Anti-injunction Act). It held no solution for the troublesome unemployment of the day but did mark a significant advance for collective bargaining. The full freedom of collective association without the interference of employers was declared as public policy.

At the time of Roosevelt's election, the U.S. and in effect the whole North American economy could be described as being in a deflationary spiral. In order for the manufacturer to sell its goods, it often had to cut its prices. After it cut its prices and sold its goods, it went back and cut wages in order to get its costs into line.

Immediately after the Presidential inauguration in 1933, a great deal of legislation was quickly passed. Much of it was intended to get the economy moving again. Some of this legislation, with the purpose of ending the downward spiral of prices, allowed employers to form associations which were allowed to exchange information on pricing. Some of the legislation was designed to create public works projects, such as the Tennessee Valley Authority, to create job opportunities for the unemployed. One of the more important pieces of legislation was the National Industrial Recovery Act (NIRA) of 1933.

Section 7A of this Act guaranteed the right of employees to organize into unions of their own choosing and to bargain collectively with employers. Although the basic purpose of the NIRA was, in the U.S. President's words, to "put people back to work", it meant far more than that to American labour. Confident in the protection of the law, labour commenced organizing and recruiting campaigns everywhere. However, in May 1935, the NIRA was declared invalid — this was a severe blow to union aspirations.

A new deal for labour made its appearance with the passage of the National Labour Relations Act (the Wagner Act) in 1935. Incorporated into this Act were the provisions of Section 7A of the NIRA. However, the incentive for union growth provided by the Act was subject to delay. Many employers, doubting the validity of the new legislation, refused either in spirit or in practice to carry out its provisions. But in April 1937 the U.S. Supreme Court validated the Act and labour got legal sanction for further advances.

5.5 CRAFT UNIONS VERSUS INDUSTRIAL UNIONS

All the early trade unions in Canada and elsewhere were associations of persons performing a certain type of skill or trade — for example, carpenters or bricklayers. Later, however, other unions came to be formed, the membership of which was open to all persons working in a certain company or industry. This new type of union came to be known as an "industrial union". The most important early example of such a union in North America was the Knights of Labor established in the 1880s, with many locals in Ontario and Quebec as well as in the United States, particularly Chicago. The craft unions were opposed to industrial unions — in large part because they feared that craft workers in a particular company or industry might join the industrial union rather than the craft one. However, the growth of manufacturing industry, with an increasing number of relatively unskilled jobs, meant that the industrial unions had more and more potential members. The craft unions, on the other hand, had a more gradual increase in the number of potential members. The Knights of Labor, one of the strongest of the early industrial unions, became gradually weaker, giving way to other industrial unions.

American Federation of Labour

The conflict between craft and industrial unions became the subject of bitter debate at the annual convention of the American Federation of Labour, or AFL, in San Francisco in 1934.

The national unions composing the AFL were of the craft or horizontal type. They were constituted of a rather homogeneous level of skilled labour stretching laterally over many different types of industries. The United Brotherhood of Carpenters and Joiners, for example, included carpenters who were employed in building a house, in a cabinet shop, or on shipboard. The important thing was the skill, knowledge, and training of the carpenter, no matter where he was found.

The non-AFL unions were of the industrial or vertical type. The mere fact that a person was employed in a certain industry made him or her eligible for membership. No particular skill was necessary. Only because of this could the great mass of workers carry their collective bargaining ambitions to fruition.

At the AFL's San Francisco convention, it was finally agreed that union charters would be issued in the automotive, cement, and aluminum industries and in "such other mass production and miscellaneous industries that in the judgement of the executive council may be necessary to meet the situation". It also authorized the council to "inaugurate, manage, promote, and conduct" an organizing campaign in the steel industry as soon as practical. During the next months, the AFL granted charters to unions in the automobile and rubber industries. In defining the jurisdiction of these unions, the executive council specifically excluded certain skilled craftsmen and maintenance employees who already came under the jurisdiction of existing craft unions. This was a source of much irritation to the industrial unions. However, the crowning blow occurred when the steel organizing drive failed to materialize. The executive council reported that "we did not deem it advisable to launch an organizing drive for the steel industry". As far as the industrial union element within its ranks was concerned, the AFL had added insult to injury.

Congress of Industrial Organizations

In November 1935, the industrial union crusaders completed plans to set up their own Committee for Industrial Organization (CIO) with John L. Lewis as chairman. The ten unions participating in the CIO were then suspended from the AFL. In May 1937, Lewis and his associates transformed the Committee into the Congress of Industrial Organizations.

The organizing efforts of the CIO in the late 1930s were helped by the provisions of the Wagner Act but ran into very strong resistance in the major industrial mass production units such as the steel, packing house, and automotive industries in the United States. Gradually over that period the CIO was successful, in spite of very considerable violence, in organizing large numbers of employees in these industries and in negotiating contracts with their employers.

The leaders of the CIO recognized that part of the reason for their success in the United States was the Wagner Act. They also realized that there was no equivalent to the Wagner Act in Canada. They believed the CIO was making a significant contribution toward improving the welfare of industrial workers in the United States and believed that Canadian workers should have the same benefits and that the CIO was the organization that could bring this about. In addition, they recognized that many of the employers that had strongly resisted the CIO in the United States had branch plants in Canada. One of the methods available to these employers to resist the CIO in the United States was to expand their operations in Canada, thereby exporting American jobs to Canadian workers. For both these reasons, the CIO unions moved into Canada to conduct strong organizing campaigns.

Along with the CIO unions, other industrial unions became more active in Canada. As a result of the general economic conditions of Canadian workers, the rise of Canadian industrial unions, and the activity of the CIO, a strike movement began in Canada in 1937. Thus, for example, in the winter of 1937, 850 workers at Empire Cottons struck against conditions branded by Ontario Minister David Croll as "brutal underpayment and shameless exploitation".

However, the largest textile strike was in Quebec at Dominion Textiles. Hours were 60 per week on the night shift and sixty-four per week on the day shift. Wages were as low as $3.50 per week for women. The workers who were members of the National Federation of Textile Workers, an affiliate of the Canadian Catholic Confederation of Labour, or CCCL, demanded a 40-hour week, a wage increase, and union recognition. The company refused to negotiate. Strike fever mounted and, in August 1937, employees went on strike at Montreal, Valleyfield, Drummondville, Magog, Sherbrooke, St. Gregoire, and Montmorency. Maurice Duplessis, just elected for his first term as premier of Quebec, proposed that Cardinal Villeneuve mediate. The union accepted and recommended a return to work. An agreement concluded later between the company and the union granted wages increases and a 50-hour week.

The automotive industry was another storm centre. Oshawa, 1937, its eye. On April 8, 4,000 General Motors workers went on strike for a forty-hour week, pay at time-and-half for overtime, recognition of shop stewards, seniority, and recognition of the union, the United Automobile Workers.

Ontario Premier Mitchell Hepburn said he would break the strike. He branded the CIO communist and sent in a special squad of Provincial Police which was assisted in turn by a contingent of the RCMP. He said he would, if necessary, raise an army too. The strikers continued to picket in numbers reaching 600 and set up their own strike police. Across Canada, many labour councils called for solidarity with the strikers. Two members of Hepburn's cabinet submitted their resignations. The strike ended with a settlement for a forty-four hour week, wage increases, recognition for the union stewards, and no discrimination against the striking employees.

5.6 THE SECOND WORLD WAR AND ITS AFTERMATH

In 1939, Canada went to war.. Production expanded enormously. Between 1939 and 1944, the annual value of manufactured goods produced increased from 3 billion dollars to 9 billion dollars. Over a million men and women were engaged directly in the "war effort". And union membership more than doubled between 1940 and 1945.

However, during the war, the Federal government introduced wage and price controls. And the unions, to support the war effort, generally followed a no-strike policy.

During the war, labour relations, which was largely a matter of provincial jurisdiction, was taken over by the Federal government, under the war-emergency provisions. Orders-in-council were passed dealing with labour relations and some of these gave labour certain rights, some of which resembled rights provided in the United States under the Wagner Act. After the war, provincial labour relations jurisdiction was returned to the provinces and provincial Labour Relations Acts were passed. While these Acts varied they had certain similarities and some of their provisions were somewhat similar to provisions of the U.S. Wagner Act.

In 1945, with the war at an end, there was considerable economic uncertainty. Whereas the 1930s were typified by economic depression and mass unemployment, the years 1940 to 1945 were typified by full employment caused by the war effort. When the war ended, some people expected full employment to continue, while others expected the economy to revert to the conditions of the 1930s.

Unions had made a great deal of progress in organization during the war years. However, the objectives of both union leaders and the union membership had been severely restricted by war-time wage and price controls. Consequently, in 1946, strikes broke out right across Canada, from Cape Breton to Vancouver Island, affecting one major industry after another, mostly in manufacturing but also in mining, logging, and transportation. The strike movement began in May when the British Columbia loggers, members of the International Woodworkers of America, walked out. Then came strikes of seamen, textile workers, and rubber workers. Later, electrical and steel workers in Hamilton went on strike. Then in the Fall, lumber workers in Northern Ontario left their jobs. Generally, these strikes had one common outcome — they were won by the unions.

Union Rivalry

During the 1940s, there was constant rivalry in recruiting union members, both craft and industrial, between the AFL and TLC on the one side and the CIO and CCL on the other. In the 1950s, however, it became apparent that it was becoming more and more difficult to obtain new members. Consequently, in June 1954, the presidents of the AFL and the CIO, George Meany and Walter Reuther, agreed to a two-year no-raiding pact. Then in February 1955, a merger of the AFL and CIO was decided upon, with George Meany as president and over 15 million members. This was followed in April 1956 by the merger in Canada of the TLC and the CCL, the main rival union federations, to form the Canadian Labour Congress (CLC), with over one million members.

The dominance of U.S.-controlled, "international unions" continued in Canada for many years. However, over the last twenty-five years, Canadian nationalism has begun to be felt more and more strongly in the union movement. One dramatic example was the formation in 1974 of the Canadian Paperworkers Union by breakaway members of the United Paperworkers International Union. And many other national unions have been formed in Canada over recent decades — for example, the Canadian Autoworkers Union. The international unions themselves, in recognition of Canadian nationalism, have gradually reduced control over their Canadian sections so as to discourage any further breakaways.

5.7 LABOUR UNIONS IN QUEBEC

The growth of labour unions in Quebec was greatly influenced by the Roman Catholic church which desired that French-Canadian workers remain French in language and Catholic in religion. To the Roman Catholic clergy, as well as to many other French Canadians, the activities of the English-speaking American and Canadian labour unions could only mean a further loss of Quebec's cultural identity. Consequently, following a lockout in the boot and shoe industry in Quebec City in 1900, that was arbitrated by the Archbishop of Quebec, new and solely French-speaking unions were formed with the assistance of the Roman Catholic clergy, in various industries in the province.

Later, following the establishment of various central councils, a permanent province-wide federation of these French-Canadian unions came into being in 1921, called the Confederation des Travailleurs Catholiques du Canada (CTCC). However, the CTCC and its affiliated unions, although French-Canadian, were not militant enough in the nineteen-twenties and thirties to attract the majority of French-Canadian unionists. In fact, well under half of such workers belonged to the French-Canadian unions.

During and after World War II, the situation changed rapidly. First, Quebec became much more industrialized, with a consequent influx of workers to the towns and cities. Second, the Catholic unionists, led by new and more aggressive non-clerical officials, became more and more dissatisfied with the large wage gap between themselves and English-speaking workers in certain industries and trades.

In 1949, this dissatisfaction erupted in a bitter and violent strike by the asbestos workers in Quebec. On the one side were the striking workers, supported by the Roman Catholic Church; and on the other, the employer, the subsidiary of a large American company, supported by the provincial Duplessis government. The latter, a supporter of the *status quo*, even went so far as to declare the strike illegal, decertify the union, and send in several hundred heavily armed police to keep order.

The QFL and the CTCC

Although the workers' gains were minimal, the CTCC acquired considerable prestige among Quebec workers for its firm stand. It also helped convince the CTCC that it should seek allies among other labour organizations rather than trying to operate independently. However, although the rival provincial federations of the Trades and Labour Congress of Canada (TLC) and the Canadian

Congress of Labour (CCL) merged in 1956 into a new CLC-sponsored Quebec Federation of Labour, the QFL remained suspicious of the CTCC and unresponsive to its overtures. Nevertheless, the two main labour organizations did co-operate on certain issues such as the strike by copper mining and smelting workers in Murdochville, Quebec. However, in 1959, the lack of support by English-speaking Canadians for the CBC producers strike in Montreal, together with a hostile attitude by the executives of the CLC parent union towards their French-speaking locals, persuaded the latter to switch their allegiance to the CTCC. This event marked the end of any further co-operation between the two central labour federations in Quebec, the QFL and the CTCC.

Confederation of National Trade Unions

At its 1960 convention, the CTCC, changed its name to the Confederation des Syndicats Nationaux (CSN), thereby dropping its identification with the Catholic Church. During the nineteen sixties, the Confederation of National Trade Unions, or CNTU, as the CSN was called in English, more than doubled its membership. This was due in part to a new more liberal Quebec labour code. Membership by the end of the decade was over two hundred thousand, including six former CLC unions.

During the nineteen seventies and the nineteen eighties, the leadership of both the CNTU and the QFL in Quebec became more radical in character, with a more aggressive stance in support of labour negotiations by member unions. Today, politically, the Quebec labour movement is sympathetic to the Parti Quebecois.

REVIEW QUESTIONS

1. What factors delayed the growth of trade unions in Canada during the nineteenth century?

2. Compare the British and American influence in the development of trade unions in Canada.

3. Explain the nature and role of trades councils in the trade union movement in the late nineteenth century.

4. Explain the reasons for the early popularity of international unions in Canada.

5. Describe and assess the significance of the Winnipeg general

strike of 1919.

6. What was the effect of the "Depression" on the Canadian trade union movement in the nineteen thirties?

7. Compare and discuss the handling of the Estevan and Stratford strikes in the 1930s with the way that strikes are handled today.

8. How did Franklin D. Roosevelt and his "New Deal" affect the trade union movement in the United States and Canada?

9. Explain and discuss the reasons for the conflict between the craft and industrial unions in both the United States and Canada.

10. Why did the CIO unions move into Canada to conduct strong organizing campaigns?

11. Why did the AFL and CIO eventually decide to merge?

12. "Canadian nationalism is slowly beginning to make itself felt in the trade union movement." Explain and discuss.

13. Why did the Church become involved in the union movement in Quebec? How long did this involvement last? How and why was its influence eventually reduced?

14. What were the effects on the Quebec labour movement of the asbestos workers' strike in 1949?

15. What were the two rival labour federations in Quebec? Why were they rivals?

16. "Through its support for the Parti Quebecois, organized labour in Quebec won many goals that would otherwise have had to be fought for on the factory floor." Explain and discuss.

CHAPTER 6: EMPLOYERS: ORGANIZATIONS, ATTITUDES AND PRACTICES

6.1 TYPES OF EMPLOYERS' ASSOCIATIONS

There are many different types of employers' associations in Canada that are involved in industrial relations. As the great diversity suggests, lack of employer unity is a key characteristic, compared with other countries such as Germany and Sweden.

Bargaining Associations. Some employers' associations — in, for example, clothing, printing, construction and trucking — act as the formal bargaining agent for their members. They are in effect, therefore, "bargaining associations". The reason for their establishment is that in these industries there are many small firms representing employers on the one hand but only one common trade union or group of unions representing the employees on the the other. Such associations, acting on behalf of their member employers, undertake the bargaining with the union, sign the collective agreement, and may even administer the agreement. Sometimes an employer association may carry out the bargaining with the union but the member firms will each sign a separate collective agreement and administer it themselves. In this case, the organization may be known as a "consultative association".

Co-ordinating Associations. Other associations such as the Railway Association of Canada act only as a "co-ordinating association" — co-ordinating the collective bargaining activities of their members.

Educational Associations. Other associations such as the Canada Construction Association and the Canada Pulp and Paper Association serve mainly as an "educational association" — educating members in all aspects of industrial relations and acting as a central depository for all information useful for collective bargaining purposes.

Lobbying Associations. Some employer organizations such as the Canadian Chamber of Commerce and the Canadian Manufacturers' Association do not participate at all, either directly or indirectly, in the collective bargaining process. Instead, they act as a spokesperson for employers in Ottawa and the provincial capitals. They are what may be called "lobbying associations".

6.2 EMPLOYERS' ASSOCIATIONS
AND COLLECTIVE BARGAINING

The practice by some employers of joining together in associations to negotiate with unions is an attempt by employers to strengthen their bargaining position. It is considered a logical move designed to counteract, to some extent, the increasing strength of labour unions in modern times.

By joining together, employers can agree beforehand on a desirable and realistic level of wages, fringe benefits and other conditions of employment and negotiate more effectively, using specialized, full-time negotiators, to achieve a settlement with the union as close to these goals as possible. Also, after a settlement has been reached, the members of the employers' association have the satisfaction of knowing that everyone is in the same boat — no employer has a competitive advantage over another, as all wage and benefit increases and non-monetary concessions are the same for all members.

Another advantage for employers of a common front is that, if there is a strike, public and government attention and, hopefully, support will be forthcoming more quickly than if an individual firm is shut down.

In some industries, such as construction, where many different types of workers are employed, it is much more convenient for employers to negotiate as an association with the various unions. Each type of worker — for example, carpenters — can be covered by a master agreement that is effective for all employers in the association. If there is no employer association, a union or group of unions may be tempted to strike one company so as to secure a generous settlement that can be used as a standard in negotiations with the other employers.

6.3 LEGAL STATUS OF EMPLOYERS' ASSOCIATIONS

There is no restriction in law on the right of employers to join together for collective bargaining purposes. In fact, certain Labour Relations Acts (or Labour Codes, depending on the province) have an accreditation procedure for employers' organizations. In British Columbia, this applies to all industries. In other provinces, only to the construction industry.

According to the Ontario Labour Relations Act, 1995, Section 1, an employers' organization is:

> "an organization of employers formed for purposes that include the regulation of relations between employers and employees and includes an accredited employers' organization and a designated or accredited employer bargaining agency".

The procedure for accreditation requires an employers' association to apply to the Labour Relations Board for accreditation as the bargaining agent for all employers in a particular sector of an industry and in a certain geographic area. The Board then has to determine that the employers' unit is appropriate for collective bargaining purposes, that it is properly constituted and that it has appropriate authority vested in it by the employer members to act as an accredited bargaining agent. Upon accreditation, the association becomes the exclusive bargaining agent for all employers in the bargaining unit. The Board, as one of its responsibilities, will try to ensure that there has been no union interference in the establishment of the employers' organization.

Duty of Fair Representation

An important responsibility for an accredited employers' association is the "duty of fair representation" of its members.

Specifically, an accredited employers' organization should not act in a manner that is arbitrary, discriminatory or in bad faith in the representation of any of the employers in the unit, whether members of the accredited employers' organization or not.

6.4 EMPLOYER ATTITUDES

In the nineteenth century, when trade unions were first established, most employers were quite hostile to them. Nowadays, with the various Labour Relations Acts or Codes that require an employer to bargain in good faith with a certified trade union, most employers accept unions as part of the industrial relations system and the collective bargaining process as a normal part of doing business. Some employers continue, however, to resist strongly any union activity. Others try to prevent unionization by offering relatively high rates of pay and generous fringe benefits. Others try to resist unionization of their employees by less acceptable means such as the dismissal of employees engaged in union activity or suggesting that employees will be worse off economically and otherwise by joining a union.

6.5 ANTI-UNION PRACTICES

In the past, employers have used many different methods for opposing unions.

Blacklists. These were lists of persons who were known to be union members or union sympathizers. Employers have been known to circulate these lists among themselves and refuse to employ anyone shown on them.

Labour Spies. Persons were often hired by employers to work in a plant and inform on any pro-union employees — who would then be dismissed. Sometimes a worker might even be blackmailed to report on his colleagues.

Intimidation. Often an employer, faced with the possibility that its employees might join a union, would try to intimidate them. The usual method was to threaten that they would be worse off if the plant became unionized — by the reduction or elimination of benefits now being received, and by a reduction in the number of jobs. An extreme way was by locking out the employees.

Today, still, there are reports of employers trying to intimidate their employees. This can occur at any one of the four main stages of the collective bargaining process—when the union is recruiting members in order to gain certification; while the union application for certification is being processed; during negotiations for a collective agreement; and during the life of the agreement itself. Also, an employer will sometimes lock out its employees.

Infiltration. One modern anti-union practice that has been reported in the press has been the infiltration of the work force by undercover operatives hired by the employer or by a related company such as a security service. The undercover operatives then try to dissuade other employees from joining a union and themselves vote against the union when a certification vote is held.

Staged Incidents. Another modern anti-union practice also reported in the press, has been the staging of incidents that provide the employer with plausible grounds for dismissing employees actively involved in union activities or known or suspected to be highly sympathetic towards unionization of the company work force. Such incidents may be staged by management — for example, by provoking an employee into an emotional outburst against a supervisor or into an act of disobedience. Alternatively, incidents can be staged by the undercover operatives mentioned previously. For example, they may start a fight with the union sympathizers that gives management grounds for dismissing all the persons involved and thus creating an appearance of fairness.

Unfair practices by management are discussed further in Chapter 10.

REVIEW QUESTIONS

1. What are the various types of employer associations involved in industrial relations?

2. What advantages do employers obtain by joining together for collective bargaining purposes?

3. What is the legal status of employer associations?

4. Outline the procedure for accreditation to be followed by an employers' organization under your provincial Labour Relations Act or Code.

5. Explain the "duty of fair representation".

6. One modern anti-union practice is "infiltration". Explain.

7. Another practice is "staged incidents". Explain.

8. In what other ways have some firms tried to prevent unionization of their employees?

9. What labour relations policy would you recommend a firm to follow? Why?

10. How do employers' labour relations policies vary in practice? Give examples.

CHAPTER 7: THIRD PARTIES — THE GOVERNMENT AND THE PUBLIC

7.1 THE PUBLIC INTEREST

The two parties most directly involved in the collective bargaining process are employers and labour unions. However, their interaction can have serious repercussions on the public — whether it be the hardship caused by a strike in an essential service such as public transportation, education, or hospital care; by the effect on prices of substantial wage increases; or by loss of worker income as a result of a union strike or an employer lockout. Consequently, the collective bargaining process is not something that the public, or its elected representatives, provincial, federal, and municipal, can afford to ignore.

7.2 GOVERNMENT INVOLVEMENT

In fact, our federal and provincial governments do have an important say in the industrial relations process. As we saw in Chapter 3 (the Constitutional and Legal Environment), the federal parliament and provincial legislatures have all enacted statutes that set out the rules covering all aspects of the collective bargaining process in the private sector. They have also passed statutes governing collective bargaining by certain types of public employees. These are described later in Chapter 20 (Public Employees).

At one time, governments usually sided with the employer, making it very difficult for workers to form trade unions or otherwise improve their conditions of work. Gradually, however, hostility changed to recognition and co-operation. Nowadays, union leaders are consulted in Ottawa and the provincial capitals and many public employees have been given not only the right to join trade unions but also the right to strike. However, certain types of public employees — for example, police officers — are still forbidden to strike in many jurisdictions and others may be threatened with government intervention should they decide to exercise their right.

Safeguarding the Public Interest

As a custodian of the public interest, our governments cannot play a merely passive role — setting up the legal framework for collective bargaining and then leaving the employers and trade unions to get on with it. If a strike goes on too long and the public suffers hardship thereby, a government may well decide to intervene. However, there are no hard-and-fast rules for such intervention. Very often the government's decision will be influenced by the political implications of such intervention. Will it help or reduce a government's chances of re-election? Also, a government must keep up with the times. Thus the legal framework of industrial relations in Canada has been amended in recent years to extend the right to strike to public employees. However, since then, our governments have for budgetary and other economic reasons imposed occasional wage controls and even ordered public service strikers back to work.

Ensuring Fair Shares

Our modern economy has been characterized by *inflation* — a steady rise in prices mainly as a result of an increase in the country's money supply. This means that, as the purchasing power of the dollar declines, a person's wages gradually buy fewer goods and services. Thus a person's real income may fall even though an increase in pay has been obtained — for example, a wage increase of 2 per cent when the annual rate of inflation is 4 per cent. In inflationary times, all workers are inevitably involved in a mad scramble to at least keep up with the rise in prices. However, the workers best equipped to do this, other than politicians, are the ones that have a union to represent them. As a result, unionized workers tend gradually to increase their share of the national economic pie, whereas non-union workers, workers denied the right to strike, and pensioners and other fixed-income receivers, gradually find themselves with a smaller share. The indexing of pensions is one attempt by government to address this problem. Generally speaking, however fixed-income receivers have been left to fend for themselves.

Keeping the Economy Competitive

An important responsibility of our governments is to keep the country economically prosperous. If excessive union power causes wages to increase too rapidly, this may jeopardize the competitiveness of Canadian products at home and abroad. However, in the late nineteen seventies, the imposition of wage and price controls by the federal government caused the increase in wages to fall behind the rate of inflation, thereby bringing about a reduction in workers' real incomes. This led in turn to accusations by labour spokespersons that the federal government had abused its power, in favour of employers. In 1982, the introduction by the federal government of the "6 and 5" wage restraint program in the public sector, followed suit by many provincial governments, was also greeted with labour outrage. Since that time, there has been no further recourse to mandatory wage and price controls in Canada. Instead the government has used monetary policy to try to control inflation. However, from time to time, the federal government does endeavour to restrict pay increases for federal civil servants.

7.3 PUBLIC VERSUS PRIVATE EMPLOYEES

One of the most perplexing aspects of modern industrial relations in Canada is the growing importance of government as an employer. Unlike the private business firm that will go bankrupt if it grants wage and benefit increases beyond its capacity to pay, the government is often regarded as having a bottomless purse. If a government department or a Crown corporation spends more than it earns, it can look to the government to provide the necessary funds to cover the deficit. Also, suppose that a Crown corporation (such as the Post Office) or any other government body that provides a service to the public, has a monopoly or semi-monopoly position. Then it can raise its charges to the public to cover the cost of perhaps above-average salaries or benefits (such as inflation-indexed pensions) received by the public employees involved. Private firms by contrast face the discipline of the market-place. If their expenses are too high, their efficiency too low, or their products no longer in demand, they can soon be put out of business. In many eyes, most public servants now enjoy a privileged position — their pay is equal to or better than that of their private sector counterparts, their fringe benefits (vacations, pensions, etc.) are often better, and their job security outstanding. The question arises: should public sector employees lead the way in better pay and fringe benefits, or should they exercise a moderating influence on the private sector employees?

REVIEW QUESTIONS

1. How do our governments have an important say in the industrial relations process?

2. How does a government decide when to intervene in a labour dispute to protect the public interest?

3. "In times of inflation, unionized employees have an unfair advantage over other members of the community." Discuss.

4. "Government control of union activity is essential to maintain the

international competitiveness of Canadian industry." Discuss.

5. "Public employees are the most privileged members of the trade union movement." Discuss.

CHAPTER 8: UNION ORGANIZATION

8.1 INTEREST IN JOINING A LABOUR UNION

At any time, some of the employees in a non-unionized firm may come to believe that they would be better off as members of a labour union. This may be because of a newspaper article, because of conversations with friends or relatives who are themselves union members, because of a real or imagined grievance or complaint at work, or because they have been approached and persuaded by members of an existing union. This interest in a union may be based on the fact that unionized employees in other firms, perhaps in the same industry or geographical area, seem to be doing much better than the non-union employees are. Certainly the hope that, by joining a trade union, employees can obtain higher rates of pay, more generous fringe benefits, improved job security, and more respect from management, is an important motivating factor.

8.2 CONTACT WITH A LABOUR UNION

Once interest in joining a labour union has been aroused, whatever the reason, one or two disgruntled employees within that firm might then get in touch with an existing labour union, perhaps by telephoning or visiting the union's local office. They would probably select a union that represents employees in other companies doing the same kind of work or making the same kind of product. The officials of the union they contact would very likely agree to discuss their problems with them or alternatively refer them to another union with more appropriate jurisdiction. Very often, however, a union does not restrict its organizing activities to only certain types of employees. Thus there are many examples of employees being represented by what would appear to be at first sight an unlikely union. A union might want to organize these employees in the hope that it would, through the larger number of employees and firms covered, improve the bargaining position of its existing members. Obviously, the larger the percentage of an industry's employees the union represents, the greater is its bargaining power. Also, the larger this percentage, the less chance there is of non-union employees hurting the union membership by taking work away from unionized employees.

8.3 THE UNION ORGANIZER

The term *union organizer* is used to describe the person who is employed on a full-time, permanent basis by many large labour unions to plan, organize, and carry out membership recruitment campaigns at plants that are not yet unionized. Such persons usually specialize in the *organizing* of certain types of employees — for example, women, ethnic groups, white-collar workers (such as bank employees) or employees in certain types of industries such as steel, fisheries, and lumbering. Because of their personality, intelligence, and specialized experience, the full-time organizers provide the spearhead for union organizing activities.

8.4 THE ORGANIZING COMMITTEE

Once the decision has been made to go ahead with an organizing campaign, the union organizer or other union official in charge will try to assemble a group of employees dedicated to the goal of unionization. This group, or *organizing committee*, would consist of people willing to devote the time and effort necessary to contact other employees, present the union's case for unionization, and ask the persons contacted to join the union by signing a union membership card.

The group, or committee, consists of union representatives, including the "organizer", and may also include the employees who first made contact with the union, and who are sympathetic to union organization. These persons must be prepared not only for a lot of hard work but also, in the case of the employees, for considerable job risk.

The provincial Labour Relations Acts or Codes prohibit an employer from discriminating against an employee for participating in union organizing activity. However, this does not always prevent employers from doing so. Consequently, it is the usual practice, based on common sense, to keep any union organizing campaign as low-key as possible, at least initially. One way to help achieve this is to keep the organizing committee fairly small.

8.5 THE ORGANIZING CAMPAIGN

The committee would make a careful assessment of the probable success of an organizing campaign. Then, if there is agreement to proceed, it would provide the necessary assistance, leadership, and expertise.

Gathering Information

The first step in the organizing campaign is to gather together as much information about the company as possible — for example, its products, customers, finances, production methods, employees, management, ownership and attitude towards employees. Information is also be collected about other firms in the neighbourhood who employ the same types of workers. Once this data has been collected, analyzed, and discussed, the committee can start to plot its campaign — particularly the type of appeal to be made to the employees to join the union — showing, for example, how the company can afford to pay better wages or how the employee needs greater job security in the face of impending technological change.

In trying to organize a small firm, representatives of the organizing committee might contact individual employees on a personal basis, usually after work, just outside the plant or at home. In a larger firm, initial contact might be made through other means such as union bulletins, mailings to the employees' homes, through newspapers, etc. The overall objective of the contact would be to persuade the employees to join the union by signing a union membership card.

List of Eligible Employees

The second step in the organizing campaign is to obtain an accurate, up-to-date list of all the employees eligible to join the union in the particular plant or company that is the object of the organizing campaign. If this cannot be obtained from within the firm (and the employer is under no obligation to provide such a list), resort must be made to other means. Using the list, the committee can record the responses received when a committee member later makes personal contact with each employee to solicit membership.

Personal Contact

The next step is for the committee members to start making personal contact with the various employees. The aim is to secure their agreement to join the union and acknowledge this agreement by signing a union membership card.

Usually, to get the campaign off to a good start, the employees who are believed to favour unionization are approached first. They are also the ones most likely to keep quiet about what is taking place. To avoid any suggestion of intimidation, the personal contact with the employee is often made on a one-to-one basis. For maximum confidentiality, it may take the form of a visit to the employee's home where the purpose of unionization, the potential benefits to the employee, and the possible disadvantages, can be openly discussed, often with the participation of the employee's spouse as well as the employee.

If lucky, the union organizer will get the employee to "sign-up" on the first visit. In many cases, however, a second or third visit may be required. On each visit, the union organizer will try to determine such matters as: the attitude of the employee and family to the union; possible "beefs" that the employee may have about pay, working conditions, immediate supervision, and the way the firm is run generally; and the employee's fears about joining the union and other possible arguments against membership. The organizer will also ask the employee to keep as quiet as possible about the contact until the union has a majority of the eligible employees signed up and is ready to make its application for certification to the Labour Relations Board.

The fact that the committee members making the personal calls are fellow-employees is usually helpful to the recruitment process. They are acquaintances, even personal friends, rather than strangers. They have shown by their own action that they are in favour of the union and they are asking the person approached to follow their example, not just to "do what we say". As a fellow-employee, the committee member shares a common lot with the prospective union member and tends to be trusted in a way that no outsider would. He or she can chat about the plant, the people, and their problems from first-hand experience and thereby quickly put the person approached at ease. However, the union organizer must ensure that the committee members are carefully briefed on what to say (including the fact that the union intends to push ahead whatever management says or does) and on how to deal with objections. Basically, what the committee members are doing, as union canvassers, is a selling job. Obviously, not everyone is suited for it.

Because house-calls are a time-consuming process, many labour unions prefer to restrict them to employees who are considered essential to the recruitment drive. The other employees are often contacted on their way to or from work, perhaps outside the company gate or at a nearby gathering place.

All-Out Public Campaign

Once management has become aware of the union's organizing activities, the union may switch from a policy of discreet recruitment to an all-out public campaign. It may then advertise its intentions in the media and in handbills for distribution outside the plant, inviting eligible employees to sign up, or perhaps to attend an open meeting to obtain further information. At the meeting, the organizer, other union officials and committee members would explain the reasons why the employees should join the union, answer questions, and invite the persons present to sign up for membership. Union membership recruitment meetings are not used as much today as they used to be. This is mainly because of the relatively poor turnouts. An exception might be a plant in which the employees have a long history of grievances, or one in which a labour issue has just arisen, such as automation, that may critically affect the well-being of a large number of the employees.

Signed Membership Cards

After the employee's signature has been obtained, the union canvasser turns the signed membership card over to the union office or to the organizer. The union will try to ensure that no cards are handed in with forged signatures. This is because such an occurrence might lead, under the Labour Relations Act, to the union being disqualified from certification as the bargaining agent for the employees of the company being organized. The Labour Relations Board will check the validity of the signatures and will accept only validly signed membership cards. The number of employees that have signed up for union membership is kept a closely-guarded secret by the union office, until a substantial majority of the eligible employees have done so.

REVIEW QUESTIONS

1. What reasons can motivate some of a non-union firm's employees to get in touch with a labour union? How is this contact usually made? What type of union would they approach?

2. Why would a union be interested in representing the employees of a firm not normally considered to fall within its jurisdiction?

3. Explain the composition and role of the union organizing committee.

4. What is the background and role of the organizer?

5. Do members of the organizing committee and other active canvassers for the union undergo any risk of losing their jobs or other retaliation by the employer? How can any risk be reduced?

6. What information can be usefully gathered by the organizing committee? What purpose does it serve?

7. How can the union obtain a list of employees eligible to join the union?

8. How do the organizing committee members approach eligible employees with a view to persuading them to join the union?

9. When might a union decide to use an all-out public campaign to recruit members? How would it go about it?

10. What can happen if membership cards are submitted with forged signatures?

CHAPTER 9: UNION CERTIFICATION

9.1 CERTIFICATION DEFINED

It is considered to be in the public interest for government to encourage harmonious relations between employers and employees by facilitating a process of orderly collective bargaining. Therefore, each province, in its labour relations statute, sets out a method by which a union may acquire the right to represent a group of employees for collective bargaining purposes. *Certification* is the procedure whereby a union obtains a certificate from the Labour Relations Board declaring that the union is the exclusive bargaining agent for a defined group of employees in a bargaining unit that the Board considers appropriate for collective bargaining.

9.2 PERSONS EXCLUDED

The provincial Labour Relations Act or Code, depending on the province, applies to most employed persons. However, there are exceptions, as follows:

1. Employees covered by the federal Labour Relations Act (e.g. bank and airline employees).

2. Persons not deemed to be employees. Thus Ontario's LRA states, in Section 1(3), no person shall be deemed to be an employee, (a) who is a member of the architectural, dental, land surveying, legal or medical profession entitled to practise in Ontario and employed in a professional capacity; or (b) who, in the opinion of the Ontario Labour Relations Board, exercises managerial functions or is employed in a confidential capacity in matters relating to labour relations.

3. Employees specifically excluded from the application of the provincial Labour Relations statute. Thus Ontario's LRA, Section 3, states that:
    This Act does not apply to:
    (a) a domestic employed in a private home;
    (b) a person employed in agriculture, hunting, or trapping;
    (c) a person, other than an employee of a municipality or a person employed in silviculture, who is employed in horticulture by an employer whose primary business is agriculture of horticulture;
    (d) a member of a police force within the meaning of the *Police Services Act*.

    (e) a person who is a firefighter within the meaning of the *Fire Protection and Prevention Act, 1997*;

    (f) a member of a teachers' bargaining unit established under the Education Act, or a supervisory officer, a principal, or a vice-principal;

    (g) a member of the Ontario Provincial Police Force;

    (h) an employee within the meaning of the *Colleges Collective Bargaining Act*;

    (i) a provincial judge; or

    (j) a person employed as a labour mediator or labour conciliator.

Some of the above persons (police, teachers, and college employees) are covered by their own collective bargaining legislation.

9.3 JURISDICTION

In Canada, there exists both provincial and federal labour relations legislation — so one of the first questions, when employees wish to become unionized, is under which labour jurisdiction they would fall.

Province of Employment

If the plant or office workers of an employer located in a particular province choose to become unionized, they would fall under the jurisdiction of that province's Labour Relations Act. Similarly, workers employed by a person located in another province would come under the jurisdiction of that province's Act. However, suppose that an employer located in one province chooses to open a second plant or office in another province. Then the employees in the new location, should they choose to become unionized, would come under the jurisdiction of the province in which they are employed and not that of the head office.

    Suppose a firm sets up its head office in one province and eventually sets up operations in all the other provinces. Then, if its employees in the ten different provinces are unionized, the firm would be dealing with ten different provincial Labour Relations Acts.

Federal Jurisdiction

Persons employed by certain firms, because of the nature of their operations, come under federal jurisdiction. Examples of these would be employees of the national railways, banks, airlines, shipping companies, and ports.

9.4 APPROPRIATENESS OF THE BARGAINING UNIT

Labour Union Application

A labour union, when it thinks it has sufficient membership support, will apply to the provincial Labour Relations Board to be certified as the bargaining agent for the employees in the group it considers to be appropriate for bargaining.

The union will give consideration, in its application, to the common interests among members of the group, geographical location, and the likelihood that the group will be acceptable to the Labour Relations Board for certification. Consideration will also be given to the question of whether the application should be made as a single-plant, multi-plant, single-employer, or multi-employer group.

Labour Relations Board Decision

Although the union, in its application for certification, will claim the unit of employees is appropriate for bargaining, it is the Labour Relations Board that makes the decision. The employer is also given the opportunity to express its view to the Board as to the appropriateness of the unit.

Standard units recognized by the Board include production units, office units, technical and professional units. The Board will also recognize *craft units* — groups of skilled workers engaged in some trade who commonly bargain together, separate from other employees. In every case, the unit must consist of more than one employee. Normally, if a manufacturing company has both a plant workforce and an office workforce, the Labour Relations Board will consider the non-supervisory plant employees as one unit appropriate for bargaining, and the non-supervisory office employees as another. As mentioned previously, certain employees would automatically be excluded. The Board may also certify a trade union as bargaining agent even before the final composition of the bargaining unit is determined, so long as the Board is satisfied that any dispute as to the composition of the unit cannot affect the labour union's right to certification.

The criteria used by the Labour Relations Board in deciding appropriate industrial units include the following: (a) the wishes of the employer and the trade union; (b) the community of interest among employees, taking into account the nature of the work performed, and the skills of the employees; and (c) the Board's general policy of not putting office staff and production workers into the same bargaining unit.

9.5 CERTIFICATION PROCEDURE

A labour union may apply to the Labour Relations Board to become the certified bargaining agent for a group of employees. In Ontario, under the LRA, Section 11, the union must deliver a copy of the application to the employer no later than the day the application is filed with the Board. The application must include a written description of the proposed bargaining unit, including an estimate of the number of persons in the unit. The application for certification must be accompanied by a list of the names of union members and evidence of their status as union members. But the trade union may not give this information to the employer.

The employer may give the Labour Relations Board a written description of the bargaining unit that the employer proposes and must do so within two business days after the day on which the employer receives the application for certification from the union.

If the Labour Relations Board is satisfied that the union has the support of 40% or more of the eligible employees, based on signed membership cards, then, under Section 8(2), the Board will direct that a secret representation vote be held. The Board may not hold a hearing, when making this decision, unless the Board directs otherwise. The secret vote will be held within five days after the day on which the application for certification is made.

After the vote has been taken, the Labour Relations Board may hold a hearing if the Board considers it necessary to dispose of the application for certification. Under Section 10(1), the Board must certify the union as the official bargaining agent if more than 50% of the ballots cast are in favour of the union.

9.6 TIMING OF APPLICATION

Under Section 7(1), a labour union may apply at any time to the provincial Labour Relations Board for certification as the bargaining agent of the employees in a unit that the union claims to be appropriate for collective bargaining. However, this assumes that no other labour union has already been certified as the bargaining agent, and that the employees in the unit are not already bound by a collective agreement.

No Other Labour Union Certified

In this case, there is no restriction on the right of a union to apply for certification as bargaining agent for the employees.

No Collective Agreement

Suppose that another labour union has already been certified as the bargaining agent but has not entered into a collective agreement with the employer. Also that the Board has not declared that the other labour union no longer represents the employees in that bargaining unit. Then a second labour union may apply to the Board for certification as bargaining agent — but only after one year has elapsed from the date the certificate was issued to the first labour union – Section 7(2).

Union Recognized by Employer but no Collective Agreement

Suppose that an employer has recognized in writing that a union is the exclusive bargaining agent of its employees but the employer and the union have not entered into a collective agreement. Then, unless conciliation proceedings are under way, another trade union may apply to the Labour Relations Board for certification as bargaining agent — but only one year after the date of the recognition agreement – Section 7(3).

Collective Agreement for up to Three Years

Suppose that another trade union has already been certified and has signed a collective agreement with the employer, but for a term of not more than three years. Then a second trade union may apply to the Board for certification as bargaining agent of any of the employees in that bargaining unit after the commencement of the last three months of operation of such an agreement – Section 7(4).

Collective Agreement for over Three Years

Suppose that a collective agreement is for a term of more than three years. Here, a second trade union may apply to the Board for certification but only after the commencement of the 34th month of the agreement's operation and before the commencement of the 37th month of its operation – Section 7(5).

    A collective agreement continues to operate if either the the union or the employer fails to give the other party notice of termination of its desire to bargain for a renewal of the agreement or for the making of a new one. In this situation, a second trade union may apply to the Board for certification during the last three months of each year that the agreement continues to operate, or after the commencement of the last three months of its operation, as the case may be – Section 7(6).

9.7 DETERMINATION OF UNION MEMBERS IN THE BARGAINING UNIT

Once an application for certification is received, the Labour Relations Board, under Section 8, may determine the voting constituency to be used for a representation vote. It does this by taking into account (a) the description of the proposed bargaining unit included in the application for certification and (b) the description, if any, of the bargaining unit that the employer proposes. If the Board determines that 40% or more of the individuals in the bargaining unit proposed in the application for certification appear to be members of the union at the time that the application was filed, the Board must order that a representation vote be taken among the individuals in the voting constituency.

9.8 VOLUNTARY RECOGNITION

An employer may voluntarily recognize a union as the bargaining agent for its employees, if it considers the bargaining unit to be appropriate and believes that the majority of its employees, without having been subject to undue pressure, have indicated their desire to be represented by that union. In this case, the employer agrees in writing to recognize the union as the exclusive bargaining agent for a group of its employees as defined in the agreement with the union. *Voluntary recognition* is an alternative to certification and is usually done privately between the employer and the union, without any government supervision.

9.9 RIGHT OF ACCESS

Sometimes employees reside on property owned by the employer, or on property to which the employer has the right to control access. Then, if necessary, the Labour Relations Board may, under Section13, order the employer to allow the representative of a trade union access to the property — so that he or she may attempt to persuade the employees to join the trade union.

9.10 SECURITY GUARDS

These are persons who monitor other employees or who protect the property of an employer. In Ontario, under the LRA, Section 14, a trade union with members other than security guards may be certified as the bargaining agent for a bargaining unit composed solely of guards. Also, a bargaining unit may include guards and persons who are not guards. However, if the employer objects, the trade union involved must satisfy the Labour Relations Board that no conflict of interest would result from the trade union becoming the bargaining agent, or from including persons other than guards in the bargaining unit. The Board must consider the following factors in determining whether a conflict of interest would result.:

1. the extent of the guards' duties monitoring other employees of their employer or protecting their employer's property;

2. any other duties or responsibilities of the guards that might give rise to a conflict of interest;

3. such other factors as the Board considers relevant.

9.11 UNIONS NOT TO BE CERTIFIED

Under Section 15, the Board may not certify a trade union if any employer or any employers' organization has participated in its formation or administration, or has contributed financial or other support to it. Nor if the trade union discriminates against any person because of any ground of discrimination prohibited by the provincial *Human Rights Code* or the *Canadian Charter of Rights and Freedoms*.

9.12 AUTOMATIC CERTIFICATION

In Ontario, until a few years ago, an employer who interfered in the unionization process could be punished, under the Labour Relations Act, by the granting, to the employees involved, of automatic union status. Currently, labour unions are asking the provincial government to restore this right of automatic certification.

REVIEW QUESTIONS

1. Do all employees have the right to join a union under the terms of the provincial Labour Relations Act? Who, if at all, is excluded?

2. Certain persons are deemed not to be "employees". Who are they? Is this logical?

3. The ABC Co. has its headquarters in Calgary and manufacturing and sales branches in Alberta, Manitoba, and Saskatchewan. Do its branch employees fall under Alberta's labour jurisdiction?

4. Under which labour jurisdiction do the following fall: (a) letter carriers, (b) firefighters, (c) teachers, and (d) hospital workers?

5. The United Assemblers Union has signed up, as members, a large number of employees from the Ace Electronics plant. How long must it wait before applying for certification?

6. Suppose another union was certified six months ago but, as far as the employees were concerned, "never did anything for us". Can the United Assemblers Union still be certified? Would it make any difference if the employer had already recognized in writing the first union as the certified bargaining agent for its employees?

7. Suppose there is a collective agreement already in force between the employer and the first union. When, if at all, can the second union apply for certification?

8. Do the following have any effect on the second union's application for certification: (a) conciliation proceedings between the employer and the union already certified, and (b) the existence of a lawful strike or lockout?

9. Who decides what group of employees is appropriate for collective bargaining? What factors would be taken into account?

10. What is a "representation vote"? When is it necessary? What is its purpose?

11. Are trade union members legally entitled to enter an employer's premises to explain to the employees the benefits of joining the union and to solicit membership?

12. Are security guards allowed to join a union? What is their legal position under the Ontario Labour Relations Act?

13. Under what circumstances is a union not permitted to be certified as a bargaining agent?

14. What is "voluntary recognition"? Why is certification more usual?

APPENDIX 9A: TERMINATION OF BARGAINING RIGHTS

Just as it is possible for a labour union to become legally certified as the bargaining agent for a group of employees, so also is it possible for a union to become *decertified*. In fact, most Labour Relations statutes provide for both certification and decertification. There are in fact many different reasons that may cause a union to have its bargaining rights terminated.

Certification of Another Union

First, under Section 62, if another labour union obtains certification to represent a group of employees already represented by a union, then the first union automatically loses its bargaining rights.

Failure to Make a Collective Agreement

Section, under Section 63(1), if a labour union does not make a collective agreement with the employer within one year after its certification, any one or more of the employees in the bargaining unit may apply to the Labour Relations Board for a declaration that the labour union no longer represents the employees in the bargaining unit.

Loss of Employee Confidence

Third, under Section 63(2), if there is a collective agreement in force, any one or more of the employees in the bargaining unit may apply to the Board for declaration that the labour union no longer represents the employees in the bargaining unit. However, in the case of an agreement for a term of not more than three years, such an application may be made only after the commencement of the last three months of its operation. In the case of an agreement for a term of more than three years, the application may be made only during the three-month period prior to the third anniversary or in the three-month period prior to each subsequent third anniversary. Then, if 40% of the employees in the bargaining unit have voluntarily signified in writing that they no longer wish to be represented by the labour union, the Labour Relations Board is required to satisfy itself that the majority of the employees desire that the right of the trade union to bargain on their behalf be terminated. It does this by holding a *representation vote*. Then, if more than 50% of the ballots are cast in opposition to the labour union, the Board will declare that the union no longer represents the employees in the bargaining unit.

Union Request

A fourth reason for terminating a union's bargaining rights is the Labour Relations Board being informed by the labour union that it no longer wishes to continue to represent the employees in the bargaining unit. This is called *termination on abandonment*, as provided for in Section 63(17).

Union Fraud

A fifth reason is the discovery that the union obtained a certificate by fraud. In such a case, under Section 64(1), the Labour Relations Board may declare the union no longer represents the employees in the bargaining unit, and any collective agreement it may have made for them is void.

Failure to Give Notice of Desire to Bargain

A sixth reason for termination is the failure of the union to give notice, within 60 days following certification, of its desire to bargain with a view to making a collective agreement. In such a case, the Labour Relations Board may, under Section 65(1), upon application of the employer or any of the employees in the bargaining unit, declare that the union no longer represents the employees in the bargaining unit. This decision may be made with or without first holding a representation vote.

Failure to Bargain

Seventh, bargaining rights may be terminated, under Section 65(2), because of the union's failure to bargain within 60 days of giving notice to the employer of its desire to bargain with a view to making a collective agreement. Or because of failure to bargain within 60 days from the collapse of negotiations but before the appointment by the Minister of Labour of a conciliation officer or mediator. The Board may terminate the union's bargaining rights following application by the employer or any of the employees in the bargaining unit, with or without a representation vote.

Voluntary Recognition

Eighth and last, the bargaining rights of a union may be terminated, under Section 66(1), upon application by any employee in the bargaining unit, or by a labour union representing any employee in the bargaining unit, where there has been *voluntary recognition*. This is a situation in which an employer and a union that has not been certified as the bargaining agent enter into a collective agreement or a *recognition agreement* (whereby the employer recognizes the labour union as the exclusive bargaining agent of its employees and the agreement is in writing signed by both parties). In such a case, the application for termination of the bargaining rights of such a voluntarily recognized union must be made during the first year of the collective agreement. If no collective agreement has been entered into, the application for termination must be made within one year from the signing of such a recognition agreement.

Conclusion

In conclusion, we should stress that, despite the many different grounds on which bargaining rights may be terminated, such an event is unusual. Certainly, an employee hoping to decertify a union would first need to talk with a good labour lawyer or labour consultant.

REVIEW QUESTIONS

1. The United Assemblers Union fails to make a collective agreement with Ace Electronics despite months of negotiations. Some of the employees complain to the Labour Relations Board that the union has been "bought" by management and they want to get rid of it. What can the Board do?

2. Suppose that the union did sign an agreement but the employees feel that they have been "sold out". What can they do, if anything?

2. Explain the meaning of the term "termination on abandonment".

4. The United Assemblers Union, through incredibly poor management, failed to give notice to Ace Electronics, within two months of the date of certification, of its desire to bargain. The Board was asked to declare that the union no longer represented its employees. What might the Board do?

5. What is meant by the term "voluntary recognition"? If this occurs, what is the union's legal position?

CHAPTER 10: UNFAIR PRACTICES

10.1 UNFAIR PRACTICES DEFINED

These are actions taken by employers or labour unions that contravene the principle of bargaining "in good faith". One example would be an employer dismissing a person, perhaps on some false pretext, for attempting to form or join a union. Another would be union organizers physically or mentally intimidating an employee into joining a union against that person's real wishes. Unfair practices vary somewhat in definition from one labour relations statute to another. Nevertheless, they can be defined generally as: actions by employers and employees, or their representatives, which are prohibited by statute — because they interfere with the proper operation of the collective bargaining process.

10.2 HISTORY OF UNFAIR PRACTICES

For many years, while unions were in their infancy, unfair practices were associated mainly with management. Thus, as we saw in Chapter 3 (The Constitutional and Legal Environment), the Wagner Act passed in the U.S. in 1935, specifically named and outlawed five such management practices:

a) interfering with an employee's right to joint a union;

b) dominating a labour union;

c) discriminating against an employee for engaging in union activities;

d) dismissing or otherwise penalizing an employee for filing charges under the Act; and

e) refusing to bargain with the union representing the employees.

The Wagner Act also provided for a National Labour Relations Board to investigate any complaints of unfair labour practices by management; to prosecute the companies and persons involved; and to hold and supervise elections to determine which union it should certify as the official bargaining unit.

As trade unions became stronger, management began to complain bitterly that employers were also the victims of unfair practices — this time by the unions. Eventually, in 1947, the Wagner Act was amended to permit unions also to be prosecuted for unfair labour practices.

In Canada, the history of unfair practices is also a long and stormy one. Employers have, on occasion, had the assistance of special police, the

R.C.M.P., and government back-to-work orders in order to break strikes. They have also used such measures as threats, bribes, dismissals, blacklistings, physical beatings, factory spies, and employer-run unions to prevent the unionization of their workers. But gradually, as in the U.S., the various labour relations statutes, both provincial and federal, have outlawed many of these practices and the provincial and federal Labour Relations Boards, together with the courts, have tried to make their elimination a reality. Labour unions have also been accused of unfair practices.

10.3 UNFAIR PRACTICES BY EMPLOYERS

For purposes of analysis, we can identify four main stages in the collective bargaining process during which employers may engage in various types of unfair practices. First, while a union is being organized; second, while its application for certification is being processed; third, while it is negotiating a collective agreement with the employer; and, fourth, while a collective agreement is in operation.

In Ontario's LRA, employers are prohibited from interfering with Unions (Section 71); with employees' rights (Section 72); and with bargaining rights (Section 73).

While a Union is Being Organized

In Canada today, under the various labour relations statutes, an agreement between an employer and a trade union is held not to be a collective agreement if an employer or employer's organization helped to establish, or administer the trade union involved.

However, an employer still has the freedom to express its views so long as it does not use coercion, intimidation, threats, promises or undue influence. Obviously, the distinction between an employer expressing its views on the one hand and attempting to dissuade its employees from joining a labour union on the other is not always clear. Consequently, there are many cases that come before the Labour Relations Boards that revolve around this point. Normally, an employer is free to explain its labour policy, including a presentation of the advantages and disadvantages of unions. However, such an exposition should not contain threats of reprisal or promises of benefit if employees join a union or not.

An employer is also forbidden from interfering with an employee's rights to join a trade union, or become an officer in one, or to exercise any other rights under the applicable labour relations statute. Specifically, the employer is prohibited from using intimidation or coercion — for example, the threat of dismissal or of a reduction in wages, or even of closing down the plant — to discourage a person from becoming a union member. However, an employer still retains the right to dismiss an employee for "just cause" — for example, because of persistent lateness, drinking, etc. Another example of interference with an employee's rights would be an employer questioning the employee about his or her union activities.

Sometimes there may be more than one union trying to "organize" a firm's employees. Whatever the employer's preference for one union rather than the other, it would be considered an unfair practice to attempt to persuade the employees to join the union that the employer prefers. Nor must the employer assist one or other of the unions in its campaign to recruit new members.

While a Union is Applying for Certification

During this period, it would also be illegal for the employer to engage in the conduct mentioned in the previous section. It would also be illegal for the employer to alter the working conditions of the employees without the consent of the trade union that has applied for certification.

If the trade union is considered to have been influenced by the employer, its application for certification will be disqualified by the Labour Relations Board. A union which receives financial help from the employer is known as a *company union* and would be ineligible for certification.

While a Union is Negotiating a Collective Agreement

A collective agreement would be disallowed under the various Labour Relations Statutes if it discriminated against anyone because of any ground of discrimination prohibited by the provincial *Human Rights Code* or the *Canadian Charter of Rights and Freedoms*.

An employer is also prohibited from including in a contract of employment any conditions that would prevent a person from joining a trade union or exercising any other rights under the applicable labour relations statute.

Failure to recognize or bargain with the certified union is another unfair practice specifically prohibited by the labour relations statutes. Should negotiations break down, the union may legally call a strike once the required period of conciliation has been exhausted. In this case, a possible unfair practice by the employer would be the dismissal of employees sympathetic to the union.

While a Collective Agreement is in Operation

An employer is expected to observe the terms of the collective agreement that has been negotiated with the trade union acting on behalf of the employees. Any disputes that arise are to be handled according to the grievance procedure set out in the agreement, with any outstanding issues being referred to arbitration. While the agreement is in force, the employer may not therefore lock out its employees. Also, an employer must reinstate any employee who has previously been engaged in a legal strike so long as the employee makes a written application to return to work within six months from the beginning of the strike. And there must be no discrimination in the terms of employment offered. The only exception to reinstatement is if the employer no longer has persons performing the same or similar work. An employer is also forbidden to discriminate against anyone who has acted as a witness or filed a complaint under the applicable labour relations statute.

While a Union is on Strike

Nowadays, in Ontario and other provinces, the hiring of professional strike-breakers by employers is considered to be an unfair practice and is specifically prohibited by law (see Chapter 15: Strikes and Lockouts).

10.4 UNFAIR PRACTICES BY LABOUR UNIONS

Under the various labour relations statutes, a trade union, or persons acting on its behalf, is also prohibited from engaging in various types of conduct. Many of these parallel the actions forbidden the employer — for example, discriminating against anyone (in this case, for trade union membership) on grounds of race, creed, colour, nationality, ancestry, sex, or place of origin, as specified in the provincial *Human Rights Code* or in the Canadian *Charter of Rights and Freedoms*.

In Ontario's LRA, trade unions are prohibited from interfering with employers' organizations (Section 71); and from interfering with bargaining rights (Section 72).

The following is a list of unfair practices that a union, or persons acting on its behalf, may commit:

1. Participating in or interfering with the formation or administration of an employer's organization or contributing financial or other support to such an organization.

2. Bargaining with or entering into a collective agreement with an employer while another trade union continues to be entitled to represent the employees in the bargaining unit.

3. Not representing fairly the employees in the bargaining unit.

4. Attempting to persuade an employee at his or her place of work, during working hours, to become or continue to be a member of a union.

5. Not making secret a strike vote or a vote to ratify a proposed collective agreement.

6. Not giving those employees entitled to vote, ample opportunity to cast their ballots.

7. Calling or authorizing an unlawful strike, or threatening to do so.

8. Suspending, expelling, or otherwise penalizing a member who refused to participate in an unlawful strike.

9. Discriminating against a person in regard to employment.

10. Intimidating, coercing, fining or otherwise penalizing a person because of a belief that he or she has made, or is about to make, a disclosure in a proceeding under the Labour Relations Act or because he or she has made an application or filed a complaint under the Act, or because he or she has participated, or is about to participate in, a proceeding under the Act.

REVIEW QUESTIONS

1. Explain how an employer might be involved in the establishment of a trade union. Why is this considered undesirable?

2. A collective agreement is not recognized as such by law if it discriminates against any person on one of the various specified grounds. What are they? Should any others be included?

3. What employee rights is an employer forbidden to interfere with under the terms of your province's Labour Relations statute?

4. Give some examples of intimidation and coercion used by employers and trade unions that the statute aims to prevent.

5. May a trade union or employer attempt, during working hours, to persuade an employee to join or refrain from joining a union? Discuss.

6. Are strikes and lockouts permitted while a collective agreement is in force? Explain the situation.

7. Does an employer have the right to insist that a vote be taken by the employees whether to accept or reject the employer's last offer? Who is permitted to vote?

8. The ABC Co.. refused to take back several employees who have been on strike, claiming that they are "trouble-makers". What is the employees' legal position?

9. During negotiations for a new collective agreement, but before the old one expired, the ABC Co. locked out its workers, claiming *that* the union demands, at the time of falling company sales, were excessive. What is the union's legal position?

10. Terry Moore, although a union member, refuses to participate in a strike called by his union, claiming that "we're just asking for trouble". What is his legal position vis-a-vis the union: (a) if the strike were called before the existing agreement expired and (b) after the agreement expired?

11. The XYZ Co., which had been steadfastly opposed to the unionization of its employees, announced after certification of a union as its bargaining agent, that it was no longer going to pay medical treatment, group insurance and other employee benefits. Can the employees do anything about this?

12. Frank Woods, a senior employee, complained to management about the non-payment of the benefits and announced that he was going to tell the Labour Relations Board about it. A few days later, he was fired because, according to management, he could no longer do his work properly. What is his legal position?

CHAPTER 11: THE NEGOTIATING PROCESS

11.1 INTENTION TO BARGAIN

Suppose that a trade union has been certified as the bargaining agent for the employees in a bargaining unit. Or has received voluntary recognition by the employer. Then the union must give written notice to the employer of its desire to bargain with a view to making a collective agreement. Also, suppose that a collective agreement has been in force. Then, under the terms of the Labour Relations Act, either party may give notice in writing to the other party of its desire to bargain with a view to renewing, with or without modifications, the agreement then in operation or to making a new agreement. The time period for giving such notice is also usually specified in the existing collective agreement. Thus, for example:

> This Agreement shall remain in force for a period of one year, from the date hereof, and shall continue in force from year to year thereafter unless in any year, not more than 90 days before the date of its termination, either party shall furnish the other in writing with notice of termination or of proposed revision of this Agreement.

During this open period, it is normal for the union to notify the company of its intention to bargain. However, before negotiations for a new collective agreement can begin, the company and the union will need to establish negotiating committees.

11.2 THE COMPANY NEGOTIATING COMMITTEE

Composition

In a medium-sized manufacturing firm of several hundred employees, the company negotiating committee would probably consist of three to five people. It would commonly include the Industrial Relations Manager, or representative, because of his/her knowledge of the collective bargaining process and labour relations in general; the plant manager, or representative, because of his/her responsibility for the operation and also for knowledge of practical operating problems; perhaps another manufacturing representative for knowledge of particular problem areas to be discussed; perhaps a specialist in wage administration, depending on the anticipated subject matter; and perhaps a specialist in work measurement. The company negotiating committee might also include an outside consultant.

The composition of the committee and the background of each of its members should be such as to demonstrate to the union that the members of the company team have a good knowledge of the relevant facts and of the various pressures influencing both management and the union. It is important, in the eyes of the union, that the company team has integrity and accepts the bargaining process; also that the committee members have the ability to listen patiently, think creatively, and to speak and write clearly, precisely, and effectively.

Attitude

The attitude of the company negotiating team is very important. In this regard, we assume that the employer's objective in the negotiations is to seek a settlement based on a reasonable and realistic assessment of the bargaining circumstances. These would include such factors as the company's financial situation, the demand for its products, wage settlements in this and other industries, and the general economic situation. Therefore the committee, both as a whole and as individuals, should adopt in the negotiations with the union, a constructive, realistic, problem-solving approach. The personalities of the persons comprising the company negotiating team should generally be agreeable and acceptable to the union and the persons themselves should demonstrate a conciliatory rather than antagonistic attitude in their discussion of the issues involved.

Organization

The organization of the committee should be clearly understood by all its members. Normally, the Industrial Relations representative on the committee acts as its chairperson. However, the chairperson of the committee might instead be the person responsible for the operation — for example, the manufacturing manager — who would then use the Industrial Relations representative as a staff advisor.

Initial Preparation

It is essential that committee members discuss the various issues amongst themselves and reach agreement as to the company's initial bargaining position before meeting with the union. The chairperson, who is normally the chief spokesperson, can then speak on behalf of the committee to the union, knowing that there is agreement within his/her group. Normally, the chairperson does all the talking for the company except in regard to certain matters which, by pre-arrangement, are handled by other persons on the committee.

Also, from time to time, the chairperson may request, during a meeting with the union, that one or more of the other persons on the committee speak in regard to certain points being raised by either side in the negotiations.

The responsibility for the successful completion of negotiations belongs to the committee as a whole. However, it should be established beforehand that, in the event of disagreement amongst the members, someone must have the authority to make decisions and have the responsibility for them. Normally this is the chairperson.

Authority

The members of the company negotiating committee should possess sufficient authority and status in the company organization to convince the union that they have the authority to reach an agreement on the company's behalf. However, the company team should not have unlimited authority to make a settlement and should not give the appearance of having such unlimited authority. The company president should refrain from becoming a member of the negotiating committee — thereby making it clear to the union that there is still somebody who can put limits on what the negotiating committee may agree to.

If the company negotiating committee is unable to reach a settlement with the union, the normal result is a strike which can be very damaging to the firm. It is vital therefore for the committee to know exactly what authority it has and how it can report quickly to top management on the progress of the negotiations, on the problems that may have arisen, and on any concessions or other measures that may be required to avert a breakdown of the talks. Consequently, the chairperson of the negotiating committee should have ready access to the president of the company. The committee head must also know exactly how far the company is willing to go in meeting union demands and whether it is willing or not to put up with a strike and the financial and other loss involved.

11.3 THE UNION NEGOTIATING COMMITTEE

Composition

In some situations, the union negotiating committee would consist, on a predetermined basis, of a select group of union representatives, such as the president of the local, the vice-president, the chief steward, etc. Each of these persons is elected by the membership. Alternatively, since the purpose of the union negotiating committee is to represent the views of the union membership, the rank and file membership might be asked to select the negotiating committee by means of a special election.

If the union has a business agent, he or she would almost certainly also be a part of the negotiating committee. If there is no business agent, and sometimes even if there is a business agent, the central union organization, the "national", will most likely supply a national representative to assist the local group in the negotiation of their collective agreement.

Whatever the manner of selection, the union negotiating committee should have a good, detailed knowledge of the firm's general operating situation and of the particular problems to be discussed. It should also have a sound understanding of collective bargaining procedure and labour relations in general.

Many of the comments in regard to the company negotiating committee are also applicable to the union negotiating committee. It is certainly important that they have a good knowledge of the relevant facts and pressures influencing both sides and that their integrity be recognized by the company negotiating committee.

Attitude

It follows almost without question that the union representatives accept the bargaining process. Certainly they should be able to speak and write precisely and effectively, and think creatively with regard to the problems that will inevitably arise. Also they should have experience in the collective bargaining process. Most unions would feel it desirable that they bring a constructive approach to the negotiations with a realistic approach to problem-solving. Also most unions would think it important that the union representatives appear to be agreeable and conciliatory in their approach to the various issues.

11.4 COMPANY DEMANDS

Important company demands, based partly on experience from operating under the previous agreement, will have been discussed many times between the Industrial Relations people and the line management who are responsible for the company's operations. However, it is considered judicious to review any arbitration decisions made during the life of the agreement. These would suggest other possible changes to the benefit of the company. The consequences of any adverse arbitration decisions that have been made will underline just how important it is for the company to get the new agreement changed.

Furthermore, a review of the grievances that have been filed may indicate areas in which the company has been having difficulty in operating under the terms of the agreement. It may also pinpoint areas of continuing and unnecessary conflict because of the provisions of the agreement. It is also judicious to give supervisors who operate under the agreement an opportunity to suggest changes.

11.5 UNION DEMANDS

As part of the process of drawing up union demands, many unions hold meetings for all union members at which individual members have the opportunity to suggest items for inclusion among such demands. Also, many unions provide special opportunities for stewards and chief stewards to make their suggestions. In addition, officers and various experts of the union would normally review the grievance and arbitration procedures. Perhaps there have been arbitration decisions which adversely affected the union and which, from the union's point of view, require changes in the agreement. The union would undoubtedly consider the advice of the union's national representative and of the local business agent in regard to the demands that should be made to solve existing problems or to avoid anticipated future problems. Furthermore, union national policy objectives might result in the placing of additional demands. The national representative and the business agent should have a good knowledge of collective bargaining trends and of settlements elsewhere and this knowledge could also influence the demands to be made by the union.

11.6 INFORMATION REQUIRED

For negotiating purposes, it is essential for both the company negotiating committee and the union one to have adequate information. To start with, both committees are probably fully conversant with the terms of previous collective agreements and recognize their importance as a reference point in the upcoming negotiations. Such terms may be above average, thereby causing a problem for the company, or below average causing a problem for the union.

Wages and Benefits

Both negotiating committees need information on the company's wage benefit package compared to that of other firms in the industry and other firms in the area. There is an abundance of this type of information available to each of the parties. Government information such as that from Statistics Canada, government wage surveys, and Ministry of Labour settlement reports are available to both sides. Information is also available from private publications. In addition, the company normally has access to information provided by various employer associations such as the Canadian Manufacturers and Exporters Association, personnel associations, Chambers of Commerce, and so on. The company may also obtain information on request from other employers. The union can obtain additional information from the various collective agreements from other unions and also by making contact with unions representing other employees in comparable firms or industries. From all this information, each party can draw conclusions about wages, employment, and other trends in the economy and in labour relations in general which are going to affect the negotiations for a new collective agreement.

Work Force

Both sides will have access to information about the work force which makes up the bargaining unit. The union members may be relatively old, perhaps making them more concerned with security and pensions; or they may be relatively young, perhaps making them more concerned with the hourly wage rates rather than benefits and job security.

Ability to Pay

The employer's ability to pay is an important factor for both sides. The employer may well look at its present relative position as an employer in the labour market, and at the overall trends and patterns in wages, fringe benefits, and so on and recognize there are many arguments for improving working conditions in his company. But looking at its overall profitability picture, it may well conclude that it is impossible to do these things at least for the present.

The union may decide, on the basis of these trends, what it thinks the company should pay and take the position that the company's ability to pay is the company's problem rather than the union's. However, the union must recognize, at least eventually, that there is a definite limit on a company's ability to pay and that, if it insists on obtaining a settlement beyond that which the company can afford, it may provide the company with no alternative other than to close the plant or endure a long strike. And conceivably, if such a strike goes on long enough, it may cause the company to go out of business, taking the employees' jobs with it.

It is possible for a company to agree to an excessive settlement to avoid a strike and to give time for the company to decide on an appropriate course of action. After the union has obtained an excessive settlement, the company may decide that there is no alternative other than to close the operation. The union can then be in a situation of having been successful in obtaining its objectives in the short run but having completely lost out in the long run. On the other hand, the company may well be able to afford better wages and improved benefits.

11.7 COMPANY-UNION MEETINGS

Location

Meetings between the two negotiating teams might be held on company premises, in a conference room or business office, or in the union hall or a similar type location, or in some neutral area such as a local hotel. The company negotiating committee is usually reluctant to meet in the union hall as it would feel itself at a psychological disadvantage going to the union in order to negotiate with it. While it is cheaper to negotiate on company premises rather than to go elsewhere, there are also some significant handicaps in this location. The people on the company negotiating committee are normally taking time away from their regular duties. If they are on the company premises, they run the risk of being interrupted by these duties or being distracted by them — with the result that less attention is paid to negotiations than is required. Also, it is important that events that arise in the course of negotiations not be misinterpreted either by company non-union employees or by employees represented by the union. Negotiations can become emotional or appear to become emotional. Therefore, when people leave a negotiation meeting, it is quite possible that their personal appearance or some off-hand remark may be misinterpreted by those not involved in the negotiations. Problems may be relatively minor in the context of the negotiations but can be easily misinterpreted by those not involved. Once put into the rumour mill, such problems may cause unfavourable reactions that are completely out of proportion, thereby unnecessarily complicating the negotiations. Therefore most companies and most unions feel that is is advantageous to negotiate in some neutral location away from the day-to-day responsibilities of both parties. Usually, negotiations are held in a hotel where, in addition to a room for the negotiations, each group has the opportunity to obtain a separate room for themselves for preparation and discussion purposes.

Frequency and Duration of Meetings

There are various opinions as to how often the meetings should be held and how long they should last. However, many people believe that meetings should be held as often as either or both parties consider it desirable — so long as they help the parties move closer to a settlement, even one issue at a time. Most companies and most unions also believe that meetings should start at a sensible time in the morning, such as 9:30 or 10:00 o'clock, giving both sides some time for preparation prior to the meeting. They also believe that they should last as long as they are serving their purpose. Either side has the privilege of suggesting, when it feels it is appropriate, that a meeting be adjourned.

However, other companies and unions believe that negotiations should fit into the overall operation of the business. In one situation, the union representative and the plant manager agreed that they would set aside one day per week — Wednesday — for the purpose of negotiations. Also that, in the interest of the overall efficient use of time, the meetings would start at 8:00 a.m., adjourn for lunch at 12:00 noon, reconvene at 1:30 p.m. and end for the day at 4:30 p.m. In practice, it seemed as though these meetings were held every Wednesday and went on for the full seven hours whether they served any purpose or not. Also, it would not have mattered whether more meetings were necessary — Wednesday, between 8:00 and 4:30, was the only time available for this purpose, whatever the need.

11.8 NEGOTIATING PROCEDURE

At the same time that the union gives notice to the company of its intention to bargain, it may also submit to the company its proposals for a new or modified agreement. Alternatively, it may reveal these proposals in subsequent correspondence, or at the first or second meeting arranged for the purposes of negotiating the agreement. The company may also have proposals to modify the agreement. If the union submits its proposals by mail prior to the first meeting, the company might respond similarly or it might notify the union only of its intent and wait for the first or second meeting before presenting its own proposals. Alternatively, the union might submit its demands at the first meeting and the company may submit its proposals also at that first meeting or perhaps at the second meeting. In any event, proposals to amend the agreement are sooner or later exchanged between the parties.

Written Proposals

The proposals submitted are normally in writing and may either propose precise changes in the agreement or may express the intention to change the meaning or content of the agreement without specifying the wording to be used in the revised agreement. Very often, after the proposals are exchanged, each party is expected to explain to the other the intent of its proposed changes so as to ensure proper understanding. Next, the other party is usually asked to justify its demands. This involves giving the origin of the problem, the reasons for the proposed changes, and an explanation as to why the proposed changes are considered to be the most satisfactory solution to the problem. After all this has taken place, serious discussion of each item will begin. Also, each party can then consider other possible solutions to each problem not just the solution proposed by the other party.

Private Assessment

At this stage, the company and the union will probably make a private assessment of each other's demands. Each party will then probably conclude that it can agree to certain proposals made by the other party and can see areas of possible compromise on certain other items. Each party may also tentatively conclude that the other side will not push certain items beyond reasonable limits, whereas certain other items are strike or lockout issues.

Monetary versus Non-Monetary Issues

Very often the parties will separate the demands into so-called monetary issues and so-called non-monetary issues. *Non-monetary issues* include such items as contract language, procedural matters, and administrative matters which do not result in direct cents-per-hour labour cost increases.

Very often, the parties will decide to discuss the so-called non-monetary items first — usually because of the assumption that such items are easier to resolve and that, by resolving them first, the overall area of disagreement will be reduced. Also, quick resolution of such items tends to give a positive impetus to the talks, acting as an early signal of progress.

Normally, the two parties will meet with each other a number of times to resolve the various issues, non-monetary and monetary, before a new or amended collective agreement is accepted by both sides.

Each party usually considers, at an early stage, the concessions that it will be willing to make to the other party — knowing that negotiations will proceed for some time with continuing pressure to make concessions. It will also give consideration as to when any concessions should be made.

Conciliation Services

Both parties will be aware of the government conciliation services available and the statutory requirement to use them before a legal strike or lockout can take place. Both parties will also be aware that a government conciliator will exert strong pressure on them to make further concessions. If, after conciliation, there is still no settlement, there will probably be further negotiating sessions before the strike deadline arrives.

11.9 NEGOTIATING TACTICS

In all the meetings between the company and the union, from the very start of negotiations, each party will be arguing for its demands and resisting those of the other party. At the same time, each party will be looking for compromise alternatives that may enable an agreement to be reached. Ideally, both parties will come away from the negotiations feeling that they have secured many of their basic bargaining goals, even though in modified form; and confident that the agreement will be acceptable to both top management and the union membership.

Bargaining Positions

The union cannot allow the company to announce a settlement without first going through the bargaining process. The union members might believe that the union has just "sold out" to the company. One of the basic reasons for employees joining a union, and agreeing to pay union dues, is the assumption that the union can obtain for its members benefits that they would not otherwise receive from the employer. In other words, the union must constantly justify to the membership its role as their bargaining agent.

When the company makes its first offer, it is almost axiomatic that the union reject it. Therefore, if the company's first offer is the maximum that it can afford, or the maximum that it can justify, the company is in effect forcing the union to call a strike or lose credibility in the eyes of its members. To be practical, the company should initially offer considerably less than it can really afford or justify. The union can then reject the offer, thereby justifying its existence to its membership, and paving the way for a series of offers and counter-offers. Eventually a settlement will be reached which the union can recommend to its members, either as a fair settlement or the best it can get without calling a strike, and certainly one that is a lot better than that originally offered by the company. Sometimes, of course, a proposed settlement is unacceptable to top management or to the union membership and a lockout or strike becomes inevitable.

Some negotiators dislike the use of a bargaining position. However, most negotiators consider it an indispensable means for achieving their bargaining objectives.

Maximum and Minimum Objectives

The bargaining goal in, for example, a wage negotiation usually has a range. From the company point of view, the lower end of the range is the maximum objective and the higher part of the range is the minimum objective. The union goal likewise normally has a range and a maximum company offer below the union's minimum expectation would result in a strike.

In the hands of a skilled negotiator, the bargaining position has a dual role: it reveals and conceals. It is used first to reveal, move by move, the maximum expectation of the negotiating team, and second to conceal, for as long as is considered desirable, the negotiator's minimum expectation.

The negotiator tries to convince his (or her) opposite number that the maximum of his target range is really the minimum. He does this mainly by the manner and timing of changes in his bargaining position. Since he has taken a much more demanding bargaining position at the beginning of the negotiations, each concession brings him closer to his maximum expectation. Each concession should also be designed to encourage or pressure the other negotiator to respond with similar concessions of his (or her) own and to provide at least as much information about his expectations as the party making the first concession has revealed about his.

Three Main Activities

The company and the union are combining three main activities in negotiations:

1. Attempting to influence each other and the employees by advocating the merits of their respective positions.

2. Indicating their strength to each other.

3. Exploring the possibilities, in terms of the other party's minimum expectations, of a settlement without an economic contest or, failing that, an economic contest of minimum duration.

These three activities are inter-related and may be treated separately only for purposes of analysis.

The need to assert strength and to explore the possibility of a settlement is at the very heart of negotiations. A negotiator must have the ability to combine the two in such a way that one does not undermine the other. The basic purpose of each party in the negotiations is to convey strength and at the same time explore possibilities for a peaceful settlement to avoid a strike.

Advocacy of a Position

Even highly experienced and sophisticated negotiators sometimes underestimate the importance of adequate preparation and effective presentation of their position. This is because there is a tendency to consider the preparation and presentation as only the preliminaries to actual hard bargaining based on relative economic strength — a feeling that logical or persuasive discussion has little or nothing to do with the actual settlement of the issues in dispute. However, although relative economic strength is vital, logic and reason have in many instances significantly affected a final settlement. A good negotiator may give the impression that he/she is not influenced by a carefully presented, logical argument. However, in consultation with his own committee, when perhaps subsequently considering different courses of action, he may well give it the consideration it deserves.

Indication of Strength

The need for the parties to indicate their strength to each other is constantly present in the negotiations. The union, in arguing its own position or probing the company's position, is constantly saying or implying we can strike you, the membership will support a strike, and we will strike you if certain minimum conditions are not met. Similarly, the employer is constantly conveying the impression to the union that the amount of money for pay and other benefits is limited, the union and its members cannot afford to strike, and if the union does, the company can take it better than the union and its members can. Both sides are subtly and indirectly suggesting that there is a possibility of a lockout or strike if acceptable minimum conditions are not met.

Although both parties are endeavouring to convey an impression of strength and the possibility of a lockout or strike, both parties are usually careful to avoid outright threats. Threats are probably the most dangerous and least effective methods of indicating strength. Negotiators are not inclined to believe something just because it is expressed as a threat. Often people who make threats find it necessary to do so because they are bluffing. If a negotiator has bargaining strength, then threats are unnecessary. If threats are made then, when the showdown comes, the negotiator may have to eat his or her own words. In delivering an ultimatum, the negotiator is asking the other side to openly surrender. Obviously, that makes it more difficult for the other side to agree. As a result, the two parties are in a position where neither can back down gracefully without weakening their bargaining effectiveness.

One way of conveying strength is by the timing of changes in bargaining positions. In retreating from a bargaining position to the area in which the final objective is to be found, the negotiator must avoid giving the other side the impression of weakness. Perhaps therefore the negotiator can proceed to his/her objective under conditions which require the other side to match this movement step by step.

Exploration of Possible Areas of Settlement

The character of the negotiations is strongly influenced by the need to work towards a deadline. Both sides know that if there is no agreement, a strike will result. And this possibility is in the background right from the beginning of negotiations. There must be a successful effort to reach an agreement or the negotiations will be followed by a strike — usually with very serious economic consequences for both sides. So the two sides will, as the deadline approaches, carefully review each area of negotiation to determine how much each can yield to reach agreement and, through a series of proposals and counterproposals, gradually settle their differences — hopefully, before the deadline arrives.

11.10 IMPOSITION OF A FIRST AGREEMENT

If no settlement is negotiated for a first agreement, some provinces provide for the imposition of an agreement on the parties. These provisions were designed to help establish a workable relationship in cases where the employer and the union have failed, through bargaining, to establish a relationship, perhaps because of unrealistic union demands or the uncompromising nature of the employer's response.

In Ontario, either party may apply to the Labour Relations Board, under Section 43(1) of the LRA, to direct the settlement of a first collective agreement by arbitration. The Board will do this, if it appears to the Board that bargaining has been unsuccessful because of one or more of the following circumstances:

a) the refusal of the employer to recognize the bargaining authority of the trade union,

b) the uncompromising nature of any bargaining position adopted by the respondent without reasonable justification,

c) the failure of the respondent to make reasonable or expeditious efforts to conclude a collective agreement, or

d)   any other reason the Board considers relevant.

Such a request may be made if the parties are unable to reach a first collective agreement and the Minister of Labour has released a notice that it is not considered advisable to appoint a conciliation board or the Minister has released the report of a conciliation board which indicates that the parties have failed to reach an agreement.

Once the Labour Relations Board has issued its direction for settlement of a first collective agreement by arbitration, the parties have seven days in which to notify the Labour Relations Board that they have agreed that the Board arbitrate the settlement. Otherwise the parties must then follow the procedure specified for appointment of a private three-person board of arbitration.

11.11 SINGLE VERSUS MULTI-EMPLOYER BARGAINING

Single versus Multiple Plants

Usually, labour unions organize and become certified to bargain on behalf of the employees in one particular plant of a business corporation. However, when negotiating with multi-plant corporations, unions normally prefer a company-wide agreement, supplemented by individual plant agreements that cover local issues. Some employers have long accepted such agreements as, for example, in the automotive industry.

Single Employer versus Multiple Employers

There appears to be no desire among labour unions to include not just all the plants in a multi-plant corporation, but all the corporations in a particular industry. In other words, most unions prefer the single-employer negotiation which is in fact the most typical form of bargaining relationship. This union preference is not difficult to understand. By being free to concentrate its attention on the major corporation in an industry that is most likely to agree to the most favourable terms for the employees, the union can obtain a settlement that can be held up as a pattern for the industry. In other words, the union will be able to put pressure on the other firms in the industry to grant similar terms, or to show why they are unable to do so. If a firm can demonstrate that it cannot afford to accept the pattern, the terms might eventually, after some hard bargaining, be altered somewhat.

With this approach, the union chooses the company from which it expects to secure the most favourable terms. It then tries to bring all the other firms in the industry up to that level, or as near to it as possible.

In general, most large employers prefer to bargain individually. They dislike having other firms decide what wages, etc. they are to pay. They prefer to maintain their own freedom, and rely on their own bargaining power, to arrive at a settlement that reflects their own needs.

Multi-Employer Bargaining

Multi-employer bargaining is considered by many unions to be the approach most likely to yield good results in industries in which there are many small firms and a high degree of competition. This is because no individual firm, faced with fierce competition, can afford to make significant wage improvements. Otherwise its costs will be out of line and its economic vulnerability increased. Only by getting all the small firms in the industry to agree simultaneously to improve wages and other benefits, can the union hope to make progress. In this scenario, no individual firm would be at a competitive disadvantage as a result. In addition, employers in such industries often prefer to negotiate with a union through an employers' association rather than by themselves. The small individual firm feels weak against the union. The employer knows that a strike can soon put it out of business, particularly if its competitors continue to operate. On the other hand, to grant a wage increase that is out of line with other firms in the industry can be equally disastrous. The answer to this problem is for all the firms in the industry to negotiate together so that all grant the same wage increase and, if necessary, all take a strike together.

11.12 RATIONALE BEHIND CONTRACT NEGOTIATIONS

Why do some labour negotiations appear to be irrational with table thumping and threats, absurd demands, and frantic all-night meetings as the strike deadline approaches? Why do not the parties rely more on facts and less on propaganda and power? And why does society permit bargaining disagreements to be settled, if conciliation fails, by the brute force of a strike?

One of the most perceptive analyses of the bargaining process has been made by Professors Richard E. Walton and Robert B. McKersie who point out, in their McGraw-Hill book, *A Behavioral Theory of Labour Negotiations*, that labour negotiations actually consist of four different systems of activity: distributive bargaining, integrative bargaining, attitudinal structuring, and intra-organizational bargaining. Each of these processes deserves examination, for each makes different demands upon negotiators and each also sheds light on the above questions.

Distributive Bargaining

By distributive bargaining, the authors mean that type of negotiation with which most people are familiar — namely, haggling over how to divide up the pie. In labour negotiations, wages are the classic example of a distributive issue.

In this situation, hard facts have only limited value in determining a wage settlement. The union will admit that wages of, say, $30.00 per hour would bankrupt the average employer who, in turn, will admit that wages of $10.00 per hour would leave it without enough good workers. But such outer limits do not greatly help in deciding whether workers who are receiving $15.00 per hour should receive an increase of, say, 40, 50, or 60 cents per hour. With this situation, each negotiator has an incentive to bluff. If the union representative really would settle for a 50 cents-per-hour increase, rather than call a strike, why not open with a demand for $1.00 per hour and plead, threaten and bluff with the employer in the hope of persuading it to grant at least 60 cents an hour to avoid a strike?

If the bluff succeeds, the union negotiator has done his (or her) job well. If it fails, he can still fall back to his true position of 50 cents. Also, for all the union representative knows, perhaps the employer has privately determined that it will go as high as 60 cents to avoid a strike and the union negotiator would consider it foolish to risk opening for less than the employer might eventually be willing to give. But the employer is also thinking in the same terms, so each party often opens with a transparently unrealistic position; each knows what the other is doing and the art of distributive bargaining is to probe for (and possibly alter) the true position of the opponent, while concealing its own as long as appropriate.

Integrative Bargaining

At the same time as the parties are conducting distributive bargaining, they may also be engaged in "integrative bargaining". This means the negotiation of an issue on which both parties may gain or at least neither one will lose. Suppose, for example, the parties have decided in principle on a job evaluation system or a dental plan. Once the contentious issues of money and principle are out of the way, both parties may well gain from a co-operative search for the best job-evaluation plan or the best dental plan. For this purpose, a different approach is needed — an open discussion of alternatives, with perhaps joint efforts to obtain the necessary facts.

Attitudinal Structuring

Collective bargaining differs from many other types of negotiations by its strong involvement in *attitudinal structuring*. This means the shaping of such attitudes as trust or distrust, friendliness or hostility between the parties. Management and union representatives must live with each other and with their agreements, day after day, on a continuing basis. This factor can promote restraint between negotiators. However, it may have just the opposite effect — the friction developed in their daily dealings under the old agreement can erupt and make a shambles of the negotiations for a new agreement.

Intra-Organizational Bargaining

The aspect of bargaining which perhaps receives the least consideration is the aspect of intra-organizational bargaining. This is the manoeuvering to achieve consensus within (rather than between) the labour and management organizations. Perhaps most people view collective bargaining as a clash between two monoliths, because each party tries to present a solid front to the other and to the public. In fact, internal bargaining is very widespread and has a strong effect on bargaining between the employer and the union.

First consider the union. There are always groups within the union that believe their interests are not being given adequate consideration. The skilled workers may believe the union pays too much attention to the unskilled. Women workers may think that their interests are inadequately considered by the men who may run the union. In a company with two plants, the union local at one may feel that its interests are subordinated to those of the other. Perhaps the younger workers think too much money is being spent on pensions whereas the older workers may think the opposite. In the election of union officers, these interest groups are in the same kind of bargaining relationship as the voter and the politician in the broader political society. Candidates for union office will try to appeal to factional interests to win votes, and the factions or special interest groups within the union will seek to use their votes to place in office the persons most favourably disposed towards their concerns.

Sometimes differences arise between the local union and the national organization (or central office). Perhaps, by way of illustration, the local leadership is convinced that management will not grant more than a 50 cents-an-hour increase but the national pattern is 70 cents. To permit a settlement at the lower figure may jeopardize what the national union can obtain in other organizations; to insist on the higher figure may involve the local union in a long and fruitless strike. The competing interests in the union must be resolved and this resolution comes about through an informal bargaining process.

Bargaining with the employer cannot even begin until this internal bargaining has taken place.

The bigger or more complex the bargaining group, the more likely it is that aspirations will be divergent and competitive rather than common. Individual groups which believe their interests are being sacrificed and their aspirations being ignored may threaten to disassociate themselves from the group as a whole. They may then try to obtain bargaining power for themselves.

In bargaining with the employer, the union negotiator must be sensitive to these internal pressures. A union often submits a very large number of initial demands, not only for purposes of distributive bargaining — to provide itself with a stock of negotiating issues — but also to demonstrate to each group in the union that its demands have been voiced to the employer. The union negotiating team can never win everything the members want, but at least they can appear to be tough and aggressive in hammering out a settlement.

On the employer's side, there may also be conflicting points of view which have to be resolved — for example between the sales manager and the treasurer. The sales manager may urge that a settlement under almost any conditions is necessary, in order to satisfy the customers, while the treasurer may argue that a settlement beyond a certain cost is unacceptable.

The company must also harmonize the objectives of the local plant and of the company as a whole. Plant management may be directed to take a stand which is either contrary to its own best judgement or not suited to its own needs, for fear that a precedent may be set which the union will seek to use in bargaining with other plants of the same company.

For the management negotiators, all of this means that they too must please the constituents on whom their jobs depend. They too can never win everything in bargaining that they would like to have, so a show of militancy may also help them to show that they are not selling out to the other party when they ultimately make concessions.

In summary, Walton and McKersie's analysis shows that the negotiation process is far more complex than it may appear to be to the casual observer. It is not just a poker game for high stakes or another buyer/seller relationship, although it contains elements of these and other types of economic and political (and theatrical) activities — nor does it impugn the integrity of labour and management negotiators to point out the ritualistic nature of the bargaining process. The players usually know the rules of the game and that serious issues are at stake.

Because there is seldom a single "right answer" to the economic issues in dispute and because the union-management relationship also involves a clash of political, psychological and organizational interests, the negotiation process inevitably bears little resemblance to a dispassionate search for what is equitable.

Expiration Date

How is this complicated management-union negotiation manoeuvering ever resolved? The answer lies in the fact that a collective agreement has an expiration date. Upon expiration of the agreement and completion of conciliation services, the union is free to strike, and the company to lock out its employees.

Negotiations for a new agreement begin before the current agreement expires, often drag on for a few weeks, and then quicken in pace and movement as the expiration date approaches — for that is the deadline when all the bluffs are called and all the speeches must end. Either the parties agree on a new agreement or both will incur the costs of a strike.

11.13 CRITICAL ROLE OF THE STRIKE

It is important to understand the critical role of a strike in the bargaining process. When labour and management disagree, how might the disagreement be resolved?

Strike Alternatives

One alternative is for the employees to quit and look for work else where. However, if this free market alternative worked satisfactorily, there would be no need for unions.

Second, the workers could marshall all the facts at their disposal and plead their case before management. However, in effect, management wins every dispute so long as the workers can only talk and management maintains the right to determine wages and working conditions.

Third, society could require both parties to submit their dispute to some authority for a binding decision. But such binding arbitration is opposed by most management and union officials. Among the reasons for this opposition is the opinion by both labour and management that better decisions are reached between the parties than if decisions were imposed by an outside arbitrator or a government agency. Furthermore, company and union officials would ask, if the government is to fix wages, why should it not also fix prices and profits and make all the other economic decisions now left in private hands, and how capable is it of making all of these decisions?

The Strike Weapon

The only alternative to the above is permitting workers to cut off their employer's income by means of a strike. No one can claim the right to strike has not been abused. But neither has anyone uncovered an alternative that is generally acceptable to both parties which permits workers an effective voice in establishing their terms of employment. However, a union can only call an effective strike when the issues are important enough to the membership to cause them to be willing, if necessary, to give up weeks or months of lost earnings to convince the employer to press their demands.

11.14 RATIFICATION VOTE

In Ontario, under Section 44(1) of the LRA, a collective agreement that is entered into, or memorandum of settlement that is concluded, has no effect until it is ratified by the members of the bargaining unit. The LRA also specifies: (a) that such a vote of ratification must be by ballots cast in such a manner that persons expressing their choice cannot be identified with the choice expressed, (b) that all employees in a bargaining unit, whether or not such employees are members of the trade union, shall be entitled to participate in the vote, and (c) that any vote shall be conducted in such a manner that those entitled to vote have ample opportunity to cast their ballots.

Also, according to the LRA, Section 44(3), a proposed collective agreement or memorandum of settlement is ratified only if more than 50% of those voting vote in favour of ratifying the agreement or memorandum.

REVIEW QUESTIONS

1. What factors influence the composition of a typical company negotiating committee? Who is usually included? Why is the company president normally excluded?

2. What should be the attitude of the company negotiating committee?

3. How much authority should the company negotiating committee have?

4. How should the committee be organized? Who should act as the spokesperson?

5. What preparations should the committee undertake before negotiations begin?

6. What is the usual composition of a union negotiating committee? How are the members selected?

7. Should the members of the union committee be "agreeable and conciliatory in their approach to the various issues"?

8. How are company "demands" prepared?

9. How does the union draw up its own demands?

10. What types of information are necessary for negotiating purposes?

11. When and where are negotiating sessions usually held?

12. What is the procedure for re-negotiating an existing collective agreement that is about to expire?

13. What is the purpose of separating company and union demands into monetary and non-monetary issues?

14. "The union cannot allow the company to announce a settlement without first going through the bargaining process." Discuss.

15. "To be practical, a company should initially offer considerably less than it can really afford or justify." Discuss.

16. "In the hands of a skilled negotiator, the bargaining position has a dual role. It reveals and conceals." Explain and discuss.

17. What three main activities are the company and union combining in negotiations?

18. Why is multi-employer bargaining sometimes preferred by a union?

19. Explain the concept of distributive bargaining.

20. What is "integrative bargaining"?

21. How do attitudes affect the process and outcome of contract negotiations?

22. How and to what extent do internal pressure groups affect contract negotiations?

23. What are the requirements, in Ontario, for ratification of a proposed collective agreement? Why are such requirements considered to be necessary? Discuss.

CHAPTER 12: CONTENTS OF A COLLECTIVE AGREEMENT

Collective agreements vary considerably. This is because they must take into account the peculiar circumstances of each firm and industry and the relative bargaining strengths of management and labour. Nevertheless, there are many similarities in the topics covered. This is because each agreement represents a serious effort to cover all aspects of the employer-employee relationship. Also, agreements achieved in one firm and industry come under the careful scrutiny of union and management elsewhere. An example of an actual agreement is contained in Chapter 26 of this book.

12.1 PREAMBLE

Here the two parties usually recognize the need to maintain orderly collective bargaining and to provide for satisfactory working conditions and prompt settlement of grievances.

12.2 RECOGNITION AND COVERAGE

In this article of the Agreement, the Company officially recognizes the union as the exclusive bargaining agent for the employees covered by the agreement. Also, the bargaining unit is defined. Thus, it may include all employees of the Company, with certain exceptions.

Example:

> All employees of the Company at the designated location below the rank of sub-foreman except employees certified in other bargaining units, security staff, plant clerical staff, scientific workers, and employees in confidential positions as listed in Appendix A.

The article may also state that foremen and higher levels of management and sub-foremen will not perform the work usually performed by members of the Bargaining Unit except as specified elsewhere in the Agreement.

Next, the article may set out the status of part-time and casual employees. Then perhaps state what has been agreed upon with regard to the *contracting out* of work by management — that is, the right of management to have outside firms rather than its own employees do work such as office cleaning.

12.3 RIGHTS OF MANAGEMENT

This article provides that all rights of management belong to the Company except for those that are specifically given up under the provisions of the agreement with the Union.

Example:

> Subject only to the provisions of this Agreement, the management and operation of the business and the employment, direction, promotion, transfer, lay-off, and suspension, discharge, or other discipline of employees for just cause shall be vested solely in the Management of the Company.

12.4 WAGES

This article sets out the rate of pay for each job covered by the agreement for each year of the agreement. It may also specify an additional cost-of-living increase tied to the Consumer Price Index. The article may also specify the starting rate for a new employee — perhaps 10 cents per hour below the base rate, with an automatic increase after so many weeks of service, followed by another increase in the base rate after so many more.

12.5 UNION SECURITY

In this article, management usually agrees to collect union dues and union initiation fees from employees and to pay them to the union.

The Company may also agree as a condition of employment that all employees who were members of the Union at the time of the signing of the Agreement must continue to be members and that any persons hired later must become members.

It may also be agreed in this article that no coercion or intimidation shall be used to compel or influence an employee to join the union and that no discrimination may be made against present or prospective union members. Also, both the Company and the union usually explicitly agree not to discriminate against any employee because of race, creed, colour, age, sex, marital status, nationality, ancestry, or place of origin.

This whole topic of Union Security, a vital one for the union, is discussed in some detail in the next chapter of this book (Chapter 13: Union Security).

12.6 OFFICERS AND STEWARDS OF THE UNION

The union agrees to appoint or elect stewards to deal with matters affecting employees in the Company's plants and to supply a list of these stewards and officers to the Company. The Company agrees to recognize the stewards and officers and to treat them the same as other employees, except as set out in the Agreement.

Example:

> A Union Steward, and any other representative of the Union shall continue to perform his regular duties on behalf of the Company and shall not leave his regular duties without obtaining permission from his supervisor who shall be given a reasonable explanation for such absence, and shall report back to his supervisor after engaging in Union duties which are permitted by this Agreement. Such a Union representative shall also report to the Supervisor of a section in which he is not employed when entering such section.
>
> A Union representative shall record all the time that he is absent from his regular duties, pursuant to this Article, in accordance with the plant time-keeping procedures.

12.7 GRIEVANCE PROCEDURE

In this article, the Company and the union first emphasize the desirability of a satisfactory **grievance procedure** which will have the purpose of settling grievances promptly. The union may then be given the right to appoint or elect a Grievance Committee to deal with matters not settled in the first, second or third steps of the grievance procedure and to supply the Company with a list of the committee members. Third, the grievance procedure is agreed upon and explicitly described.

In Chapter 16, we explain and discuss grievance procedures.

12.8 DISMISSAL OR SUSPENSION

Such an article may provide that an employee who believes that he has been unjustly dismissed (permanently lost his job) or suspended (temporarily lost his job) may have his case handled as a **grievance**.

12.9 ARBITRATION

In this article, the Company and the Union agree to settle any alleged violation of the agreement by **arbitration** — that is, by referral to a neutral third person or persons who will study the dispute and make a decision about it that is legally binding on both the Company and the Union. A possible decision of the Arbitration Board may be, however, that the matter in question is not arbitrable. The inclusion of such an Arbitration article is required by the provincial Labour Relations Act. In this way, all disputes arising during the life of the Agreement must be resolved peacefully, without resort to strikes or lockouts.

In Chapter 17 (Arbitration), we look at this matter more closely.

12.10 HOURS OF WORK AND OVERTIME

Such an article may specify the standard hours of work as not more than 8 hours daily and 40 hours weekly, on five days per week. It may also specify the payment to hourly-rated employees of one and one-half the regular rate of pay for overtime work.

12.11 HOLIDAY PAY

This article usually provides for the payment by the Company of regular pay on specified holidays, and double time for work on these holidays. It might also deal with employees on sick pay or receiving Workers' Compensation; employees who are absent immediately before or after a public holiday; and employees who are on vacation during a public holiday.

12.12 SENIORITY

Seniority is usually defined in terms of accumulated service in the bargaining unit, with credit for certain other types of service.

The article may state that seniority begins when a new employee has completed his/her three-month probationary period and is retroactive to the commencement of his/her employment. It is lost if the employee voluntarily quits, fails to return on recall, or has been on lay-off in excess of the allowable time to which he/she is entitled.

12.13 NOTICE OF LAY-OFF

Here the Company may agree to provide employees with a specified number of days of prior notice of lay-off.

12.14 LAY-OFFS AND RECALLS

This article stipulates the order of lay-off should it become necessary to reduce the working force. Usually this is on a seniority basis, with the more junior members being laid off first. The order of recall is also usually set out in this article, again on a seniority basis, with the more senior employees being recalled first, but usually with a requirement that the senior employee be qualified to perform the work formerly done by the junior employee. Shift preference based on seniority and recognition of seniority, despite transfers between different company plants, might also be covered in this article.

12.15 TRANSFERS AND PROMOTIONS

In this article, the basis for the permanent and temporary transfer of employees from one department to another is agreed upon. Employees may be given the right to request a return to their regular department or to request a transfer from their present department.

Vacancies and promotions are often handled on the basis of seniority, provided an employee possesses suitable qualifications for the job or can qualify reasonably quickly. The application of seniority in transfers and promotions, as well as in lay-offs and recalls, is discussed in detail in Chapter 19 of this book.

12.16 AUTHORIZED ABSENCE FROM WORK

In this article, the Company may agree to grant or consider granting an employee a leave of absence without pay, if a written application is made providing sufficient reason. The Company may also agree to permit absence from work for reasons of pregnancy; appearance in court; full-time appointment with the union; attendance at union schools, conventions or conferences (by a limited number of employees for a limited time); election to public office; or attendance at the funeral of an immediate relative.

12.17 OFF-SHIFT PREMIUMS

The Company usually agrees to pay a premium of so many cents an hour, in addition to the basic rates of pay, to employees working at certain times during the day and on regularly scheduled Saturdays and Sundays.

12.18 REST PERIODS

This article specifies the number of rest periods that an employee may take:

Example:

> The Company agrees to grant rest periods of 10 minutes each during the morning and afternoon shifts, provided the working time of the shift exceeds $2^1/_2$ hours. A rest period of ten minutes shall be granted in overtime, provided the overtime shift exceeds $2^1/_2$ hours after the return from the second meal period. The union agrees that, except in cases of personal necessity, employees shall not ask for additional time off during the working day. The union agrees that rest periods must not be abused.

12.19 VACATIONS

In this article, the amount of vacation with pay to which an employee is entitled is set out. Usually, the number of weeks increases according to the number of years of service — ranging, for example, from two weeks after one year's service to five weeks after twenty years' service. The method of calculating vacation pay is also specified — for example, the normal weekly hours at the regular hourly rate. The article may also specify the time at which the vacation pay may be taken and the preference, if any, given to vacation requests.

Example:

> Vacations may be granted at any time subject to the demands of the business, but the Company will make a sincere effort to grant vacations at times requested by employees. Senior employees in each department will be given preference. No vacations shall be granted between October 1st and December 31st unless by special arrangement with the Plant Superintendent.

The article may also deal with vacation credit owing on termination of employment. Also, it may stipulate that there is to be no carry-over of vacations from one year to another.

12.20 SAFETY AND HEALTH

In this article, the Company may agree to be responsible for the safety and health of its employees.

Example:

> The Company shall make reasonable provision for the safety and health of employees during the hours of their employment. Protective devices on machinery and other devices deemed necessary properly to protect employees from injury shall be provided by the Company. This, however, shall not be construed to include such personal necessities as safety boots or any article which becomes the personal property of the employee. Should such reasonable provisions not be made or such protective devices not be provided, the matter may be subject to the grievance and arbitration procedures.

12.21 TOOLS, LICENCES AND CLOTHING

This article may cover the provision by the Company of tools, clothing, and necessary licences.

12.22 SICK PAY AND WELFARE PLAN

This article may provide for income during absences due to illness; specify the amount of life insurance to be provided each employee by a Group Life Insurance Plan fully paid for by the Company; and specify the continuation of existing Hospitalization, Medical-Surgical, and Major Medical Plans.

12.23 UNION NOTICES

This article covers the use of plant bulletin boards.

Example:

> The Company agrees to extend to the Union the use of plant Bulletin Boards provided that the use of such Bulletin Boards shall be restricted to the posting of notices of Union Meetings, recreational, and social affairs. Such notices shall have received the prior approval of the Supervisor, Industrial Relations, or his nominee.
> The Union agrees that it will not distribute or post or cause or permit to be distributed or posted on the property of the Company, for or on its behalf, any pamphlets, advertising or political matter,

cards, notices or other kinds of literature except with prior written permission of the Supervisor, Industrial Relations, or his nominee.

12.24 STRIKES AND LOCKOUTS

In this article, the union agrees not to undertake strikes or slowdowns and the Company not to lock out its employees during the life of the Agreement.

Example:

> The Union agrees that there shall be no slowdown, strike or other work stoppage or interference with work. The Company agrees that there shall be no lockout.

12.25 DURATION OF AGREEMENT

This article stipulates how long the Agreement is to be in force. One, two, and three-year agreements are the most common.

REVIEW QUESTIONS

1. What is usually contained in the preamble to a collective agreement?

2. Which employees are usually excluded from coverage?

3. What is meant by "contracting out"? Why would reference be made to this in a collective agreement?

4. What "rights" may be specifically reserved for management in a collective agreement?

5. What is the Consumer Price Index? Why does it appear more and more frequently in collective agreements?

6. What are "union dues"? Why does management agree to collect them on behalf of the union? Does every employee in the bargaining unit have to pay them?

7. Does management have to agree, in the collective agreement, that union membership be a condition of employment?

8. What privileges are usually included in an agreement for union officers and stewards?

9. Should a person who believes that he has been unjustly dismissed or suspended have the right to have his or her case treated as a grievance? Or is this an infringement of the employer's management rights?

10. What is meant by "arbitration"? Why is such a clause always included in a collective agreement?

11. How is "seniority" usually defined? When does it normally begin? When it it lost?

12. What is the purpose of a seniority clause? What are the advantages and disadvantages of employee seniority (a) for the employee and (b) the employer?

13. What principle is usually followed in lay-offs and recalls? How satisfactory is this procedure?

14. A supervisor in a large electrical products manufacturing firm complained to a friend that the three workers that he had just finished training had been "bumped" out of the plant and he now had to start all over again. Explain and discuss.

15. Explain the need for off-shift premiums.

16. Do the employer and the union have a completely free hand in deciding what vacations employees will receive? Should employees be free to choose when to take their vacation, with reasonable notice to management? Discuss.

17. "An employee's safety and health, even at work, is basically his or her own responsibility." Discuss.

18. Why does management so strictly control the posting of union notices?

19. What are the various types of strikes and slowdowns that would be forbidden by the collective agreement? What is meant by a lockout?

CHAPTER 13: UNION SECURITY

13.1 UNION SECURITY DEFINED

The fact that a labour union is certified as the bargaining agent for the workers in a particular plant does not automatically mean that all eligible employees must become union members. This will depend on the terms of the collective agreement.

A labour union, in its written agreement with the employer, will often therefore negotiate the inclusion of what is known as a *union security clause*. This is a clause that requires management to assist in the collection of monthly payments to the union from its employees. These payments are called *union dues* and their automatic deduction from an employee's pay cheque is called a *checkoff* of union dues. The union security clause may also require all eligible employees to become members of the union.

The situation in each firm, as regards these matters, will depend on the agreement that has been negotiated between management and the union. In fact, there are five basic types of union security clause: compulsory checkoff, voluntary checkoff, union shop, dues shop, and closed shop, as explained in the following pages.

13.2 UNION DUES

As in many other organizations, the members of a labour union are required to pay a regular monthly fee, known as "union dues", to the union local. Even though a person may not have chosen to join the union, he or she may have to pay these union dues. By trying to get as many employees as possible to become union members, the union not only helps ensure that it is certified as the bargaining agent, but also obtains a solid financial base for its activities.

13.3 COMPULSORY CHECKOFF

Some provinces, including Ontario, require that collective agreements contain compulsory checkoff clauses.

In Ontario, the LRA, Section 47(1), provides that, where a union so requests, there shall be included in the collective agreement a compulsory checkoff provision. This provision requires the employer to deduct from the pay of all members of the bargaining unit, whether they are union members or not, the amount of regular union dues and to remit them to the union forthwith.

13.4 VOLUNTARY CHECKOFF

In practice, it was not easy for unions to collect dues from their members. And without the dues, the unions found difficulty in covering their expenses. Consequently, pressure was exerted on employers in labour agreement negotiations to undertake to deduct from an employee's pay an amount of money equal to union dues and to forward it to the union. However, employers agreed to do this, only if they first received a written authorization and direction from the employee to do so. This was known as the "voluntary checkoff" of union dues. Nowadays, however, provincial labour relations statutes have made compulsory checkoff the rule, rather than the exception.

13.5 UNION SHOP

In the early days, the unions felt that the voluntary deduction of union dues, although a step in the right direction, did not go far enough. This was because only a portion of a firm's employees would agree to have union dues deducted from their pay. As a result, the cost of union representation, although for the benefit of all, was being borne only by some. The unions considered it unjust that workers who were not union members should be "free riders"— that is, obtain the benefits of union activity without sharing the cost. Therefore, the unions battled hard to make union membership and the compulsory deduction of union dues from each employee's pay a requirement of employment. Where in fact an employer agreed to these conditions, the situation is known in the labour movement as a "union shop".

Many firms now have this arrangement — one in which all present and future employees are required to join the union and become paid-up union members.

13.6 DUES SHOP

Some employees have felt strongly that they should not be forced to join a union if they do not wish to do so. And many employers have agreed that union membership should be a matter of individual conscience and decision. As a compromise, Ivan C. Rand, former Chief Justice of the Supreme Court of Canada, suggested that collective agreements might require all employees to pay normal union dues but give them the choice of becoming union members or not. This is known as the *modified Rand Formula* and has gained considerable acceptance among employers and labour unions. A firm which operates in this way is known in the labour movement as a "dues shop" (also "agency shop" in the U.S.). With this arrangement, there is no obligation for an employee to become a member of the union. However, there is an obligation for the employer to deduct from the employee's pay an amount equal to union dues and to forward this money to the union. In this arrangement, the dues are considered to be a charge for services performed by the union as bargaining agent for all the employees.

The dues shop is quite widespread. Some unions prefer this arrangement because no union member can justifiably claim that he or she was forced to join the union.

13.7 CLOSED SHOP

In a union shop, explained previously, a person has to become a member of the union in order to be employed there. However, this requirement normally applies only after he or she has become an employee. It is the employer, therefore, who decides who is eligible to be employed.

In a "closed shop", on the other hand, a person must already be a union member before he/she can be hired. Thus a person who wishes to work for the employer must first obtain union membership and must remain a member in good standing. Since a closed shop virtually transfers control of hiring from management to the union, this type of arrangement has been strongly opposed by employers.

A closed shop is common in the construction industry and in the longshoring industry. Workers are supplied to employers by the union by means of *hiring halls* where persons are assigned work by the unions. A closed shop is uncommon in manufacturing or office union situations.

13.8 STATUTORY PROTECTION

In Ontario, under the LRA, Section 51, a collective agreement may contain a provision requiring, as a condition of employment, membership in the trade union or granting a preference of employment to members of the trade union or requiring the payment of dues or contributions to the trade union. The collective agreement may also contain a provision for permitting an employee who represents the trade union involved to attend to the business of the trade union during working hours without deduction of time or wages. The agreement may also contain a provision permitting the trade union involved, the use of the employer's premises for trade union purposes without payment therefor.

13.9 RELIGIOUS GROUNDS FOR EXEMPTION

In Ontario, under the LRA, Section 52, an employee in a bargaining unit who, because of religious beliefs, objects to belonging to a union or making a financial contribution to a union may be exempted from doing so. Instead, that person must agree to pay an amount equal to the union dues to a charity which is selected by the employee and the union or, failing agreement, by the Labour Relations Board.

13.10 CONTRACTING OUT

The term *contracting out* refers to the practice by some employers of having certain activities in the manufacturing process, plant maintenance, delivery, etc. performed by outside firms, with their own employees, on a contract basis. Obviously, such a practice takes work away from members of the employer's own unionized work force and gives it to outside workers who are usually lower paid.

Many collective agreements do not make any reference to contracting out since employers consider this to be one of their management rights.

13.11 SUCCESSOR RIGHTS

When a company sells its business to another company, the question arises as to the rights of the employees now that they are working for a new employer.

In Ontario, the LRA, Section 68, specifically provides protection for such workers. According to the Act, a "successor employer" is an employer to whom a predecessor employer has sold its business. This successor employer is then bound by any collective agreement that its predecessor employer was bound by, until the Labour Relations Board declares otherwise. Also, the trade union that is the bargaining agent for any employees of the predecessor employer, or has applied to become their bargaining agent, or is attempting to persuade the employees to join the trade union, continues in the same position in respect of the business as if the successor employer were the predecessor employer. The LRA also specifies certain conditions under which the Labour Relations Board may amend the bargaining unit after a business has been sold, or even terminate the bargaining rights of the trade union involved.

REVIEW QUESTIONS

1. What are regular "union dues"? What are they used for? Where do they go?

2. Is compulsory checkoff of union dues required by statute in your province? Which employees in the bargaining unit, if any, are exempted from this requirement? Outline the pros and cons of a compulsory checkoff.

3. Distinguish between the dues paid by an employee who is a member of the bargaining unit, but not a member of the union, and the dues paid by one who is a union member.

4. Why does the union consider it only fair that non-union members who are members of the bargaining unit pay the same regular union dues as union members?

5. What is meant by the term "union shop"?

6. What is the Rand Formula? How does this satisfy both the union and the employees who do not want to join the union?

7. Distinguish between a union shop and a closed shop. A closed shop can sometimes give rise to abuse. Explain and discuss.

8. Can an employee be exempt from union membership because of religious reasons?

9. What is meant by the term "contracting out"? Should employers have a free hand in this matter? Discuss.

10. What happens to the rights of union members when the employer's business is sold?

11. Explain the concept of "successor rights".

CHAPTER 14: CONCILIATION

14.1 CONCILIATION DEFINED

The term *conciliation* refers to the use of an outside third party called a *conciliator* to assist a company and the union representing its employees, to arrive at a mutually satisfactory collective agreement. Following certification or voluntary recognition, either party may request that the provincial Minister of Labour appoint a conciliation officer to provide such assistance. Such conciliation is often requested after direct negotiations between the company and the union have broken down, either for a first agreement or renewal of an existing one. It is required by statute in many jurisdictions some weeks prior to the date upon which the company is legally entitled to lock out its employees or the union to call its members out on strike, because of failure to reach a new collective agreement. Its purpose is to help the company and the union to reach a new collective agreement, without the hardship involved in a lockout or strike. With conciliation, the only means available to the conciliator to bring the parties to agreement is persuasion. Therefore, there is never any guarantee that the parties will in fact reach an agreement before the lockout and strike deadline arrives. Much will depend on the skills of the conciliator and the desire of the company and the union to settle their differences without a lockout or strike.

14.2 CONCILIATION REQUIREMENT

In Ontario, under the LRA, Section 79, even though no collective agreement is in operation, a union does not have the right to strike, and an employer does not have the right to lock out its employees, without having exhausted the conciliation procedure specified by the Act. The LRA provides that, on the request of either party for conciliation services, the Minister of Labour will appoint a *conciliation officer*. There is also provision in the Act for appointment of a three-person *conciliation board* should the conciliation officer fail to obtain a settlement within the time allowed. In practice, conciliation boards are not usually appointed and the conciliation process is that of the conciliation officer alone. Under the LRA, a union has the right to strike and an employer has the right to lock out its employees 14 days after the Minister of Labour has released the report of the conciliation officer to the parties involved. There are similar conciliation-type provisions in the Labour Relations statutes of other provinces.

14.3 MEDIATION

The term *mediation* is often used instead of conciliation as it also means the use of an outside third party (called a *mediator*) to bring the two parties to an agreement by peaceful persuasion. However, the term is most commonly used to describe such negotiations when undertaken either on the eve of a strike or lockout, or during the existence of one. Such mediation is undertaken at the request of one of the parties involved or at the suggestion of the government. Whereas conciliation is required by provincial statute prior to a strike or lockout, mediation is usually a voluntary process. However, both processes are similar in that they involve the services of a third person, usually a professional, to bring the parties to agreement by persuasion. Unlike arbitration, discussed later, there is no compulsory or imposed settlement. With conciliation or mediation, the parties directly involved always have the right to reject the conciliator's or mediator's suggestions.

In Ontario, the Ministry of Labour has designated a select group of people as mediators. Usually, they are former senior conciliation officers. Under Section 19 of the LRA, the Minister of Labour may appoint a mediator instead of a conciliation officer or conciliation board. The Minister will often appoint one of these people as a mediator during the fourteen-day waiting period before the union has the right to strike. This is sometimes at the request of one or both of the parties. The mediator will meet with the parties and endeavour to get a settlement without a strike. If his/her efforts fail and there is a strike or lockout, he or she may well meet with the parties again from time to time, to attempt to resolve their differences. Both conciliation officers and mediators in this context are full-time employees of the Ministry of Labour.

Sometimes the company and the union will appoint a mediator agreed upon by themselves rather than one appointed by the government. Mediators may also be drawn from the ranks of lawyers, retired judges, university professors, and consultants who have developed, usually through past experience, expertise in industrial relations matters and acceptability to people in the industrial relations area. Such persons are available for employment on an *ad hoc* basis, as the need arises.

14.4 CONCILIATION VERSUS ARBITRATION

A clear distinction must be made between conciliation (or mediation) on the one hand and arbitration on the other. The conciliator (or mediator) has no power to impose a settlement on the disputing parties. He or she can only make suggestions. The purpose is to bring the parties to an agreement by persuasion. An arbitrator by contrast has the right, after investigating the matter or matters in dispute, to impose a legally binding settlement. This power may be conferred by statute, as it is for many public sector employees. In their case, compulsory arbitration, rather than the strike weapon, is the only permitted way of resolving outstanding labour-management disputes in negotiations for a new agreement. On occasion, in order to avoid or settle strikes, the federal parliament or provincial legislatures have passed special legislation requiring employees to end a strike and return to work with a settlement to be imposed by arbitration.

14.5 THE CONCILIATION PROCESS

Let us assume that a conciliation officer has been appointed to help resolve a dispute. The first step in the process is for him or her to get in touch with the company and the union and arrange a combined meeting at a place and time in the near future.

Prior Research

Next, the conciliation officer may undertake some research into the dispute, the parties involved, and the nature and problems of the industry concerned. In this way, the conciliator has some basic knowledge upon which to draw at the first meeting. The conciliator does not need to waste valuable time, the others' as well as his/her own, learning the essentials. However, some conciliators believe that it is better to attend the first meeting with a completely open mind and that prior reading about the matter prevents this. Thus, there are two schools of thought as to the preparations that should be made.

First Meeting

At the first meeting, often a relatively short one, the conciliator will try to determine, first of all, whether the two parties are serious about the conciliation process or whether they merely wish to go through the motions of conciliation so as to fulfill the requirements of the law. The conciliator will then try to determine the issues that have been resolved, those that are still outstanding, and the present attitudes of each party towards the outstanding issues. He or she may also try to assess, to some extent, the personalities of the negotiators for the opposing sides.

Separate Meetings

Often, the next step is for the conciliator to arrange separate meetings with the company and the union negotiating teams. At such meetings, he or she will attempt to determine the concessions that each party is willing to make in order to reach a settlement and the extent of each party's desire for a settlement. With this knowledge, the conciliator can start making suggestions for the solution of the problems, involving give-and-take on both sides. In reality, the parties are usually quite secretive about their bargaining positions and stubborn and reluctant to make concessions. Apart from what they may feel about the righteousness of their cause, the negotiators must also keep in mind how any settlement may be perceived by the company directors and shareholders and the union membership. However, in the back of everyone's mind, is the fact that until the conciliator hands in his or her report to the Minister, the countdown to a strike deadline cannot commence. Hopefully, as conciliation continues, the two parties will draw closer together and, finally, as the threat of a strike or lockout approaches, reach an agreement. But, of course, conciliation does not always work out this way. And sometimes, even when the conciliator believes that he or she has brought about a settlement, the unexpected can occur — for example, that the agreement is rejected by higher management or the union membership.

14.6 ROLE OF THE CONCILIATOR

In practice, some parties to an industrial dispute merely observe the letter of the law with respect to conciliation. They hold meetings with the government-appointed conciliation officer at an early stage of the negotiations but do not make serious use of the services offered. Others make use of the conciliator's services only after negotiations have been carried on for some time, hoping that he or she may be able to break a negotiating impasse.

Impartial Go-between

Very often, the existence of an impartial "go between" has proven of inestimable value. Because of personality, intelligence, and past experience of the conciliation process, the conciliator may be able to make suggestions for solutions that enable both parties to move closer towards an agreement without abandoning their major goals. Perhaps both parties are fearful of modifying their formal negotiating positions. However, they may be willing instead to confide in the conciliator. With such additional information, the conciliator may be able to suggest an acceptable area of settlement to both parties and help bring the two parties together. Perhaps on his or her own initiative, with diligent probing and questioning, the conciliator can guide, coax, cajole, educate and even pressure both parties into making or accepting proposals which will in the end bring about a settlement.

Willingness to Listen

A good conciliator or mediator is one who is always willing to listen. During direct negotiations the employer is trying to convince the union and the union is trying to convince the employer of the validity and justness of their position. At conciliation, the company and the union will also try to convince the conciliator as to the reasonableness of their point of view. They will often try to do this with long and detailed presentations.

Waiting Period

One common frustration for conciliation officers is that, no matter what they do or say, there is a waiting period of fourteen days after the release of their report to the parties before there can be a strike or lockout. As a result, no matter what recommendations the conciliator may make, or what logic he or she may present, the union's real answer may be that the employer has another fourteen days in which to improve its offer. Alternatively, the employer may say that, no matter what it offers, the union can turn it down and spend the next fourteen days trying to get some more.

How Mediator's Job Differs

The mediator, on the eve of a strike, is in a much better position to get the parties to agree. Immediately before the strike deadline, the union knows that the alternative is for the union to accept the offer now or perhaps be on strike tomorrow. The company also knows, immediately before the strike deadline, that either a settlement will be made now or perhaps no goods will be produced tomorrow. The mediator also knows this and it makes his or her job very different to that of the conciliation officer.

Early Settlement

If a settlement is reached before the deadline, some managements would believe their negotiators had not bargained hard enough. Similarly, the union membership might not be convinced that their representatives had secured the best settlement possible. As a result, there is a tendency for top management and the union not to approve a settlement unless negotiations have continued right up to the deadline. In such a situation, the mediator has to recognize the importance of the timing of any settlement.

Sometimes an early settlement can spell trouble. In one company, the company and union teams would normally negotiate right up to the settlement deadline, reaching a settlement only at the last minute. The conciliator in the most recent contract negotiations thought this practice unwise and by his competence and persistence caused the company and the union negotiators to reach a settlement somewhat prior to the deadline. However, when the union took the settlement to their membership, it was voted down — the only apparent logic for this being that the membership did not believe the union had obtained the best settlement it could without going right to the deadline. Similarly, when the company negotiator reported to his principals, they also reacted that, since he had settled so soon, he had not secured the best deal possible. The conciliator failed to recognize that both negotiators needed to give their principals the impression that they had bargained as hard as possible.

Judicious Pressure

One of the functions of the conciliator is to apply pressure to the parties to get them to make concessions which will bring about a settlement. However, this pressure has to be applied very judiciously. The conciliator must recognize that there is an appropriate time to apply pressure, also an appropriate time at which to apply maximum pressure. He or she must also recognize that the negotiating parties, whatever the pressure applied, need to be given time to modify their positions.

Assessment of Positions

Another part of the conciliator's job is to assess the negotiating positions of the parties, the target settlements, and the ultimate settlements that both parties are prepared to make. The conciliator cannot go in and ask those questions directly and expect to have them answered, so he or she will probably go slowly — perhaps listening hard to find out what the company and union will and will not do — and then asking indirect questions. Perhaps the parties will do things they have said they will not do. However, unless the company makes it clear that it intends to have a lockout or the union a strike, it is only logical to assume that both want a settlement. If they do, there must be some flexibility in their respective demands. If they are reasonably close in their demands, then not a great amount of flexibility is required. If the conciliator can eliminate the strike and lockout issues from both sides, presumably what is left is negotiable. Perhaps the conciliator can coax both parties into making slightly more concessions in the negotiable area. If the conciliator can establish that the only problem left is to see who makes the final move, perhaps he can go to the company and say in confidence that if the union would do this, would you do that? With some encouragement, he or she can go to the union with a similar proposition. If the conciliator gets some encouragement, perhaps he or she can recommend to the committees jointly, or perhaps more safely separately, that a settlement can be reached on that basis and have both parties agree.

In many situations, the employer's negotiating team starts off by looking for the ideal settlement desired by the employer, and the union, the ideal settlement desired by the membership. Over a period of time, one or both parties may come to recognize that their original objective is impractical. As a result, in order to avoid or end a strike or lockout, the union may settle for what is merely acceptable to its members, or the company for what will barely satisfy its top management.

14.7 CHANGING CIRCUMSTANCES

Negotiations often proceed for a considerable period of time during which circumstances may change. The company may then be faced with the choice of paying somewhat higher wages than it had planned or, for example, losing a large order or a significant share of a market. As another example, the employees and the union may have previously concluded that certain demands must be met. However, during the period of negotiations, they may find that other unions are settling for less and that a pattern of settlement has developed which they are compelled to accept without accomplishing their original objectives. Also, general economic conditions may have changed. Thus when the company and union started negotiations, the economy may have been prospering and the company's financial prospects seemed encouraging. However, if a general economic downturn, or an industry downturn, develops during the course of negotiations, this will reduce the union's optimism as to the possible settlement. These changes can occur during the life of a strike as well as during the life of negotiations for a new collective agreement.

14.8 CONTRACT RATIFICATION

Before a newly negotiated contract is signed by union officials, the union may wish to have it approved or "ratified" by the union members. Such a ratification takes the form of a vote at a meeting, usually at the local union hall, which members of the bargaining unit are invited to attend. If the members reject the proposed new contract, the union negotiators may go back to the bargaining table to try to resolve the problem.

14.9 FEDERAL EMPLOYEES

A conciliation board or conciliation commissioner may be appointed to investigate an industrial dispute involving federal employees or other federal employees under federal jurisdiction and to make recommendations for a settlement. However, unlike an arbitration report, such recommendations are not binding on the employer or employees. They represent what the conciliation board or commissioner feels is an acceptable settlement, taking into account all the facts involved.

Since such recommendations are not binding, the question arises: what good do they achieve? In fact it has been argued that they do more harm than good — encouraging the party whose bargaining goals are most favoured in the recommendations from softening its bargaining position. Such a softening may be essential, if a negotiated settlement is to be reached. For this very reason, a federal task force on Canadian industrial relations recommended some years ago that conciliation boards be cut back in favour of conciliation officers (or mediators). In other words, that more positive steps can be achieved by having a conciliator act as an intermediary, helping the parties to reach a negotiated settlement, rather than by having a board to pass judgment and produce a set of recommendations binding on no one. In practice, such conciliation board reports may have helped bring about and prolong strikes rather than hasten a settlement. Because of this, Ontario some years ago effectively gave up the practice of appointing conciliation boards.

REVIEW QUESTIONS

1. What is meant by the term "conciliation"?

2. When is conciliation required?

3. Distinguish between conciliation and mediation. What do they have in common?

4. What types of persons act as conciliators and mediators? By whom are they appointed?

5. Distinguish between conciliation and mediation on the one hand and arbitration on the other.

6. What preparation should a conciliator undertake before starting his or her conciliation efforts. Explain.

7. What might the conciliator attempt to do at the first meeting with the union and employer negotiating teams?

8. Why can the conciliator's role be so valuable in negotiations?

9. What problems does the conciliator face? Why is the conciliator's task more difficult than the mediator's one?

10. Why is the timing of a settlement so important? Why is an early settlement usually undesirable?

11. How can a conciliator exert pressure on the negotiating parties? Why is such pressure necessary?

12. What assessments does the conciliator have to make? How does he go about making them?

13. How can changing circumstances affect negotiations? Give examples.

14. What is a "ratification vote"? Who is allowed to participate?

15. Sometimes a union may reject an employer's final offer and call a strike even though a majority of the employees may be willing to accept the offer. Is this situation (a) desirable? and (b) inevitable?

CHAPTER 15: STRIKES AND LOCKOUTS

Failing a settlement through negotiations and conciliation, a union has the legal right to call its members out on strike, and an employer the legal right to lock out its employees. A *strike* is the temporary refusal of the employees to continue working for the employer. A *lockout* is the temporary refusal of the employer to continue providing work for its employees and may involve the temporary closing of the employer's establishment. The term *work stoppage* is now also used, particularly in statistical documents, to describe such events — thereby avoiding the need to assign responsibility for the breakdown in labour-management relations. The number of person-days lost in Canada in recent years through work stoppages is shown in Table 15.1. The total includes all industries, not just those shown separately.

15.1 LEGAL REQUIREMENTS

Collective Agreement in Force

Where a collective agreement is in operation, then, under Ontario's LRA, Section 79(1), no employee bound by the agreement shall strike and no employer bound by the agreement shall lock out such an employee.

No Collective Agreement

In this situation, no strike or lockout is permitted until the Minister of labour has appointed a conciliation officer or mediator. And then seven days must elapse from the date of release of the report of the conciliation board or mediator. Or fourteen days from the date that the Minister of Labour has notified the parties that he or she does not consider it advisable to appoint a conciliation board.

Mandatory Strike Vote

In Ontario, a secret vote must now be held by the employees in a bargaining unit, before they can go on strike. And a majority of those voting must vote in favour of a strike in order for it to be legal.

Thus, according to the Labour Relations Act, 1995, Section 79(3):

> If a collective agreement is or has been in operation, no employee shall strike unless a strike vote is taken 30 days or less before the collective agreement expires or at any time after the agreement expires and more

than 50 per cent of those voting vote in favour of a strike.

And Section 79(4):

> If no collective agreement has been in operation, no employee shall strike unless a strike vote is taken on or after the day on which a concili-ation officer is appointed and more than 50 per cent of those voting vote in favour of a strike.

15.2 TYPES OF STRIKES

When a union declares a strike, its members usually leave the employer's premises and go home, perhaps stopping by the union hall or other meeting place. In other words, there is *walkout*. Sometimes, however, the union mem-bers stay on the job but slow down the pace of their activity. This is known as a *slowdown*. Often it serves as a prelude to a full strike, giving warning to the employer of the employees' dissatisfaction. Although causing aggravation to the employer and its customers, union members are still employed and con-tinue to receive their pay. This state of affairs may continue until a settlement is reached, or the employer loses patience and sends the workers home, or attempts other disciplinary measures. Similarly, union members may remain at work but observe many of the detailed rules governing their jobs which may have previously been ignored in order to maintain a reasonable rate of production. As a result, fewer goods are produced or poorer service is given to customers. Such a form of industrial action is termed *work-to-rule*.

Another form of strike in which union members withdraw their services but stay on the work premises is a *sit-down strike*. As a matter of interest, this type of industrial action was successfully used by the United Automobile Workers' Union in 1937 to secure recognition by General Motors Corporation. In more recent times, union members, when faced with plant closings and loss of jobs and even pensions, have resorted to similar types of action. One important advantage of a sit-down strike from the union's point of view, is that it makes it more difficult for the employer to bring in replace-ment labour. Another advantage is that the forcible removal of the striking workers can become a highly publicized event, likely to arouse public sym-pathy and to focus public attention on the labour-management dispute.

Occasionally, other unions may call their members out on strike to support the strikers. This is called a *sympathy strike*. However, such an action is con-sidered to be illegal.

Sometimes, the workers on a job may, according to their different skills, be represented by several different unions rather than by just one. In such cir-cumstances, there can occasionally be disputes as to which workers (for example, labourers or bricklayers) are entitled to perform a particular type of

Table 15.1 — *Time Lost in Work Stoppages in Canada, in thousands of person days, 1990–2000*

Year	Mining	Manufacturing	Construction	Transportation	Trade	Community, business & personal services	TOTAL
1990	411	2,474	1,150	400	170	549	5,154
1991	153	788	35	110	144	1,306	2,582
1992	276	910	151	121	114	625	2,202
1993	115	501	157	65	240	524	1,603
1994	72	657	21	234	219	413	1,618
1995	24	722	202	277	73	281	1,607
1996	137	898	93	112	424	1,546	3,343
1997	164	1,272	0	85	463	1,563	3,573
1998	92	624	326	84	43	782	2,436
1999	151	921	6	279	79	945	2,499
2000	164	472	16	70	92	750	1,659

Source: Human Resources Development Canada, *Research Bulletin*

Note: includes all strikes and lockouts, legal or illegal, lasting one-half day or more and amounting to 10 or more person-days lost. Time lost by workers indirectly affected, such as those laid off because of a stoppage by other employees, is not included.

work. Inevitably the employer will tend to favour the workers with the lower rate of pay so long as they can perform the work competently. The union representing the higher-paid workers may then call its members out on strike to protest the awarding of the work to the members of the other union — work that should, by custom, belong to its own members. Such a strike is known as a *jurisdictional strike.* Somewhat similar in origin is the calling of a strike by a union to protest the "contracting out" of work formerly performed by its members — for example, maintenance, cleaning or security services. Instead of having its own employees do the work and having to pay them wages and benefits, the employer may find it cheaper and more convenient to engage the services of an outside firm.

15.3 PURPOSE AND EFFECTIVENESS OF A STRIKE

A labour union, by means of a strike, is trying to exert financial and, to some extent, public pressure on the employer to accept the union's demands as to the terms for a new collective agreement. However, to be successful, the union and its striking members, must be able to stop or at least substantially reduce the firm's production or other operations. Otherwise, the employer sustains no immediate financial loss, no loss of customer goodwill, and no permanent loss of customers to competitors.

When a strike takes place, the employer is sometimes able to continue production by using other non-union employees such as supervisory personnel and by hiring new workers (known to the strikers as "scabs") to perform the tasks formerly done by the striking workers. Usually, however, the firm cannot continue to operate during a strike, except in a crippled fashion. And the strike is a highly effective means of persuading the employer to modify its bargaining position.

Sometimes, however, the union may fail to halt production. As a result, the union may continue to weaken itself financially by paying strike pay to its members and by paying advertising and other expenses, without moving any closer to a favourable settlement of the dispute. The individual union members may suffer even more severely, receiving only strike pay, if anything, instead of their regular wages.

The longer a strike goes on, the better the settlement that the union must obtain in order to make all the financial and other hardships worthwhile. Otherwise, the extra pay, etc. will not be sufficient to offset the financial losses taken during the strike. The worst of all worlds is to have a long strike and a meagre settlement. The best is a short strike and a generous settlement. Consequently the decision to strike, irrespective of any social or political implications, should not be taken lightly but must be based on a careful appraisal of all the factors involved: rates of pay elsewhere; the economic climate; the ability of the employer to pay; the public demand for the employer's product; possible public reaction; and so on. Some strikes have in fact been followed by the permanent closing of the employer's establishment and the permanent loss of jobs, a highly undesirable and unforeseen outcome. On a less drastic scale, strikes have sometimes been followed by the contracting out of some types of work, such as maintenance, unless expressly forbidden as one of the terms of a new settlement.

15.4 LOCKING OUT THE EMPLOYEES

In order to cover ongoing expenses and make a profit, an employer must continue to produce and market its goods or services. Obviously, therefore, the employer will not lightly decide to lock out its workers. The only factors that will make such a decision a logical one include: the belief that it is a necessary measure to place economic pressure on the union to come to a settlement; the belief that such a lockout will only need to be of short duration; perhaps the previous declaration of a strike by the union; the existence already of a slow-down or work-to-rule movement among its employees; or the belief that the union and its members are in no financial position to withstand a continued loss of wages and benefits.

If the employer is to be successful in its lockout, the loss of wages and benefits by the union members must create financial hardship. If, however, the union has a large strike fund, it may, at least for some time, be able to negate or at least mitigate the economic effects of the lockout. Also, if other unions provide financial assistance, this will reduce the impact of the lockout. The longer the lockout continues, the greater the hardship on the employees and the greater the pressure on the union to come to a settlement.

15.5 UNLAWFUL STRIKES AND LOCKOUTS

The calling of a strike, or the declaration of a lockout, must conform with the provisions of the relevant provincial or federal labour relations statute. An *unlawful strike* is a strike that contravenes one or more provisions of the labour relations statute and lays the union and its members open to charges and possible fines and/or periods of imprisonment, if found guilty. Similarly, an *unlawful lockout* is a lockout that also contravenes one or more provisions of the statute and which lays the employer open to similar charges and possible penalties. It would be unlawful, for example, for a union to call a strike during the term of an existing collective agreement. It would also be unlawful for a union to call a strike prior to the expiration of the waiting period after conciliation and after the termination of the collective agreement. Also, of course, it would be unlawful for the union to call a strike in an industry whose workers, because of the essential nature of their services, are not by statute, permitted to strike. Similarly, it would be unlawful for an employer to lock out its employees in any of these circumstances. In Ontario, it would also be unlawful to call a strike or go on strike without the required secret strike vote.

According to Ontario's LRA, Section 81:

> No trade union or council of trade unions shall call or authorize or threaten to call or authorize an unlawful strike and no officer, official or agent of a trade union or council of trade unions shall counsel, procure, support, or encourage an unlawful strike or threaten an unlawful strike.

Section 82 prohibits unlawful lockouts by an employer or employers' organization.

15.6 UNAUTHORIZED STRIKES

So far, we have assumed that all strikes are called by the union. In practice, this may not always be so. Those that are not, are termed *unauthorized, unofficial or wildcat strikes*. Sometimes a union leadership will lose touch with the mood of its membership and work too slowly to correct injustices that the membership may feel strongly about. Unofficial leaders, perhaps younger and more dynamic, may capture support of the union members and persuade them to "down tools". This may occur just before the union's declaration of a strike or perhaps in direct defiance of union orders to stay on the job. An unofficial strike may be lawful or unlawful, depending on when it takes place. Thus, if a wildcat strike takes place during the life of a collective agreement, it is unlawful. If it take place, once the union is in a legal strike position after negotiations and conciliation, it is lawful.

15.7 PICKETING

To hamper the employer in its efforts to maintain production and sales during a strike, the union will arrange for its members to picket the employer's premises. *Picketing* is the stationing of union members at the entrances and exits of the struck plant to discourage the movement of materials, parts, and non-striking and replacement workers (the so-called "scabs") into the premises and the shipping of finished goods out of them. Union members are required to take turns on the picket line and help prepare placards and other signs. Payment of strike pay is often conditional on picket duty. Picketing workers are sometimes joined by members of their families and by other supporters including, occasionally, politicians.

Picketing is supposed to be non-violent, involving only the physical presence of the striking workers in modest numbers and the use of signs and verbal communications: to explain their point of view and to solicit support from non-striking workers of the employer or employees of other firms who need to visit the premises in the course of their work — for example, to deliver materials or collect products. In practice, tempers may occasionally become frayed and the presence of the police may be required to keep order at the factory gates. If violence breaks out, or police orders are ignored, the offenders may be arrested and charged with one or more criminal offences such as obstructing a police officer in the course of his or her duty or committing assault.

Although unusual in Canada, *secondary picketing* occurred extensively in the United Kingdom some years ago, notably in the various coal miners' strikes. Such picketing involves the placing of pickets comprised of striking union members and their supporters outside the premises of firms which supply materials, parts, fuel, transportation and other services to the firm that is being struck.

15.8 BOYCOTTS

Another method that a union can adopt to increase pressure on the employer is a *boycott* of the employer's products. This means that union members and their supporters refuse to buy the firm's products so long as the strike or lockout continues. However, to have any great impact on the employer, the boycott must be widespread. It must involve a large segment of the buying public rather than just the strikers and their immediate supporters. Thus there must be a great deal of public sympathy for the striking workers, if a boycott is to succeed.

15.9 INJUNCTIONS

Another weapon that management may use is the *injunction*. This is a court order forbidding the persons to whom it is directed from carrying on a certain activity. Formerly, court orders were used to forbid a wide variety of union activities. Nowadays their use appears to be restricted to persons damaging the employer's property, committing acts of violence, trespassing, and engaging in acts of intimidation — for example, mass picketing. An injunction may be granted if the court is convinced that damage will otherwise be done to the employer's property and that this damage could not be compensated for by a monetary award. An injunction can also be used against any conspiracy to commit personal injury, to induce breach of contract, or to interfere with contractual relations. The injunction carries the weight of the law behind it.

There are several types of injunctions. A *restrictive injunction* orders a person to stop doing something — for example, to stop intimidating workers. A *mandatory injunction* orders a person to do something — for example, to remove barriers. Because of the time it takes for a dispute to be tried in court, a judge may grant a temporary injunction. This may be for a fixed period of time, in which case it is called an *interim injunction*; or it may be for an indefinite period until the matter is finally judged in court, in which case it is called an *interlocutory injunction*. An *interim injunction* is one made for a short period and without notice to the other party. When a case is tried in court, the judge may grant a *permanent injunction* if he or she finds in favour of the plaintiff and considers an injunction a necessary remedy.

The use of the injunction has been strongly criticized by labour unions on the grounds that by limiting pickets, for example, a strike is made ineffective. In other words, they consider that the use of the injunction confers an unfair bargaining advantage on the employer.

15.10 REPLACEMENT OF STRIKERS DURING A LEGAL STRIKE

In all jurisdictions in Canada, except Quebec, employers are permitted to hire new employees during a strike and assign to them work previously done by strikers. Therefore a small employer, particularly of relatively unskilled employees, may be able to hire enough replacement employees to continue normal operations during a strike.

For a very large employer, it is impractical to hire and train enough new employees to maintain a high level of production during a strike. Similarly, it is usually impractical for an employer of large numbers of highly-trained technical employees to find sufficient appropriately-qualified replacement people to carry on normal production during a strike.

15.11 PROFESSIONAL STRIKE BREAKERS

It is now considered to be an unfair labour practice in some provinces for employers to use professional strike breakers during a strike.

In Ontario, according to Section 78(1) of the LRA:

> "No person, employer, employers' organization or person acting on behalf of an employer or employers organization shall engage in strike-related misconduct or retain the services of a professional strike breaker and no person shall act as a professional strike breaker."

The Act further states, in Section 78(2), that, for the purposes of Subsection (1):

> "Professional strike breaker" means a person who is not involved in a dispute whose primary object, in the Board's opinion, is to interfere with, obstruct, prevent, restrain or disrupt the exercise of any right under this Act in anticipation of, or during, a lawful strike or lockout.
>
> 'Strike-related misconduct' means a course of conduct of incitement, intimidation, coercion, undue influence, provocation, infiltration, surveillance or any other like course of conduct intended to interfere with, obstruct, prevent, restrain or disrupt the exercise of any right under this Act in anticipation of, or during, a lawful strike or lockout."

REVIEW QUESTIONS

1. Explain the terms: (a) strike, (b) lockout, and (c) work stoppage.

2. Why would union members go on a slow-down or engage in a work-to-rule action rather than leave their jobs?

3. Why would union members engage in a sit-down strike rather than go home?

4. What is a sympathy strike? What other actions might be taken?

5. What is a jurisdictional strike?

6. What is the immediate purpose of a strike?

7. What determines the effectiveness of a strike?

8. How can an employer overcome the effects of a strike?

9. What factors should be taken into account by a union before it calls a strike?

10. Why would a firm lock out its employees? What would determine the success of such a lockout?

11. When would a strike or lockout be unlawful? What are the possible legal implications for the union or employer?

12. What is an unofficial or wildcat strike? Why would it occur? Would it be legal or illegal?

13. Explain the nature and purpose of picketing. Why are police sometimes required?

14. What is secondary picketing?

15. A boycott has been used more as a political weapon than as an industrial one. Discuss.

16. What is necessary, if a boycott is to be effective?

17. Explain the use of injunctions by employers.

18. Should employers be allowed to hire replacement workers during a strike? If so, what should be the right of such workers after the strike is over? Discuss.

19. What are "professional strike breakers"? Are they legally permissible? Explain and discuss.

20. Why does Ontario require a secret vote by members of a bargaining unit, before a strike can take place? Discuss.

CHAPTER 16: GRIEVANCE PROCEDURE

16.1 GRIEVANCE DEFINED

Every collective agreement contains a *grievance procedure* — the steps by which a dispute between management and labour during the life of the agreement may be amicably settled. A *grievance* is usually considered to be an alleged violation of the collective agreement. A complaint (for example, "it's too hot in here") may not constitute a grievance. The person who files a grievance is called the *grievor*.

The grievance procedure shown in Exhibit 16A provides no definition of a grievance and this is true of many grievance procedures. Many people consider it desirable to have a definition but in practice there is a problem as to how to define, in a manner acceptable to both union and management, the concept of a grievance. One approach is to define a grievance as "an alleged violation of a collective agreement". When the company proposes such a definition to the union, one of the likely responses of the union is to say: What about the employee complaint that is not an alleged violation of the agreement? Should he or she not also have the right to process such a complaint? There is also some advantage to the employer in having such complaints processed. In this way the company finds out what problems are bothering its employees. Certainly, in the interest of good employee relations, the employer should be interested in resolving such problems.

One very practical approach to resolving this dilemma is to allow any matter bothering an employee to be processed through the grievance procedure. However, when such matters are processed, a distinction is made between those that allege violations of the collective agreement and are therefore subject to arbitration, and those that do not allege any violations. The latter will be handled as complaints that are not subject to arbitration. Hopefully, the employer is interested in resolving both kinds of problems in a proper manner.

16.2 TIME LIMIT FOR FILING A GRIEVANCE

Nearly all collective agreements have a time limit for filing a grievance. These time limits range from say 24 hours up to 6 months or a year, with the occasional one having no time limit at all. Perhaps the most common types of time limit are in the range of 30 to 60 days after the event which gave rise to the grievance.

16.3 STEPS IN A GRIEVANCE PROCEDURE

A grievance procedure specifies the steps which must be followed in settling an alleged violation of the collective agreement. These steps vary according to the particular collective agreement, but may be as follows:

1. The employee first asks the supervisor's help in settling the complaint — for example, why the employee did not receive the proper overtime pay.

2. If no satisfactory solution is found, the employee will report the grievance to the shop steward, who is the unpaid union representative in each shop, or section, of the plant. Very often, the employee will go directly to the shop steward rather than first talking to the supervisor. The shop steward, who is normally permitted time off from his or her job in the shop to process grievances, will normally put the matter in writing and then attempt to settle the grievance with the shop supervisor.

3. If the supervisor's decision is not acceptable to the employee, the chief steward for the plant may take the matter up with the department superintendent.

4. If the grievance is still not resolved to the employee's satisfaction, the union may ask for a meeting of the firm's Industrial Relations Manager and the Union's Grievance Committee.

5. If this meeting fails to achieve a decision acceptable to both sides, arrangements are made for an arbitrator or an arbitration board to settle the matter. This arbitrator is an outside person (such as a university professor), acceptable to both labour and management, who will listen to the two viewpoints, ask questions, and finally make an award. *Arbitration* is the making of a decision, or award, which is legally binding on both the employer and the union. The provincial Labour Relations statutes make compulsory the inclusion of an arbitration provision in all labour agreements. The cost of the arbitrator is usually shared equally by management and the union. In the next chapter, we look in some detail at arbitration.

16.4 EXAMPLE OF AN ACTUAL GRIEVANCE PROCEDURE CLAUSE

Exhibit 16A (below) contains an example of an actual grievance procedure:

EXHIBIT 16A: *Example of a Grievance Procedure Clause in a Collective Agreement*

Article 6

GRIEVANCE PROCEDURE

6.01 It is the mutual desire of the parties hereto that complaints from employees shall be adjusted as quickly as possible, and it is generally understood that employees shall not file a grievance until they have first given their supervisor an opportunity of adjusting their complaint.

6.02 The complaint shall be taken up as a grievance only within six months of the event giving rise to the complaint.

6.03 *Step No. 1* — Between the Employee, Steward, and Supervisor. An employee with a grievance may discuss the matter with his/her steward who may present the grievance in writing, signed by the employee, to the supervisor indicating the time and date of receipt. The supervisor shall give an answer in writing to the steward within two working days.

6.04 *Step No. 2* — Between the Employee, the Chief Steward, and the Manufacturing Manager or nominee. If settlement of the grievance has not been reached under Step No. 1, then this step shall commence within four working days following receipt by the steward of the answer in Step No. 1. The Manufacturing Manager or nominee shall give an answer in writing to the Chief Steward within three working days of receiving the grievance.

6.05 *Step No. 3* — Between the Employee, the Union, and the Manager, Industrial Relations or nominee.

If a settlement of the grievance has not been reached under Step. No. 2, then this step shall commence within ten calendar days following receipt by the Chief Steward of the answer in Step No. 2. The Manager, Industrial Relations, or nominee, shall arrange a meeting within one week of receiving the grievance and shall give an answer in writing to the Union within not more than five working days following such meeting. The union will be given a minimum of forty-eight hours' notice prior to such meeting. Union representatives at the third step of the grievance procedure may consist of the President of the Local, the Chief Steward, and the Steward representing the grievor, and one Union representative who is not an employee of the Company, and any employee possessing factual knowledge bearing on the matter in dispute. The Union may appoint an alternate to act in place of any of the foregoing employees, when such employee is unavailable at the time of a third step grievance hearing.

6.06 A grievance which is not processed within the time limits set out in this article, or which is not posted to arbitration within thirty calendar days after the answer has been given under Step No. 3 hereof, shall be deemed to have been settled or abandoned.

6.07 If the Company fails to comply with the time limits set out in this Article, the grievance may be entered at the next step.

6.08 The Company shall have the right to have present, at the third step of the grievance procedure, any officers, officials, or agents of the Company.

6.09 It is recognized that the Company shall have the right to take up a grievance with the Union relating to the conduct of the Union, its officers, or any other Union representatives, or the conduct of the employees, or concerning the application or interpretation of any provision of this Agreement. The grievance shall first be presented in writing to the Union and a meeting will be held within one week between the Company and the Union. The Union shall answer the grievance within one week of such meeting.

6.10 It is recognized that the Union shall have the right to take up a grievance with the Company relative to the violation, misinterpretation, or non-application of any provision of this Agreement. The grievance shall be first presented in writing to the Company and a meeting will be held within one week between the Union and the Company. The Company shall answer the grievance within one week of such meeting.

6.11 Any adjustment arising out of the settlement of a grievance relating to a claim for retroactive payment shall be limited to a period of six months prior to the date on which the grievance was first presented hereunder.

Complaint Stage

At the beginning of the procedure just set out, there is provision for a complaint stage prior to filing a grievance. This step, designed to help resolve problems, exists in some grievance procedures but not in all. It provides an opportunity for employees with a complaint to discuss with their supervisor the nature of the problem. Perhaps the supervisor is not aware of the problem. Perhaps he or she does not realize the effect it has on the employee. Sometimes, in this way, the problem can be quickly resolved. The complaint procedure tends to be informal; there is nothing in writing. Often, a discussion of the complaint enables the supervisor to take some action that will resolve the matter.

Unions are reluctant to agree to a compulsory complaint procedure that requires employees to discuss their problem with their foreperson without the presence of their union representative. Such a procedure tends to inhibit employees from raising complaints and perhaps, because of lack of knowledge of the collective agreement, encourages employees to agree to things that they would not have agreed to if there had been proper union representation. Also from the union point of view, it does not give the union the opportunity to bring to bear its experience in other parts of the company or to express its concern as to how the action might affect other employees.

Handling Grievances

In this particular example, the first step in the grievance procedure is between the employee, the steward and the supervisor. The second step is between the employee, the chief steward and the manufacturing manager or nominee, and the third step between the employee, the union and the manager of industrial relations, or nominee.

Logic Behind the Grievance Procedure

Perhaps the logic behind this arrangement is that the first step gives an opportunity for the employee to tell his or her story, for the union steward to point out the alleged violations of the agreement, and for the supervisor to be able to quickly correct the matter if the grievance is deemed justifiable.

If the problem is not resolved at the first step, then the logic is to allow the employee, the chief steward — hopefully with more experience than the shop steward — and the manufacturing manager, again hopefully with more experience and authority than the supervisor, to deal with the problem. Sometimes, the more senior manager can look at the problem with less emotion and perhaps bring more experience to bear on it. He or she will then overrule or uphold the supervisor's decision.

Similarly, the chief steward, again hopefully with more experience than the steward, may perhaps see weaknesses in the union position or alternatively, argue the union position more effectively and thereby bring about its resolution. In Step 3, the union representation would normally include an outside union representative who probably has much more experience and much more training, and perhaps better judgment than the inside union representatives. As a result, the outside representative may bring more to bear on the decision-making process, and also may argue the union case more effectively than the others.

On the company side, the Manager, Industrial Relations, should have a good knowledge of what the employee can or cannot win in arbitration. Being removed from line management, he or she may perhaps make a judgment somewhat different to that which the line management would make.

Therefore, since the same problem is being looked at in each of three different steps, it is in effect being looked at by three different groups of people who should consider all the various aspects of the problem. Hopefully, this procedure should result in the employee and the union being accorded their legitimate rights. Where the employee and the union do not have the rights they claim, this should hopefully become apparent to them and the problem be resolved without recourse to arbitration.

In order to expedite the problem solving, and to prevent procrastination or uncertainty on either side, there is, at each step, a time limit on both the union and the company. Failure to meet any of these time limits can result in the grievance being automatically processed to the next stage, or automatically considered to have been withdrawn or resolved.

16.5 RETROACTIVE PAYMENT

One of the items that may have to be resolved is the amount of retroactive payment that can result from a grievance about rates of pay. Some agreements provide no time limit to retroactive pay; others provide that there will be no retroactive payment prior to the date of filing of a grievance. In practice, a company may argue that, even if there has been a violation of the collective agreement, there should be no payment for the period prior to the date of filing of the grievance. This is because no one has called attention to the alleged violation of the agreement. Surely, the company may argue, it should not be held responsible for retroactive payment for the period prior to its being made aware of such a problem.

The counter-argument could be that the employee is entitled to the payment, because it is required by the collective agreement. It is the company's fault that it was in violation of the agreement. The only redress available to the employee for the violation is compensation. The employer's requirement to pay what is required under the collective agreement should not be limited by the fact that the employee did not immediately file a grievance. From these and other conflicting arguments, agreement should eventually be reached on the amount of retroactive payment.

In many collective agreements, a maximum period for retroactive payment is set out. In our example, the period is six months prior to the date on which the grievance was first presented. Many other agreements provide maximum time limits, such as 30 days, 60 days, 90 days or perhaps a year prior to the date of filing the grievance.

16.6 RIGHT OF COMPANY AND UNION TO FILE GRIEVANCES

It is fairly common in a collective agreement for the company and the union to set out specifically the right of each to file grievances (as distinct from an employee's right). However, it is unusual for a company to file a grievance. An example of a *company grievance* would be in regard to a work stoppage or in regard to the conduct of the union, its officers or any other union representatives, or it might want simply to file a grievance in order to deal with the interpretation of a certain provision in the collective agreement.

A *union grievance* filed under this provision of the collective agreement relates to something that no individual employee would be able to deal with effectively. It might, for example, be the violation, misinterpretation or non-application of a provision of the agreement that affects a large number of the employees. Thus the union might file a grievance questioning the method of calculating statutory holiday pay, or the requirements for employee entitlement to it. As another example, it might file a policy grievance with regard to the conditions under which employees are entitled to receive overtime payment. Both of these grievances differ from the claim of any individual employee with regard to statutory holiday payment or overtime payment.

16.7 THE GRIEVANCE RATE

The *grievance rate* is the number of grievances filed in relation to the number of union members in the company. Some firms enjoy a low grievance rate while others suffer from a high one. In the latter case, something is obviously wrong — either on the management side or on the union side.

Factors that help determine the rate of grievances in a firm include the following:

1. Union-employee relations

2. Past history of union-employer dealings

3. Personalities of key union and company officials

4. Pay and seniority

5. Technological changes

6. Union policies

7. Grievance procedure

8. Management policies

1. Union-Employer Relations

The better the relations, the lower is likely to be the grievance rate, and vice-versa. Good relations help reduce the number of grievances because employees are less likely to be militant, raising technicalities and bringing cases just for the purpose of harassing management; also employees are more likely to settle their complaints orally with the foreperson. If bad relations exist, a trade union will tend to stir up grievances just to strengthen the solidarity of the union and to provoke and upset management. In such a situation, a larger proportion of disputes turn into written formal grievances rather than being settled quickly at the foreperson level.

A low grievance rate does not always mean that relations are good. Nor does a high rate necessarily mean they are bad. Sometimes a low grievance rate accompanies bad union-management relations — for example, if the employer has recently defeated the union in a long strike. Grievances in the company are few, mainly because management is tough and the defeat of the union in a strike has left the union too weak to challenge the employer. A low grievance rate may also indicate that many disputes are settled outside the formal grievance procedure.

A high grievance rate may sometimes exist, despite good management-labour relations, because the union does not screen complaints properly or because the particular work situation produces a great many problems or disputes.

2. Past History of Union-Employer Dealings

The amount of experience that union and management have previously had in dealing with each other has a decisive influence on a firm's grievance rate. Unreasonable positions may be taken by one side or another or even by both, just because they do not know what is reasonable. As a consequence, the grievance rate is a lot higher than it should be. Also, when a union is newly certified, it may lack leaders who are willing and able to distinguish between complaints that are violations of the labour agreement and ones that are not. Often the union stewards, trying to win approval from the rank and file employees, accept too easily as grievances the complaints brought to their attention.

3. Personalities of Key Union and Company Officials

Sometimes an individual with a strong personality will tend to impose his or her view as to the way that the union or management should be treated. The other officials are relegated to a back seat. There have often been drastic changes in the labour relations climate and hence in grievance activity following changes in either management or union representations or both.

4. Pay and Seniority

The pay system used in a plant can greatly affect the rate of grievances. Even with an hourly system there are disputes about job grades, overtime rates, and so on. However, the use of incentive pay standards can result in many more disputes. Every piece rate or every production standard used to determine bonus payments may be challenged. Piece work and bonus plans inevitably result in different earnings by different employees and groups of employees. This can give rise to jealousy, suspicion and claims of unfair treatment which eventually bubble to the surface in the form of grievances.

Another source of friction is the application of seniority in transfers and layoffs. If the firm is thriving, there is little or no need for transfers or layoffs. Consequently, few grievances will result. However, if production has to be curtailed and the labour force reduced, the opposite will be the case. This is especially so if the seniority system includes some room for management judgement, such as the relative skills and ability of the persons involved.

5. Technological Changes

Many workers view with suspicion any change in production technology because of the belief, often based on past experience, that the main purpose of such change is to reduce the number of workers required, to place greater demands upon them with no additional pay, or to replace many of the present employees with lower paid, less skilled workers. Changes in production technology and work methods can be a major source of grievances.

Changes in managerial methods and policies, particularly ones that require transfers, promotions or layoffs, are also likely to raise issues that produce grievances. If a firm is losing money, or finding that its production costs are becoming too high relative to those of its competitors, it will probably undertake drastic changes in its organization and work methods. This often brings about a rash of grievances.

6. Union Policies

Some unions deliberately encourage their members to bring forward grievances. Others discourage them from doing so, trying to settle the matter without filing grievances. Some unions are fairly neutral. Whatever the case, union policy can greatly influence the rate of grievances in a firm.

At the shop floor level, the fact that a steward is elected rather than appointed may greatly affect the number of grievances filed. The elected steward, in order to maintain or promote personal popularity with the union members, might encourage them to make claims even though many of such claims stand little chance of success. Position in the union hierarchy, rivalry for presidency or for places on the union grievance committee, can also affect the militancy of attitude of the union leaders in their relations with management — that is, their willingness to confront rather than co-operate with management.

7. Grievance Procedure

The way in which grievances are handled has a lot to do with grievance rates. If, for example, the collective agreement provides for a large number of shop stewards compared with the number of employees, for payment to shop stewards and committee members for time spent on union business, and no time limit or other checks on the activities of union representatives, then the number of grievances might be higher.

8. Management Policies

Both the number of grievances and the manner of their settlement can be affected by the policies pursued by management. If management wishes to keep the number of grievances small, it should try to ensure a management-labour contract that is generally regarded by union members as a fair one. Also, before making any changes in work methods, output quotas, methods of remuneration, and so on, it should consult with the union to gain its understanding and, if possible, support. Certainly, management should not try to operate outside the collective agreement.

16.8 VALUE OF A GRIEVANCE PROCEDURE

In conclusion, we should ask ourselves: just how useful is the grievance procedure?

Employees' Point of View

From the employees' point of view, there is no doubt that a grievance procedure provides a straight-forward, clearly-defined way in which to have a grievance reviewed and resolved. In the "old days", employees would most likely just have had to grin and bear any perceived injustice. With a grievance procedure, by contrast, they can have their "day in court", assisted if necessary, at the appropriate time, by competent, articulate union officials and even a labour lawyer in presenting their case. No longer can their complaints be ignored by the forepersons or supervisors or their employment terminated at will by the company because of their "beefs". Also, since a grievance procedure sets out certain time limits for each of its steps, employees know that their grievances will be heard and answered within the time limits provided. Then, perhaps most of important of all, the employees know that, should the employer and the union fail to agree on a remedy for their grievances, or even to agree on whether the "grievance" is in fact a grievance, there is provision for an outside third party, to arbitrate the matter.

Employer's Point of View

From the employer's point of view, a grievance procedure may or may not be welcome. On the positive side, it does provide an orderly procedure for handling employee complaints. It also acts as a communications device, letting the employer know fairly quickly just what matters — for example, unfair treatment by a supervisor or dangerous working conditions — are sources of discontent on the factory floor. That is why many employers are willing to accept a wide variety of complaints for handling under the grievance procedure. Furthermore, a grievance procedure plays an important role as a "safety valve", letting an employee blow off steam before a grievance committee rather than turning to sabotage, or to low productivity, as silent revenge for the company's failure to recognize his or her complaints. The absence of a grievance procedure could even mean, should a dispute arise, that the labour force as a whole may end up putting down their tools and going on an official or unofficial strike or making other interference with work. On the positive side, therefore, the grievance procedure can be an important means of boosting employee morale. In line with modern managerial thinking, this can only mean better labour productivity. On the negative side, some employers feel that employees and the union abuse the grievance procedure, filing unnecessary complaints and grievances, wasting valuable management and labour time, undermining the authority of first-line, or shop-floor management, and incurring unnecessary arbitration expenses.

Public's Point of View

From the public's point of view, it is undoubtedly better for management and labour to talk rather than fight about their differences. In a strike or lockout, the public often suffers as well as the parties directly involved. Also, in a society that prides itself on being civilized, a grievance procedure can undoubtedly be the most rational way to settle such differences. But, of course, like every procedure, it is open to abuse. It is the responsibility of both the company and the union to ensure that the grievance procedure is used in the way intended — not as a means or irritating or confounding the other party.

16.9 DUTY OF FAIR REPRESENTATION

Commonly, under a collective agreement, an employee has the right to file a grievance and have the grievance processed through the grievance procedure and perhaps on to arbitration. However, the processing of the grievance is controlled by the union.

Normally, if the grievance is without merit, the union and the grievor will agree that the grievance be withdrawn.

However, cases do occasionally arise where the grievor insists on having the grievance processed to arbitration even though the union, for whatever reason, may not wish to proceed. From the grievor's point of view, failure to proceed would prevent a third party resolution of the matter. So there arises the question of the union's duty of fair representation on the employee's behalf.

In general, the Labour Relations Boards have accepted the principle that the individual employee does not have an absolute right to have his or her claim arbitrated. However, because of its duty of fair representation, the union must give an employee's grievance proper consideration before refusing to take it to arbitration.

Thus, according to Section 74 of Ontario's LRA:

> "A trade union, or council of trade unions, so long as it continues to be entitled to represent employees in a bargaining unit, shall not act in a manner that is arbitrary, discriminatory or in bad faith in the representation of any of the employees in the unit, whether or not members of the trade union or of any constituent union of the council of trade unions, as the case may be."

REVIEW QUESTIONS

1. What is a "grievance"? How might the definition vary depending on the firm and union involved? What time limit, if any, is involved in filing a grievance?

2. Outline the steps usually involved in a grievance procedure. Explain the logic behind such a system. How is unnecessary procrastination avoided?

3. Why is a formal grievance procedure considered a necessary part of a collective agreement?

4. How should any claim to retroactive pay, as the result of a grievance, be handled?

5. Contrast, with examples, grievances that might be filed by the union and ones filed by the company.

6. What is the "grievance rate"? What does a low grievance rate imply? A high grievance rate?

7. The main factor that determines whether a firm has a high or low grievance rate is its level of pay and fringe benefits. Discuss.

8. Technological change has always been a fertile source of labour unrest. Discuss, with reference to current examples.

9. Discuss, from the employee's point of view, the advantages and disadvantages of a grievance procedure.

10. How desirable is a grievance procedure, from the employer's point of view?

11. Should a person who believes that he has been unjustly dismissed or suspended, have the right to have his case treated as a grievance? Or is this an infringement of the employer's management rights?

12. Can a union refuse to support an employee's request to file a grievance or to process it to arbitration?

CHAPTER 17: ARBITRATION

17.1 ARBITRATION DEFINED

Arbitration is the use by two parties to a dispute of a third, impartial person (called an *arbitrator*) or group of three persons (called an *arbitration board*) to settle the outstanding issue. The decision of the arbitrator or arbitration board is binding on both parties to the dispute either by voluntary prior agreement or by law. In practice, the parties involved in a dispute resort more often to an arbitration board than to a single-person arbitrator. This provides assurance that each side, through its representative on the board, will have its point of view forcefully expressed. Whereas the role of a conciliator, conciliation board, or mediator is to recommend terms of a grievance or contract settlement, the same is not true of an arbitrator or arbitration board. Their task is to make a legally binding award.

17.2 PURPOSE OF ARBITRATION

Arbitration has been used since the nineteenth century in Canada and elsewhere in resolving labour-management disputes without recourse to strikes or lockouts. However, it is only the advent of collective bargaining in the public sector in recent years that has made arbitration such a widely used method of resolving employer-trade union contract negotiation. This is because public sector employees, although now having the right to bargain collectively, do not also usually have to the right to strike. Hence the use of arbitration as a dispute-resolving mechanism. In the semi-public sector also, including hospitals and universities, binding arbitration may be a required or optimal method of resolving contract disputes, depending on the province.

In normal contract negotiations, the function of each party is to convince, or pressure, the other side to agree to its position or to reach an acceptable compromise.

In arbitration, the aim of each of the parties becomes one of trying to convince the arbitrator to decide in its favour or to impose an acceptable compromise.

Pros and Cons of Compulsory Arbitration

One important advantage of compulsory arbitration in public sector labour-management disputes is that it protects the public from the inconvenience and hardship of a public sector strike. It also helps protect the interests of the public sector employees themselves, in the absence of the right to strike. Without compulsory arbitration, the employer might be unlikely to give serious consideration to union demands. It could just set its own terms and conditions of employment.

A big disadvantage of compulsory arbitration is that it puts into third-party hands the right to settle a dispute — not the parties directly involved. It has also been claimed that arbitrators in making their awards, ignore the interest of taxpayers, who will indirectly bear the cost of expensive settlements. In times of large federal and provincial government budgetary deficits, this disadvantage is a vital concern to the governments involved. Another criticism has been that compulsory arbitration discourages genuine bargaining. One or other of the parties may believe that resort to arbitration will result in a better deal for its side.

17.3 TYPES OF DISPUTE

There are two main kinds of labour disputes that are often the subject of arbitration. The first is what is known as an "interests dispute"; the second, what is called a "rights dispute".

An *interests dispute* is one that arises between an employer and a union in the course of negotiations for a new collective agreement. In such negotiations, the employer and the union can agree to replace the employees' right to strike and the employer's right to lock out its employees, with final and binding arbitration. However, this is done very exceptionally.

A *rights dispute* is one that occurs between an employer and a union with regard to the interpretation of the collective agreement that governs their relationship. Thus, for example, an employer may argue that it should not reimburse shop stewards for time spent on company-union meetings during their non-working hours whereas the union might argue that it should. The matter officially filed by the union, known as a grievance, may defy settlement within the company whatever the amount of discussion that takes place between union and company representatives. Only an impartial third party, the arbitrator or arbitration board, can resolve the matter. In all provinces, every collective agreement must now contain a provision for compulsory arbitration of alleged violations of the agreement that are not otherwise settled.

17.4 ATTITUDE TOWARDS ARBITRATION

Union Reluctance

Unions generally are reluctant to agree to outside arbitration because of their traditional conviction that they can only get their demands satisfied by strike action or by the threat to strike. History convinces them that outside parties have usually been unsympathetic and opposed to them and they associate arbitration with these outside parties.

Employer Reluctance

The employer is concerned with its right to manage the company. Some employers feel that this right includes determining wages, benefits, and other conditions of employment, as well as work arrangements, and that they should not give up these rights to an arbitrator. Some managers feel that as they are being paid for operating the business their responsibilities should include the foregoing. They would be giving up their responsibilities to the shareholders if they delegated these functions to an arbitrator. In addition, they fear the kind of decision that an arbitrator might make. This fear reflects their concern with the arbitrator's possible lack of knowledge, or lack of understanding, of the economic and other consequences of the arbitration decision.

17.5 ARBITRATION REQUIREMENT

The use of arbitration may be voluntary. However, most labour–management arbitration is of a compulsory nature. This is because the various Labour Relations statutes require the inclusion, in every collective agreement, of a clause that provides for compulsory arbitration of any alleged violation of the agreement that cannot be settled at any one of the stages of the grievance procedure.

Thus, according to Section 48(1) of Ontario's LRA:

> Every collective agreement shall provide for the final and binding settlement by arbitration, without stoppage of work, of all differences between the parties arising from the interpretation, application, administration or alleged violation of the agreement, including any question as to whether a matter is arbitrable.

If no arbitration clause is included, then the collective agreement is deemed to contain the one set out in the Labour Relations Act.

According to Section 48(2):

> Where a difference arises between the parties relating to the interpretation, application or administration of this agreement, including any question as to whether a matter is arbitrable, or where an allegation is made that this agreement has been violated, either of the parties may after exhausting any grievance procedure established by

this agreement, notify the other party in writing of its desire to submit the difference or allegation to arbitration and the notice shall contain the name of the first party's appointee to an arbitration board. The recipient of the notice shall within five days inform the other party of the name of its appointee to the arbitration board. The two appointees so selected shall, within five days of the appointment of the second of them, appoint a third person who shall be the chair. If the recipient of the notice fails to appoint an arbitrator, or if the two appointees fail to agree upon a chair within the time limited, the appointment shall be made by the Minister of Labour for Ontario upon the request of either party. The arbitration board shall hear and determine the difference or allegation and shall issue a decision and the decision is final and binding upon the parties and upon any employee or employer affected by it. The decision of a majority is the decision of the arbitration board, but if there is no majority the decision of the chair governs.

Compulsory arbitration occurs after the last step in the grievance procedure set out in the collective agreement. However, only a small percentage of grievances actually go this far.

17.6 ARBITRABILITY

Not all disputes during the life of a collective agreement may be taken to arbitration. Usually, a collective agreement will specify that only disputes involving an alleged violation of the agreement are arbitrable. If necessary, the arbitrator will decide whether a dispute is arbitrable.

Therefore, even if one party, employer or union, argues that a particular issue is not arbitrable, the other party can submit it to arbitration. Each party would present its arguments as to why it thinks the matter is arbitrable or not and the arbitrator or arbitration board would make the final decision. If the arbitrator's ruling is that the matter is arbitrable, the arbitrator would go on to hear and decide the case. Otherwise, there would be no arbitration.

17.7 ARBITRATOR OR ARBITRATION BOARD

Although the various Labour Relations statutes provide for arbitration by either an arbitrator or an arbitration board, in practice the vast majority of collective agreements in Canada specify the latter. If an agreement fails to include an arbitration clause, it is deemed to contain the one set out in the statute which, in Ontario, now provides for an arbitration board.

The advantage of a single arbitrator is that the hearing is faster and cheaper. However, some people think that a three-person arbitration board reduces the chances of poor decisions or arbitration awards that have unfortunate or unanticipated ramifications.

Arbitration boards usually consist of three persons: an impartial chairperson and a person nominated by each of the parties to the dispute. The company nominee would probably be a lawyer or consultant experienced in labour relations from the management viewpoint, or perhaps an employee of another company. The union nominee would probably be a lawyer or a consultant, experienced in labour relations from the union point of view, or a representative of some other union. The procedure is for the parties to appoint, first of all, their nominees to the Board and then for the nominees to endeavour to agree on the choice of an impartial chairperson. Arbitration board chairpersons are most usually law professors, other university professors, or other persons experienced in labour arbitration.

An arbitration board, as well as being able to render a decision, provides an opportunity for the company and the union to mediate, or negotiate, a last-minute settlement rather than rely on the arbitrator's decision, for better or for worse. The disadvantages are, first, the longer time involved in choosing the board and in hearing and resolving the dispute. Second, being partisan in nature, each party's nominee may indulge in long, time-consuming reviews of the proceedings in an effort to persuade the chairperson to look more favourably on that party's point of view.

17.8 AD HOC ARBITRATORS OR PERMANENT UMPIRES

Usually an arbitrator or arbitration board is chosen by the company and the union for each specific dispute. Because of this, the term "ad hoc" ("for the purpose") is sometimes applied to them, as compared with a permanently appointed arbitrator, sometimes known as an "umpire".

Choosing an arbitrator or arbitration board can be a slow and complicated process. To do this for each dispute might seem to be an unnecessary expense. However, the company and the union, by choosing this route, avoid being saddled with a person in whom they may not have confidence. Also, such a person may not have the range of technical knowledge required to deal satisfactorily with a variety of industrial problems.

An ad hoc arbitrator, by contrast, provides flexibility — being chosen for his or her particular knowledge and experience as demanded by the nature of the dispute. Also such a person need be paid only for services rendered. Furthermore, if an ad hoc arbitrator enjoys the respect of both parties, he or she can continue to be used. In this way, full use can be made of this person's increasing knowledge of the company and the union, the employees, the technology, work methods, and so on.

17.9 CHOOSING AN ARBITRATOR

The procedure for choosing an arbitrator or an arbitration board, to settle a dispute, is usually set out in the arbitration clause of the collective agreement. The following is an example:

> Within seven days of the notice of desire to arbitrate, each of the parties shall notify the other of the name of its appointee to an Arbitration Board. The two appointees so selected shall, within seven days of the appointment of the second of them, appoint a third person who shall be the chairperson. If the two appointees fail to agree upon a chairperson within this time, the appointment shall be made by the Minister of Labour upon the request of either party.

If the procedure has not been set out in the collective agreement, then the standard arbitration clause set out in the Labour Relations Act is deemed to be included in the agreement.

It is common practice, after the company and union nominees have been appointed, for one nominee to contact the other with regard to the appointment of a chairperson. One or both nominees may have candidates to suggest. Usually agreement is reached fairly readily between them, and the agreed upon person is asked to be chairperson of the arbitration board.

17.10 THE ARBITRATION HEARING

The next step, after the employer and the union have chosen an arbitrator or arbitration board, is the hearing of the dispute.

The dispute may be a difference between the parties relating to the interpretation, application or administration of the collective agreement, including any question as to whether a matter is arbitrable, or an allegation by one party that the agreement has been violated in some way by the other party.

Normally the arbitration hearing is held in a conference room in a hotel or similar place. The tables are usually arranged in a T-shape. At the head of the T sits the arbitration board with the chairperson in the middle and a union nominee and a company nominee on either side.

Down the length of the T sit the parties to the dispute — the persons appearing on behalf of the company on one side of the table and the persons representing the union on the other. The arbitration case is presented for each side by a person normally known as *counsel*. In the case of the company, the counsel might be a lawyer, it might also be a consultant, or perhaps an employee specialized in labour relations, or conceivably a person such as a plant manager. On the union side, the counsel might perhaps be a lawyer, but is more likely to be the union's business agent or a representative from the union's head office. The counsel on either side is in charge of and responsible for the presentation. Normally, the hearing, although of a judicial character, is conducted in an informal, and even friendly way.

Most grievances are filed by an employee or by the union and allege that the employer is in violation of the collective agreement. At the hearing, the union usually begins and tries to establish that there has been such a violation.

To ensure the basic fairness of the arbitration hearing, certain basic principles are normally observed. Each of the parties involved must be:

1. notified of the place and time of the hearing

2. given the opportunity to attend

3. quite free to introduce evidence

4. able to cross-examine fully all adverse witnesses

5. able to make concluding statements

17.11 METHOD OF PROCEDURE

The method of procedure depends on the circumstances. It is usual for the party that has initiated the arbitration action ("the moving party"), most often the union, to start off by submitting to the arbitration board a copy of the collective agreement and also a copy of the grievance which is subject to arbitration. The company and the union, either before the hearing or at the hearing, might agree upon a "statement of fact" (or "statement of issue") to be submitted to the arbitrator. The union then proceeds to submit its evidence. This is most commonly done by the union counsel, who would call on witnesses to testify on the union's behalf, much as in a court of law. The union counsel would call its first witness and ask appropriate questions, designed to have the witness state the evidence necessary to uphold the union's position. After this evidence has been presented, the company counsel has the opportunity to cross-examine the witness. When the examination and cross-examination has finished, the witness normally returns to his or her place and plays no further part in the proceedings, unless recalled to the witness stand. Using the same procedure, the union then calls further witnesses, as it considers judicious. The union may also want to submit certain other kinds of evidence, such as documents and other cases similar to their own, if favourable to their argument.

Normally, the burden of proof rests with the party that has initiated the arbitration. And to win the case, this party must show that its claim is correct. In discipline cases, the burden of proof is on the employer.

Very often, the party making an arbitration claim will argue that the wording of a particular provision in a collective agreement is ambiguous. In this regard, the arbitrator will look carefully at the *past practice* of the parties to determine whether their past behaviour implied a certain interpretation to a provision of the agreement that is now alleged to be ambiguous. Under what is known as the "reserved rights" theory, management usually takes the position that, except as specifically restricted by a collective agreement, it retains unilateral control over hours, wages, and all other employment conditions. This is because, prior to collective bargaining, the employer exercised unilateral control in these matters (i.e. not sharing it with the employees).

As soon as the union has completed submitting its evidence, the counsel for the employer has the opportunity to submit his or her evidence. He or she proceeds in the same manner, calling witnesses, examining them and then having them subject to cross-examination by the union counsel. The employer also has the opportunity to submit documentary evidence, relevant cases, exhibits, etc. to uphold its position. The chairperson, or the company or union nominee, may ask additional questions of the witnesses or with regard to other evidence.

After all the evidence has been submitted by both sides, the union counsel has the opportunity to argue his or her case based on the evidence submitted. When the union counsel has finished, the company counsel then has the opportunity to do the same and will attempt to refute the union's arguments. After that, the union counsel gets an opportunity to refute the arguments presented by the company's counsel. This completes the arbitration hearing.

The remaining task for the arbitration board is to make its decision, based on the grievance submitted, the applicable collective agreement or sections of the collective agreement, and the evidence submitted at the hearing. The arbitration decision becomes one of deciding, based on the evidence submitted, whether or not there has been a violation of the agreement. If there has been, the grievance will be upheld. If there has not been a violation, the grievance will be dismissed.

Sometimes, the evidence presented is contradictory. One key task of the arbitrator or arbitration board is to sort through the evidence, assessing its relevance, authenticity, and importance.

In making its decision, an arbitration board may take into account decisions made previously in similar cases. However, unlike judges in common law courts, an arbitration board is not always bound by such decisions.

Normally, the company nominee on the arbitration board is convinced that the company's position is correct, and the union representative that the union's position is correct. As a result, each endeavours to convince the chairperson of the arbitration board that only its position is valid. The chairperson then reviews the evidence and makes a decision. Normally, if the chairperson upholds the grievance, the union nominee signs it, making it a majority award. If the chairperson dismisses the grievance, the company nominee signs it, also making it a majority award. In the former case, the company may well write a dissenting opinion. In the latter case, the union nominee may do so. Occasionally, the arbitrator may make a decision which suits neither the company nor the union nominee. In that case, the chairperson's award becomes the board's award with perhaps two dissenting opinions.

17.12 IMPLEMENTING THE ARBITRATOR'S DECISION

In most cases, whatever the award, the parties involved in the dispute are willing to implement it.

However, if an employer, trade union, or employee fails to comply with an arbitration decision within a given period to time, the decision may be enforced by means of a court order.

Normally, arbitration awards have the same effect in law as if they were awards of a court. Sometimes, however, an arbitration award may be set aside or "quashed" by a court, on appeal, usually for one of four reasons.

First, if the court believes that natural justice was denied — for example, one of the parties was not given a fair hearing.

Second, if the arbitrator exceeded his powers.

Third, if there was bias or fraud involved in the arbitration.

Fourth, if there was an error of law on the face of the award (e.g. if the arbitrator twisted the meaning of the contract).

17.13 COSTS OF ARBITRATION

The company and the union share equally the costs of the chairperson of the arbitration board. These costs include the arbitrator's fee for time involved in hearing and deciding the case and writing the decision, and his or her travel and accommodation expenses. Normally, the company and the union each pays for its own additional expenses.

17.14 SETTLEMENT OFFICER

In Ontario, there is provision for the appointment of a settlement officer to try to bring about a settlement before an arbitration hearing begins.

Thus, according to Section 49(6) of Ontario's LRA:

> The Minister may appoint a settlement officer to confer with the parties and endeavour to effect a settlement prior to the hearing by an arbitrator appointed under subsection (4).

17.15 FINAL OFFER SELECTION

"Total package selection" is a form of arbitration in which, unlike the normal type of arbitration, the arbitrator must choose, without modification, either the final offer of the union or the final offer of the company. However, this method of resolving industrial disputes has been received with little enthusiasm by labour and management. This is because a negotiated settlement, or even a normal-type arbitration award (in which the arbitrator has taken into account both the union's and the company's points of view) is more likely to satisfy both parties.

Some of the persons who favour final offer selection would prefer an "issue by issue" approach. Under such a system, known as "final offer by item", the arbitrator would have the right to choose, on a item-by-item basis, either the union or the company proposal. Thus the final settlement would embody both union and company proposals rather than consist of one complete final offer package or the other.

Advocates of final offer selection, whatever its form, say that it encourages the union and the employer to put forward more reasonable proposals than they otherwise would, each side hoping that the arbitrator will choose the more reasonable proposed settlement.

17.16 CONSENSUAL MEDIATION-ARBITRATION

In this form of assistance, a third party is appointed to mediate the differences between the union and the employer. Any issues still outstanding after the mediation efforts have been made, are then settled by the mediator who makes his or her award after having studied the rival submissions. Med-arb is sometimes criticized on the grounds that it is difficult for one person to act as both mediator and arbitrator in the same dispute.

Ontario's LRA, Section 50(1), states:

> Despite any grievance or arbitration provision in a collective agreement or deemed to be included in the collective agreement under section 48, the parties to the collective agreement may, at any time, agree to refer one or more grievances under the collective agreement to a single mediator-arbitrator for the purpose of resolving the grievances in an expeditious and informal manner.

17.17 INCREASED USE OF ARBITRATION

Labour arbitration in Canada has mushroomed since the 1930s because of two factors: first, the enactment of labour relations legislation providing for compulsory arbitration and, second, the growth in the number of workers represented by labour unions and covered by collective agreements.

REVIEW QUESTIONS

1. What is "arbitration"? How does it differ from conciliation?

2. Explain with an example, an "interests" labour dispute.

3. What is a "rights" dispute? Explain with an example.

4. Is it necessary to include an arbitration clause in a collective agreement? If so, why?

5. Does compulsory arbitration apply to the negotiation of a new collective agreement? If not, why not?

6. "Not all disputes are arbitrable." Explain, with examples.

7. Compare the merits of an arbitration board with those of a single arbitrator. Why is the former the most usual?

8. Why do most firms use ad hoc arbitrators rather than permanent ones?

9. What is the procedure for choosing an arbitrator?

10. How is the arbitration hearing organized? Who takes part?

11. Explain the way in which the arbitration hearing is normally conducted.

12. Suppose the company or the union refused to accept the arbitration board's decision. How can it be enforced?

13. What costs are involved in an arbitration hearing?

14. How are arbitrators selected by the Ministry of Labour in your province?

15. What is "final offer selection"? Why are employers and unions unenthusiastic about it? In what form might it be more acceptable?

16. What is "mediation-arbitration"? What are its merits?

17. Why is arbitration now used so frequently in labour-management disputes?

CHAPTER 18: DISCIPLINE

18.1 CONDUCT OF EMPLOYEES

Most collective agreements give the employer the right to make reasonable rules and regulations governing the conduct of its employees and the right to take *disciplinary action* (i.e., impose some form of sanction or punishment) if they are broken. Also, most collective agreements give an employee and the union the right to file a grievance if they consider that a disciplinary action was taken by the employer without "just cause". In fact, many of the grievances that are filed by a union during the life of a collective agreement relate to problems of employee discipline.

If such disputes are not settled by union and management during the early stages of the grievance procedure, they are then subject to arbitration. In arbitration, the union will attempt to show that the employer did not have just cause for its action, while the employer will attempt to show that it did. The arbitrator's decision will be binding upon both parties.

Need for Discipline

In every organization, *discipline* (i.e. a system of punishments for breaches of rules and regulations) is necessary to maintain a working climate in which subordinates willingly and promptly carry out the instructions of superiors, abide by the accepted standards of business and personal conduct, and use common sense in performing their duties on the organization's behalf.

Most company employees act in a disciplined, responsible manner and are only irritated if forepersons, supervisors and other management personnel constantly make disciplinary threats — "do this or else". However, there are some employees who, for one or more reasons, are unwilling to work properly and to abide by the established rules and standards of conduct, even after these have repeatedly been brought to their attention. In such cases, disciplinary action by management may well be necessary.

Many companies have concluded from experience that it is very difficult to anticipate all the possible kinds of violations that may take place and all the unusual circumstances that may surround them. Consequently, the amount of disciplinary action called for in any given situation must depend partly on the nature of the circumstances involved, as judged by company management.

18.2 TYPES OF DISCIPLINARY ACTION

The usual types of disciplinary action that may be taken by management are the following:

1. verbal warning

2. written warning

3. suspension

4. discharge

Verbal Warning

This type of action is normally taken to deal with all offences of a relatively minor nature — for example, being late for work — particularly if it is a first offence. The verbal warning gives the supervisor an opportunity to discuss the breach of discipline with the offender and to try to discover the causes of it, with a view to their possible future elimination. An interview between the supervisor and the employee also presents the employee with an opportunity to "get something off his chest", perhaps an explanation or a complaint, to see his own errors, and in some cases to suggest the means of self-improvement.

When a supervisor gives a verbal warning to an employee, he should state clearly to the employee that it is in fact a verbal warning and that it will go on the employee's record. The supervisor should then record the fact that this warning has been given — so that the employee's history file can be amended to include the date, nature of, and reasons for such a warning.

Written Warning

This is normally given to an employee who has already received a verbal warning for the same or a similar offence. However, such a warning is sometimes given without any previous verbal warning, if the offence is sufficiently serious. It is desirable that the written warning be given to an employee only after the supervisor has given him or her an opportunity to explain the misconduct. Written warnings are normally issued on a special form with one copy to the employee, probably another one to the union, and a third one for the employee's file in the personnel department. In issuing a written warning, the supervisor should stress to the employee that it is a serious matter and that further breaches of discipline may lead to more serious disciplinary action, perhaps even discharge.

Suspension

This action is normally taken after an employee has already received one or more written warnings. However, it may also be taken in the case of an employee who has not previously received a warning but who commits a very serious type of misconduct. Most commonly, the period of suspension is from one to fourteen days, although in some instances much longer periods of suspension may be considered necessary.

Discharge

This is the most serious disciplinary action of all and is normally taken only after an employee has been given every opportunity to improve his or her performance, following the issuance of warnings and/or suspensions. Occasionally, a very serious and flagrant breach of discipline may result in discharge even when no previous warning or suspension has been given.

However, even in such serious cases, it is considered wise first of all to provide the employee with an opportunity to present the employee's version of the incident. Following such an interview, it may still be necessary to order the employee to stay away from work until notified otherwise. In some circumstances, it is considered desirable to remove an employee immediately from the company premises to await a final decision as to whether he or she is to be discharged.

If it is subsequently decided to discharge the employee, he or she should be notified by the supervisor, usually in the presence of another member of management, and depending on the collective agreement or the relationship that exists with the union, also in the presence of a union representative. It is usually advisable, because of possible emotional outbursts, to inform the employee of his or her dismissal in a room or other place away from the work area.

18.3 DISCRETIONARY VERSUS AUTOMATIC SYSTEMS OF DISCIPLINE

The comments above refer to a system in which the amount of disciplinary action taken varies according to management's judgment of the offence and the particular circumstances of the case. However, some organizations have a more automatic system of discipline. In effect, they have a pre-determined and stated punishment for each offence. Suppose, for example, that a person is late so many times during a week or other given period. The first time, the employee will receive a warning, the second time a suspension, and the third time a discharge. For certain offences, the first time may result in a suspension and the second time in a discharge. Perhaps for a third group of offences, the first time may mean discharge. This system has the advantages, first, of making it clear to each employee exactly what the penalty will be for a particular offence; second, of ensuring that the company's action is always consistent; and third, of saving the time required to make a more careful judgment. However, one of the problems that arises is management's difficulty in anticipating each possible offence and to make a judgment that is both fair, and seen to be fair by the employee concerned. For example, if the rule is for an employee to receive a warning after being late three times, no room is allowed for exceptions based on peculiar circumstances. Again, if exceptions are allowed for peculiar circumstances, a decision must presumably be made in advance as to the peculiar circumstances which would be considered exceptions and which would not. And, as stated before, it is extremely difficult to anticipate all of these unusual circumstances.

18.4 DISCIPLINE GRIEVANCES AND ARBITRATION

Faced with a discipline grievance, an arbitrator must determine, first, whether the alleged offence by the employee actually occurred and, second, if it did occur, whether the penalty imposed by the employer was appropriate.

Factors that might be taken into account by the arbitrator in making his or her award include the following:

1. If a *rule* has been broken, was it known to the employee?

2. Has the company been consistent in the way it has enforced its rules and standards? Have all violations been handled in the same way?

3. Did the employee know that failure to comply would result in a penalty? Was he or she warned in writing? Was a final warning sent?

4. What was the employee's prior work record? Have there been any previous offences?

5. How serious was the offence?

6. How long has the person been employed at the company?

7. Was the offence committed by impulse or was it premeditated?

8. Were there any unusual or mitigating circumstances involved?

18.5 CULMINATING INCIDENT

Sometimes, a severe penalty such as dismissal may be justified for an offence because that particular offence is in effect the climax or culmination of a series of offences. Normally, the offence committed would not merit such a severe penalty. Thus, for example, an employee might be discharged for a particular incident just because that person has a long history of the infraction. This particular offence was the "last straw". However, for an employer to argue that the offence was a "culminating incident", it must be prepared to prove to the arbitrator that (a) the culminating incident actually occurred, (b) the incident constitutes an offence that would normally incur a penalty, and (c) the employee had been previously warned about the unsatisfactory aspects of his or her work record.

18.6 SUBSTITUTION OF PENALTY

Sometimes, in a discipline case, an arbitrator or arbitration board may substitute another penalty for one that has been imposed by the employer.

Thus, Ontario's LRA, Section 48(17), states:

> Where an arbitrator or arbitration board determines that an employee has been discharged or other wise disciplined by an employer for cause and the collective agreement does not contain a specific penalty for the infraction that is the subject-matter of the arbitration, the arbitrator or arbitration board may substitute such other penalty for the discharge or discipline as to the arbitrator or arbitration board seems just and reasonable in all the circumstances.

REVIEW QUESTIONS

1. What disciplinary powers does management usually retain under the terms of a collective agreement?

2. How does the union ensure that its members are not unjustly treated?

3. What exactly is discipline? Why is it necessary in a business firm?

4. When should a verbal warning be issued to an employee?

5. How and when should a written warning be issued?

6. What is the purpose of a suspension? How effective is it?

7. How and when should an employee be discharged?

8. Is it better to have a pre-determined and stated punishment for each possible offence rather than a discretionary system?

9. Explain the concept of a "culminating incident".

10. Does the employer always have the "last word" in disciplinary matters?

CHAPTER 19: SENIORITY

The term *seniority* means a person's status in a company based on the number of years and months of service relative to other employees.

19.1 SENIORITY CLAUSE

Nearly every collective agreement has a *seniority clause*, in which the employer and the labour union affirm the principle of job preference for one employee over another, according to length of service with the company. This seniority clause also usually defines how the principle of seniority is to be applied in layoffs, recalls, promotions and transfers. Thus, for example, employees with the longest continuous service are usually the last to be laid off and the first to be recalled. They are also given priorities in promotions and transfers. But this is usually subject to their *ability* to perform the available work. Many collective agreements also provide for the application of seniority in work assignments, shift preference, allocation of days off, and vacation times. These latter applications may be spelled out in the seniority clause or may be scattered throughout the collective agreement in appropriate places.

19.2 SENIORITY VERSUS ABILITY (OR MERIT)

The principle of seniority has been accepted in many areas as an equitable and objective decision-making criterion. In union-management relationships, the concept has existed ever since the earliest collective agreements. However, it has been the source of considerable controversy, especially as related to promotions, job assignments and layoffs. Even though labour unions and managements often agree that length of service is an important factor in determining these matters, they often start to disagree when seniority versus ability (or *merit*) arguments arise. Many managements seek to place greater weight on ability or merit while many unions place more emphasis on seniority.

19.3 DIFFERENT TYPES OF SENIORITY/ABILITY CLAUSES

In practice, there are many different types of seniority/ability clauses in collective agreements. The four types listed below serve to illustrate the range of such provisions:

1. Promotions, demotions and layoffs due to lack of work will be solely on the basis of seniority.

2. The most senior applicant shall be promoted, and the most junior shall be demoted or laid off due to lack of work, provided the senior has sufficient ability to do the job.

3. Where skill, ability, and physical fitness are relatively equal, seniority shall govern which employee is promoted, demoted, or laid off due to lack of work.

4. Promotion, demotion, or layoff due to lack of work shall be made on the basis of skill, ability, and physical fitness to be determined solely by the employer.

Clauses like 1 and 4 are very rare. Employers are generally unwilling to accept seniority as the sole criterion for the promotion of employees, or for their demotion or layoff due to lack of work. Conversely, employees, as represented by their unions, are generally unwilling to give the employer unilateral control over promotions, demotions, or layoffs, due to lack of work. The result is usually therefore a contract clause like 2 or 3. Clause 2 provides that as long as the senior person can perform the job satisfactorily, that person is entitled to it, even if other applicants have greater ability. Under clause 3, the applicant with the greatest seniority would get the job even if that person had no more ability than the other applicants.

19.4 PROBLEMS IN APPLYING SENIORITY/ABILITY PROVISIONS

Regardless of the type of clause found in the collective agreement, certain administrative problems are likely to arise in promotion situations. How is "ability to do the job" to be defined? When does an employee have the ability to do the job, and when not? What does "relatively equal" mean? Hence the large number of seniority disputes that eventually go to arbitration.

Some of the criteria for judging ability are the following: work experience on the job; work experience related to the job; results of a proficiency test; education; and previous training.

Where the seniority clause is of the "sufficient ability" type (no. 2 on our list), arbitrators have generally held that when a junior employee is promoted or held on the job despite lesser seniority, management has the burden of proof to show clearly that the senior employee was not competent to perform the job.

Where relative ability clauses are present (no. 3 on our list), most arbitrators will place the burden on management to prove that the senior employee was not qualified. However, the requirements are less stringent. In either type of clause, minor differences in ability will not be sufficient to allow the promotion of a junior employee over a senior one, or the retention of a junior employee despite lesser seniority. As a result, a junior employee may be promoted ahead of a more senior employee, or held in a position despite lesser seniority, only when he or she has clearly superior ability.

19.5 JOB DISPLACEMENT OR "BUMPING" RIGHTS

In the absence of clear differences in ability, it is generally accepted that the most senior employees should have the greatest job security. In most situations, this means they are the last to be laid off and the first to be recalled.

In order for this to happen, it is often necessary for a senior employee to displace, or "bump" a more junior employee. However, the right of a senior employee to replace a junior employee is often restricted by the requirement that he or she be able to do the work satisfactorily. Usually the seniority clause specifies the work areas in which workers may exercise their seniority rights when a reduction in the work force becomes necessary.

In situations in which broad displacement or "bumping" rights exist (i.e., where senior employees can displace junior employees in other types of work), there may be a whole chain of displacements or "bumps" triggered by a single layoff. Because of the tremendous administrative problems involved in any chain-bumping situation, managements tend to favour seniority systems which permit the exercise of bumping rights on a restricted basis only. Unions, on the other hand, tend to favour plant-wide bumping rights, unrestricted by differences in classifications, even if it means expenditure of time and money by the employer in training replacements and loss of productive efficiency during the changeover of personnel.

19.6 SENIORITY SYSTEMS

Many seniority systems can be grouped under the following headings:

1. *Departmental or Classification Only*
Under such a system, employees who are no longer needed in their present jobs because of lack of work may displace junior employees in their own department or classification provided that they can do the work. If they are unable to do so, they are laid off.

2. *Departmental or Classification plus Plant-wide Seniority*
Under such a system, employees who are no longer required, due to lack of work, are able to bump junior employees in their own department or classification. If they fail to do so (because of inability to do the job), they may then exercise their seniority to displace employees junior to them somewhere else in the plant, again provided that they can do these persons' jobs.

3. *Group (or Job Family) Seniority, plus Restricted Plant-wide Seniority*

Under this system, various types of jobs in a firm are grouped together. These groups are called "job families". Usually, employees would only have the right to displace other, more junior employees in their own group. Another group of jobs, usually the least skilled ones, are designated as, say, a "labour pool" into which any employee with seniority is able to bump. Thus, in this kind of situation, an employee, if no longer required for a job, is able to displace a junior employee in his or her own group or job family and failing this, is able to displace a junior employee in the labour pool.

4. *Lines of Progression*

With this seniority concept, certain jobs are designated as entry jobs. These jobs are the only jobs for which new employees are hired. These entry jobs may be grouped into a labour pool. All jobs within the bargaining unit are then grouped into various lines of progression. An employee is assigned to the bottom job in the line of progression either upon being hired into an entry job or, alternatively, when being promoted from the labour pool. After that, the employee is promoted when there is a vacancy in the designated job immediately above his or hers in the line of progression, and so on up to the top. Therefore, in the event of a work shortage, each employee moves down one notch into the job that he or she had done before. Eventually, the junior in the line of progression is moved down into the labour pool and, if necessary, the most junior person in the labour pool is laid off.

Conclusion

In some situations, plant-wide seniority is workable; in others, departmental seniority is more practical. Sometimes the group or lines-of-progression system, combined with a labour pool, works effectively. The possible variations are almost endless.

19.7 LAYOFF AND RECALL SYSTEM

An appropriate layoff and recall system is a major item on the bargaining agenda of most labour unions and managements and one that is obviously very important to both. Seniority rights are very important to employees and to the union, and a system must be worked out in collective agreement negotiations which is acceptable to both management and the union.

Usually, the most critical time under a seniority system is when an employee is about to be laid off. It is at this stage that the employee is most likely to claim that he or she has the ability to perform another job held by a person with less seniority. The effect of a layoff on an employee is obviously much more important to that person than the effect of a transfer. From the employer's point of view, great care must be taken to ensure that the right person is laid off. Otherwise, a grievance may be filed on behalf of the person laid off. If the grievance goes to arbitration, as well it may, and the employer loses, it may be required to compensate the employee who was incorrectly laid off, for lost wages. As a result, some collective agreements provide that an employee is entitled to a trial period under certain conditions to establish whether or not he or she can do the job. Some other agreements, instead of permitting a trial period, provide for a training period. Such trial or training periods are normally limited to a specific period of time. In order to obtain such a trial period, an employee must normally provide reasonable evidence that he or she would be successful in it.

Trial or training periods can greatly reduce the number of grievances resulting from the application of seniority clauses. They can also help convince the employee who is unhappy about being laid off that he or she does not in fact have the qualifications required to perform a different, although less senior job.

19.8 EXAMPLE OF SENIORITY CLAUSES IN A COLLECTIVE AGREEMENT

The following is an example of seniority clauses in a collective agreement:

1. With regard to the order of layoff, should it become necessary to reduce the workforce:

   First: Probationary employees provided, however, that employees remaining who have completed the probationary period can perform the required work satisfactorily or can qualify reasonably quickly for the required work. Those who can qualify reasonably quickly will be given an opportunity to do so. Those given such trial must have within one week demonstrated they will be able to perform the required work satisfactorily.

   Second: Employees possessing departmental seniority attached to the department the staff of which is being reduced, on the basis of seniority, provided, however, that employees remaining can perform the required work satisfactorily or can qualify reasonably quickly for the required work in their department. Those who can qualify reasonably quickly will be given an opportunity to do so on the same basis as set out in the previous clause.

   Third: Employees possessing departmental seniority in other departments on the basis of seniority, provided, however, that employees remaining can perform the required work satisfactorily.

2. With regard to the order of recall when the work force is to be

increased:

> *First:* Employees possessing plant seniority, in order of seniori-
> ty, regardless of the departments in which they were previously
> employed, provided they can perform the required work satisfac-
> torily. Senior employees who have elected to accept layoff rather
> than transfer will be eligible for recall only to departments elect-
> ed by them in writing at the time of layoff or at a subsequent
> time within their allowable breaks.
>
> *Second:* Employees possessing departmental seniority in the
> department in which the staff is being increased, in the reverse
> order to that in which they were laid off, provided they can per-
> form the required work satisfactorily.
>
> *Third:* Employees possessing departmental seniority in other
> departments in order of seniority as vacancies occur provided
> they can perform the required work satisfactorily.

REVIEW QUESTIONS

1. What is a "seniority clause"? Why is it necessary in a collective agreement?

2. What problems can arise in applying the principle of employee seniority?

3. What are the four basic types of seniority/ability provisions mentioned in the text? How do they differ? Which are the most commonly used?

4. What is a "relative ability" clause?

5. Why is it that so many seniority disputes go to arbitration?

6. A system of plant-wide bumping rights is a fair and efficient way of handling a temporary or permanent reduction in a firm's work force. Discuss.

7. Explain the following seniority systems:
    (a) departmental or classification only
    (b) departmental or classification plus plant-wide seniority.

8. What is meant by group or job-family seniority, plus restricted plant-wide seniority?

9. Explain "lines of progression" as a seniority system.

10. Which seniority system is the best? Discuss.

11. What type of seniority system is used in the example of actual seniority clauses included in this chapter?

12. What are the advantages and disadvantages of employee seniority for (a) the employee, and (b) the employer?

13. What seniority principle is usually followed in lay-offs and recalls? How satisfactory is this procedure?

14. A supervisor in a large electrical products manufacturing firm complained to a friend that the three workers he had just finished training had been "bumped" out of the plant and he now had to start over again. Explain and discuss.

CHAPTER 20: PUBLIC EMPLOYEES

20.1 THE PUBLIC SECTOR

Today in Canada about one out of every five employed persons works in the public sector.

Types of Public Employees

Such public employees include: (a) *direct public employees* — that is, persons employed by government departments; (b) *public agency employees* — that is, persons employed by government agencies, commissions, crown corporations, etc.; and (c) *publicly subsidized employees* — that is, persons employed by institutions such as universities and hospitals that receive most of their funds from the government.

Collective Bargaining Rights

For many years, public sector employees were forbidden to join unions and were denied the collective bargaining rights that private sector employees were coming to take for granted. However, in the last two decades, this situation has drastically changed. The vast majority of public employees are now unionized and their leaders have succeeded in obtaining significant improvements in wages and other conditions of work. However, the pattern of unionization varies considerably from one group of employees to another.

Public versus Private Sector Employees

Previously, public sector employees were regarded as persons receiving relatively lower pay than private sector employees, but enjoying substantial job security. Today, the pay and fringe benefits, including indexed pensions, are often more favourable than in the private sector. However, the job security has become less and less assured as governments strive to reduce or prevent substantial budget deficits.

20.2 UNIONIZATION OF FEDERAL PUBLIC EMPLOYEES

Unionization of federal public employees in Canada began towards the end of the nineteenth century. In 1891, for example, the Federated Association of Letter Carriers was established as a national organization. Later, in 1907, the

Civil Service Association of Ottawa was set up to represent headquarters employees. Then, in 1909, the Civil Service Federation of Canada was established, combining in one loose alliance the Civil Service Association, the postal associations, and a few other groups. In 1920, the Professional Institute of the Public Service of Canada was set up with the aim of improving the status and conditions of service of professional employees in the Public Service. Also in that year, an association called the Amalgamated Civil Servants of Canada was formed to improve conditions of work for civil servants generally. This was later merged, in 1958, with the Civil Service Association to form the Civil Service Association of Canada. This Association was then merged in the 1960s with another union, the Civil Service Federation, to form a new union, the Public Service Alliance of Canada.

Staff Associations

Over the years, staff associations have been formed in many different government departments. In addition to social functions, they have been instrumental in presenting employee complaints to management, and regular patterns of consultation have often been established. Successive governments have recognized the right of public employees to become members of such associations. These associations have also been active since 1957, following the establishment of the Pay Research Bureau in that year, and of the Advisory Committee on Pay Research in the following year, in the planning of comparative rates of pay and conditions of employment for public employees.

Consultation Process

The process of consultation between management and the staff associations with regard to pay and other working conditions that had gradually been established over the years was formalized by the Civil Service Act of 1961. This Act made provision for consultation between the staff associations on the one hand and the Civil Service Commission and the Minister of Finance on the other. However, in practice, this system of consultation proved cumbersome and inefficient. As a result, the staff associations began to look more and more in the direction of collective bargaining as a means of protecting the interests of their members. This attitude was strengthened by the recommendations of a Royal Commission on Government Organization which suggested greater autonomy for each government department.

Demand for Collective Bargaining Rights

The growing demand by federal civil servants for collective bargaining rights bore fruit in 1965 when a government-appointed Preparatory Committee on

Collective Bargaining in the Public Service recommended drastic changes in the existing job classification and pay systems and proposed legislation to permit collective bargaining. This activity resulted in the passing by the Federal Parliament in 1967 of the Public Service Staff Relations Act, or PSSRA.

20.3 PUBLIC SERVICE STAFF RELATIONS ACT

Scope of Collective Bargaining

According to Section 56 of the PSSRA, contract negotiations are restricted to matters not already covered by other legislation. This means that matters of employment such as hiring, merit rating, promotions, demotions, transfers, layoffs, and dismissals, which are already covered by the Public Service Employment Act, are excluded from the negotiations. Also, pensions are excluded because the Public Service Superannuation Act already covers them. However, wages, hours of work, seniority, etc., are all legitimate topics for negotiation. Distribution of work, manning of equipment, job descriptions, and job evaluations are not.

Persons Excluded

Certain types of employees are excluded from collective bargaining:

- persons employed in a managerial or confidential capacity,

- persons whose duties include those of a personnel administrator including persons required to deal formally on behalf of the employer with regard to grievances,

- persons paid fees of office,

- part-time employees,

- casual employees with less than six months of service,

- members of the RCMP,

- members of the Armed Forces.

Actions Prohibited

Under the Act, the employer is prohibited from: (a) discriminating against a person because he or she is a member of an employee organization or is exercising rights given under the Act, (b) imposing conditions of employment that interfere with an employee organization, and (c) intimidating an employee to join or not to join an employee organization.

Public Service Staff Relations Board

This Board is responsible for administering the PSSRA. The members of the Board, which can vary from six to ten, including the Chairperson and Vice-Chairperson, are appointed by the Governor-in-Council, on the advice of the Federal Government. Half the members must represent the employers' interests and half the employees' interests. To carry out its function, the Board has the power to make regulations of general application on a variety of subject matters such as representation issues, complaints, the hearing of questions of law and jurisdiction, and the establishment of rules of procedure for its own hearings. Its investigations of complaints include prohibited acts committed by an employer or by an employee organization, or failure to implement the decision handed down by arbitration. The Board also has the task of defining bargaining units and certifying bargaining agents.

20.4 CERTIFICATION

Before an employee organization can negotiate with an employer for a collective agreement, it must be certified as a bargaining agent by the PSSR Board.

Requirements for Certification

Application for certification may be made either by a single employee organization or by a council of employee organizations (two or more employee organizations that have joined together for collective bargaining purposes). An employee organization can be certified only if: (a) the employer does not participate in the administration of the organization in such a way as would impair the fitness of the organization to represent the employee interests in the bargaining process; (b) the employee organization has no monetary affiliation with a political party; (c) it does not discriminate against employees because of sex, race, nationality, colour, or religion; and (d) it is made up only of occupationally-related employees. In this latter respect, the Board has defined 72 different occupational groups in the Public Service. These fall within five basic occupational categories: professional and scientific; technical; administrative and foreign service; administrative support; and operation. However, the 72 bargaining units defined relate only to employees in the "central administration" for whom the Treasury Board acts as the employer.

In order to be certified, an employee organization must, after application, satisfy the Board with documentary evidence that (a) the employees wish that organization to represent them as their bargaining agent, and (b) the representatives of the organization were authorized to make the application for certification.

Certified Bargaining Agent

Upon certification, the employee organization becomes the bargaining agent for the bargaining unit in negotiations with the employer for a collective agreement. Such a collective agreement then becomes binding on all employees in the occupational group until such time as the certification of the organization is revoked. The employee organization, once certified, is also given the exclusive right to represent all employees in that bargaining unit in the presentation and adjudication of grievances relating to the interpretation or application of the collective agreement or arbitral award.

Termination of Bargaining Rights

The Board can revoke certification if it discovers, as the result of a representation vote of the employees, that the employee organization no longer represents a majority of the employees in the unit. Such a representation vote may be held during initial certification, as well as during the last two months of the life of an agreement, or at any time if no collective agreement is in force. Certification of a bargaining agent can also be revoked if that organization voluntarily gives up its certification, or if it is discovered that the bargaining agent obtained certification by fraud. Also, the certification of a bargaining agent for a council of employee organizations can be revoked if there is a change in the constituent membership of the council, or for any other reason that the Board accepts. If certification is revoked, then any collective bargaining agreement that the bargaining agent has negotiated will immediately cease to be in effect, unless a new bargaining agent specifies otherwise.

20.5 CONTRACT NEGOTIATIONS

Unlike private sector negotiations, the bargaining agent must specify what method it will use to resolve a dispute if one should arise. It can choose either arbitration or a conciliation board (which allows for the occurrence of a strike). To begin negotiations, either party can give written notice to the other party that bargaining should begin. This notice can be given at any time if there is no agreement or award in force. If an agreement or award is in force, then the notice must be given within the two months before the agreement or arbitral award ceases. An *arbitral award* is the decision given by the Arbitration Tribunal about a disputed matter. Previous terms and conditions of employment will continue in force until such time as a new collective agreement is reached and entered into by both parties.

Not more than twenty days after a notice to commence collective bargaining has been issued, the bargaining agent for the employees, and the officers representing the employer, *must* meet and make *every* reasonable effort to conclude a collective agreement. Both parties, in their negotiations, must be aware that no part of a collective agreement can be in conflict with the Government Employees Compensation Act, the Government Vessels Discipline Act, the Public Service Employment Act, or the Public Service Superannuation Act.

20.6 COLLECTIVE AGREEMENT

A collective agreement, once negotiated and signed, must remain in force either for a specified period, or for at least one year, although amendments can be made at any time during the term of the agreement. Unless some other date is specified by either the agreement or the Board, a collective agreement becomes binding on both parties, on the first day of the month after an agreement is reached, and must be implemented within 90 days after the agreement is reached.

20.7 CONCILIATION

Suppose the two parties are unable to reach a collective agreement, even though they may have been negotiating in good faith. Then either party may, by notice in writing to the PSSRB, request the assistance of a conciliator in reaching agreement.

Whether the bargaining agent has specified arbitration or a conciliation Board as the dispute settlement process, it has the right to request a conciliator before invoking either the arbitration or the conciliation board mechanism. The appointment of a conciliator is not, however, compulsory. The parties may, if they wish, bypass the conciliator step and proceed directly to the dispute settlement stage. The chairperson of the PSSRB appoints the conciliator, who then confers with the parties and attempts to assist them in reaching an agreement. The conciliator has fourteen days from the date of his or her appointment, or such longer period as may be determined by the Chairperson of the Board, to report his or her success or failure to the Board. The purpose of the conciliator is to bring the parties together and assist them in reaching agreement. His/her task is to maintain negotiations between the two parties in the hope that such further negotiations will result in the conclusion of a collective agreement. The conciliator cannot make directives, but can offer suggestions.

The Chairperson of the PSSRB may refuse to appoint a conciliator if he or she decides that a conciliator would be unable to help the parties reach an agreement. In this case, or if a conciliator has been appointed and was unsuccessful, or if no conciliator was requested, either party can request the Chairman of the Board to refer the matter in dispute to the Arbitration Tribunal or to an ad hoc conciliation board. The choice would depend on the process for resolution of a dispute chosen by the bargaining agent prior to commencing negotiations. Arbitration results in a decision that is final and binding on both parties; whereas, in conciliation, the parties are free to accept or reject the report and recommendations of the conciliation board. If arbitration has been chosen, the bargaining agent cannot call a strike, and the employees in the bargaining unit cannot engage in strike action. If, on the other hand, a conciliation board (not to be confused with a conciliator) has been chosen, the employees in the bargaining unit, with the exception of certain designated employees, may ultimately engage in a strike to enforce their "demands".

20.8 HANDLING OF GRIEVANCES
Grievance Defined

Under the PSSRA, a grievance is considered to be any written complaint of an employee for which there is no other administrative procedure for redress under any other Act of Parliament, notably the Public Service Employment Act and the Financial Administration Act. The subject matter of a grievance may be: (a) the interpretation or application of a collective agreement or arbitral award; (b) the application of any statement regarding terms and conditions of employment that has been issued by the employer; (c) any other occurrence or matter that affects an employee's terms or conditions of employment — so long as there is no other administrative procedure for redress; and (d) his or her classification. The right to resort to the grievance process is accorded to all employees who are entitled to collective bargaining under the PSSRA, as well as to persons who are "excluded" from the application of the Act because they are employed in a confidential or managerial capacity.

Matters Excluded

Matters that are excluded as grievances from PSSRA because they come under the Public Service Employment Act are appeals arising out of the application of the "merit" system. They include appeals relating to (a) appointment (including promotion); (b) demotion or release because of incompetence or incapability; (c) dismissal for violation of provisions of the Public Service Employment Act, dealing with political activity; and (d) revocation of appointment because of fraudulent practices during an examination held by the Commission. Under the Financial Administration Act, a person can appeal a suspension or dismissal made in the interests of the safety or security of Canada or any allied state.

Representation

On grievances relating to the interpretation or application of a collective agreement or an arbitral award, employees must, by law, have the approval of, and be represented by, their bargaining agent. In all other cases, employees may submit the grievance personally, or may have an employee organization represent them.

Grievance Procedure

When employees have a complaint, they are expected to discuss and try to resolve it with their immediate supervisor. However they may, if they wish, resort immediately to the grievance procedure. This involves, at the first level, submitting their grievance on a special Grievance Presentation Form to their immediate supervisor or local officer-in-charge, who then transmits the information to the appropriate parties. There is a maximum of four levels to which a grievance can go, each level representing a higher level of managerial authority. In some locations, there are less than four levels. Under the PSSRA Regulations, management is required to respond to a grievance received at any level, within 15 days from the time the grievance was received at that level. If a response is not made within the specified time, employees are entitled to present their grievance at the next level. At the final level, management *must* respond to the grievance. If an employee is not satisfied with the decisions given at any level, except the final level, he or she can return the grievance to the immediate supervisor or local officer-in-charge, for processing to the next level by submission of a Grievance Transmittal Form. The grievance must be presented by the employee at subsequent levels not later than the tenth day after he or she received a reply to the grievance at the lower level, or not later than fifteen days past the date that the employer was required to reply to the grievance at the previous level. The final level involves a decision taken by or in the name of the Deputy Minister.

Adjudication

Certain types of grievance may be referred to adjudication even though they may have passed through the final level in the grievance process. *Adjudication* is the process established under the PSSRA by which an employee can have a grievance resolved by an independent third party. It may be done by a board of adjudication or by an adjudicator. The adjudication decision is binding for both the employee and the employer. Grievances that may be referred to adjudication are those relating to (a) the interpretation of application of a collective agreement or arbitral award, or (b) disciplinary action resulting in discharge, suspension, or financial penalty. Adjudicators are appointed by the Governor-in-Council on the recommendation of the PSSR Board.

20.9 TREASURY BOARD VERSUS PUBLIC SERVICE UNIONS

The Treasury Board, led by its president, represents the federal government and indirectly the taxpayer in its bargaining for pay and other conditions of work with the thirteen unions (excluding the two postal unions) that represent the federal public service employees. The publicly-stated policy of the Treasury Board is to pay the fair market wage for civil servants. However, the Treasury Board bases its notion of a fair market wage on the results of surveys by the Pay Research Board, a government agency. In arriving at a mean wage, the Treasury Board uses all employers in a comparative group with 200 or more employees, both union and non-union. The public service unions, notably the Public Service Alliance of Canada, state that their goal is to maintain real wages for their members and to make up for losses to inflation in previous rounds of bargaining and that the Pay Research statistics not only tend to be out-of-date but should include only unionized firms. They would also prefer that more attention be paid to the cost-of-living index, something that the Treasury Board refuses to do, even questioning its validity as a real measure of inflation. So far, only one group of public service employees, the postal workers, have been able to negotiate the inclusion of a cost-of-living clause in their collective agreement with the Treasury Board. The unions also question the bargaining philosophy of the federal government which is that it must not, with its wage supplements, be in a position of leading the private sector. As regards the public interest, union officials, although apologetic about the inconvenience to the public of strikes by union members, feel that they are the only way to achieve their goals.

20.10 THE RIGHT TO STRIKE

A key issue in any discussion of public service employees is whether they should have the right to strike to help achieve their goals. Because of the essential nature of the services provided, the general public is often put to great hardship and inconvenience when such strikes take place. This means that the government of the day, wishing to maintain its political popularity, is under great pressure to reach a settlement however financially generous it may be. This in turn can lead to similarly generous settlements with other public service unions who can use each settlement in a leap-frog approach to obtain ever better terms. Once private sector employees see that their public service counterparts have done so well, they in turn refuse to settle for anything less, and so the inflationary circle continues.

From the union point of view, the extension of the right to strike to the public service unions in the nineteen-seventies was a right long overdue. The right to strike is considered an essential weapon for the achievement of the unions' goals. Without it, public service employees believe that they would be left way behind their private sector counterparts. And the unions argue that, even with it, they are not keeping up with inflation.

The alternative to the right to strike in the public service is compulsory arbitration whereby an independent party makes an award that is binding on both the government as employer and on the union that represents the public service employees concerned.

20.11 PROVINCIAL PUBLIC EMPLOYEES

Each province has its own statutes governing collective bargaining by provincial government employees.

In Ontario, for example, the Ontario Crown Employees Collective Bargaining Act, 1993, covers direct public employees and public agency employees. An Ontario Public Service Labour Relations Tribunal certifies unions as the bargaining agent for appropriate groups of employees. Certain matters are excluded from collective bargaining. No strikes or lockouts are permitted and any outstanding issues must be submitted to binding arbitration.

20.12 MUNICIPAL EMPLOYEES

Most municipal employees enjoy the same collective bargaining rights as workers in the private sector. However, some types of essential municipal employees such as the police and firefighters may, depending on the province, have their bargaining rights restricted by provincial statute. Such employees have to belong to separate bargaining units and are forbidden to strike. Any disagreement about a new collective agreement must be settled by binding arbitration.

20.13 PUBLIC SECTOR DISPUTES

Private versus Public Sectors

In the private sector, a union can call a strike, or the employer lock out its employees, and this can continue until the union, employer, or both, are hurt enough that one or the other, or both, decide to modify their positions and agree to a settlement. In the meantime, the customers obtain the product or service from another supplier, and the only ones hurt are the employees, the union, and the employer.

In the private sector, one of the factors that brings about the settlement is the pressure on the employer's profit and the recognition by the employees that there is a limit on what the employer can pay, because there is a limit on what the customer will pay.

However, in the public sector, where the employer's revenue comes from the government, the pressure is not the same as in the private sector. The employer can go to the government and ask for more money which the government can get by increasing taxes. The customers are also the taxpayers and the voters who can complain to the government if they are not getting the service they are paying for in their taxes. It is not the same as a dispute between the employees, the union, and an employer in the private sector.

In addition, there are certain services which the government is not prepared to see refused because of a labour dispute. One illustration, in some jurisdictions, is the hospital service.

The Public Interest

Our society, through legislation, has decided that strikes are not acceptable in certain relationships where collective bargaining is practised but which involve the public interest. In such cases, the right to strike has been replaced with the requirement of binding arbitration.

In some jurisdictions, legislation has been passed relating to certain types of public employees (for example, police and firefighters) which does not prevent collective bargaining but makes strike action illegal and final and binding arbitration a legal requirement.

In Ontario, for example, nurses and other hospital employees are not excluded from the Ontario Labour Relations Act. However, the Hospital Labour Disputes Act provides that once negotiations for a collective agreement have gone through conciliation without any settlement being reached, the matters in dispute shall be decided by arbitration. In other words, nurses and other hospital employees, although having the right to bargain collectively, do not also have the right to go on strike because of the essential nature of their work. Similarly, the employer may not lock out the employees.

20.14 FACT-FINDING

One type of third-party assistance not so far mentioned in this chapter is "fact-finding". This involves the appointment of a fact-finder at the request of one or other of the parties involved in a labour-management dispute or at the initiative of a public commission charged with administering a statute governing negotiations with that particular public sector. The fact-finder is given so many days in which to research the dispute and prepare a report. After delivery of the report, the parties involved are then given so many days in which to achieve a settlement, using the report for assistance. If no settlement is reached, then the report can be made available to the public media. Fact finding seems to have been most helpful, when the fact-finder includes specific recommendations in his or her report, rather than just an analysis of the situation.

REVIEW QUESTIONS

1. What are the various types of public employees in Canada? How large is this public sector?

2. The extension to public sector employees of collective bargaining rights, including the right to strike, has been a mixed blessing. Discuss.

3. What was the role of staff associations in the federal public service? What were their limitations from the member's point of view?

4. What was the Civil Service Act of 1961? Why was it considered inadequate?

5. According to the PSSRA, negotiations on behalf of federal public employees are restricted to matters not already covered by other legislation? Explain the significance of this.

6. Which persons are excluded from collective bargaining under the PSSRA?

7. What actions are prohibited under the Act?

8. Explain the composition and the role of the PSSR Board.

9. In order to be certified under the PSSRA, an employee association must fulfill certain criteria. What are they?

10. What documentary evidence must the employee association produce after application for certification?

11. Under what circumstances can certification be revoked?

12. What must the bargaining agent for the employees specify before any negotiations take place?

13. How soon must negotiations begin?

14. What must be the duration of any collective agreement? When does it become binding on the parties? How soon must it be implemented?

15. How and when is a conciliator used?

16. How are grievances defined under the PSSRA?

17. Explain the grievance procedure.

18. What is meant by "adjudication"?

19. What is the Treasury Board's pay policy for federal public employees? Why are the public service unions unhappy with it?

20. What are "essential services"? Should employees performing such work be denied the right to strike? Discuss the pros and cons.

21. What collective bargaining rights do provincial public employees have in your province?

22. All municipal employees enjoy the same collective bargaining rights as workers in the private sector. Discuss.

23. How is arbitration used in public sector labour-management disputes?

24. Assess the usefulness of "fact-finding" in labour-management disputes.

CHAPTER 21: INDUSTRIAL HARMONY

21.1 INDUSTRIAL HARMONY DEFINED

Over the years, research has shown that companies in which a high degree of "industrial harmony" prevails, continue to do well in the marketplace. By "industrial harmony," we mean a situation in which management and employees co-operate willingly in the pursuit of the company's commercial objectives and in which a high level of employee satisfaction exists.

21.2 SIX KEY REQUIREMENTS

There are, we believe, six key requirements for harmony in a business organization. These are now examined in turn.

#1 — Company Motivation

The first requirement is the willingness of a company to look at "harmony" as a "vehicle" to deal with problems such as safety, quality, production quotas, and absenteeism. With any number of problems available, it is quite easy to see how a company would be motivated to promote "harmony" for the sake of the benefits received through, for example, better safety performance, less work disruption, lower production costs, greater quality effectiveness, and better waste control.

#2 — Company Policy

Once there is corporate motivation, a company policy on harmony must be stated and encouraged at the very highest level of management. The policy is usually written out in specific terms, but sometimes it is just verbally stated, or even acted upon without declaration. Regardless, it is the actual promotion of "harmony" that indicates the existence of such a policy, whether written or not.

Material in this Chapter is used, with permission, from *Industrial Harmony: A Study of the Advances and Benefits of Personal and Corporate Satisfaction*, by Frank Kehoe, and published by Harmony Labour Publications, Dundas, Ontario.

#3 — Communication and Implementation of Policy

The third requirement is for the corporate harmony policy to be communicated to the employees and then implemented. Most commonly, the policy is accompanied by a tangible plan of action — even if the "plan" is to "make a plan of action" in order to focus the whole corporate community on the pressing problems and concerns. Each company with a knowledge of the communication process will attempt, by its policy, to engender a climate in which employees feel free to provide feedback and direction to the employer. The companies most successful in promoting harmony listen to and act upon the participative, involved, and co-operative responses of the employees.

Sometimes, in the implementation of such a program, there is need for training and development of the human resources. It is reasonable to suppose that everyone in a corporation involved with the communication and implementation of programs to promote harmony, will, in one way or another, become trained and/or developed to handle efficiently this increased communication.

#4 — Functional Change

Some rearrangement of tasks within the company may be necessary to improve employee morale. Also, employers are encouraged to contribute to the decision-making process.

#5 — Structural Change

If there is corporate commitment to promoting industrial harmony, there may well be the need to streamline the corporate structure. One way is to bring the top level of management closer to the front-line employees by structural change, usually by removing intermediate levels of management. The effect of this "flattening" of the management pyramid by the removal of intervening layers of supervision, not only allows for greater fluidity in communications but creates a need for front-liners to take on more responsibility. The streamlining of companies also has a direct financial benefit in reduced overhead.

#6 — Mutual Respect and Trust

Companies have found this requirement a critical factor in their approach to industrial harmony. However, only if management can adequately communicate its respect for the employees, can it expect to receive their respect in return. This does not necessarily need to be a lengthy process. It hinges on key players who exhibit leadership in giving respect and, in time, earning "a high degree of trust." Trust, naturally, comes out of mutual respect proven over time. The proof is in the actions of the parties concerned — both management and employees.

21.3   EMPLOYEE SATISFACTION

The fulfilment of all the key requirements, outlined above, should lead to greater employee satisfaction within an organization. The employer must be seen as motivated and committed to promoting industrial harmony, as evidenced by a policy that is clearly and effectively communicated to the employees. Implementation of training programs is also necessary, if employees are to perceive the employer as serious in its attempts to promote harmony. Employers look serious if resources of the company are turned to training and development at all levels. Functional change is one of the most radical approaches in Canadian companies. It is obvious that the employer means well when employees are given greater opportunity to help manage themselves and their activities. Because many employees enjoy added responsibilities in assisting in the management of a company, there is a tendency for structural change to take place as well — with the company reducing its levels of management so that the top executives are closer in touch with the employees, and communications are more direct.

These actions, as evidenced over time, gain the respect of the employees. It shows the company's willingness to change. If communicated properly and consistently, the employees will reciprocate respect for management, and the mutual respect will create a climate of trust. In this way, employees will be better satisfied with the workplace environment and will, if properly encouraged, be willing partners in a new vision for employment and commercial success.

Employee satisfaction comes from the nurturing of both physical and psychological environments by a management which does what it can to promote the enjoyment of work.

If there is employee satisfaction, individuals will have a different attitude toward what they do to earn a living. Alert, enthusiastic and happy employees will be of benefit to themselves, their families, their co-workers, their friends, their community, and, of course, their companies.

Employee satisfaction may seem to be relative and the measurement of such may be very subjective. However, there are some visible guidelines.

First, the six key requirements will be present.

Second, there are "harmony indicators" which give some evidence as to whether the company is successful in its recognition of and action with respect to the requirements. Examples of "harmony indicators" are: excellence in housekeeping, high degrees of friendliness and cordiality between workers and management, low absenteeism, minimal work disruptions, low employee turnover rates, good safety records, low alcohol and drug abuse, no acts of vandalism and/or violence. Statistics (where available) for these ongoing "harmony indicators" may be compared with the ongoing statistics for unit labour costs, productivity levels, production levels, and product quality to get an overall picture of "harmony" and its effects within a corporation.

21.4 POTENTIAL TO SURVIVE

A corporation's ability to create harmony within its organization will increase tremendously its potential to survive. It should be recognized that there is untapped value in most employees. Progressive companies, destined for success, will find the means to encourage employees to contribute. And satisfied employees will wish to contribute to the continued success of the company.

Employees will wholeheartedly endorse a company which welcomes and rewards their contribution of energy and ideas.

REVIEW QUESTIONS

1. What is meant by the term "industrial harmony"?

2. What elements are required to bring about such harmony in a business organization?

3. Why would a business firm be motivated to implement a policy of "industrial harmony"?

4. How can a company best devise a policy of industrial harmony

5. How should management go about implementing an "industrial harmony" policy within an organization?

6. What is meant by the term "functional change", as used with regard to industrial harmony?

7. What structural change may be required within an organization to help bring about greater industrial harmony?

8. How can mutual respect and trust between management and employees be increased within an organization?

9. What is meant by the term "employee satisfaction"?

10. What factors can increase employee satisfaction? What factors decrease it?

11. How can "employee satisfaction" be measured?

12. How can industrial harmony improve a company's chances of survival within a competitive marketplace?

CHAPTER 22: CASE STUDIES OF INDUSTRIAL HARMONY

22.1 INTRODUCTION

The objective of this research was to look at the conditions and relationships in selected Canadian companies that have led to high employee satisfaction. The focus has been on employer-employee relationships and the employer's attempts to bring harmony to the work place. By promoting employee satisfaction, corporations have received the "bonus" of harmony as evidenced by better safety records, lower absenteeism, better quality and service, significant waste control, and, importantly, greater industrial efficiency and cost competitiveness.

The companies studied may or may not have shown our investigators the best or "last word" on appropriate approaches to the harmony situation. But they have all attempted to address the need for industrial harmony as a most significant aspect of the current research in the business sector.

Due to the time involved in completing the research and getting this material into print, there have been some changes in corporate names and organizational structures. Rather than trying to be absolutely up-to-date, we have used the names current at the time.

The following notes have been generated from the interviews that our researchers conducted. The companies involved have wanted to share their experiences with others so that the whole business sector may benefit. The companies interviewed have almost unanimously declared that their programs for industrial harmony are not the "last word" in employer/employee relations. In one case, the company was not entirely sure which course it was taking to promote harmony — but promote harmony, it did — as evidenced by the friendly and co-operative employees who seemed very familiar with and supportive of the management philosophy.

22.2 ABITIBI-PRICE

Problems between labour and management, resulting in serious, prolonged, and expensive strikes, led Abitibi-Price to evaluate and develop a human resource strategic plan.

Abitibi-Price has tried to improve employee relations based on a plan which came as an outgrowth of an overall company policy. This plan called for a well-informed workforce.

Senior management was not after any "quick fix" solution and realized that an integrated approach to the situation, as it existed, was the only reasonable approach.

Strategies of co-operation, participation and involvement, and communication were integrated with job structures, job design, and management systems. Management saw the need to involve those persons who properly should have the responsibility for making this approach happen successfully — the line operators.

Along with the "shifting" of responsibilities to line-operating people, there was a shift to decentralized decision-making.

Senior management was concerned that the traditional adversarial aspects of industrial relations must be reduced. To help with the change process, the company's top executives in personnel, industrial relations, and communications were enlisted to assist in the activities involved in implementing the overall concept. Because of the fifteen thousand employees and twenty-five union locals represented at Abitibi-Price, there was certainly need for expert handling of the plan all the way through the organization.

The communication program was vital. Video tapes, manuals, workshops and discussion sessions were all used to introduce the newly emerging "team" culture. It obviously required more than a communication program — but at least this was in place.

Initially, a manual was developed to inform managers of the three main themes of the plan: co-operation in employee relationships; participation and involvement as a leadership style; and communication, the key to trust and credibility.

The implementers of the plan knew that their aim was to change the culture of the organization from the known and traditional culture which included: a traditional/hierarchical style of management, adversarial labour confrontation, and excessive "red tape". The new culture was to reflect the "team" style of organization. This was all outlined in the manual.

People received the manual in a workshop — not in an in-basket. There was some resistance noticed because many felt that the personnel department was "doing it all". The research group sensed that, in retrospect, top management should have placed more emphasis on the involvement of the line organization in the promotion and implementation of the program.

The managers in each location, were encouraged to develop an effective human resource strategy in conjunction with the local unions. The overall program was taken back to the union locals. The various union local leaders were invited to make comments on the program and management was prepared to listen — and they apparently did. Greater productivity, one of the anticipated spin-offs of the "better relations" program, has begun to be in evidence. Abitibi-Price is cautious about appraising its degree of success in the plan. However, there have been some demonstrable cost savings already indicated.

At one mill, there is a communication program with considerable inter-action amongst the key groups. Employees give suggestions on how to control costs and productivity. Employees work with unions and manage-ment in trying to focus the program objectives. And although management suggested the use of video tape programs as a base of information it was the employees who determined for themselves how these videos could best be applied.

At this same mill, the union people requested a showing of film clips that were developed for use in any of the programs. The film clips "set the stage" for meaningful discussion and involvement of the employees.

For example, one of the film clips asks the question, "Are we going to close down, or are we going to try and improve the situation?"

To promote the program in this mill, there were mobiles saying "Let's keep on working together." There were also posters saying "Thanks...your suggestion saved $26,000."

Three customers of Abitibi-Price were interviewed. They talked about their customer relations with the company and the need for consistent quality of product. This enhanced the employee's perception of being involved with customers and end-products — and thus allowed the employees more of a feeling of being part of a "team" which delivers.

At one mill, a number of steps were taken to promote better employee communication and involvement. For example, the organization was "flat-tened" by the removal of some management levels. "Involvement teams" were established. Coloured hard hats, to signify "rank", were no longer used.

This mill manager showed the company-wide approach — "no imposition of the plan". All mill managers were encouraged to develop their own programs based on the general program designed by the central planning and development group. By involving the mill manager's creativity and willing-ness to carry this program forward, the company was able to engender com-mitment all the way down through the organization.

Senior management encouraged all managers to divulge more and more information. It was considered wise to maximize "common interest" in the company at all levels and thus, even profit information was made available. As a result, people have been sharing ideas and "good" things are happening. There is increasing awareness and understanding at all levels of the organiza-tion.

While some managers may wonder what benefits all this communication will have, senior executives are asking their managers to manage with a balanced leadership style.

The cultural change is seen by some managers as threatening. Others are insecure. Still others say they manage the "new way" already — but the process takes time. Managers are coming to understand the depth of Abitibi-Price's commitment to what hopefully can be accomplished. Senior executives realize that there is still a distance to go in order to realize their goals as substantially as they hope. Senior executives are not trying to tell their people what to do — they are trying to help their people understand the nature of the industrial environment more fully.

Senior management has offered assistance to each plant wishing to develop its own program — including training for potential trainers. Guidelines of objectives are provided along with methods of measuring the accomplishment of the objectives. A number of measurement "tools" are listed in the back of the manual — with both short and long-term assessment guides. However, it is also recognized that employee satisfaction is not always found simply in scoring a question on a scale of one to ten.

Meanwhile, the company's industrial relations group is finding a way to live harmoniously with the unions, and lessen the opportunities for conflict.

Top level management recognizes that this is a long process in developing a future way of working. There will be success stories and there will be some false starts but there is no question about the commitment to the overall direction.

22.3 NORANDA

Noranda has twenty-six mining operations in North America. Many of the "mining towns" are almost completely dependent on the fortunes of the company. Thousands of individuals depend on Noranda directly for their "bread-and-butter". It was reported that mining is not always a lucrative business. Mobility of personnel is widely recognized in the operation of mining installations.

Noranda became concerned about the national productivity figures, economics and the negative economic forecast. If the forecasts turn out to be valid there would be disaster for many people.

Senior management knew that there was a very positive attitude in a lot of companies and some of the many good managers are coming up with positive approaches to handling current corporate concerns. Management knew that the positive and constructive approaches must be communicated.

Safety, always a matter of corporate concern, was the motivation for Noranda to continually enhance their communications program in this area.

The communication of their caution ultimately led to increased harmony in the corporation.

Partly because employee injuries were too frequent, Executive Committee for Accident Prevention (ECAP) was set up. This committee was also investigating why injury frequencies were declining in some locations and not declining in others.

ECAP visited various properties in the mining sector to observe the safety programs, to see what they could learn, and to lend support and encouragement to mines practising good safety measures. Employees were able to talk to committee members and impressed the committee with their understanding of health, environment, and safety concerns.

Noranda executives confirmed that good general communications resulted in safety improvements. Better performance was also noted in other areas as a direct result of the corporate emphasis on communications.

With the objective of "better productivity", the president of Noranda encouraged a corporate policy on employee involvement, worker satisfaction and work enhancement.

Noranda's top managers had a number of questions to help guide them in the development of their policy — a policy which was to lead the way to a different "corporate culture".

- What were perceived to be the problems?

- What caused their present approach to managing employees?

- After diagnosing a problem, what plans did they make to deal with it?

- What successes are they having?

- How do they measure success?

- What is the corporate philosophy?

Noranda did come up with answers to help it develop its policy into an implementable plan and reflected on its need to be impartial and objective.

Noranda had experience in implementing change. It was one of the first in the mining sector to have a profit-sharing program.

The profit-sharing program became a vehicle for communication as the employees had more and more reasons to be involved with pertinent company information. It also gave the employer and employees opportunity to find common ground — the shared interest in corporate profitability.

Noranda took other steps to plan and develop its programs for enhancing employee relations and creating more harmony in the work place.

The company contacted Ford concerning the auto company's successful employee involvement program.

Noranda also developed communication audits in an attempt to measure the effectiveness of its two-way communications.

The company encouraged employees to take part in numerous groups that seemed to develop, and even previously-established occupational health and safety groups were integrated into the overall program of groups in which employees could participate. Corporate policy and occupational health and safety audits were also designed.

Crews also became involved in the creation of cost-saving approaches. At some locations, the crew jointly decides with the supervisor at the beginning of the shift what work is to be done and the part each crew member will be responsible for. The supervisor acts as a co-ordinator.

The crews identify productivity changes whenever possible. In one location an estimated 20% increase in productivity has occurred during the last two years.

One area where there has been tangible success is in the scheduling and maintenance programs for equipment. Employees care about the availability of equipment — it is their responsibility, and employees have been handling this responsibility competently. An example was given regarding an operator taking a machine out and repeatedly damaging the fuel tank. The operator finally assessed the problem as being one of design and suggested changes to the supervisor who set up the operator/mechanic liaison. The problem was corrected in the machine shop by the relocation of the fuel tank. The availability of this equipment has been increased from 60% to 75 or 80%.

Hourly employees are being recognized and supervisors are less insulated behind a wall. Employees have seen their positive effect in attempting to solve problems and because of the conscious effort on the part of both employees and management, employees are offering more assistance to management in operations previously viewed as "outside" their domain. Employees, feeling more a part of the operations are no longer afraid to question certain decisions. Employees know that decisions by management can be changed.

In one of the assay offices, an employee suggested that excess capacity of the office be used for doing work for other companies. This extra work is now 10% of the office's work — and brings in an additional quarter million dollars in sales each year. Thus, the utilization of this excess capacity, as suggested by an employee, and as acted upon by management, improved overall profit performance.

Employees seem interested in the company's money and the resulting cost savings. Employees also take a caring attitude about their equipment as evidenced by their references to "my machine".

The increased two-way communication has seemingly resulted in other satisfactory results. As one indication, there has been a considerable improvement in the absenteeism rate at one operating unit — down 33% from previous levels.

Management stated that they are consciously strengthening employee involvement and participation in the work planning and decision-making process in certain of the operating units. The process will apparently take some time before being put into active use at some other locations.

Most people in the company, at all levels, need to change, and where the managers resist, there is a peer pressure developing. The employees are not being asked to do more. They are being asked to have a different perception and to act on it in their own best interest. It means that they are working "smarter" not "harder".

Senior management made reference to the success of the "golden rule" philosophy as they saw increasing efficiency in production by counting on the constructive input of the employees and the effectiveness of a well-planned communications program.

22.4 CORPORATE FOODS

Strong support at the top of the organization for a program of communications and participation was a dominant feature of Corporate Food's attempts to promote industrial harmony. Corporate Foods management has maintained the respect of their employees and is known for its credibility during negotiations.

Top management sought to operate at the mid-point between management by autocratic authority and management by delegation. Because the operation was relatively small, it was easier for senior management to communicate with all levels of the corporation and it was easier for employees to know and understand the scope of the entire operation.

Industrial harmony, according to Corporate Foods personnel, depended on the credibility of management, personal contact, and awareness of the importance of employee recognition.

The overall organization has five levels, no job descriptions, no suggestion plan, and no organizational chart. There are no quality circle programs. Outside consultants were once brought in to help set up such a program but were not successful because they did not have the same type of credibility and communication style as internal management.

Senior management recognized that good communications were certainly valuable for safety programs but communications developed, as part of a safety program, were also seen as possible springboards to other areas of need. For example, the truck drivers, who are crucial to the company's operations, as members of the Teamsters Union, meet four or five times a year on their days off to discuss safety. Although their meetings were mostly "moan and groan" sessions, they did reduce accidents and compensation claims for accidents, were almost eliminated. And as a result of "spillover" comments, the drivers were understood better and management seemed to listen more when the drivers began giving their views on a variety of topics.

Corporate Foods has a system of employee meetings. The superintendent and foreman give a general overview of how the company is doing in the marketplace and how the particular plant is doing within the Corporate Foods organization. There is a perceived need for the various plants to compete for survival. To survive there would need to be a free exchange of ideas at and between all levels in any particular plant.

In addition, Corporate Foods encourages communications in their safety meetings, at the yearly plant picnic, as well as at a weekend retreat for all sales and production and accounting personnel, foremen and plant managers, Christmas parties, golf tournaments, and long-service award dinners.

This tightly-knit company of between six hundred and seven hundred employees is not without the odd problem. There are four or five discipline cases each year with about the same number of grievances.

Discipline cases are related to the failure of employees to meet the standards required. Management has made it known that there is an open-door policy and that problems with people or their work can always be resolved. Corporate Foods does not fire people from the floor. They give people the opportunity to solve the problem and, if that does not work, people are asked to go home and contemplate the problem until they are willing to resolve it.

The three-day life cycle of the company's bakery products gives the whole organization a sense of urgency. This same attitude seems to prevail in all areas, including industrial relations. Every opportunity is taken to improve the company's communications. This also occurs during negotiations with the unions. Top management insists, for example, that while talking about union demands, negotiations must also focus on corporate and production problems as well. In this way, the unions become more fully aware of the nature of the company. The "by-product" of these successful negotiations is increased company credibility with the unions and the employees.

22.5 MITSUBISHI

Management by "common sense" was the approach senior executives were committed to at Mitsubishi. With this approach, employees were not "just numbers" nor were they mere adjuncts to the machine tool. In fact, employees were expected to take initiative and act — rather than waiting to be told. Quality is seen as an employee responsibility — not as a separate function. And quality of the product is of such high priority that no product is released until it meets all requisite specifications even if this affects the volume of production.

The Mitsubishi operation was previously run by another company. Mitsubishi re-opened the plant and hired the previous company's personnel on a scale of ability and seniority ranking. Because of the practice of hiring experienced workers, there is less need for training to do certain jobs since many of the rehirees are thoroughly knowledgeable of the plant and its operations. Most training, therefore, is on the job. There is some job rotation through various sections but supervisors are somewhat reticent in getting this practice into full swing. As a result, top management is planning a communications program for supervisors. The program will emphasize "leadership" and "problem-solving".

Mitsubishi has recently gone to a three-shift operation which has created a half-hour overlap on the shifts. Supervisors have been using this time to communicate with the employees on job-related information.

General meetings with all employees occur at least twice a year for management to explain their plans and programs.

The organization structure is seen as "loose" and somewhat unstructured, certainly a change from the way that the previous company's operations were viewed. Senior management indicated its desire to put a little bit more structure into the operations but not at the expense of the employees. So, the climate is kept as open as possible in order to encourage employee involvement and participation.

22.6 MATSUSHITA

Top level management indicated their commitment to good employee relations, communication and participation.

While the assembly of television sets is virtually done the same way at Matsushita plants as any other television manufacturing facility elsewhere in the world, the difference is in how the employee is treated. At Matsushita the emphasis is on the employee as a partner — not as just a labourer for the dollar. This means getting input from the employees on every manufacturing decision. The philosophy is that employees should enjoy working at Matsushita.

Foremen and supervisors who have joined the company from similar jobs elsewhere had some misconceptions about the company. In some cases it took the new supervisors a couple of years to "catch on" to the management style of Matsushita. The company was not "totally disorganized" as these new supervisors had thought — it was merely functioning under different management approaches.

The operation has continued to be profitable even as the shakeout in television manufacturing reduced the numbers of companies from twelve to five. Matsushita makes only televisions and uses the Canadian operation to partly serve the United States even though there is an American plant. North American production allows Matsushita to have better quality control as opposed to units shipped from Japan. Canadian production is slightly less expensive than American production.

Because of the marketplace, Matsushita marked down the price of its Canadian products by seven per cent. The employees were consulted on the requirements of the marketplace and the needs for such a price-cutting measure. Actually, employees are quite aware of the wages of people in other companies who are making televisions. While having competitive wages with these others, employees at Matsushita are also aware that they are still below average in wages in the manufacturing field as a whole.

Turnover at Matsushita is only about four per cent, which is considered extremely low. It has, no doubt, more to do with a corporate attitude toward employees rather than the free coffee, birthday gifts, two weeks' bonus pay at Christmas and other thoughtful gestures. However, since company policy is strictly against lay-offs, and supervisory personnel are adept at treating people as individuals, it is obvious that the attendant good atmosphere and lack of bullying by supervision would encourage longer-term employees.

Information is a significant commodity at Matsushita. Generally speaking, there is a daily morning meeting. And employees are called together if there is an important event happening or about to happen. There is an employee representation committee which meets upon request to talk about anything the employees suggest. There is one employee for each section of the company, elected by their section. The personnel manager, and occasionally the plant manager, will join in at these meetings. The committee focuses on wages and benefits once a year and keeps current on industry conditions. When there are disciplinary problems, which are rare, they are discussed in the committee. About eighty per cent of the committee's recommendations are accepted by the company. The committee discusses safety problems and attempts to solve them. By all reports, the meetings are enjoyable, the employees receive important information, senior management gets feedback, and the open flow of information, with no secrets, enhances the harmony between employer and employees.

Because the committee meetings are sometimes held after work hours, other employees are welcome to come into the committee sessions. Morning meetings are short and usually take place before the start of a shift by five or ten minutes. The purpose of these meetings is to let the group leaders quickly pass information so that employees can stay informed of conditions on an up-to-the-minute basis. Even so, there is some desire on the part of employees to have more involvement.

In general, there are few decisions made by one person because the company attempts to operate, as much as possible, by consensus. It takes longer this way, but as a result, everybody understands the decisions and the reasons for them. Most agree that their decision-process is the best way to do it.

Matsushita employs 250 people, of which 220 are hourly employees and thirty are clerical, supervisory, or management. Seventy per cent of the workforce is male.

Like many other companies, Matsushita welcomes the request for job changes by employees. The company not only respects the employee's wishes, but also realizes that the more jobs an individual can do, the more flexible that company is. However, there is no push for routine job rotation.

Successful managers at this plant would be viewed as flexible, a little bit "laid back," good listeners, and not too domineering. In a word, "approachable". At Matsushita nobody is considered "better" than anybody else, certainly a plus for harmonious employer/employee relations.

The company realizes that it must be careful when hiring supervisors from outside the Matsushita system because of the incomplete perceptions of outside supervisors when they see the operations at Matsushita. In addition, supervisors joining Matsushita from outside must be people-oriented and certainly not "status" conscious, in keeping with the overall approach that employees are special people (partners, in fact) and should be respected for that.

22.7 CONCLUSIONS

Company Motivation

Companies have been forced, by recurring problems, to look directly at what is happening in the work place. Inefficiencies, poor quality products, inadequate production rates, accidents, absenteeism, and other evidences of disharmony have been startling reminders to companies of their responsibilities to keep costs down and quality up. Any factors causing problems to the "bottom line" are powerful, motivating factors. For this reason, companies have attempted to state fairly, in formal or informal ways, the rights and responsibilities of employees.

Abitibi-Price previously had had labour problems resulting in prolonged and expensive strikes. The company wanted to reduce the adversarial relationships with its unions and its employees. The company believed it would have better employee relations and better productivity through a well-informed work force.

Noranda became concerned because of the frequency of on-the-job injuries and wished to find the most effective way of improving safety performance.

At Corporate Foods, a manufacturer of bread and other short shelf-life products, management knew that work slowdowns or inefficiencies of any sort would greatly handicap their company's efforts to compete. Management recognized that employee communications and involvement would result in better union relations, more co-operation, and minimized interference with the operation.

At Matsushita, management simply believed that employee involvement and participation is better for the company in terms of ultimate profit performance.

At Mitsubishi (another company with successful Japanese management), it was declared that the objective is to maintain very high quality and couple that with high productivity. To assist in meeting these objectives, the company is highly committed to good employee relations through communication and employee participation.

Company Policy

Whether stated explicitly or not, all of the successful companies that we have studied do have a policy designed for creating harmony. Management realizes the benefits of having a policy which creates an open and informed work place, knowing that such a policy, when implemented, will encourage not only better employee relations but also greater participation in the company's full operation.

At Abitibi-Price, a decision was made at the highest level of management to implement a policy that would require changing the culture of the organization. They were going from a traditional and hierarchical management to a "team" approach. To get the type of improvement the company wanted required an integrated approach. The task was to integrate the strategies of co-operation, participation/involvement, and communication with job structures, job design, and management systems. Obviously, to communicate the changing culture in the organization required a clear statement of philosophy which guided the corporate policy.

Noranda's management has, for many years, been in agreement that a good communication program could assist many key matters such as safety, employee turnover, and employee relations. Through the president of the company, the ideas of employee involvement, worker satisfaction and work enhancement became corporate policy — a policy articulated with the objective of better productivity.

Corporate Foods is a smaller and less formal organization, and although

there is strong support at the top for a program of communication and participation, there is not a formalized statement of policy with respect to industrial
harmony. However, there is an "open door policy" and management is
always willing to discuss problems.

At both Matsushita and Mitsubishi, top level management is highly committed to good employee relations through communication and participation.
At Matsushita, the philosophy that guides management is that employees
should enjoy working there. As a result it has become procedure to treat
employees like partners. Mitsubishi's policy for treating employees was management by "common sense".

Communication and Implementation

All of the companies take their communication seriously — as a special tool
or program, which requires implementation in order to involve employees.

Training and development is also used in the same way. It must promote
involvement in company affairs and give employees a greater perspective.
Training and development can take place at any level, and although supervisory training historically was the approach taken — possibly due to cost con-
siderations — companies are now more open to give training opportunities to
a broader range of employees. In this way the company considers that it is
fulfilling its responsibility to enhance harmony in the corporate setting.

Abitibi-Price developed a manual on "Human Resource Strategies" which
involved top level people of the company, with representatives from industrial relations, personnel, communications and management. The manual
confirmed that the legitimate role of the union was being recognized. It
assured them that management was not trying to interfere with the
union/membership relationship nor the bargaining process. The company had
invited the union's participation in reviewing the human resources strategy
and it listened to the union's constructive suggestions. The general push was
to divulge more and more information through effective communication.
Managers were encouraged to release information. Each manufacturing and
woodlands operation developed its own action plan. Assistance was provided
on request, which included the assistance of experienced personnel to train
the trainers. The human resource plan was not a template or enforced master
plan which could be applied to all operations. Plant managers were encouraged to show initiative. Each of the managers set his/her own objectives and
ways to measure the achievement of these objectives. The managers can
judge where they are now and where they want to be in three to five years.
The manual refers to a number of measurement devices for both short and
long-term assessment.

Senior management at Noranda talked to Ford and others about employee involvement and attended a three-day seminar involving managers from the Mines and Metals group on "An Approach to Quality Circles". They talked to others about Quality Circles. They looked at it from a broader sense and across departments. The union was brought into the discussions to avoid any problems. Communication audits were developed in an attempt to find out how accurately information was being dispersed through the company. The Occupational Health and Safety Groups evolved into a broader type of communication. Large numbers of projects were developed to establish "crew involvement". Crew involvement means that employees in a certain area help make decisions about their scope of work. Decisions made by any other process or individual are now open to questions and employees realize that decisions can be changed. Some of these projects were fairly effective on cost savings and all were effective from an "understanding" point of view.

At Corporate Foods, management refers to a free exchange with employees. It was also indicated that communication developed as part of a safety program can also be used as a springboard to aid in other areas through different communication programs. As indicated previously, Corporate Foods management has an open-door policy. They are always willing to listen and react to people's problems concerning company conditions.

Employee meetings take place in the various plants by departments. The superintendent and the foremen run the meetings and give a general overview of Corporate Foods and how their individual plant is doing within the company and in the marketplace. Even in contract negotiations with the union, management insists on taking the opportunity to talk about other things besides union demands. Company concerns, production problems, and safety issues are among the topics communicated between employer and employees, even during the sensitive times of contract negotiation.

At Matsushita, meetings are quite literally, the order of the day. Generally speaking they have a meeting every morning and when a significant event happens another meeting is called.

Matsushita also has an employee representation committee which meets upon request to talk about anything. When these committee meetings are held after work there is no objection if other employees want to come and sit in. The company expects than an informed employee will wish to be involved in the company to a greater degree and for this reason everyone even knows the profit and loss situation. As far as maintaining harmony within the working group, they are developing "involvement circles" in one department to assist workers in improving work place conditions.

At Mitsubishi, there are periodic meetings held throughout the year to update employees regarding the operating and financial situation and to explain the company programs and plans and how employees can make the best contribution. In addition to these general meetings, many supervisors are holding weekly meetings with their employees to discuss production or safety issues or other items of interest to the employees. Mitsubishi is planning on a communication program with their supervisors and expects to get it started this year.

To implement policy, most companies have introduced some training and development programs.

Abitibi-Price is offering its managers training in order to change the corporate culture to provide an appropriate balance between centralized and decentralized management. Because some supervisory personnel feel threatened by the impending changes, Abitibi-Price has seen the need to work with management to develop a greater understanding of the process.

Matsushita provides on-the-job training for newly placed employees, and while this can seemingly impede worker productivity in the initial stages of a job change, Matsushita believes that this method of training can create better harmony — and better productivity in the longer term.

Functional Change

Companies that were studied seemed to take almost for granted that employees would assist in the management process when encouraged to participate. Companies made adjustments to increase employee involvement. In each case, companies noted that employees needed to express their views and that management needed to listen.

As employees provided more direction, it became obvious that they took to the directions more favourably — it was after all, their own recommendations that they were being asked to accept.

Employees helped, it seemed, in every conceivable area of management: safety, equipment maintenance, sales, services, absenteeism, quality control, traffic control and time management.

Management, at the companies we researched, was continually surprised by the "added" resource found in employees, a resource, which when used, constantly pointed to greater production efficiencies and hence greater profit performance.

At Abitibi-Price, an example was that task forces of union and management people took a hard look at the maintenance groups. In some cases, because the recommendations were made by the task forces and not imposed from the top down by management, there was generally a better acceptance by the employees.

At Noranda, management listened to what the employees said regarding their safety program and took action. Management adopted the recommendations because they were good. The employees accepted them because they were their own and therefore made sense to them. Hence, safety performance at Noranda is much improved. As a spin-off to the successful safety program large numbers of crew involvement projects were developed to assist in other areas. Some of these projects were quite effective on cost savings and all were effective in creating an understanding between management and employees. At some locations they now have crew involvement at the start of the shift. The crews and supervisors jointly decide as to who will do what work.

At Noranda, productivity improvement was evident because of shared involvement. In one example, a piece of heavy machinery was continually breaking down in normal use. An employee suggested design changes to the supervisor who then set up the employee/maintenance liaison in order to implement the corrective measures. The subsequent availability of the machinery reached all time highs as a result of these co-operative efforts.

What may have started out as an off-handed employee remark about the underutilized assay office being available for external assay work, resulted in a quarter million dollars of sales annually for assay services. Again, employees closest to a situation were able to demonstrate a useful perspective which enhanced the management, and ultimately, profit performance of the company.

Employee assistance is also a highlight at three other companies studied. At Corporate Foods, the truck drivers, for example, make recommendations concerning everything from safety to sales. At Mitsubishi and Matsushita, the line employees have increasing influence over management decisions. At Mitsubishi, for example, where there is an attempt to introduce an environment in which employees can participate in the decision-making process, some employees are determining how to best utilize overlapping shift time. At Matsushita, employee involvement circles (different from "quality circles") have been initiated in one department. The company hopes that this concept will spread to other departments. Employee involvement circles are involved in many manufacturing decisions. Management realizes that this may cause a lengthier decision-making process, but it makes for better results because the employees understand the decisions and the reasons for them. Employee involvement circles are seen to increase employee co-operation and thus better, more effective implementation of decisions.

Structural Change

Companies studied have realized that structural change can be rendered quite easily. Top executives that were for so long isolated from the hourly employees, are now seeking ways to be closer to the operations and to reduce unnecessary costs. Employees are showing themselves to be so well-versed in the matters of production efficiency that they are now being asked in many companies to make presentations to top executives on the state of the production process. For management to listen more acutely to employees, there was often structural change in the company to allow for less intermediary distortion.

Usually, with this "functional" change, top management realizes that intermediate "managers" are less essential to the organization. Almost every company talks of the flattening of the corporate structure to better accommodate the new mode of operations.

The Abitibi-Price program includes giving more responsibility to line operating people with a corresponding shift to decentralized decision making. In addition, Abitibi-Price is attempting to flatten the organization for a more streamlined operation.

Utilizing experiences from other properties, Noranda is also flattening their organization in newly developing operations. In one operation, due to come on stream next year, the customary six levels of management are being reduced to three. It is anticipated that the new streamlined shape of the organization will increase efficiency in corporate communications as well as produce cost savings.

Corporate Foods, with some 500 employees, has always considered itself to have an extremely flat organization, with only five levels of management from president to the machine operator.

Mutual Respect and Trust

- Management "listening"
- Management openness to communication from all levels.
- Management recognition of people as individuals with the right to know and share in corporate decisions.

These are examples of how corporations create a respectful and trusting climate within their companies. Obviously, promoting input from employees shows respect. But management validates the trust of employees by following up on employee recommendations. The most successful companies take their employee suggestions and recommendations seriously — all the way to full implementation where and whenever practical. In the event that recommendations are not acted on, the employee is advised of the reasons.

At Abitibi-Price, top management lets people know that they recognize the legitimate role of the union. The company decided to take its overall hopes for an employee-involvement program down to the union local. They invited the union's input and respectfully listened. Management showed their trust in the union viewpoint by adjusting their own preferences for programming to reflect suggestions received from the union. For example, at one mill, to demonstrate further their respect for the employees, the practice of wearing various coloured hard hats that distinguished managers from others was ended.

Again, "listening" was a key for Noranda, as crews were asked to talk about how the work should be done.

At Corporate Foods, management refers to the importance and concern for recognition, personal contacts and trust. Employees are considered to have the right to know, so that in their employee meetings in the various plants and departments, the superintendents and the foremen give the employees a general overview of how Corporate Foods and the individual plant is doing in the marketplace.

At Matsushita, employees are treated like partners. Supervisors treat people on an individual basis and it is rare to have a disciplinary problem. There is generally a good atmosphere and supervisory personnel do not bully their subordinates. Like other companies showing respect for their employees, they keep them well-informed. When any significant event happens, they call their employees together, have a meeting and talk about it. When there is a disciplinary problem, it is discussed with the employee committee. The committee makes a recommendation and about 80 per cent of the time the company accepts the recommendation.

Sometimes meetings with the employee committee are held after work and, when that is the case, there is no objection if other employees want to come and sit in on the meetings. Nothing is held in secret because the "partners" are expected to have the right to know what is happening.

At Mitsubishi, everyone is treated virtually the same and everyone is listened to. The fundamental guiding philosophy is that employees are people and not machine tools. Management at Mitsubishi wants to create an environment in which employee suggestions and concerns are considered.

CHAPTER 23: FORD MOTOR COMPANY OF CANADA

23.1 INTRODUCTION

Over the years, from its beginning in 1903, the Ford Motor Company has been part of the fabric of industrial America. However, like its rivals, notably General Motors Corporation, it has seen its fortunes wax and wane. Currently, it has been going through a new period of turbulence. As a result, a new chief executive officer, William Clay Ford Jr., the great-grandson of founder Henry Ford, has now taken charge. The former C.E.O., Jacques Nasser, ran the Company from January 1999 to October 2001 — an almost three-year reign.

In the following pages, we describe the industrial harmony program that was introduced at Ford of Canada during the Nasser period. Then we summarize the events that have battered the company in more recent times. Finally, we can ask ourselves what actually went wrong at Ford — to cause profits to turn into losses and for dividends to shareholders to be chopped in half, to save on cash. Was it the "industrial harmony" program, was it poor management, was it uncontrollable outside events, or just bad luck?

23.2 IMPROVING PRODUCTIVITY

The engine plants in the Ford organization compete for survival. If there is not enough business to sustain all plants, the least cost-effective plants face the prospect of closing. For this reason, each plant wishes to be as profitable and as productive as possible. The Canadian Auto Workers Union accepts this concept. This was reason enough for senior plant executives to look for any programs which may help the production efficiencies in their plants.

Visit to Japan

In an attempt to find suitable approaches to improve production efficiencies, many management representatives and some union representatives went to Japan to witness first hand what was happening with some of the automobile production facilities there. They saw commitment on the part of employees and learned that this commitment came from the Japanese worker's involvement in the operations and from established communication programs. As a result, employees took pride in their work and manufactured high-quality products.

Although it was recognized that the Japanese culture was not transportable to North America, the Ford representatives believed that a program of involvement and communication would result in a higher quality product. Quality was a key issue at Ford.

The conclusions of the Ford representatives were approved by the chairman and top executive and a new policy was issued committing Ford to a new approach in communications and other programs to enhance production.

Pre-employment procedures

The programs even started with pre-employment procedures. Ford was impressed with the system used by the Japanese to select the best employees from the pool of applicants. Enthusiastic Ford personnel responsible for operations in Mexico were quick to adopt a system whereby they could attract and hire the top 10% of the Mexican work force.

In the Essex Engine plant, they now hire only those candidates with high school diplomas. In addition, Ford uses a quality-control inspection test which 25% of the qualified candidates cannot pass. Ford justifies its rigorous employment standard because of its job posting system. At one Ford operation, many employees are transferred, within the plant, each year. Due to increasing statistical process control in the operation, employees must be able to demonstrate greater mathematical capabilities.

The Essex Engine plant has introduced a new pre-employment, 20-hour orientation program. The program covers: knowledge and job requirements, productivity, quality control, safety, and work practices.

23.3   EMPLOYEE INVOLVEMENT PROGRAM

For regular employees, Ford developed the Employee Involvement Program, a program normally adjusted by local plant management according to their specific needs.

At the Essex Engine plant, the newly endorsed theme of "involvement", came packaged with a manual as one of the initial contact points between employer and employee. There were many tangible developments as a result of this employee-centred program that indicated a whole new range of employer and employee attitudes:

- A group of hourly employees gave a presentation on savings, quality and profit improvement to the president of Ford in Canada — all with the encouragement of the fully-committed union plant chairman. In fact the union plant chairman realizes that he can now call the plant manager at any time to discuss problems with an unprecedented level of frankness.

- Hourly employees now talk to the plant manager and feel comfortable doing so.

- The foremen, on the company's behalf, invite employees to off-plant premises for business discussions. The company contributes to the cost of food and refreshments. These foremen-arranged meetings attract approximately ninety per cent of the hourly employees — on a non-paid basis.

- Foremen are given the opportunity to take Dale Carnegie training courses. The foremen endorse this fully, not only because it helps, but because it is fun, it makes them feel good, and it gives them access to valuable resource material.

- There is a new selection procedure for supervisors. The stringent testing of supervisor candidates allows for only about a 50% success rate in those who apply for the supervisory positions.

- There are periodic communication sessions regarding general concerns that allow employees to express to management their opinions on a wide range of problems.

23.4   SICK LEAVE AND ABSENTEEISM

Sick leave was considered a problem because, if significant numbers of employees are away from work, drawing workers' compensation, or sickness and accident insurance, costs quickly become much higher than they should be. The union became convinced, when approached by the company, that capable employees could return to work. Apparently the company had information which proved that there was abuse of the system. Union leadership, when shown the facts by the company, passed the facts on to the people concerned. Perhaps it was the realization that the company would have successfully won in an arbitration case, or perhaps it was the case of a new understanding in the plant. Whatever it was, the Essex Engine operation, with the best Ford plant performance in Canada with only four hundred people out on sickness and accident, improved even more dramatically by reducing the figure to only 145 during a twenty-four month period. There are also statistics related to this plant's safety record that demonstrate the effects of accident prevention.

Absenteeism was also seen as an area for improvement. Six per cent absenteeism means having 6% more employees on payroll than needed. Fringe benefits are also paid to absentee employees. With fringe benefits in many companies costing approximately 25–30% of the wages, the costs of absenteeism really detract from the profitability of an organization.

The Essex Engine plant, with an absenteeism rate of 3.5%, has taken steps through their "involvement" program to reduce absenteeism as much as possible.

What was the Essex Engine plant doing to achieve such favourable absenteeism rates? Perhaps it was the humane treatment of those employees with another and more serious problem — alcohol abuse.

Absenteeism was just one of the problems related to unhealthy alcohol usage. Safety was another.

Ford has a program to assist employees who seek help. There is a committee, made up of a cross-section of employees, which will monitor and advise on alcohol and drug-related problems.

The committee, when required, will suggest that employees take treatment at a local rehabilitation clinic. The treatment takes 90 days and the company pays the bill which, after OHIP, is $1,800. At any one time there can be 12 to 15 employees receiving treatment. The committee does not impose their recommendations on employees unless the employees are supervisory and thus their staff is in jeopardy with regard to safety concerns. At such a time, a supervisor must take the treatment or be replaced.

Once treatment is over, the employees are told that, if treatment is required again, they will be discharged. Employees sign a one-year waiver of grievance against discharge for that reason.

The program for alcoholic rehabilitation is successful in 80% of the cases.

23.5 MANAGEMENT TRAINING PROGRAM

Ford also has a management training program in which three subordinates identify their supervisor's management style. This is discussed with the supervisor and the training group. Supervisors are encouraged to take whatever action is required to deal with the perceptions of their subordinates — and to change their supervisory behaviour if it is warranted. This is a cautiously-monitored program because Ford recognizes that different management styles are necessary for different people.

The plant manager establishes a committee which takes the training and assessment program down through the organization. There is a realization that some supervisors are not interested in this program.

Ford encourages employees to solve their problems as immediately as possible — on a verbal basis and the company has shown some commitment to discourage formal written grievances.

Supervisors who are unwilling to change their styles to adapt to the new modes of management are put under pressure to comply. The alternative may be to take voluntary, early retirement.

The training of supervisors involves a variety of techniques from demonstration modelling and simulations to the discussion of real-life problem situations.

Reference was made to Ford's million dollar training budget with the comment that "Japan has to keep on training — and the employee can ask for the training which he or she wants." Ford is committed to a world-wide reputation based on quality products and realizes that to compete on this scale requires every asset and resource possible — particularly highly trained employees.

Structurally, Ford has executed some fairly drastic measures. For example, the Essex Engine plant has reduced its supervisory levels to four which has helped to sustain its reputation as a finely-tuned operation.

23.6 CORPORATE CITIZEN ROLE

Ford representatives point with pride, equal to their pride in cost-saving measures, to their corporate citizen role, a role that the employees happily take part in.

Per capita donations, by employees in the Windsor area, to the welfare of the community in the United Way campaign were more than double any other Ford plant in Canada. Comments were made that a competitive manufacturer's plant, also in Windsor, with twice the employees, was unable to match the total generosity of the Windsor employees.

Windsor-area employees have also been involved in selling daffodils for cancer research and, recently, have helped find a donor of a liver for a non-employee. Ford provided space, phones, office equipment and personnel to help in this vital search.

The Essex Engine plant will be providing sports facilities for the employees. Whether an employee's interest is softball, soccer, volleyball, or just working out in the exercise room, there will be athletic services available to just about everyone. Again, this is a demonstration of the company's respect for the employee — an employee having many and varied social and personal needs now more fully recognized by the company.

23.7 INDUSTRIAL HARMONY AT FORD

As we have already indicated, Ford of Canada has been very active in improving the working conditions of its employees. So let us review how the six key requirements of industrial harmony have been present at Ford.

Company Motivation. The increasing success of the Japanese automotive industry in the late 70's was a significant factor in motivating Ford to look for new ways of doing business. A perception that Japanese quality was superior to that of the North American automobile manufacturers was taking its toll in the marketplace.

Harmony Policy. Many of the Ford representatives (particularly those who had been to Japan to research their system) concluded that emphasis on employee involvement and communication resulted in a high level of commitment on the part of Japanese employees. This conclusion resulted in senior management approval for a policy of increased employee involvement at Ford. A one-page letter, signed by the President, stating this policy is included in this Chapter, as Appendix 23A.

Communication and Implementation of Policy. At Ford, after the top executive endorsed a program of increased employee participation, an eight-step process for the implementation of Employee Involvement (EI) was developed, a copy of which is provided in Appendix 23B. Ford has also conducted various opinion surveys among employees, an example of which is shown in Appendix 23C.

Ford–U.S., the parent company, undertook the recruitment of experts in the area of Participative Management. The function of these experts was to train other people in the Company. They trained line supervisors in participative management skills and improved communication systems.

The experts also trained staff representatives with the objective of having the staff representatives train others in the organization.

In the Essex Engine plant, communication sessions are held regularly to discuss general concerns. At these meetings, employees can express their opinions on a wide range of problems. There is also a new program in which foremen invite employees to meet away from plant premises to discuss business. Also, an employee newspaper was begun to improve communications.

Ford has also introduced Teleometrics training for supervisors. In this process, supervisors are assessed by subordinates. This assessment, plus further discussion helps supervisors identify their management style.

While not every company can warrant a million-dollar budget for training as Ford does, it is clear that such a commitment to training is provided in the employee's best interest.

Functional Change. At Ford in Oakville it is too early yet to assess, in an absolute way, the value of its Employee Involvement efforts. However, some obvious improvements have been implemented with regard to facilities and authority levels.

Also, to encourage employee participation, Ford is now giving salary review information to the employee. At Ford Windsor, information concerning absenteeism and compensation for sickness or accident was shown to the union. The union accepted the facts presented and put pressure on employees who were abusing the system to return to work as quickly as possible.

Structural Change. The North American Ford organization is trimming its company structure and has eliminated many of the approximately fifteen levels of management. In the Essex Engine plant, for example, there are now only four levels of management.

Mutual Respect and Trust. "Discussion" was a key item for Ford. As an example, at the Essex Engine plant it was stated that the union plant chairman can now discuss problems with management and receive a respectful hearing. In addition, and certainly more indicative of a changing "climate", hourly employees now "talk to the boss and feel comfortable" doing so.

23.8   BUSINESS LEADERSHIP INITIATIVE PROGRAM

One of the measures that the Ford Motor Company had begun to implement, on the initiative of its former C.E.O., Jacques Nasser, was what Ford calls the "Business Leadership Initiative" program, or BLI for short.

Under this program, directed at all 350,000 Ford employees worldwide, the aim is to make everyone act more like owners and entrepreneurs, rather than as hourly-paid employees. (In fact, Ford employees together own 20% of the company's shares). Also, the CEO expects to reintroduce, among Ford employees, an owner's traditional feeling of pride and proprietorship.

Under BLI, Ford's 55,000 managers are being encouraged to participate in "100-day projects" aimed at cutting costs and resolving production and other problems. In this approach, the emphasis is on "shareholder value": what it means and how it can be improved. Ford managers are also encouraged to participate, as teams, in community-improvement projects. To improve BLI's chances of success, Ford is taking BLI participation by managers into account in its compensation and performance-review process.

23.9   CRISIS AT FORD

Soon after Jacques Nasser became C.E.O. at Ford in January 1999, the Company was on the verge of overtaking General Motors as the largest automaker in the world. This followed the purchase by Ford of Land Rover and the car business of Volvo AB. However, as it turned out, Ford never did overtake GM.

Firestone Tires

The first setback was Ford's involvement in a costly legal battle with tire-maker and long-time partner Bridgestone-Firestone Inc. The cause of the dispute was tire blowouts. Ford had installed Firestone tires as original equipment on its Ford Explorer sport utility vehicles. However, when driven on the highway, the tread had sometimes separated from the tires, causing the vehicle to roll over and the occupants to be injured or killed. The ensuing recall and legal settlement are estimated to have cost Ford over U.S. $3 billion.

Other Problems

In another dispute, Ford had to compensate car and truck owners because of problems with their vehicle ignition systems that had been blamed for 11 deaths. Another problem was lack of new or redesigned vehicle models for the coming year. Also, shortage of cash caused the company to slash in half its dividends to shareholders and to cancel a program to provide each employee with a personal computer and internet access for a nominal fee.

New Approach

New C.E.O., William Clay Ford Jr. (or Bill Ford), announced in 2001, when he took over leadership at Ford, that "everything's up for review. Everything we have, every assets, every piece of geography, we're going to take a good, hard look at it". He also stated that "I think we lost our focus in several areas". Basically, the new C.E.O.'s aim was to make the company profitable again and restore its damaged reputation.

Towards the end of 2001, Vice-President Nick Scheele, in a thorough review of company operations, was examining staffing, assembly plants and other areas for cutting costs. Already, a voluntary plan had been announced for reducing the number of salaried employees by 4,000 to 5,000, including 200 in Canada.

Outside analysts have stated that Ford needed to get back to basics. Under Nasser, who wanted to be an "agent of change", the company had invested in too many diverse areas. For example, in Canada, Ford had become one of the largest scrap yard owners and the owner of Young Drivers of Canada.

By the end of 2001, Ford Motor Company was operating at less than 80% of its manufacturing capacity in North America. The aim was to bring that number above 90%. Also, to cut costs, Ford was expected to close some plants, reduce the number of shifts, and lay off thousands of hourly workers, as well as office staff. At that time, Ford was employing about 16,000 production workers in Canada and 103,000 in the United States. In order to make significant labour cutbacks, Ford would need the co-operation of the United Auto Workers union whose labour agreement with the company expires only in 2003.

Financially, the Ford Motor Co. lost $5.45 billion (U.S.) in 2001 — the first annual loss since 1992. In 2000, by contrast, it made a profit of $3.5 billion. Arch-rival, General Motors Corp., made a profit of $601 million (U.S.) in 2001.

Ford of Canada

At Ford of Canada, a new president, Alain Batty, was appointed in March 2001. This was at a time of declining sales, declining market share, and declining production. Batty's first steps have been directed at improving dealer relations and sharpening the company's marketing efforts. It is not yet clear how the company's industrial harmony program will be affected. However, the head office emphasis on cost-cutting, better product quality, and improved productivity, may well lead to clashes with the employees and the union that represents them, the United Automobile Workers' Union. In fact, Buzz Hargrove, the president of the Canadian Auto Workers Union has promised to make the proposed shutdown of Ford's Ontario Truck Plant in Oakville, in late 2003 or early 2004, the key issue in contract talks with Ford Motor Co. of Canada later in 2002. Also critical is the potential downscaling of production at the adjacent Oakville Assembly Plant which makes the Ford Windstar minivan. Of the Truck Plant's 1,200 employees, about half are nearing retirement. Of the remainder, some will be able to bump less experienced workers at the largest Oakville Assembly Plant which has 3,500 employees.

Ford Still Struggling

By 2005, Ford was still struggling to maintain vehicle market share in North America. Although more profitable in 2004, much of its profit was from the company's vehicle financing operations. Overall, sales revenue was down 13% in 2004. Major problems in 2005 are intense competition and soaring health-care costs for employees. As expected, the Ford truck assembly plant in Oakville was closed in July 2004, with a reduction in the adjacent minivan operation. On the positive side, Ford is now building a $1.2 billion flexible manufacturing plant in Oakville to start production in late 2006, producing three vehicles including minivans.

APPENDIX 23A: POLICY LETTER RE EMPLOYEE INVOLVEMENT AT FORD OF CANADA

Policy Letter B-14
Office and Division Heads
General Managers and Plant Managers
Persons Designated by the above
All Holders of the Methods and Procedures Manual

Subject: *Employee Involvement*

It is the policy of the Company to encourage and enable all employees to become involved in and contribute to the success of the Company. A work climate should be created and maintained in which employees, at all levels, can achieve individual goals and work satisfaction by directing their talents and energies toward clearly defined Company goals.

To the extent practicable, management is expected to operate within the following guidelines:

• Management systems, procedures, and practices should take into account that human resources are among the Company's most important assets and that imagination, ingenuity and creativity are widely distributed throughout the entire workforce, as are dedication and the desire to contribute.

• Methods of managing should encourage employee participation in identifying and solving work-related problems.

• Communication programs and procedures should be implemented that encourage frequent, timely and constructive two-way communication with employees concerning work-related problems. Employee work suggestions and ideas should be solicited, and employee questions should be answered as completely as possible.

There is no simple or universal prescription associated with human resources management. All members of management should identify and evaluate available methods and employ those most suited to their particular set of circumstances.

The Vice-President — Industrial Relations is responsible for interpretation of this policy.

President

APPENDIX 23B: PARTICIPATIVE MANAGEMENT AND EMPLOYEE INVOLVEMENT AT FORD OF CANADA*

A.1 BACKGROUND AND PROCESS

I would like to welcome each of you who have elected to attend this session on "building quality through people". I hope many of your expectations will be fulfilled during the course of the afternoon.

During the next 40 minutes, Bob and I will outline for you some of our experiences with employee involvement and participative management at Ford of Canada.

First, I will take you through some of the background leading up to the need to change our management style and then I will explain the steps we used to implement the change. Following that, Bob will comment on the relationship between employee involvement and participative management and the role that relationship plays in our quest for continuous improvement.

By the end of the 1970's, The Ford Motor Company faced some of the greatest challenges in its 75 year history:

- Competitive quality had shifted consumer preference to foreign made cars — especially the Japanese — due to their reputation for high quality and gas mileage.

- Diminishing profitability of our North American automotive operations due in part to warranty costs resulting from quality problems, and

- Changes in job expectations of both our salaried and hourly employees due to higher educational levels and increased economic security.

To meet these challenges, our senior management concluded that we must expand our efforts to tap the ingenuity, imagination and creativity of all members of our work force in every aspect of our business — research, engineering, manufacturing, marketing and sales. This meant providing opportunities for greater involvement of employees in the day-to-day activities of our business.

Toward this end, Ford of Canada issued a policy on employee involvement in November of 1979. This policy signalled an intent on the part of the company to shift from a culture that was impersonal, authoritarian, and management-centred to one that is personal, participative and employee-centred.

---

* Paper presented by Hilda H. Hall and Robert A. P. Rideout, Personnel and Organization Department, Ford of Canada, at the 11th Annual Compensation and Human Resources Conference of the Conference Board of Canada in Toronto. Reprinted with kind permission of Ford of Canada.

Before proceeding, an explanation of what we mean by employee involvement would be useful.

Employee involvement, or simply EI, is the process by which employees at all levels have the opportunity to participate actively in the key managerial processes affecting job-related matters.

Key managerial processes refers to the traditional aspects of a manager's job, that is, planning, organizing, goal setting, decision making, and the like.

Although we will be making some references to our experiences in a unionized environment, the primary focus of our presentation today will be on the salaried non-union workforce.

The EI process in both the hourly and salaried setting is being implemented through similar processes. The primary difference in the process for hourly employees is the inclusion of the union as a full partner in the process.

The process for implementing EI for salaried employees at Ford includes the following steps:

Step 1 — management commitment
　　　2 — assign planning responsibility
　　　3 — diagnosis and setting objectives
　　　4 — plan change and prepare the organization
　　　5 — implement change strategy
　　　6 — evaluate and fine tune
　　　7 — acceptance as a way of doing business

I would like to comment briefly on each step in the process.

Step 1 — Management Commitment

The first step is always the same — leadership commitment. It is also probably the most critical step. The leadership must demonstrate their commitment through their words, their financial support and most importantly, by example.

Step 2 — Assign Planning Responsibility

A planning or steering committee is formed. The role of the committee is to ensure that EI objectives are clear, guidelines are followed, communications are managed, responsibilities are assigned, and procedures and approaches are identified. The committee also provides ongoing support for projects and resolves problems as they arise.

Recommended for early consideration by the committee is the use of an independent consultant from outside the organization. EI can benefit from the services of a consultant, particularly during the early stages when consultants can provide important initial direction and assistance to the committee. The outside consultant serves in an advisory capacity and should not become a permanent part of the organization's EI effort.

The existence of a planning or steering committee will also demonstrate to employees that management is committed to carrying out EI plans.

Committee members should be in positions high enough to influence key decisions. Although it is desirable to have cross-functional representation, it is also important that those persons whose areas of responsibility will be most directly affected have a voice on the committee.

The planning or steering committee usually consists of the following key management representatives:

- various multi-functional managers

- a representatives from the Human Resources Department

- employee involvement administrator

Our experience indicates that the typical committee consists of approximately eight members of management. Too large a committee makes it unwieldy and slow. Too small a committee may not be adequate to ensure that differing views are heard and that varied experience is available for overall guidance.

There may be situations where it would be advisable to have some non-management employees on the committee.

Step 3 — Diagnosis and Setting Objectives

One of the first activities the committee should undertake is an organizational diagnosis.

Diagnosis refers to the process of gathering information about work relationships and the work environment. Through employee interviews, opinion surveys or other means, factors are identified which may facilitate or impede attainment of EI objectives. The diagnosis can also be used as an aid in selection of the work group or department for a pilot project. Finally, diagnosis also provides benchmark data which may be used later in evaluation.

An outside consultant can be extremely helpful at this step in the EI process since organizational diagnosis by opinion survey, interview or a combination of the two requires skillful administration and data interpretation.

Our organizational diagnosis investigated the following work place dimensions:

— *Supervisory Practices* — How do employees' immediate supervisors act on the job? Are they effective?

— *Employment Practices* — How do employees relate with employees in their department, in their departments, on other shifts?

— *Task and Role Characteristics* — What is the nature of the work involved? What is expected of employees?

— *Work Group* — How do co-workers relate to one another? How do they function as a group?

— *Problem Solving Process* — How are problems identified within the work situation? How are they solved?

— *Job Satisfaction* — To what extent are employee needs being met by the work situation?

— *Involvement/Commitment* — To what extent do employees personally identify with the job? Are they committed to achieving common goals?

— *Performance* — What is the quantity and quality of work produced by employees and the organization?

— *Recognition* — Is there adequate recognition for good performance?

— *Organization Maintenance* — What are the organization's absenteeism and turnover rates?

Once this information is obtained, specific objectives are determined.

Step 4 — Plan Change and Prepare the Organization

The committee selects one or more strategies such as team development or EI groups to pursue the objective.

Preparing the organization for EI requires the establishment and execution of a detailed communications plan to assure that employees receive adequate and timely information regarding the EI process. Such communications could include letters from the steering committee, group meetings, articles in company newspapers, and so on.

For example, employees should know of the establishment of an EI effort and should be kept abreast of local projects as they evolve.

Preparing the organization requires a strong commitment to education and training. The type and amount of education and training will depend on organization factors identified by the diagnosis and the particular approach selected by the steering committee. These include:

— Education directed at increasing the knowledge of EI principles, concepts and methods.

— Supervisor training directed at developing skills in participative problem solving, leading group meetings and communications, and

— Employee training focused on group problem-solving methods.

Step 5 — Implement and Change Strategy

Target groups are determined for initial efforts. The members of the group should be given information and training.

They should be informed of:

— the background of the company's EI effort

— the pilot nature of their involvement and how it may shape the implementation of EI in the future

— the role of the EI administrator and the steering committee.

They should be given training in group problem solving and any additional training as deemed necessary by the steering committee on such subjects as group process, effective meetings, and listening skills.

Step 6 — Evaluate and Fine Tune

Following project initiation, the pilot should be carefully monitored to assure that the EI process develops in a constructive fashion and that necessary support and organization resources are being provided. Such monitoring will enable fine-tuning as all parties learn more about the effective implementation of such efforts.

In addition to monitoring the process, it is necessary to measure on a planned basis the extent to which the pilot is attaining its objectives. These objectives, as well as the means for their measurement, should have been established by the steering committee prior to initiation of the project. Such measures may include in-house quality indicators, performance, and employee reactions.

Step 7 — Acceptance as a Way of Doing Business

The feedback from the experience with the pilot site will provide the steering committee with a working knowledge of the EI process. With this experience at hand, they can avoid potential problems and facilitate further expansion of the EI process. To ensure orderly and successful expansion, it is essential that the committee develop a long-range plan that covers such issues as site selection, order and implementation, timing, training, communications and resources.

As is the case with any human resource intervention there is no one way to implement EI. The process I have just outlined is one that has been used at Ford locations throughout North America with great success.

Notwithstanding the viability of the process generally, there are four personal insights I would leave with you.

1. The continuous commitment and support of the senior management of the organization are essential to the success of any EI effort.

2. A lot of fanfare about the implementation of this new style of management runs the risk of raising unrealistic expectations with regard to the extent and timing of the change. I believe there is an opportunity for senior management desirous of greater employee involvement to quietly set about modeling a participative style of managing, and ensuring that such is the case with each successive level of supervision.

3. The successful implementation of an EI process will depend significantly on appropriate staffing. The requisite time, training, and tenacity precludes the possibility of the human resource specialist doing the job "off the corner of his or her desk".

4. To change an organization's style of management will require an inordinate amount of patience on the part of all responsible for its implementation. There will be setbacks, detractors, and frustrations. Depending on the degree of change required, the move to a participative style of management may require several years. On this issue, we often console ourselves with the knowledge that it took us our first 75 years to fully develop our autocratic style of management, it is unlikely that a complete change will be achieved quickly...but it has begun.

A.2 EXPERIENCES IN PARTICIPATIVE MANAGEMENT

It is indeed a pleasure to be invited to speak to you today about Ford's experiences in the area of increasing the involvement of salaried employees in key managerial processes. I say pleasure, because we are very proud of what we have done, what we are doing and what we are planning to do in this area.

My colleague has explained the reasoning that went into Ford's decision to change from an authoritarian to a participative style of management. Against that framework, I would like to share with you some of our experiences in actually implementing the change at our central office in Oakville.

Ford has emerged from a depression in our industry a healthier, more vibrant, and more dynamic company. We have reduced our costs, increased our market share, improved our product quality, and introduced some trend setting new models.

The prime moving force behind this record turnaround was, in a few words, greater efficiency and effectiveness! We have cut our operating costs significantly. Our break-even volume has been lowered and we have learned to live lean.

Where possible, head count reductions were made through voluntary attrition, for example, we offered special early retirement to many employees.

Employees who had to be laid off benefited from improved separation payments and extended recall periods.

Nonetheless, those were painful and difficult actions. Personally, I hope we never have to experience anything like it again.

Through co-operative efforts, our employees, unions, and management have made incredible strides towards greater efficiency and effectiveness while rededicating the total company to our number one priority — product quality.

The co-operative efforts I refer to were due in no small measure to the employee involvement process. However, as we gained experience with EI in the white collar setting, we realized that there was another important dimension to the process.

That dimension was the participative style of management that would provide employees at all levels with the opportunities to participate actively in key managerial processes affecting job-related matters.

The employee involvement process was accordingly redesignated participative management/employee involvement or as we call it — PM/EI.

PM/EI is one of our major thrusts in assuring the long-term viability of The Ford Motor Company. Our PM/EI process is at the root of Ford's efforts to institutionalize a corporate culture which espouses the values so key to survival and prosperity in today's highly competitive automotive market — such things as quality, flexibility, adaptability, efficiency, effectiveness, and customer orientation.

As my colleague mentioned earlier, we have concluded that we must move away from a human resources management system that is impersonal, authoritarian, and management-centred to one that is personal, participative, and employee-centred if we are to remain competitive. This need for change was reinforced in the recent "best seller", *In Search of Excellence* — a study of the best run companies in the U.S. There are few executives within Ford Motor Company who have not read it.

PM and EI are really two sides of the same coin. PM is concerned with participation as viewed from the manager's perspective and is likely to be present when a manager agrees with indicators such as, "I involve employees in the decision making process; I make an effort to obtain employee opinions; I involve employees in group problem-solving." These are indications that the manager believes he or she is receptive to involvement on the part of employees.

EI is concerned with participation as viewed from an employee perspective and is likely to be present when an employee agrees with such indicators as, "I participate in the decision making process; sufficient effort is made to get my opinions; I participate in group problem solving." These are indications that the employees are involved and contributing to organizational goals and the quality of their work life.

Our approach to PM/EI recognizes that the nature of most white-collar jobs is fundamentally different from blue-collar jobs. Salaried employees are involved in auditing, reviewing, supervising, analyzing, inventing, developing, and advising. Obviously, these tasks can be done efficiently or inefficiently. But more importantly, from an organizational standpoint, the question must be asked: are we working effectively? Are we spending our energies and resources on the right subjects?

The difference in the nature of white-collar and blue-collar jobs also has implications for the PM/EI process. Most hourly EI projects have centred around problem-solving teams where the efforts have been directed at product quality and making work more meaningful. Many white-collar projects have had the same focus. However, in order to deal with the effectiveness issue, the PM/EI process for white-collar employees includes involvement in such management processes as goal setting, planning, and decision making.

A major element of the PM/EI process is training. The practice of participative leadership requires certain skills in such areas as oral and written communications, listening, team building, interpersonal skills, problem solving and leadership styles.

We recently concluded the last of eight 4-day PM/EI workshops that dealt with many of these subjects. Every manager in our organization, from the president on down, has attended this off-site training.

A few general observations should be made about Ford's PM/EI process.

First, there is no such thing as a typical example. PM/EI efforts are very decentralized. Our corporate staff provides general support to components. However, each component has the freedom to approach PM/EI in its own way. Thus, a great deal of variety exists.

Second, the number of locations, number of groups and number of participants involved are not closely monitored. This process cannot be evaluated based on numbers. An emphasis on numbers leads to artificial efforts to increase numbers without the quality necessary to make the process successful. We have enough anecdotal evidence to convince us that PM/EI makes sense. Our top management and most of our employees believe PM/EI can lead to an improved quality of work life and better accomplishment of organizational goals.

Third, PM/EI is a philosophy of doing business rather than a clearly identifiable activity. Problem-solving groups and quality circles are readily identifiable PM/EI activities. But many of the things we do, and refer to as PM/EI, are not separate from our day-to-day managerial processes. For example, a manager calls a meeting of his or her department to develop objectives for the year — a now common occurrence. But that kind of meeting is a significant departure from the old way where the manager developed the objective and gave each member of the work group his or her assignments. Thus, the PM/EI philosophy is permeating our everyday methods of operating at Ford.

As a result of the PM/EI process at our central office, the following actions have been taken:

A learning centre was opened in partial response to employees identifying increased training as an opportunity for mutual benefit. The centre is equipped with audio and video skill building and general interest programs. Employees are encouraged to use the learning centre during regular working hours.

As a result of employee requests for some latitude in the area of working hours, an alternative start-time program was instituted. Under this program employees may arrange to start work at a variety of times instead of only at 8:30 a.m. as was previously the case.

On the recommendation of the employees in our Fleet and Leasing Department, increased approval authority was authorized for lower levels of management. This action has improved the efficiency of the department and the competitiveness of our company. A "spin-off" benefit was realized when similar action was taken in our Truck Sales Department, and our Regional Sales Offices across Canada.

Our Accounts Payable Department identified upgraded facilities as the primary opportunity to improve departmental efficiency. As a result, the entire area was refurbished with "state-of-the-art" office furniture.

Our performance review program was revised to provide a substantial increase in the involvement of the employees in setting the criteria on which their performance will be rated.

We do a lot more information sharing: department managers meet monthly with their staffs; the Vice President of General Sales invites all employees to attend a monthly sales review presentation; and the President meets quarterly with all employees to inform them of the state of the company and future plans.

Increasing numbers of employees are getting involved in planning, goal-setting, problem-solving, and decision-making meetings. Employee-initiated contact with management and newsletters are some other methods by which communication is being enhanced.

The impact of all this on the utilization of white-collar employees is enhanced effectiveness and efficiency.

The foundation of PM/EI is based on the philosophy that the goals of the organization and the goals of individuals are not inherently in conflict. We are making some basic-theory kinds of assumptions about people and moulding our PM/EI efforts and our overall approach to management around that philosophy.

You have probably noticed that I have talked very little about measurable productivity improvement.

Basically, we do not believe in spending a lot of time trying to quantify productivity improvement within the white collar workforce.

Such measurement tends to over-emphasize the selected criteria to the detriment of other important elements of doing business.

Such an approach frequently sacrifices long-term improvement for short-term results.

It also tends to place a disproportionate emphasis on the needs of the organization versus the needs of the people. Sometimes we find that if we take care of the needs of our employees, the needs of the organization are fulfilled in the process.

Quantifying productivity gains is a costly, time-consuming activity. We believe the time that would be spent measuring can more productively be spent doing the things that need to be done.

Rather than focusing our energy, time and effort on quantifying white-collar productivity, we are concentrating on a notion we call "continuous improvement".

Continuous improvement is really very simple. In whatever we do, we are aiming to do it better. It means always striving for improvement. It means continually setting new goals and objectives and challenges to conquer. We are asking ourselves questions such as, "are we doing it better than last year? How can we do it even better next year and the years beyond?"

As we reach toward the next century, we, at Ford, are convinced that our success will be determined by how well we tap the potential of our people — our greatest competitive resource.

We plan to realize the fullness of that potential through our ongoing commitment to participative management and employee involvement.

A.3 EIGHT BASIC STEPS IN LAUNCHING EI

I would like to share with you what we have found to be the essential elements or steps of employee involvement. They are:

Step   1 — management involvement and support
       2 — establishment of a steering committee
       3 — diagnosis of the organization
       4 — selection of pilot area
       5 — preparation of the organization
       6 — establishment of local pilot project
       7 — evaluation and fine tuning
       8 — generalization and extension

I would like to comment briefly on each step in the process.

Step 1 — Management Involvement and Support

Commitment to employee involvement starts at the top of the organization.

Commitment and support are demonstrated through actions e.g., active participation on an employee-involvement steering committee. Employees will know that management is serious when employees receive training, and when the time and opportunity necessary to solve problems are made available, and solutions are actually implemented.

Another important demonstration of local support is the communication of operating information as well as information about EI plans and progress.

Step 2 — Establishment of a Steering Committee

The role of the Steering Committee is to ensure that project objectives are clear, employee involvement guidelines are followed, communications are managed, responsibilities are assigned, and procedures and approaches are identified. The Committee also provides ongoing support for projects and resolves problems as they arise.

One of the first actions recommended for consideration by the Steering Committee is the use of an independent consultant from outside the plant. Most projects can benefit from the services of a consultant with EI-type experience. This is particularly true during the early stages when consultants can provide important initial direction and assistance to the Steering Committee. The outside consultant serves in an advisory capacity and should not become a permanent part of a facility's EI effort.

The existence of a Steering Committee will also demonstrate to employees that management is involved and committed to carrying out employee involvement plans.

A typical steering committee usually consists of key management representatives. It might include the:

— Various (multi-functional) Managers

— A representative from the Industrial Relations Department

— EI Administrator.

Experience indicates that the typical steering committee consists of approximately eight members of management. Too large a committee makes it unwieldy and slow. Too small a committee may not be adequate to assure that differing views are heard and that varied experience is available for overall guidance.

There may be situations where it would be advisable to have some non-management employees on the Steering Committee.

Steering Committee members should be in positions high enough to influence key decisions and at a minimum represent groups whose support will be critical to project success. They should also have the credibility necessary to convince employees of their commitment and support. And finally, although it is desirable to have cross-functional representation, it is also important that those persons whose areas of responsibility will be most directly affected have a voice on the Committee.

Step 3 — Diagnosis of the Organization

One of the first activities in which the Steering Committee should get involved is an "organizational diagnosis".

Organizational diagnosis refers to the process of gathering information about work relationships and the work environment. Through employee interviews, opinion surveys or other means, factors are identified which may facilitate or impede attainment of employee-involvement objectives. The diagnosis can also be used as an aid in selection of the work group or department for a pilot project. Finally, diagnosis also provides benchmark data which may be used later in evaluation.

An outside consultant can be extremely helpful at this step in the EI process since organizational diagnosis by opinion survey, interview or a combination of the two, requires skillful administration and data interpretation.

A good organizational diagnosis would investigate the following workplace dimensions:

— *Supervisory Practices* — How do employees' immediate supervisors act on the job? Are they effective?

— *Employee Practices* — How do employees relate with employees in their department, in other departments, on other shifts?

— *Task and Role Characteristics* — What is the nature of the work involved? What is expected of employees?

— *Work Group* — How do co-workers relate to one another? How do they function as a group?

— *Problem-Solving Process* — How are problems identified within the work situation? How are they solved?

— *Job Satisfaction* — To what extent are employee needs being met by the work situation?

— *Involvement/Commitment* — To what extent do employees personally identify with the job? Are they committed to achieving common goals?

— *Performance* — What is the quantity and quality of work produced by employees and the organization?

— *Recognition* — Is there adequate recognition for good performance?

— *Organization Maintenance* — What are the organization's absenteeism and turn-over rates?

Step 4 — Selection of Pilot Area

It is recommended that all EI efforts begin with a small-scale project in a pilot area.

The Steering Committee should consider optimizing the following factors in the selection of a pilot area.

— *Receptive climate* — supervision and employees should be generally receptive to participating in a pilot project and willing to volunteer for such an effort.

— *Stable workforce* — to the extent possible, a unit should be selected where the likelihood of supervisors and employees being displaced is minimal.

— *Self-contained unit* — the unit should have clearly identifiable products or services which result from the inter-related efforts of a single work group.

Step 5 — Preparation of the Organization

Preparing the organization for employee involvement requires establishment and execution of a detailed communications plan to assure adequate and timely informing of employees regarding the Employee Involvement effort. Such communications could include letters from the Steering Committee, group meetings, articles in newspapers, etc.

For example, employees should know of the establishment of an EI effort and should be kept abreast of local projects as they evolve with even greater information given those on whom the projects will have the greatest impact.

Preparing the organization requires a strong commitment to education and training. The type and amount of education and training will depend on organizational factors identified by the diagnosis and the particular approach selected by the local Steering Committee. These include:

— Education for management directed at increasing knowledge of employee involvement principles, concepts and methods.

— Supervisor training directed at developing skills in participative problem solving, leading group meetings and communications, and

— Employee training focused on participative problem-solving methods.

The supervisor and employee training would be provided initially to participants from a pilot location and later extended to other work groups.

Step 6 — Establishment of Local Pilot Project

After selection of a pilot site with careful attention to the criteria just mentioned, it is vital that the leaders and members of the pilot group be given preparation for what they should expect from the effort. Each participant in the pilot project should be aware:

— Of the background of the company's EI effort.

— That the project is a pilot and as such will have considerable effect on whether and at what pace EI will be expanded within the larger organization.

— That participation is voluntary and may be withdrawn at any time.

Participants in the pilot project should:

— Be trained in group problem-solving methods.

— Be given an understanding of the Steering Committee's make-up and functions.

— Know the role of the EI Administrator and the relationship of the Administrator to the Steering Committee and to the problem-solving group(s).

— Know that the focus of EI groups is on work-related problems as contrasted with Company policy issues.

— Be given additional training as deemed necessary by the Steering Committee on such subjects as group process, effective meetings, listening skills and the like.

Step 7 — Evaluation and Fine Tuning

Following project initiation, the pilot should be carefully monitored to assure the involvement process develops in a constructive fashion and that necessary support and organizational resources are being provided. Such monitoring will enable fine-tuning as all parties learn more about the effective implementation of such efforts.

In addition to monitoring the process, it is necessary to measure on a planned basis the extent to which the pilot is attaining its objectives. These objectives, as well as the means for their measurement, should have been established by the Steering Committee prior to initiation of the project. Such measures may include in-house quality indicators, performance, and employee reactions.

Step 8 — Generalization and Extension

The feedback from the experience with the pilot site will provide the Steering Committee with a working knowledge of the EI process. With this experience at hand they can avoid potential problems and facilitate further expansion of the EI process. To ensure orderly and successful expansion, it is essential that the committee develop a long-range plan that covers such issues as site selection, order of implementation, timing, training, communications and resources.

APPENDIX 23C: THE FORD PULSE: 1994 FORD OF CANADA OPINION SURVEY*

"A Dialogue for Improvement — Your Opinion Counts."

"An assessment by Ford people of our relationships, reputation, and vitality."

Introduction to the Survey

The Ford Pulse is a survey of the opinions of Ford of Canada employees. Through this survey, management hopes to learn more about your opinions concerning work and the work environment, relationships, and important business issues facing the Company.

All Canadian Vehicle Division employees are being asked to participate in the survey. Your participation is completely voluntary. The results will be combined by computer for various employee groups so that individual responses cannot be identified.

To protect the anonymity of your responses no report will be generated for a supervisor if fewer than five employees respond. If fewer than five employees respond under any one identification number, the data will only be collected at the next higher organizational level.

What you say in this survey is completely confidential. Do not sign your name.

How to Complete the Ford Pulse

1. As you go through the Ford Pulse, you will notice various response formats such as "Strongly agree" to "Strongly disagree," "Very satisfied" to "Very dissatisfied," "Very good" to "Very poor," etc. *Please be alert to changes in these response formats.*

2. *Circle only one answer choice for each question.* If a question does not apply to you or you have no idea how to answer it, go on to the next question.

3. Some questions may appear to be repetitive. These questions, while referring to the same general area, express somewhat different ideas.

Reprinted with permission of Ford of Canada. The name "Ford Pulse" was contributed by Hilda Hall and Bob Rideout and the *Opinion Survey*, under that name, was used at all Ford locations.

4. The following definitions apply to terms used throughout the Ford Pulse:

— *Company & Ford* — refer to Ford of Canada.

— *Job* — refers to your current job.

— *Quality* — is a broad term that is defined ultimately by the customer (internal and external) who uses our products and services. Customers want products and services that meet their needs and expectations — at a cost that represents value.

— *Supervisor* — refers to your immediate supervisor, that is, the person to whom you report on a day-to-day basis.

— *Work group* — refers to the people you work with on a day-to-day basis who report to your supervisor. If you are a supervisor, "work group" refers to the other people who report to your superior, *not* your subordinates.

5. Do not spend a lot of time on each question. We would rather have your first thought — your first reaction. Be *completely frank*. Your answers will be useful only if they express the way you really feel.

6 If you are completing the survey on site: put the completed survey in the confidential envelope and return it to your on-site co-ordinator.

If you are completing the survey off-site: put the completed survey in the confidential envelope and return it directly to Questar.

Identification Number

Please enter the identification number of your immediate supervisor in the boxes below. If your immediate supervisor is not shown, use the number for his/her immediate supervisor.

Demographics

This information will allow us to make comparisons among different groups of employees and comparisons with similar groups of employees in other organizations.

Your responses to all questions will be strictly confidential; individual responses will not be seen by anyone within this organization. We appreciate your help in providing this important information.

The demographic data (i.e. Age, Gender, Position, Company Service) will only be collected at a total organizational level to ensure your anonymity.

Please answer each of the following by circling the number next to the description which best fits you.

A. Age

1   Less than 25 years of age
2   25–34 years
3   35–44 years
4   45–54 years
5   55 years or more

C. Position

1   Salary Grades 1–4
2   Salary Grades 5–8
3   Management Roll
4   Supplemental Compensation Roll
5   Private Salary Roll and above
6   Hourly

B. Gender

1   Female
2   Male

D. Company Service

1   Less than 1 year of service
2   1–5 years
3   6–10 years
4   11–15 years
5   16 years or more

Supervision

1 = Strongly Disagree
2 = Disagree
3 = Neither Agree nor Disagree
4 = Agree
5 = Strongly Agree

1. My supervisor inspires high performance
   through his/her personal leadership   1   2   3   4   5

2 My supervisor does a good job of building
   teamwork in his/her work group   1   2   3   4   5

3. My supervisor "sells" new ideas from my
   work group effectively   1   2   3   4   5

4. My supervisor is a good listener   1   2   3   4   5

5. My supervisor does a good job of keeping
   me informed   1   2   3   4   5

6. My supervisor treats everyone fairly   1   2   3   4   5

7. My supervisor clearly explains my job
   assignments   1   2   3   4   5

8. My supervisor gives me feedback that helps
   me improve my performance   1   2   3   4   5

9. My supervisor implements my suggestions
   for solving work-related problems   1   2   3   4   5

10. My supervisor encourages continuous
    improvement   1   2   3   4   5

11. I feel encouraged to come up with new
    and better ways of doing things   1   2   3   4   5

12. My supervisor emphasizes the importance
    of meeting the needs of internal customers
    (people inside the Company who use our work) 1   2   3   4   5

13. My supervisor requires that people do
    high-quality work   1   2   3   4   5

14. When choices have to be made, my
    supervisor usually places quality above
    other business objectives (production
    schedules, budget, etc.)   1   2   3   4   5

15. Sufficient effort is made to get the
    opinions and thinking of people who
    work here   1   2   3   4   5

16. I participate in setting work-related
    objectives   1   2   3   4   5

17. Overall, how good a job do you feel is
    being done by your immediate supervisor?
    1 = Very good
    2 = Good
    3 = Fair
    4 = Poor
    5 = Very poor

Job/Company

1 = Strongly Disagree
2 = Disagree
3 = Neither Agree nor Disagree
4 = Agree
5 = Strongly Agree

18. I look forward to coming to work	1	2	3	4	5
19. My work gives me a feeling of personal accomplishment	1	2	3	4	5
20. I feel valued as an employee of the Company	1	2	3	4	5
21. I like the kind of work I do	1	2	3	4	5
22. My job makes good use of my skills and abilities	1	2	3	4	5
23. Conditions in my job allow me to be about as productive as I could be	1	2	3	4	5
24. I have enough information to do my job well	1	2	3	4	5

25. How do you rate the Company in providing job security for people like yourself?
    1 = Very good
    2 = Good
    3 = Fair
    4 = Poor
    5 = Very poor

1 = Very dissatisfied
2 = Dissatisfied
3 = Neither satisfied nor dissatisfied
4 = Satisfied
5 = Very satisfied

26. Considering everything, how would you rate your overall satisfaction in the Company at the present time?	1	2	3	4	5
27. Considering everything, how satisfied are you with your job?	1	2	3	4	5
28. How satisfied are you with the recognition you receive for doing a good job?	1	2	3	4	5
29. How satisfied are you with the information you receive from management on what's going on in the company?	1	2	3	4	5

30. How satisfied are you with your involvement
    in decisions that affect your work?   1   2   3   4   5

31. How would you rate the Company as a
    company to work for compared to other
    companies?
    1 = One of the best
    2 = Above average
    3 = Average
    4 = Below average
    5 = One of the worst

Work Group/Teamwork

1 = Strongly Disagree
2 = Disagree
3 = Neither Agree nor Disagree
4 = Agree
5 = Strongly Agree

32. My work group lives up to the Company's
    Mission, Values, and Guiding Principles   1   2   3   4   5

33. My local organization (Plant, Depot,
    District, Branch, Office) lives up to the
    Company's Mission, Values, and Guiding
    Principles   1   2   3   4   5

34. The people I work with co-operate to get
    the job done   1   2   3   4   5

35. In my work group, expectations about the
    quality of our work are clear   1   2   3   4   5

36. Day-to-day decisions and activities in my
    work group demonstrate that quality is a top
    priority   1   2   3   4   5

37. There is close co-operation among
    departments to achieve quality   1   2   3   4   5

38. I know my department's objectives
    (quality, cost, timing, etc.)   1   2   3   4   5

39. My work group uses feedback from our
    internal customers (people inside the
    Company who use our work) to improve
    the quality of our work   1   2   3   4   5

40. I know the requirements of my internal
    customers (people inside the Company who
    use my work)   1   2   3   4   5

41. Diversity among employees (e.g., race, sex,
    nationality, age, background, personality,
    thinking style) is valued in my work group   1   2   3   4   5

42. How would you rate the overall quality of
    work done in your work group?
    1 = Very good
    2 = Good
    3 = Fair
    4 = Poor
    5 = Very poor

Quality Emphasis

1 = Strongly Disagree
2 = Disagree
3 = Neither Agree nor Disagree
4 = Agree
5 = Strongly Agree

43. Individuals are recognized for their
    contributions to quality   1   2   3   4   5

44. Groups are recognized for their
    contributions to quality   1   2   3   4   5

45. Measures of quality exist to help assess
    my job performance   1   2   3   4   5

46. I am involved in developing measures of
    quality for my work   1   2   3   4   5

47. The quality of products or services I
    provide my customers is an important
    part of how my performance is viewed   1   2   3   4   5

48. The Company's values concerning quality
    have been communicated clearly to me   1   2   3   4   5

49. My work group receives adequate feedback
    from internal customers (people inside the
    Company who use our work)   1   2   3   4   5

50. I have been involved in continuous
    improvement efforts   1   2   3   4   5

Workload/Stress

1 = Strongly Disagree
2 = Disagree
3 = Neither Agree nor Disagree
4 = Agree
5 = Strongly Agree

51. My workload allows me to satisfy my
    customers' requirements   1   2   3   4   5

52. I do not feel excessive work-related stress   1   2   3   4   5

53. Work-related stress does not interfere with
    doing my job well   1   2   3   4   5

54. My work group has the resources
    (personnel, finances, equipment, tools, etc.)
    necessary to do quality work   1   2   3   4   5

55. The amount of work I am expected to do
    on my job is:
    1 = Far too much
    2 = Too much
    3 = About right
    4 = Too little
    5 = Far too little

Empowerment

1 = Strongly Disagree
2 = Disagree
3 = Neither Agree nor Disagree
4 = Agree
5 = Strongly Agree

56. I can make some improvements at work
    without checking first with my supervisor   1   2   3   4   5

57. I have the authority to make decisions that
     improve the quality of my work   1   2   3   4   5

Training & Development

1 = Strongly Disagree
2 = Disagree
3 = Neither Agree nor Disagree
4 = Agree
5 = Strongly Agree

58. I have received the training I need to do a
     quality job   1   2   3   4   5

59. I am given a real opportunity to improve
     my skills in the Company   1   2   3   4   5

60. In my work, I find it easy to apply the
     training I have received   1   2   3   4   5

61. How satisfied are you with the training you
     received for your present job?
     1 = Very satisfied
     2 = Satisfied
     3 = Neither satisfied nor dissatisfied
     4 = Dissatisfied
     5 = Very dissatisfied

Miscellaneous

1 = Strongly Disagree
2 = Disagree
3 = Neither Agree nor Disagree
4 = Agree
5 = Strongly Agree

62. People in my work area are protected from
     health and safety hazards   1   2   3   4   5

63. I believe my supervisor will do something
     about issues that are identified in this survey   1   2   3   4   5

64. To improve, we need the kind of feedback
     this survey provides   1   2   3   4   5

65. How satisfied are you with your physical
    working conditions?
    1 = Very satisfied
    2 = Satisfied
    3 = Neither satisfied nor dissatisfied
    4 = Dissatisfied
    5 = Very dissatisfied

Leadership

1 = Strongly Disagree
2 = Disagree
3 = Neither Agree nor Disagree
4 = Agree
5 = Strongly Agree

66. My supervisor has established a climate of
    openness and trust   1   2   3   4   5

67. My supervisor involves employees in
    decision making   1   2   3   4   5

68. My supervisor ensures that employees
    function as an effective team   1   2   3   4   5

69. My supervisor transfers to employees the
    necessary authority to accomplish tasks   1   2   3   4   5

70. My supervisor ensures that all decisions are
    made based on what's best for Ford, not on
    just what's best for the department   1   2   3   4   5

71. My supervisor provides both positive and
    negative performance feedback   1   2   3   4   5

72. My supervisor provides the discipline,
    accountability and support required to
    ensure objectives are achieved   1   2   3   4   5

73. My supervisor ensures communication
    between departments   1   2   3   4   5

74. My supervisor ensures communication
    within the department   1   2   3   4   5

75. My supervisor works with employees to
    improve performance and develop capabilities   1   2   3   4   5

76. My supervisor ensures employees receive
    opportunities for development assignments
    in other related functions. 1 2 3 4 5

77. My supervisor rewards and recognizes
    employees who make improvements in
    key process areas. 1 2 3 4 5

Compensation and Benefits

1 = Strongly Disagree
2 = Disagree
3 = Neither Agree nor Disagree
4 = Agree
5 = Strongly Agree

78. From what I hear, our benefits are comparable
    to or better than those of other companies 1 2 3 4 5

79. If I perform better on my job, I will get
    more money 1 2 3 4 5

1 = Very poor
2 = Poor
3 = Fair
4 = Good
5 = Very good

80. How do you rate your total benefits
    program (insurance, medical, etc.)? 1 2 3 4 5

81. How do you rate the amount of pay you
    get on your job? 1 2 3 4 5

82. In comparison with people in similar jobs
    in other companies, I feel my pay is:
    1 = Much higher
    2 = Slightly higher
    3 = About the same
    4 = Slightly lower
    5 = Much lower

Personnel Relations

1 = Strongly Disagree
2 = Disagree
3 = Neither Agree nor Disagree
4 = Agree
5 = Strongly Agree

83. If I were treated unfairly by my supervisor,
    I would discuss the matter with higher level
    management   1   2   3   4   5

84. If I were treated unfairly by my supervisor,
    I would discuss the matter with Employee
    Relations   1   2   3   4   5

85. People around here view harassment
    (sexual, racial, and other) as unacceptable   1   2   3   4   5

86. It is unlikely that I will actively look for a
    new job outside the Company in the next year 1   2   3   4   5

87. I would rather work in this Company than
    most others I know about   1   2   3   4   5

88. Concerns about my benefits are responded
    to adequately by Personnel Services   1   2   3   4   5

89. How satisfied are you with your opportunity
    to get a better job in the Company?
    1 = Very satisfied
    2 = Satisfied
    3 = Neither satisfied nor dissatisfied
    4 = Dissatisfied
    5 = Very dissatisfied

Standards

1 = Not applicable
2 = Strongly Disagree
3 = Disagree
4 = Neither Agree nor Disagree
5 = Agree
6 = Strongly Agree

90. I understand my role in implementing
    Dealer-to-Customer Standards   1   2   3   4   5   6

91. I am personally involved in actions to help
    meet Dealer-to-Customer Standards   1   2   3   4   5   6

92. I receive adequate training to help meet
    superior purchase or service experience
    Standards   1   2   3   4   5   6

93. My management fully supports my actions
    to achieve superior purchase or service
    experience Standards.   1   2   3   4   5   6

94. I am recognized or rewarded for my
    contributions in supporting superior
    purchase or service experience Standards   1   2   3   4   5   6

95. I believe my department is committed to
    implementing Standards to achieve
    Customer Satisfaction   1   2   3   4   5   6

96. I believe the Company is committed to
    implementing Standards to achieve
    Customer Satisfaction   1   2   3   4   5   6

Miscellaneous Supplemental

1 = Strongly Disagree
2 = Disagree
3 = Neither Agree nor Disagree
4 = Agree
5 = Strongly Agree

97. My work group is committed to doing a
    good job   1   2   3   4   5

98. I change personal priorities at times in order
    to meet important work deadlines   1   2   3   4   5

99. Departments here co-operate to get the
    job done   1   2   3   4   5

100. In my work group, everyone's opinions get
     listened to   1   2   3   4   5

101. Senior corporate management shows by its
     actions that quality is a top priority in the
     Company   1   2   3   4   5

102. I understand the Company's Mission,
     Values, and Guiding Principles statement   1   2   3   4   5

103. My work group conducts it business with
     integrity   1   2   3   4   5

104. I am interested in alternate work schedules
     (e.g., job sharing, part-time, sabbaticals)   1   2   3   4   5

105. How would you rate the overall effort to
      reduce costs in your work group?
      1 = Very good
      2 = Good
      3 = Fair
      4 = Poor
      5 = Very poor

Your Suggestions

1. In my view, the three biggest opportunities for improvement at Ford of
   Canada involve: (please circle only three)

1	Equipment	9	Morale
2	Workload	10	Problem Solving/
3	Training		Decision Making
4	Communication	11	Innovation
5	Working Conditions	12	Recognition
6	Over Controlled	13	Compensation
7	Clear Goals/		(Benefits and Pay)
	Procedures	14	Job Security
8	Career	15	Supervision
	Opportunities	16	Other

2. Of the three issues that you identified in response to (1) above, which one is
   the top issue that Ford of Canada should address? (Please circle *only one*.)

   1   2   3   4   5   6   7   8   9   10   11   12   13   14   15   16

3. Please refer to your choice of the top issues, and provide your suggestions
   on what needs to be done in this area. (Response to this item is optional.)

Thank you for participating in the Ford Pulse

CHAPTER 24

WARRINGTON INDUSTRIES LIMITED
(Collective Bargaining
Simulation #1)

Little Progress in Renegotiating the Collective Agreement

Warrington Industries Limited, a fairly old, but steadily growing Toronto electrical firm, is faced with the task of re-negotiating the two-year collective agreement that it has with the Associated Electrical Workers Union, Local 672. Despite intensive bargaining by the negotiators for both sides, little progress has so far been made. Unfortunately, the present agreement which covers only the Toronto plant, is due to expire soon.

Non-unionized Quebec Plant

The company also owns a plant in Quebec which, so far, is not unionized. The Quebec employees are paid less than their Ontario counterparts. The number of workers in the bargaining unit at the Toronto plant, which has been in operation for about 35 years, is 955. Recently, about 200 Toronto employees were laid off. The Quebec plant, now seven years old, employs 800 persons most of whom have been hired during the last three years.

Financial Situation of Toronto Plant

Last year, the Toronto plant's total sales revenue was just under $63 million, compared with $69 million the previous year. Net income after tax was $3.1 million last year and $3.9 million the year before. Of this amount, two-thirds was distributed in the form of dividends to shareholders, and one-third reinvested. Total assets of the Toronto plant now amount to $21 million as compared with short-term liabilities, mainly to its bank and suppliers, of $6 million and a long-term mortgage loan on the land and buildings of the Toronto plant of $5 million. The loan, which bears a 10% per annum interest rate, is due for repayment in 12 years' time. The money was used three years ago mainly to expand and modernize the Quebec plant. Despite the unsettled political climate, the company's board of directors see a bright future for the firm's operations in that province. Much of the output of the Quebec plant is now shipped to the U.S.,Western Europe, and other foreign markets, as well as to Canadian markets.

Products Manufactured

The products manufactured are the same at both the Toronto and Quebec plants, consisting mainly of commercial and residential heating equipment, including thermostatic controls. Solar heating panels are now being produced in limited quality and company officials are optimistic that this area will experience the biggest growth in the years ahead. Most of the plant's output is sold to building firms and building suppliers. Employees work on a two-shift basis with a 20-cent per hour bonus for those on the second shift.

No Official Strikes

So far there have been no official strikes at either the Toronto or Quebec plants. However, the union came very close to calling one in Toronto, at the time of the previous contract negotiations. It was only averted by management's last-minute agreement to make union membership a condition of employment. Despite strenuous efforts, the union has been unable to obtain sufficient support among the Quebec plant employees to be certified as their official bargaining agent. It seems likely that another Quebec-based union may gradually secure the required worker support.

Wages Paid

In the Toronto plant, the average wage is now about $15.20 per hour whereas in the Quebec plant it is about $13.20. The present agreement includes a COLA provision whereby an increase of 0.5 in the Consumer Price Index entitles an employee to a 1-cent increase in his or her hourly rate of pay. Because of inflation, this is considered an extremely important fringe benefit. The adjustments in wage rates are made on a quarterly basis. Other benefits include: ten paid holidays; a vacation plan under which employees receive 2 weeks' annual paid vacation after one year of employment and 3 weeks after five years; medical premiums paid by the company; and a contributory pension plan in which the company matches the employees' contributions. Altogether, these cost the company about $1.85 per hour worked.

Management-Labour Relations

Management-labour relations have been quite good at both plants. However, an incident at the Toronto plant two months ago resulted in an illegal temporary work stoppage, or "wildcat" strike. One of the shop stewards was dismissed from work after an argument with a foreman. The shop steward was alleged to have used abusive language and to have threatened the foreman with physical violence ("I'll knock your teeth out"). Following his dismissal, employees in the department in which the steward worked put down their tools and went home. They then picketed the plant and managed to stop production for three days until management agreed to reinstate the steward.

Wildcat Strike

Because of the wildcat strike and the resultant loss of production, the company threatened to attempt to collect damages from the union. The company argued that there had been a breach of Article 35 of the Agreement which stated that:

> "There will be no strikes, slowdowns, or other interruption of production because of labour disputes during the contract period. Employees who engage in such prohibited activity are subject to discharge."

The union protested that it had not given its official support to the strike. But the company argued that the union should have prevented its members (a) from going on strike and (b) from picketing the plant. The company also argued that it was the belligerent attitude of the union's official, the shop steward, that had precipitated the crisis. Although the shop steward had been temporarily reinstated in his job, the company feels strongly that any settlement with the union should include disciplinary action against him.

Handling of Grievances

Under the present Agreement, any grievances must be handled according to a standard procedure that culminates, if necessary, in binding arbitration. However, the right to arbitration does not apply to grievances about production standards as management has retained the right, under the management rights clause of the Agreement, to determine them unilaterally. Nevertheless, there has been quite a large number of grievances about production standards — mainly to the effect that they were "unreasonably high". However, most of these were rejected by management.

Seniority

Another point of contention between labour and management has been the application of seniority in promotions and layoffs. According to the Agreement, the company must take into account both length of service and ability when deciding on promotion. Specifically, the Agreement states that seniority should apply when a senior employee has the same qualifications for the job as a junior employee. Bidding for promotion occurs on a departmental basis. In practice, the company has leaned heavily towards ability, or "merit", and promoted junior employees. This has resulted in a number of grievances, about half of which have been upheld by the arbitrator. With regard to layoffs, the company has generally honoured the seniority clause in the agreement. This has meant therefore that many junior employees have been laid off in Toronto over the last three years. Supervisors in the plant have bitterly complained that the company is losing many of its best employees. This situation has been aggravated by the existence in the Agreement of plant-wide "bumping" rights for employees who are to be laid off, even though the layoff may be only a temporary one. Under the Agreement, shop stewards and other union officials are given "super-seniority". In other words, they are protected from layoff. On average, a steward spends about twelve hours per week of company-paid time on union business. Some foremen complain that stewards often use "union business" as an excuse for "goofing off". However, this is strenuously denied by the union whenever the matter is brought up.

Overtime Work

According to the present Agreement, management can require employees to work overtime. Early this year, however, a large number of employees refused to do so when called upon. Only when threatened with dismissal did they comply and then only unwillingly. Management has the right under the Agreement to choose the persons who are to work overtime. However, this right has led to charges by the union that foremen often exercise favouritism in this respect, permitting some people rather than others to earn extra money.

Skilled Trades

At the Toronto plant, there are five types of maintenance trades: carpenters, electricians, plumbers, mechanics, and tool and die workers. In the past, each type of skilled tradesperson performed only tasks related to his particular trade. Recently, on grounds of efficiency, management has insisted that, if no appropriate skilled work needs to be done, the tradespersons should do other jobs allocated to them.

Subcontracting

This year the company decided to subcontract out several tasks previously performed by the electricians, plumbers, and carpenters. This has aroused the ire of the union as some of these tradespersons were later laid off. However, the union has been unable to do anything about it except to complain. This is because, under the Agreement, the company retains the right to subcontract work when it deems it advisable.

New Technology

Another issue that has arisen more and more frequently in the Toronto plant is the introduction of new technology. These more automated methods of production have meant a reduction in the workforce. Many of the workers laid off have found great difficulty in finding alternative employment and some are still unemployed. Management has indicated that competitive firms are more highly automated. Also the latest round of tariff cuts is expected to make foreign competition even fiercer.

Women in the Plant

Women comprise 12 per cent of the work force and complain that they are not treated as well as the men.

Age

The average age of employees in the Toronto plant is 45.

Discipline

Management has frequently complained to the union that workers are slow returning from their "coffee breaks" (a 10-minute rest period every four hours). Occasionally, a worker has been reprimanded or even dismissed for being drunk on the job.

ASSIGNMENT

Each management and union team should, by negotiations, try to resolve the differences between them as the basis for a new Labour Agreement.

JACKSON ELECTRICAL ASSEMBLIES
(Collective Bargaining Simulation #2)

Jackson Electrical Assemblies Ltd. is an electrical manufacturer, located in Oakville, Ontario, which has grown steadily in recent years but which is now faced with the task of renegotiating its collective agreement with the Associated Electrical Workers' Union, Local 762.

Waiting for Conciliator's Report

Despite intensive bargaining by representatives of both sides, little progress has so far been made. Conciliation services have been used and the parties are waiting for the report of the conciliation officer to be released by the Minister of Labour recommending that no conciliation board be established. This will mean the Union then has the right to strike within 14 days.

No offer has been made by the company to the union.

Two Plants

The company also owns a plant, located in Brockville, Eastern Ontario, which so far has not been unionized. The employees in Brockville are paid less than those in Oakville.

The number of employees in the bargaining unit in the Oakville plant which has been in operation for about 20 years is 1,100. Last year about 100 of the Oakville employees were laid off. The Brockville plant, now 5 years old, employs 500 persons most of whom have been hired in the last 4 years.

Financial Situation

Last year the Oakville plant's total sales revenue was just under $60 million compared with about $67 million the previous year. Net income after tax was about $2.9 million last year and $3.7 million the year before. Of this amount about 2/3 was distributed in dividends and 1/3 reinvested. Total assets of the Oakville plant amount to $31 million as compared with short term liabilities, mainly to its bank and suppliers, of $6 million. There is also a short-term loan of $4 million owing to the employees' pension plan. Long-term liabilities consist solely of a $10 million mortgage loan on the Oakville plant. The loan bears a 12% annual interest rate and is due for repayment in 10 years. The money was used mainly to expand and equip the Brockville plant.

Bright Future

The company's board of directors see a bright future for the Brockville plant because its location on highway 401 and the St. Lawrence Seaway provides ready transportation to the Ontario market and foreign markets and its location, compared to Oakville, offers no significant disadvantage in reaching the Western Canadian market.

The products manufactured in the two plants are largely the same and are related primarily to the commercial and residential construction markets. Management is confident that these markets will develop successfully in the years ahead.

Employees work on a two shift basis, with a 20¢ premium for the second shift.

Union-Company Relations

The Oakville plant was organized by the Union 10 years ago. Management was convinced that employees had been misled by the union to join the union. In the first negotiations, the union rejected the company's "final offer" and threatened to strike. The company's reaction was that our employees will not support a strike. However, the union called a strike, which was 100% effective. Three days later, the company agreed to the union demands in order to settle the strike.

Since then, in each set of negotiations, settlement has been reached on a reasonably amicable basis without a strike. The settlements have related closely to industry patterns.

Brockville Plant

Since the company opened its second plant in Brockville, the union has tried to organize it without success. While wages in Brockville are lower than those paid in Oakville, apparently because of the relatively high unemployment rate in Eastern Ontario and perhaps because of the lower living costs, employees seem to value the opportunity of working for the company. They seem to feel that wages are relatively good for the area which, apparently to them, is a more desirable location.

Other unions have demonstrated their interest in representing the employees in the Brockville plant.

Wages and Benefits

In the Oakville plant, the average wage is $14.80 per hour while in the Brockville plant it is $12.95. There is no provision for a cost-of-living allowance in the Oakville agreement.

Benefits include 10 paid holidays, vacations of 2 weeks after 1 year and 3 weeks after 5 years, medical premiums paid by the company, and a contributory pension plan in which the employer matches the employees' contributions. The cost of these benefits to the company is about $1.65 per employee hour.

Production Standards

Generally, relations have been reasonable in both plants. However, recently in the Oakville plant, the company had been correcting, or as the union said, tightening production standards. In one department, this resulted in an illegal work stoppage.

The company threatened to try to collect damages from the union through the grievance procedure. The union exerted considerable pressure and the company announced it would not proceed, in the interest of good employee relations.

Management has retained the right to set production standards and as a result they are not subject to arbitration. Many employees think the production standards are unreasonably tight.

The company has increased its activity regarding the introduction of new labour-saving technology. This has resulted in a reduction in the work force, with employee concern for more such changes in the future.

Management has indicated that competitive companies are highly automated and that the latest round of tariff cuts under the North American Free Trade Agreement will make U.S. competition more severe.

Management is also concerned about increased production costs involved in compliance with occupational health and safety regulations and employee equity plans.

Takeover Bid

Lately, there have been rumours that a U.S. firm is planning a takeover bid for the Canadian company. It has been speculated that, if this happens, one of the company's plants may be closed.

ASSIGNMENT

Each management and union team should, by negotiations, try to resolve the differences between them as the basis for a new Labour Agreement.

SHAW ENTERPRISES LTD.
(Costing Increases in Wages and Benefits)

Shaw Enterprises Ltd. operates a plant employing 100 full-time workers each of whom is normally scheduled to work 40 hours per week. The average wage rate is calculated to be $10.00 per hour.

Calculation of a One-Cent-Per-Hour Wage Increase

Assume that each employee works 2,080 hours per year (40 hours x 52 weeks).

For each 1¢/hour wage increase per employee, the extra yearly cost to the company is calculated as follows:

Per employee
(2,080 hours per employee) x ($0.01 increase) = $20.80 per employee

For all employees
$20.80 x 100 employees = $2,080/year increase in total wages

Assume that overtime worked costs the company an extra 10% payment per employee. Then the total annual cost of a 1¢/hour wage increase is:

$2,080 x (10% of $2,080) = $2,288

Proof
Calculation of Total Wages/Year at $10/hour

100 employees x 2,080 hours	208,000 hours
x $10.00	$2,080,000
plus overtime factor of 10%	$ 208,000
Total Wages Paid to 100 Employees Per Year	$2,288,000

Calculation of Total Wages/Year at $10.01/hour

100 employees x 2,080 hours	208,000 hours
x $10.01	$2,082,080
plus overtime factor of 10%	$ 208,208
Total Wages Paid	$2,290,288

Increase in yearly cost:

$2,290,288 minus $2,288,000 = $2,288

Algebraic Equation to Calculate Yearly Increase in Total Cost

Assuming a 40 hour work week, 52 weeks worked per year and a 10% over-time ratio,

let x = # of employees
let y = cent/hour increase union is demanding
EQUATION: 2080xy + (10% of 2080xy)
        or 2080xy + (.1 $\times$ 2080xy)

Plugging in for our first example of a ... 1¢/hour increase,

$\qquad$ 2080 (100) (.01) + [.1 $\times$ (2080) (100) (.01)]
$\qquad$ = 2080 + 208
$\qquad$ = 2288

for a 5¢/hour increase

$\qquad$ 2080 (100) (.05) + [.1 $\times$ (2080) (100) (.05)]
$\qquad$ = 10,400 + 1,040
$\qquad$ = 11,440

Costing One Additional Plant Holiday

The union proposes one additional plant holiday in the first year of the agreement.

The increased cost to Shaw Enterprises would be as follows:

One employee: 40 hours/week $\times$ 52 weeks = 2080 hours/year. Therefore 1¢/hour equals $20.80

An employee, earning $10.00/hour for 8 hours, earns $80.00 per day. Therefore one day equals approximately 4¢/hour (80/20.80). Therefore:

Cost for one employee per year: $0.04 $\times$ 2,080 = $83.20
Cost for all employees per year: $83.20 $\times$ 100 employees = $8,320

Costing Medical Benefits

The union demands that Shaw Enterprises pay for certain medical and dental benefits for the 100 employees, 40% of whom are single, and 60% of whom are married and have families.
Medical Costs: $29.75/month single rate
$\qquad$ $59.50/month family rate

Therefore 40 employees $\times$ 12 months $\times$ $29.75 = $14,280.00
$\qquad$ 60 employees $\times$ 12 months $\times$ $59.50 = $42,840.00
$\qquad$ Total cost to Shaw Enterprises per year $57,120.00

Costing a Reduction in Vacation Qualifying Period

The union demands a reduction in the qualifying period for 3 weeks vacation to 10 years of service instead of 12 years.

Seniority lists are needed for this costing procedure. In Shaw Enterprises, 20% of the employees have 10 or more years of service but less than 12.

Therefore: 20% of 100 = 20 employees who would benefit from the extra one week's vacation.

If these 20 employees were to be replaced by the company for one week at equal cost;

> 20 employees x 40 hours x $10.00/hour = $8,000 extra cost

The company's annual hours are

> 2,080 hours per employee x 100 employees = 208,000 hours

Therefore, the average annual increase cost equals approximately 4¢/hour ($8,000/208,000) or, on the average, $80 per employee ($8,000/100).

Cautionary Remarks

All the above cost calculations are based on the assumption that employees work 40 hours per week and 52 weeks per year. However, in practice, actual time worked may be less or more because of:

a) sickness, lateness, and absenteeism

b) holidays and vacations

c) layoffs

d) fluctuations in overtime worked

   In addition, the labour cost is not just the wage cost. It is also necessary to include the cost of so-called fringe benefits such as group insurance, pensions, bonuses, parking, cafeteria, etc. Also, the cost per hour will vary with the number of hours worked by each employee, since the cost of the employee benefits will be spread over a larger or a smaller number of hours.

ASSIGNMENT

1. The A.M. Company has 500 employees in their Winnipeg plant who are now earning an average of $20.00 per hour. The union is demanding a 15¢/hour wage increase per employee. What will the increase in yearly cost be to the company? (Assume a 40 hour work week, 52 weeks worked and a 10% overtime factor).

2. The union demands a reduction in the qualifying period for 3 weeks vacation, to 5 years of service, instead of 10 years. What will be the increase in yearly cost to the company?

    (Assume that 30% of the employees have 5 or more years of service but less than 10 years).

CHAPTER 25: CONSOLIDATED ELECTRICAL PRODUCTS (Collective Bargaining Simulation #3)

25.1 COMPANY BACKGROUND

Consolidated Electrical Products Inc. is a medium-sized manufacturing firm located on the outskirts of a large Canadian city. In its fairly old plant, it makes light apparatus such as visual landing aids for aircraft pilots; and electric heating units for high-rise apartment buildings and private homes. Last year, it did a substantial amount of export business as well as secure and complete several lucrative government contracts.

Top Management

The president and major stockholder of the company is Albert Walters, who started the firm in a rented garage almost twenty years ago. Assisting him in top management are Jack Morley, Vice-President Manufacturing; Peter Saccomano, Vice-President Marketing; and Jennie Chow, Vice President, Finance. All three vice-presidents have had many years of experience in this and other industries. However, the vice-president marketing has only been with the firm for eleven months. He replaced Graham Cook, the former marketing manager, who left to join another firm. The president has threatened, albeit subtly, that all the vice-presidents' jobs will be on the line if the firm's overall performance in its traditional domestic product lines does not improve.

Plant Environment

So far the firm has been characterized by the fact that it pays above-average wages and rarely lays anyone off. Also, the employees, although unionized, get on quite well with management, particularly at the supervisory levels. However, this situation may well change if management goes ahead with its plan to establish a methods department, raise production quotas, and replace present equipment with new, up-to-date labour-saving machines.

Employee Benefits

The employees have a benefit package providing medical-surgical hospital benefits, a sick benefit plan to provide 60% of earnings during absence due to illness for up to 52 weeks, and life insurance coverage of $10,000 per employee, all of which is paid 75% by the company and 25% by the employee.

The company also contributes an amount equivalent to 5% of each employee's earnings into a pension fund which will be used to buy a pension for each employee at age 65.

Work Force

The work force was substantially increased last year to cope with the extra orders, and now numbers 640.

Contract Negotiations

The firm's present collective agreement with the International Assemblers Union of America is due to expire this year. Negotiations for a new agreement are to be conducted by two teams:

For the firm:

> Director of Industrial Relations
> Vice-President Manufacturing
> Assistant to the Director of Industrial Relations
> Plant Manager

For the union:

> President, Union Local 265
> Business Agent, Union Local 265
> International Representative
> Department Steward, Machine Shop

The existing agreement is shown in Chapter 26 of this book. For purposes of this simulation, N/C alongside an item, means that no change is permitted.

25.2 PARTICIPANT'S ROLE IN THE SIMULATION

In this simulation, you are required to act as a member of one of the teams, as directed by your Instructor. So that the whole class can participate, there will be more than one set of negotiations going on at the same time, with the teams labelled A, B, C, etc.

Your task is to help negotiate a new collective agreement that is satisfactory to the persons you represent — either the firm's shareholders or the union members.

Evaluation of Your Performance

Your performance will be judged by your Instructor, on the basis of (a) the way in which you and your team conduct negotiations, (b) the written reports submitted by you or your team, and (c) the collective agreement finally made and the extent to which it corresponds with your team's initial objectives.

25.3 STEPS INVOLVED IN THE SIMULATION

1. *Getting Organized*

   - Instructor divides class into negotiating teams:

Company, Team A	Union, Team A
Company, Team B	Union, Team B
Company, Team C	Union, Team C

   - Each team:
     — allocates roles to members,
     — agrees when to meet out of class, if necessary,
     — discusses firm's and employees' situations,
     — examines the existing collective agreement.

2. *Making Plans*

   - Determine bargaining objectives.

     — Make a list of changes required, showing priorities,

     — Estimate the cost of the changes.

   - Decide on an initial negotiating position.

   - Decide on an intermediate negotiating position.

   - Decide on your target final position.

   - Summarize your conclusions in a Planning Report. This is to be given to your Instructor before negotiations begin.

3. *Conducting Negotiations*

   - Company and union teams submit their initial proposals to each other, together with supporting arguments. At the request of either team, clarifications should be made.

- Each team gives its initial reaction to the other team's proposals and comments on the implications of such proposals.

4. *Reviewing Negotiations*

- Discuss the reaction of the other team to your initial proposal.

- Discuss the other team's initial proposals.

- Estimate the other team's priorities.

- Estimate the other team's acceptable minimum.

- Determine your acceptable minimum.

5. *Reaching an Agreement*

- Go over the agreement, article by article.

- Try to reach an agreement first on non-controversial points.

- Gradually work through the more controversial points.

6. *Written Report*

- At the completion of negotiations, submit a written report to your Instructor.

- Show in the report your final settlement (or, if there is no settlement, the position of your team and that of the team with whom you were bargaining).

- Show the various steps you took in the bargaining process.

- Show how you deviated from your plan as previously set out in your Planning Report.

  NOTE: Your Instructor will tell you how many negotiation meetings are to be held. He or she may also decide to bring in a government conciliation officer. If no agreement is reached, the employees will go on strike and the company will lock them out. There is no provision for arbitration.

25.4 COSTING DATA

Overtime

Assume the average amount of overtime worked by each employee is 4 hours per month.

Call-in Pay

Assume this happens once per year per employee and that extra paid hours return no extra work to the company.

Holiday Qualifications

If you remove this qualification on holiday pay, assume a 2% loss in productivity during the day before and day after the holiday, i.e., a total of 4% of a day's pay per holiday.

Holiday Overtime

Assume this happens once per employee per year.

Vacation Pay

Years of service:	Number of employees
Less than one	58
One but less than three	20
Three but less than five	402
Five but less than ten	81
Ten but less than fifteen	37
Fifteen but less than twenty	42
	640

Wages

In addition to any wage increase, negotiated incentive wages will increase.

Fifty per cent of the employees in the bargaining unit are on an incentive wage payment plan and they average 20% above their base rates.

Employment Benefits

Report added costs in terms of cents-per-hour equivalent. For example, if the negotiated change provides pension benefits at a cost of 3% of payroll, report a cost equal to the cent-per-hour equivalent of 3% of payroll.

You may, however, bargain exact benefits indicating details and cost.

Shift Work

On average, 1/3 of the employees are on the second shift. There is no third shift.

Job Levels

The number of employees in each job level is shown in Table 25.1.

Table 25.1 — *Number of Employees in each Job Level*

1	—	120
2	—	0
3	—	94
5	—	183
6	—	65
7	—	12
8	—	85
9	—	43
10	—	8
11	—	10
12	—	20
		640

25.5 MANUFACTURING INDUSTRY DATA

Table 25.2 contains a summary of wage adjustments in seventeen collective agreements covering 5,750 union-represented employees. The average length of all the agreements is two and a half years. Eleven firms have frozen wages in the first year, with five of the freezes continuing into the second year and two into the third year. The average hourly rate of pay is $17.85, with $19.85 for top skilled employees and $15.24 for general labour. Seven of the agreements have active cost-of-living allowances.

Table 25.3 summarizes the annual paid holidays, vacations with pay, and shift premiums provided for in the seventeen agreements.

Canada Labour View Reports

Current detailed information about recently signed collective agreements in different industry sectors is contained in *CLV Reports: Facts and Trends*, published weekly by Carswell, & Thomson Company, One Corporate Plaza, 2075 Kennedy Road, Toronto, Ontario M1T 3V4.

Table 25.2 — *Summary of Wage Adjustments in Seventeen Collective Agreements*

Co. No. / No. of Employees	Wage Adjustments		Rates of Pay	
1. 54	First Year	– wage freeze	Labour	– $ 9.35
	Second Year	– wage freeze	Plant M'tce	– $18.93
	Third Year	– 3.0%, average 40¢	Average	– $12.98
2. 73	First Year	– wage freeze	Labour	– $18.92
	Second Year	– 1.0%, average 19¢	Refrig. Mech	– $20.05
	Third Year	– 2.5%, average 48¢	Average	– $19.32
3. 24	First Year	– 30 ¢, average 2.4% plus $100 lump sum	Labour	– $12.18
			Lead Hand	– $12.68
	Second Year	– 60¢, average 4.7%	Average	– $12.40
4. 350	First Year	– wage freeze	Labour	– $16.06
	Second Year	– 2.0% , average 36¢	Elect. Tech.	– $18.66
	Third Year	– 2.0%, average 36¢	Average	– $17.80
5. 70	First Year	– wage freeze	Labour	– $16.65
			Trades	– $19.74
	COLA: remains inactive over term of agreement		Average	– $17.22
6. 103	First Year	– 1.0%, average 14 ¢	Labour	– $10.88
	Second Year	– 3.0%, average 45¢	Specialty Fitter/Welder	– $18.04
	Third Year	– 3.0%, average 46¢		
	COLA: 1 ¢ for each 0.125 change in CPI (1981=100), adjusted quarterly		Average	– $15.29

7. 244
First Year	– wage freeze, $350 lump sum	Labour	– $17.97
Second Year	– 1.5%, average 28¢	Tool & Die Maker	– $ 21.78
Third Year	– 1.9%, average 36¢	Average	– $ 20.32

COLA: 1¢ for each 0.3 change in CPI (1971=100), adjusted and paid quarterly as lump sum

8. 35
First Year	– wage freeze	Labour	– $17.97
Second Year	– 30¢, average 2.3%	Tool & Die Maker	– $ 21.78
		Average	– $ 20.32

9. 965
First Year	– wage freeze	Start Rate	– $11.12
Second Year	– wage freeze, plus attendance bonus of 20¢ per hour worked	Tractor-Trailer Driver	– $ 15.23
		Average	– $ 14.00

10. 2,100
First Year	– wage freeze	Labour	– $18.84
Second Year	– 2.0% to wage groups 1 to 8	Tool Maker	– $ 22.72
	2.5% to groups 9 to 17	Average	– $ 19.61
	average labour 2.06%, or 40¢		
Third Year	– 2.0% to groups 1 to 8		
	2.5% to groups 9 to 17		
	average about 2.06%, or 40¢		

COLA: 1¢ for each 0.096 change in CPI (1986=100)

11. 90
First Year	– wage freeze	Labour	– $14.26
Second Year	– wage freeze	Electrical M'tce	–$ 16.90
Third Year	– 2.0%, average 29¢	Average	– $ 14.64

COLA: inactive in first year, 1 cent for each 0.3 change in CPI (1971=100) in excess of 6.0% a year, adjusted quarterly, capped at 25¢

12.	139	First Year	– 3.0%, average 59¢	Technician	– $ 17.09
		Second Year	– 2.0%, average 40¢	Master Operator	– $ 26.13
				Average	– $ 20.59
13.	185	First Year	– 2.0%, average 31¢	Inspector-Assembler	– $14.44
		Second Year	– 2.0%, average 32¢	Millwright	–$ 20.39
		COLA: 1 cent for each 0.35 change in CPI (1986=100) in excess of 2.0% above a December base each year		Average	– $ 16.04
14.	265	First Year	– 3.0%, average 56¢, plus 20 cents to skilled trades, etc.	Labour	– $19.09
		Second Year	– 3.0%, average 58¢	Journeyman Mech.	–$ 21.31
		Third Year	– 3.5%, average 70¢	Average	– $ 19.51
15.	420	First Year	– 5¢, average 0.5%, an early adjustment plus a $300 signing bonus	Labour	– $ 11.05
		Second Year	– 5¢, average 0.4%	Tool & Die Maker	– $ 18.86
		Third Year	– 7.5¢, average 0.6%	Average	– $ 12.05
		COLA: 1¢ for each 0.4 increase in the all-Canada CPI (1971=100), adjusted quarterly			
16.	300	First Year	– wage freeze, plus $150 lump sum	Labour	– $ 14.20
		Second Year	– $250 lump sum	Tool & Die Maker	– $ 20.69
		Third Year	– $350 lump sum	Average	– $ 15.08
		COLA: 1¢ for each 0.45 change in CPI (1961=100), adjusted every six months			
17.	375	First Year	– wage freeze, plus $250 lump sum	Assembler	– $ 12.14
		Second Year	– $300 lump sum	Prod. Mech. I	– $ 15.39
		Third Year	– $300 lump sum	Average	– $ 12.29

Table 25.3 —*Annual Paid Holidays, Vacations with Pay, and Shift Premiums in Seventeen Agreements*

Co. No.	Paid Holidays	Vacations with Pay (weeks after years)	Shift Premium
1.	12	3 after 5, 4 after 10, 5 after 20	0¢ – 70¢ – 40¢
2.	12	3 after 5, 4 after 10, 5 after 20, 6 after 30	0¢ – 55¢
3.	13	3 after 6, 4 after 13, 5 after 20	N/A
4.	14	3 after 5, 4 after 10, 5 after 15, 6 after 25	0¢ – 75¢ – 75¢
5.	12	3 after 4, 4 after 10, 5 after 18, 6 after 28	0¢ – 80¢ – 80¢
6.	13	3 after 5, 4 after 12, 5 after 20	0% – 5% – 7%
7.	13	3 after 3, 4 after 10, 5 after 20, 6 after 30	0¢ – 50¢ – 75¢
8.	13	3 after 5, 4 after 13, 5 after 22	0¢ – 30¢ – 45¢
9.	11	3 after 5, 4 after 9, 5 after 20	0¢ – 40¢
10.	13	3 after 4, 4 after 12, 5 after 20	0¢ – 50¢ – 50¢
11.	12	3 after 4, 4 after 12, 5 after 21, 6 after 30	0¢ – 50¢ – 65¢
12.	12	3 after 1, 4 after 10, 5 after 20, 6 after 25	0¢ – 87¢ – $1.50
13.	13	3 after 4, 4 after 11, 5 after 23, 6 after 30	0¢ – 55¢ – 75¢
14.	12	3 after 5, 4 after 10, 5 after 20, 6 after 25	0¢ – 43¢ – 64¢
15.	13	3 after 5, 4 after 15	0¢ – 30¢ – 45¢
16.	14	3 after 5, 3 after 10, 4 after 12, 5 after 20	0% – 5% – 7%
17.	13	3 after 5, 4 after 12, 5 after 20	0¢ – 25¢ – 50¢

Table 25.4 — *Consolidated Electrical Products — Consolidated Statement of Income and Retained Earnings*

	Year Just Ended	One Year Ago	Two Years Ago	Three Years Ago
Sales	74,573,012	58,747,936	57,338,733	47,683,300
Cost of Sales	55,581,679	44,459,022	40,936,250	33,751,199
Gross profit	18,991,333	14,288,914	16,402,483	13,932,101
Deduct:				
– Selling, admin. & distribution expense	11,507,692	9,027,412	8,148,173	6,743,533
– Interest on long-term debt	1,474,511	1,160,277	865,568	587,624
– Other interest	1,199,024	419,487	556,425	288,063
	14,181,227	10,607,176	9,570,166	7,619,220
Income before Taxes	4,810,106	3,681,738	6,832,317	6,312,881
Provisions for Income Taxes	1,845,782	1,552,413	2,907,000	2,774,000
Net Income for Year	2,964,324	2,129,325	3,925,317	3,538,881
Retained Earnings at Beginning of Year	17,422,504	16,713,203	14,116,841	11,538,010
	20,386,828	18,842,528	18,042,158	15,076,891
Less: Dividends and relates taxes thereon	1,445,878	1,420,024	1,328,955	960,050
Retained Earnings at End of Year	18,940,950	17,422,504	16,713,203	14,116,841
Earnings Per Share	$ .58	$ .42	$ .77	$ .70

Table 25.5 — *Consolidated Electrical Products — Financial Highlights for Each of the Last Four Years*

	Year Just Ended	One Year Ago	Two Years Ago	Three Years Ago
Sales	74,573,012	58,747,936	57,338,733	47,683,300
Net Income	2,964,324	2,129,325	3,925,327	3,538,881
— Per Share $	.58	.42	.77	.70
— As a % of Sales	4.0%	3.6%	6.8%	7.4%
— As a % of Capital Employed [1]	9.9%	7.5%	15.7%	15.2%
— As a % of Shareholders Equity [2]	14.4%	10.8%	22.9%	24.5%
— Dividends paid to Shareholders $	.28	.28	.26	.19
Capital Expenditures	6,616,259	2,882,022	3,447,361	4,533,761
Working Capital	18,164,842	15,525,238	19,227,339	11,875,298
— Current Ratio	1.8 to 1	1.7 to 1	2.7 to 1	1.9 to 1
Shares Outstanding:				
— Class A and Class B	3,494,400	3,482,254	3,468,550	3,452,650
— Class C and Class D	1,611,672	1,611,672	1,609,272	1,609,272
— Number of Shareholders	3,185	3,151	3,170	3,206
— Salaries, wages and employee benefits	35,890,003	26,680,858	24,120,627	23,242,749

[1] Net income as related to capital employed represents earnings adjusted for the net cost of interest on long-term debt and is calculated on total assets less current liabilities at the beginning of the year.
[2] Shareholders' equity at beginning of year.

CHAPTER 26: COLLECTIVE AGREEMENT

AGREEMENT entered into this 1st day of November, 20XX

BETWEEN

CONSOLIDATED ELECTRICAL PRODUCTS INC.
(hereinafter called "The Company")

AND

INTERNATIONAL ASSEMBLERS UNION OF AMERICA (I.A.U.),
and its Local 265
(hereinafter called "The Union")

INDEX

General Purpose

The general purpose of this Agreement between the Company and the Union is to establish and maintain orderly collective bargaining relations, to provide a procedure for dealing with grievances, and to set forth formally, the rates of pay, hours of work and other working conditions that have been agreed upon.

Article 1 — *Recognition and Scope* (N/C)

1.01   The Company recognizes the Union as the collective bargaining agency for all employees of its Plant located at _____, save and except foremen, persons above the rank of foreman, office and sales staff and students hired on a co-operative basis with a school or university programme.

Article 2 — *Relationship* (N/C)

2.01   a) The parties hereto mutually agree that any employee to whom this contract applies, may exercise, or refrain from exercising, his right to become a member of the union.

b) It is agreed that there shall be no discrimination, coercion or intimidation by the Company, the Union or their respective representatives against any employee because of Union activity or lack of activity, Union membership or non-membership, or for reasons of race, sex, colour or religion.

2.02   During the term of this Agreement, the Company agrees that there shall be no lockout and the Union agrees that there shall be no slowdown, strike, or other work stoppage or interference with work.

2.03   The Union agrees that unless duly authorized:

a) Union meetings will not be held on Company premises.

b) No employee or Union official will solicit membership in the Union, collect dues, or engage in any Union activity on Company time, during his working hours, or the working hours of any employee, except as provided for in this Agreement.

Violation by an employee of any of the foregoing provisions shall be cause for discipline up to and including discharge by the Company, but such actions are to be subject to the provisions of the Grievance Procedure.

2.04   The union agrees that, in recognition of the fact that efficient and economic production is in the interest of both parties, it will promote amongst its members good workmanship and regular attendance. It is further agreed by the Union that the employees will at all times protect the property of the Company against damage by themselves or others.

2.05   In the interests of promoting understanding of the Agreement, the Company will supply present and future employees with a copy of this Agreement.

Article 3 — *Management Rights* (N/C)

3.01   It is recognized that management of the plant and direction of the working force are fixed exclusively in the Company, which maintains all rights and responsibilities of management not specifically modified by this Agreement.

The exercise of such rights shall include but not be limited to:

a) The right to hire, assign, increase and/or decrease the working forces, promote, demote, transfer and make temporary lay-offs for lack of business materials.

b) The determination of: the number and location of plants, the products to be manufactured, the methods of manufacturing, schedules of production, kinds and locations of machines and tools to be used, processes of manufacturing and assembling, the engineering and design of its products, and the control of materials and parts to be incorporated in the products produced.

c) The making and enforcement of rules and regulations, not inconsistent with this Agreement, relating to discipline, safety and general conduct of employees, and to suspend and discharge or otherwise discipline employees for just cause.

3.02   To enable the Company to keep its products abreast of scientific advancements the Company may from time to time, without reference to seniority hereinafter set forth, hire, teach, transfer or assign duties to technically trained men and technical students and deal with them as it deems advisable. This practice, however, shall not adversely affect the employees in the bargaining unit.

3.03   The Company agrees that these functions will be exercised in a manner not inconsistent with the terms of this Agreement.

3.04   Claims of discriminatory upgrading, demotion or transfer, or a claim that an employee has been suspended or discharged without just cause may be made the subject of a grievance and dealt with as provided in this Agreement.

Article 4 — *Reporting for Work*

4.01   An employee who reports for work at the normal starting time of his shift shall be given four hours' work and will be paid his regular hourly rate. If work is not available, he will be paid for four hours at his regular hourly rate.

4.02   Section 4.01 will not apply under the following conditions:

a) Where the employee has been informed a minimum of six hours in advance of his regular starting time that he is not to report for work.

b) Where the interruption of work is due to power failure, fire, lightning, flood, tempest, or any other condition of any kind whatsoever beyond the control of the Company.

c) Where the employee is not willing to perform alternate work of a reasonable nature.

d) Where the employee fails to keep the Company informed of his latest address and telephone number.

4.03   An employee is expected to give prior notice when reporting for work following an illness which exceeds one working day. Such notice must be given to the Company by no later than 12:00 noon on his normally scheduled work day immediately prior to the day that he is available to return to work. In the event that such notice is not given, he will not qualify for work or pay pursuant to Section 4.01.

4.04   Employees who are called in outside their regular shift hours will receive a minimum of three (3) hours' work or pay at the appropriate premium rate provided under Section 6.02. This shall not apply if such is immediately prior to or succeeding his regular shift; or if a break is requested by the employee.

Article 5 — *Working Conditions*

5.01   The Company shall continue to make reasonable provisions for the safety and health of its employees at the factory during the hours of their employment. The Union will co-operate with the Company in maintaining good working conditions and will assist in assuring observances of necessary safety rules.

5.02   The Company welcomes from the Union, its members or any employee, suggestions regarding safety and health.

5.03   A Safety and Health Committee is to be appointed with responsibilities as indicated in Appendix D to this Agreement.

Article 6 — *Hours of Work and Overtime*

6.01   The normal hours of work shall be 40 hours per week consisting of five eight-hour shifts Monday to Friday inclusive. This is not to be read or construed as a guarantee to provide work for any period whatsoever.

6.02   Hours of work in excess of 8 hours per day, Monday to Friday, inclusive, and hours of work on Saturday and Sunday, will be treated as overtime hours and will be paid for at a premium rate as provided under Section 6.03(b) below, except that when employees change shifts at their own request, they shall not be entitled to such premium rate by reason of the fact that they have worked two eight-hour shifts in the 24-hour day.

6.03   a) In computing daily overtime hours, a day shall be the twenty-four hour period following the regular starting time of the shift on which the employee is working.

b) Overtime hours worked will be paid for at a premium rate calculated on the basis of one and one-half times an employee's hourly wage rate except in the case of Sunday, when that day is the second day following an employee's normal work week (that is, Monday to Friday, inclusive), in which case the overtime hours worked will be paid for at a premium rate calculated on the basis of two times an employee's hourly wage rate.

6.04   As far as possible, overtime hours worked will be equally distributed amongst the employees. Each employee is expected to co-operate with the Company in the performance of such work and the Company agrees to accept reasonable grounds for the employee declining to perform such work.

6.05   For the purpose of calculating payment for time worked under this Article 6 and under Article 7, time worked on a scheduled shift commencing prior to 10:00 p.m. shall be treated as if worked on the calendar day on which such shift commences. Time worked on a scheduled shift commencing at or after 10:00 p.m. shall be treated as work performed on the immediately following calendar day.

Article 7 — *Specified Holidays*

7.01   During the term of this Collective Agreement, the Company agrees to pay an employee, as provided under Section 7.03 below, for the following specified holidays without requiring an employee to render service:

> New Year's Day
>
> Good Friday
>
> Victoria Day
>
> Dominion Day
>
> Labour Day
>
> Thanksgiving day
>
> Christmas Day

The last half of his regular shift immediately prior to each of Christmas Day and New Year's Day up to a maximum of four (4) hours.

Three additional days to be observed each year in December, as agreed.

7.02   An employee shall qualify for payment of the aforementioned holidays subject to the following conditions:

a) If he works his full scheduled shift on the work day immediately preceding and immediately following a holiday referred to in Section 7.01 and has not reported for work more than one (1) hour after his scheduled starting time.

b) If he has worked one or more full scheduled shifts in the pay period in which a holiday falls and is prevented from complying with the provisions of 7.02(a) above, as a result of a lay-off, leave of absence or illness verified by a doctor(s), when required by the Company.

c) If he has worked one or more full scheduled shifts in the ten (10) normally scheduled working days immediately preceding or immediately following the Christmas Holiday period and is prevented from complying with the provisions of 7.02(a) above, as a result of a lay-off, leave of absence, or illness verified by a doctor(s) when required by the Company.

d) If, in the opinion of the Company, he is prevented from complying with the provisions of Sections 7.02(a), (b) or (c) due to circumstances beyond his reasonable control.

7.03 (N/C)   The specified holiday pay as referred to in this Article will be calculated on the basis of the employee's hourly wage rate multiplied by the number of hours in the employee's standard work day.

7.04   An employee required to work on the day on which the specified holiday is observed as referred to in 7.01 will receive overtime pay as shown in Article 6, in addition to the specified holiday pay.

Article 8 — *Vacations With Pay*

8.01   Annual vacations will be paid on the following basis:

i) Three weeks after 5 years' continuous service if completed by December 31st.

ii) Two weeks after one year's continuous service if completed by July 31st.

8.02   Vacations will be scheduled by the Company and shall be completed within the calendar year. It is not permissible to postpone the vacation period or any part thereof from one year to another.

8.03   (N/C) The allowance for each week of vacation will be determined by multiplying the employee's hourly wage rate by the number of hours in the employee's regular weekly schedule. This will not include hours for which overtime premium is paid.

a) An employee with less than 12 months' continuous service will be paid a vacation allowance calculated on the basis of four per cent (4%) of the employee's earnings during the period from the employee's date of hiring to July 31.

b) An employee who has been laid off, or an employee who has had leave for a period in excess of 60 working days during the vacation year (August 1st to July 31st) will be paid vacation pay to an amount of 4% or 6%, whichever figure is applicable, of his gross earnings during the year.

8.04   (N/C) a) An employee with less than 12 months' continuous service with the Company, whose service is discontinued, will be paid four per cent (4%) of the employee's earnings.

b) An employee with more than 12 months' continuous service with the Company, whose service is discontinued, will be paid two per cent (2%) for each week of vacation entitlement.

Article 9 — *Wages*

9.01   The regular hourly rates set out in Appendices A-1 and A-2 shall remain in effect for the duration of this Agreement.

9.02   a) The Company shall have the right to establish and implement new job classifications and hourly rates not covered by this Agreement. Such new job classification(s) and hourly rates shall have provisional status for a period of 90 working days.

b) Following the 90 working day provisional period, the Union shall be advised of the finalized regular hourly rate.

c) An employee who receives such regular hourly rate for such job classification, or the Union, may lodge a grievance under Section 13.02(c) of this Agreement within fifteen days of the effective date applicable under Section 9.02(b).

d) In any arbitration of such a grievance, the Arbitrator shall be limited to determining whether or not the new rate is in proper relationship to existing undisputed rates established for job classifications covered by this Agreement.

9.03   An employee alleging that the wrong job classification has been applied to him or that the job content of his finalized job classification has changed to the degree that a new job classification should be implemented may file a grievance. Such a grievance will be filed under Article 13.02(c) of this Agreement.

9.04   a) In any case of a grievance under Section 9.02(c) above, any adjustment shall be made as of the date the rate was first implemented by the Company.

b) In any case of a grievance under Section 9.03 above, any adjustment shall be from the date of the grievance.

Article 10 — *Shift Bonus*

10.01   When employees are engaged on a regularly scheduled shift commencing before 6:00 a.m. or after 12:00 noon, they shall be paid a bonus of twenty (20) cents per hour for all regularly scheduled shift hours worked. There shall be no shift bonus allowed for hours paid at overtime premium rates.

Article 11 — *Seniority* (N/C)

11.01   The seniority of each employee covered by this Agreement shall be established after a period of probation of 60 worked days, and shall then count from the date of employment with the Company.

11.02   a) Plant-wide and Section seniority lists shall be established and compiled by the Company and posted on bulletin boards in the Plant. The lists shall be fully revised by the Company at least once every six months. Copies of the seniority lists shall be supplied to the Union.

b) The plant seniority list shall be made up in the following sections:

1) Feeder Maintenance Section

2) Paint and Assembly Section

c) An employee's name shall be included on both Plant-wide and Sectional seniority lists when he has completed 15 months' service with the Company. Prior to the completion of 15 months' service with the Company, his name shall be included on the Sectional seniority list only.

11.03   a) Seniority will be the major factor governing lay-offs and transfers due to lack of work, subject to the provisions that employees with higher seniority have the necessary skill and ability to perform the normal requirements of the work available.

b) Subject to the provisions of Section 11.03(a) hereof, employees who are laid off shall be recalled in reverse order to that in which they were laid off, subject to their ability to perform the work required. A laid-off employee must advise the Company of his intention to return within 3 working days and must report for work within 7 days from the day such registered letter is mailed, except in the case of verified illness.

c) When a reduction in working force is necessary, all probationary employees will be laid off first provided that the retained employees have the necessary skills and ability to perform the work available.

d) The provisions of this Article will not apply in cases where there is a temporary shortage of work and the Company may then lay off an employee up to a total of 15 working days in each calendar year without regard to the seniority provisions of this Agreement. In calculating the 15 working days above, a lay-off for the second half of a shift or portion thereof will be deemed a half day, and shall be counted against the 15 working days.

Time lost for the following causes will not be subject to the seniority provisions of the Agreement. Neither will it be counted in the 15 day exception referred to herein:

i) Time lost by an employee during the annual vacation shutdown as a result of such employee's vacation entitlement being less than the shutdown period.

ii) Time lost by an employee due expressly to a shutdown caused by fire, lightning, flood, tempest or due to circumstances beyond the Company's reasonable control, causing damage to the Plant, or part of it, or its equipment.

e) An employee who is about to be laid off under under the provisions of the Article will be given at least 5 working days' notice of such layoff. This shall not apply to a layoff under the provisions of Section 11.03(d), but in such case as much notice as possible will be given.

11.04   An employee shall maintain and accumulate his seniority under the following conditions:

a) During a layoff not to exceed twelve months.

b) During absence due to illness not to exceed fifty-two consecutive weeks.

c) During leave of absence granted by the Company in writing.

11.05   Seniority shall be maintained only as follows:

a) During absence due to illness not to exceed fifty-two consecutive weeks for which the Company may require written verification.

b) During a period of layoff in excess of twelve months but not in excess of twenty-four months.

11.06   An employee shall lose his seniority under the following conditions:

a) If an employee leaves the employ of the Company.

b) If an employee is discharged for just cause, and such discharge is not reversed through the grievance procedure provided herein.

c) If a person fails after a lay-off to return to work within seven days after the Company gives such person notice of recall, by registered mail to his latest known address.

d) If a person fails to notify the Company of his intention to return to work within three working days following the date on which he is recalled under Section 11.03(b).

e) If an employee overstays a leave of absence without the written permission of the Company; except where he overstays such leave due to illness verified by a doctor's certificate when required by the Company or other cause, verified in writing, which is in the opinion of the Company beyond the control of the employee.

f) If an employee is laid off for twenty-four consecutive months.

11.07   Notwithstanding his position on the seniority list, a Section Steward who has at least one (1) year's service will be retained in his department provided there is work available for him which he is qualified to perform in accordance with the provisions of Section 11.03(a). Subject to the same conditions, the Local President will be retained within the bargaining unit.

11.08   An employee with seniority who has been absent from work due to illness or accident and, when medically cleared to return to work, is unable in the opinion of the Company to perform the requirements of the job performed by him immediately prior to such illness or accident, may be eligible for an open job provided he has the skill and ability to perform such open job.

Article 12 — *Probationary Employees* (N/C)

12.01   a) An employee shall be considered to be on probation until he has completed 60 worked days with the Company, at which time his name shall be included on the seniority list and dated from commencement of the probationary period. When a probationary employee is transferred to another department he will be required to complete 60 worked days from the date of initial transfer before acquiring security rights. On completion of this 60 worked days, the seniority of the employee will be counted from the hiring date in the original department.

b) The Company has full rights to discharge probationary employees, if in the opinion of the Company, they do not meet the standard required of them by the Company. Such discharge cases will not be subject to the Grievance Procedure. A grievance may be filed by a probationary employee who has been discharged and who alleges that such discharge is an act of discrimination by the Company for reasons of the employee's Union activity.

Article 13 — *Grievances* (N/C)

13.01   A grievance is defined to be any question between the Company and one or more of the employees, as to the application, interpretation or violation of the terms of this Agreement, or any matter involving hours or working conditions covered by this Agreement, or if it is claimed that discriminatory practices are being performed or that an employee is not being paid the proper rate within the rate range of his classification.

13.02   A grievance must be filed within 30 days from the date of the occurrence which gave rise to the grievance except grievances alleging violation of Section 11.03(a) or (b) of Article 11 which must be filed within 7 days of the date of the alleged improper transfer or layoff or thirty (30) calendar days from the date when an employee commences work who has allegedly been improperly hired in place of the grievor. If such a grievance is sustained, liability on the part of the Company will be limited to a maximum of seven (7) calendar days immediately preceding the date on which the grievance is lodged.

The following is the procedure for adjusting grievances:

a) It is recognized that when an employee has a just or reasonable complaint, his immediate supervisor should be informed as quickly as possible and that an employee should not consider that he has a grievance until his immediate supervisor has had an opportunity of adjusting the complaint.

b) If after complying with Section 13.02(a) above, and failing reasonable satisfaction, an employee with a grievance may take the matter to the Union Steward of his Section, and the Union Steward, with the employee, may present the grievance in writing to the foreman. A grievance must be signed by the employee concerned. The foreman shall give a reply within three full working days.

c) If the foreman's disposition of the grievance is unsatisfactory, his section Union Steward may confer with the Chief Steward and if the latter decides to take up the grievance with the Plant Manager or his designated alternate he shall do so in writing, within three working days after the receipt of the foreman's answer.

The Plant Manager or his designated alternate shall give a reply within three full working days.

d) If the disposition of the grievance by the Plant Manager or his designated alternate is unsatisfactory, the grievance may then be referred to the Union Grievance Committee, made up of three members who shall be employees of the Company, and such committee may take the grievance within three working days after the receipt of the Plant Manager's answer or his designated alternate's, and a meeting will then be held within 10 full working days. At this stage, the Union Grievance Committee may be assisted by a duly authorized official of the Union, and any employee possessed of factual knowledge touching on this matter. A reply shall be given within ten full working days.

13.03   Grievances not filed within the time limits of three days as shown in Sections (c) and (d) hereof shall be considered settled or disposed of.

13.04   a) If a grievance has not been settled under the procedure set forth in Section 13.02 and it is alleged that such a grievance involves misinterpretation or violation of this Agreement, such alleged misinterpretation or violation may be referred to arbitration if it is so requested within thirty (30) days after the final answer is given, as in Section 13.02 of this Article.

b) When a grievance is posted for arbitration, it shall state the Article and Section of this Agreement, which have allegedly been breached.

c) Such a grievance should be submitted for final decision to a Board of Arbitration as follows:

Within five working days of the election to arbitrate, each of the parties shall select a representative and the two so selected shall designate a third member of the Board who shall act as Chairperson. In the event that the two representatives originally selected shall be unable to agree on the third member within seven working days of their appointment, the Minister of Labour of the Province of Ontario shall have the power on the application of either party, to appoint an impartial Chairperson.

d) The unanimous or majority decision of the Board of Arbitration shall, with respect to matters coming within the jurisdiction of such Board pursuant to the provisions of this Agreement, be final and binding on both parties hereto.

e) Such Board of Arbitration shall have no jurisdiction to alter, change, amend or enlarge the terms of this Agreement.

f) Expenses which may be incurred in connection with the Chairperson will be borne equally by both parties to this Agreement.

13.05 It is understood that the Company may bring forward and give to the Union at any time any grievance:

a) With respect to the conduct of the Union, its Officers or Committeepersons.

b) With respect to the conduct of the employees generally.

c) With respect to the application or interpretation of this Agreement.

The grievance shall first be presented in writing to the officials of the Union and a meeting will be held within seven (7) calendar days with the Union and its representatives. Failure to agree within a period of four (4) calendar days subsequent to the meeting will permit the Company to refer the matter to the Board of Arbitration as herein aforementioned, within thirty (30) calendar days.

13.06 The Union may file a grievance alleging violation, misinterpretation of non-application of any provision of this Agreement. Such a grievance will be entered by the President of the Union Local with the Plant Manager, who, within forty-eight (48) hours, will notify the union at which stage the grievance will be processed.

13.07 The Company shall not, under any circumstances, be subject to any liability for any period more than thirty days prior to the date a grievance was filed in writing.

Article 14 — *Discharge and Suspension Cases* (N/C)

14.01 A claim by an employee, who has completed his probationary period, that he has been unjustly discharged or suspended from his employment shall be treated as a grievance, if a written statement of such grievance is lodged with the Plant Manager within three working days after the employee ceases to work for the company.

14.02 Such special grievance may be settled by confirming the Management's action in dismissing or suspending the employee, or by reinstating the employee with full compensation for time lost, or by any other arrangement which is just and equitable in the opinion of the parties or a Board of Arbitration.

14.03   Except where two (2) or more employees are suspended or discharged, the employee, if he so requests, shall have the right to see his steward prior to leaving the Plant, at a time and place designated by the Company.

Article 15 — *Stewards*

15.01   The Company acknowledges the right of the Union to appoint or elect a Steward to assist employees in presenting their grievances, for each of the following sections of the Shop (one of these Stewards may be designated as "Chief Steward"):

1) Feeder Maintenance Section.

2) Paint and Assembly Section.

15.02   An employee will not be eligible to serve as a Steward or as a member of any Union Committee until he has established seniority with the Company.

15.03   The Union acknowledges that Stewards, as well as other members of the Union Committees and Union Officers, will continue to perform their regular duties on behalf of the Company and that such persons will not leave their regular duties without first having received permission from their supervisor. Any Union representative who is privileged by the Agreement to take up Union business in a Section other than his own will first report to the foreman of that Section.

15.04   A Steward may assist in the presentation of grievances in the Section which he represents, with the exception that when a steward is absent from the Section, the Chief Steward may assist in presenting grievances for that Section.

15.05   The Company will pay for 50 per cent of time lost on grievance handling with the Company supervision to a maximum of 1 1/2 hours' pay in any one week to the Department Steward and the President of the Union Local (when the latter is acting as a member of the Grievance Committee). In addition, the Chief Steward will be compensated on the same basis as the above to a maximum of 2 1/2 hours' pay in any one week.

Article 16 — *Notices*

16.01   The Company agrees to post in its plant, Union notices on Union activities, subject to the following conditions:

a) Such notice shall first receive the stamped approval of the Management prior to posting.

b) No change shall be made in any such notice, either by the Company or by the Union, after it has received the stamped approval of the Management.

16.02   The Union agrees that it will not distribute or post or cause or permit to be distributed or posted on the property of the Company, for or on its behalf, any pamphlets, advertising, or political matter, notices, or other kinds of literature except with the written permission of the Management having been first obtained.

Article 17 — *Bereavement Pay*

17.01   Subject to the following regulations the Company will make payment of wages to an employee who is absent solely due to a death in his immediate family.

a) Such employee must have completed sixty (60) worked days.

b) Such employee except for the death and funeral would otherwise be at work.

17.02   Members of the employee's immediate family are defined for the purposes of this Agreement as spouse, son, daughter, father, mother, sister, brother, father-in-law and mother-in-law.

17.03   An employee will receive payment for time lost from his regularly scheduled hours on the following basis:

a) Payment will be made on the basis of the employee's hourly wage rate for the employee's regularly scheduled shift up to 8 hours per day, exclusive of overtime and other forms of premium pay, for up to three days' absence.

b) The time to be paid for may be any three consecutive working days from the day of death through the day after the funeral, inclusive.

c) When requested by the Company, the employee will furnish satisfactory proof of death of the member of his immediate family.

17.04   An employee will not be eligible to receive payments under this Agreement for any period in which he is receiving other payments in the form of vacation pay, specified holiday pay, disability benefit, or Workers' Compensation.

Article 18 — *Jury Duty Pay*

18.01   An employee who is called for Jury Duty will receive for each day of absence therefor the difference between pay lost, computed at the employee's hourly wage rate and the amount of jury fee received, provided that the employee furnishes the Company with a certificate of service signed by the Clerk of the Court, showing the amount of jury fee received.

Article 19 — *Information to the Union*

1901. A copy of all general notices which are posted on the Plant bulletin boards, which deal with hours, wages, or working conditions, will be sent to the President of the Local Union.

19.02 A list of employees hired, quit, recalled, laid off, discharged or permanently transferred shall be sent each pay period to the President of the Union.

Article 20 — *Leave of Absence*

20.01 The Company may grant leave of absence without pay for personal reasons, and such leave will not be unreasonably withheld.

20.02 Upon written request by the Union, and if reasonable notice is given, the Company will grant leave of absence without pay of up to two (2) employees for one day per month. The aggregate total of days not to exceed twelve (12) days per year, for the purpose of carrying out business for the Local.

20.03 The Union may appoint or elect an employee(s) to attend a convention or conference and such employee(s) will be granted leave of absence without pay by the Company if reasonable notice is given. The employee will maintain and accumulate seniority during such leave of absence.

The following conditions will apply:

a) each leave must not exceed 7 days.

b) no more than 3 leaves will be granted to an individual employee in any one year.

c) not more than 2 employees will be granted leave at any one time.

d) no more than 25 days total leave of absence will be granted in any one year.

Time spent by an employee on negotiation preparations and processes, or while attending a hearing of a Board of Arbitration in connection with a dispute or grievance involving the parties to this Agreement, shall not be subject to (a), (b) and (d) above.

The Union agrees that, except for leaves for negotiation purposes, the Company may withhold leaves requested and ask the Union to substitute other employees if the number of leaves requested in respect of any job or section interferes with the operating requirements of the Company.

20.04   Subject to the following conditions the Company will grant leave of absence without pay to a pregnant employee at her request:

i) Such employee must have one year's seniority.

ii) The Company may require medical verification of the employee's conditions.

iii) Leave will normally be granted for a period of three months prior to confinement and two months following confinement.

Nothing in this Section shall restrict the Company from requiring a pregnant employee prior to her confinement to go on such leave of absence or for such longer period as the Company decides on the grounds that her physical condition while at work constitutes a hazard to herself, her fellow employees, or is interfering with her ability to perform her work.

Article 21 — *Transfer and Recall Payment*

21.01   A transfer is defined as a change in an employee's occupational classification, which is entered in the Company's employment records, or a change of more than three continuous weeks in duration.

21.02   On a transfer from a higher to a lower paying job at the request of the Company, the employee will be paid his pre-transfer rate for the duration of the transfer.

21.03   An employee who is transferred to a higher paying job at the request of the Company, when there is work for him on his regular job, for the purpose of utilization of his applicable skills, and not as a result of other causes, shall be paid the job rate for the duration of such transfer.

21.04   An employee who is recalled from layoff to a job in which he has a previous record of employment, and on which he has attained the Job Rate, shall be paid the Job Rate, provided that he has not been off the job for a period in excess of one year.

Article 22 — *Check-off*

22.01   During the term of this Agreement, the Company will recognize dues deduction authorization cards of present employees and will deduct in accordance therewith for each pay period of two weeks an amount equivalent to Union Dues except as otherwise provided in this Article.

22.02   An employee hired or entering the bargaining unit during the term of this Agreement will be required within 30 days after his date of employment or transfer to complete an Employee's Checkoff Card (in the form set out in Appendix B) assigning to the Union, through payroll deductions, an amount equivalent to that provided under 22.01. The same requirement shall apply to any present employee within 30 days after the date of this Agreement for whom no Employee Check-Off Card is on record with the Company.

An employee who has revoked such authorization pursuant to Section 22.03 shall, on the effective date of this Agreement have such authorization reinstated.

22.03   When the dues deduction authorization card has been signed by the employee and deposited with the Company, deduction will be made, in accordance with the provisions of this Article, for the term of this Agreement, and any extension or renewal thereof, subject, however, to the employee having the absolute right to revoke such authorization at any time within the 10 day period immediately preceding the expiration of this Agreement or renewal thereof. During this time an employee may leave with his foreman a notice thereof, which will become effective immediately. Upon receipt of such notice, the company will notify the Union of the employees who have so revoked such dues deduction.

22.04   There will be no coercion or intimidation of any employee by either the Company or the Union in regard to the dues deduction arrangement.

22.05   Union dues are deductible in each pay period for which an employee receives pay, except where such pay is insufficient to cover dues deduction in which cases the omitted deduction will be recovered in the next pay period in which there is sufficient pay.

22.06   The Union agrees to keep the Company harmless from any claims against it by an employee which arise out of deduction under this Article.

22.07   An employee who returns to work from lay-off, sickness, or leave of absence or who re-enters the bargaining unit, shall have current deductions automatically reinstated upon return to work, except as otherwise provided in this Article.

22.08   It is agreed that before an employee enters the bargaining unit, the Chief Steward, or a Departmental Steward deputized by the Chief Steward, shall have the right to interview such employee during a five-minute period at a time and place to be designated by the Company. The expense of such interview will be borne by the Union.

22.09   Upon written authorization from an employee (in the form set out in Appendix B), the company will deduct an initiation fee of $10.00.

Article 23 — *Duration and Termination*

23.01   This Agreement shall remain in effect from the 18th day of September, 20xx to the 17th day of September, 20xx and unless either party gives to the other party written notice of termination or of its desire to modify the Agreement, then it shall continue for such period as the parties agree upon. (Two-year duration).

Notice that modifications are required or that either party intends to terminate the Agreement may only be given within a period of ninety (90) to seventy (70) days prior to the expiration date of this Agreement.

23.02   Negotiations shall begin within fifteen (15) working days following notification as provided in the preceding Section 23.01, or within any extension mutually agreed to by the parties.

SIGNED by the parties hereto on the first day of December, 20XX, at the City of_____.

CONSOLIDATED ELECTRICAL PRODUCTS INC.:

R.F. Cook
_____

J. Morley
_____

E.J. McQuillan
_____

G.R. Cross
_____

INTERNATIONAL ASSEMBLERS UNION OF AMERICA

On behalf of Local 265:

J. Holmes
_____

K. Roessler
_____

INTERNATIONAL ASSEMBLERS UNION OF AMERICA:

F.K. Swinnerton
_____

D. Rohlay
_____

APPENDIX A-1: WAGE STRUCTURE (YEAR 1)

Effective September 18, 20xx

Job Level	Job Title	Hourly Rate
1	Paint Line Operator	$13.99
	Assembler	
2	Cleaner	14.06
3	Utility Operator	14.13
	Machine Operator – Light	
4	Repair R.M.R.	14.23
5	Assembly Line Attendant	14.34
	Wrapper and Loader	
	Material Handler	
6	Paint System Helper	14.51
	Machine Operator – Heavy	
	Crate Maker	
7	Storekeeper – Trucker	14.66
8	Service – Material	14.79
	Receiver – Shipper	
	Spray Painter	
	Shear and Brake-Set Up & Operate	
	Receiver – Storekeeper	
9	Welder	14.93
10	Paint System Operator	15.12
11	Set Up – Assembly	15.34
12	Set Up and Maintenance	15.49
	Maintenance	

APPENDIX A-2: WAGE STRUCTURE (YEAR 2)

Effective September 18, 20xx

Job Level	Job Title	Hourly Rate
1	Paint Line Operator	$14.99
	Assembler	
2	Cleaner	14.56
3	Utility Operator	14.63
	Machine Operator – Light	
4	Repair R.M.R.	14.73
5	Assembly Line Attendant	14.84
	Wrapper and Loader	
	Material Handler	
6	Paint System Helper	15.01
	Machine Operator – Heavy	
	Crate Maker	
7	Storekeeper – Trucker	15.16
8	Service – Material	15.29
	Receiver – Shipper	
	Spray Painter	
	Shear and Brake-Set Up & Operate	
	Receiver – Storekeeper	
9	Welder	15.43
10	Paint System Operator	15.62
11	Set Up – Assembly	15.84
12	Set Up and Maintenance	15.99
	Maintenance	

APPENDIX B: EMPLOYEE'S CHECK-OFF CARD

I authorize the Company to deduct from each pay period of two weeks an amount equivalent to Union dues and to remit the same promptly to the Financial Secretary of Local 265 of the International Assemblers Union of America.

I understand that this authorization is binding on me commencing from the date hereof subject to my right to revoke such authorization within a 10-day period immediately preceding the expiration date of the Agreement or renewal thereof.

DATE ....

SIGNATURE ....

DEPARTMENT ....

BADGE NO. ....

I also authorize the Company to deduct from my next first pay of the month, the sum of $10.00 for my Union initiation fee.

DATE ....

SIGNATURE ....

APPENDIX C: DUES DEDUCTION CANCELLATION

I hereby authorize and direct the Company to discontinue immediately the deduction from each pay period of two weeks an amount equivalent to Union dues, authorized by me pursuant to the Agreement between the Company and Local 265 of the International Assemblers Union of America.

DATE ....

SIGNATURE ....

ADDRESS ....

BADGE NO. ....

APPENDIX D: SAFETY AND HEALTH

1. The safety and health of employees is a major concern of the Company and the Union. The Company and the Union both have a responsibility and a desire to eliminate or reduce exposure of employees to accidental injury or to conditions detrimental to their health. It is the objective of the parties to ensure that no condition be allowed to exist in the workplace that is likely to cause injury or illness to its employees.

2. The Company and the Union agree to exert joint efforts to develop and maintain high standards of safety, health, and housekeeping in the workplace in order to prevent industrial injury and illness.

3. The company will provide, without charge, such special protective clothing, equipment and devices as the Company determines are required for the purpose of preventing industrial injury or illness.

4. There will be a Safety and Health Committee consisting of the following members:

    a) One (1) employee appointed by the Company who will act as Chairman, and

    b) One (1) employee appointed by the Company; and

    c) Two (2) hourly-rated employees appointed by the Union. It is understood that the Company may require the Union to temporarily substitute another employee as its appointee on the Safety and Health Committee in the event that the attendance of the regular Union appointee at the meetings of the Committee interferes with the operating requirements of the Company.

    The number of appointees mentioned in (b) and (c) above may be varied through consultation between the Company and the Union.

    The parties agree it is preferable that the timing of appointments be staggered to ensure continuity.

5. The Safety and Health Committee is responsible for:

    a) promoting safety, good housekeeping and accident and industrial illness prevention measures;

    b).seeking the necessary information to properly identify

        i. practices and procedures

ii. materials and equipment

that may be a source of danger or hazard to employees;

c) recommending to management

    i. accident prevention measures

    ii. health protection measures

    iii. programs promoting safety, health and good housekeeping;

d) maintaining and keeping minutes and records of its proceedings and making them available for examination by an inspector appointed under The Industrial Safety Act or similar legislation; and

e) sending copies of minutes, recommendations, etc., to, among others, the Division Manager, the Manager of the Safety Department, and the Union.

6. The Safety and Health Committee will normally meet monthly except during the month of December or when the Plant has a shutdown for two (2) or more weeks in a month; in these months a meeting need not be held.

7. The Safety and Health Committee will conduct a regular monthly inspection of some portion of the workplace and such inspection shall normally not take more than one (1) hour unless specifically authorized by management. It is agreed that the inspection referred to herein shall not interfere with the regularly scheduled work of any employees or interfere with productivity in any way. In selecting the work location to be inspected, the Committee may have regard to specific suggestions by the Company, the Union or members of the Committee.

8. Members of the Safety and Health Committee are entitled to such time from work as is necessary to attend the scheduled meetings of the Committee and to conduct the inspections outlined in (6) and (7) above without loss of wages for the time so spent.

9. The Company will provide the Safety and Health Committee with a copy of the following documents for each lost time accident:

a) the initial report to the Workers' Compensation Board; and

b) the Foreman's Report of Accident.

10. The Company will post and keep posted in a conspicuous place, the names of the members of the Safety and Health Committee.

11. If an employee has reasonable cause to believe that an unsafe condition exists as a danger to himself or another employee

a) he shall immediately notify his supervisor.

b) the supervisor in the presence of the employee shall investigate the matter and if it is agreed that the condition is unsafe, the supervisor will take all necessary steps to correct the condition and attempt to provide alternate work for the affected employee until such condition is corrected. While alternate work is not available the affected employee will be paid his hourly wage rate for the balance of the shift and two additional shifts, following which he will be treated in accordance with the provisions of Article 16.

c) if the supervisor does not agree that the condition is unsafe, but the employee maintains that it is unsafe, the supervisor will notify the Production Manager, or his representative, who will, without undue delay, notify the Industrial Safety Branch of the Ministry of Labour and request an immediate investigation and decision by an inspector. The supervisor will also advise the Manager of the Safety Department. In the meantime, the supervisor will attempt to provide alternate work for the employee. If alternate work is not available the affected employee will be treated in accordance with the provisions of Article 16. However, if the decision of the inspector is:

i. the condition is safe, such employee will be returned to the job as soon as possible;

ii. the condition is unsafe, such employee will be returned to the job as soon as possible after the unsafe condition is corrected and will be compensated for any loss of regular wages for up to the balance of the shift and two additional shifts.

12. The supervisor and the employee concerned are to be present during the investigation conducted by the inspector from the Industrial Safety Branch of the Ministry of Labour as a result of the request outlined in 11(c) above. In addition, and provided they are available, the one (1) Company-appointed and the one (1) Union-appointed member of the Safety and Health Committee will be present during the investigation. The employee and such members in question are entitled to such time from work as is necessary to be present during the investigation, without loss of wages for the time so spent.

13. While an inspection is being conducted by an inspector from the Industrial Safety Branch of the Ministry of Labour, he is to be accompanied by the supervisor (or his alternate) for each area that is inspected, as well as

the one (1) Company-appointed and the one (1) Union-appointed member of the Safety and Health Committee. These two (2) members of the Safety and Health Committee are entitled to such time from work as is necessary to accompany the inspector without loss of wages for the time so spent.

14. The member of the Safety and Health Committee appointed by the Union designated in 12 and 13 above, shall be considered to be the "employee authorized by a trade union" or the "authorized representative" referred to in the Employees' Health and Safety Act, or similar legislation.

The "Production Manager" means the senior supervisor responsible for production in the Plant, or a part thereof.

15. A copy of any decision or order or direction or report issued by an inspector from the Industrial Safety Branch of the Ministry of Labour will be sent to the appropriate Safety and Health Committee, to the Union, and posted in a conspicuous location in the workplace.

16. The Company will issue a set of Safety Rules to each employee and, depending on the nature of their work, additional manuals such as:

    a) Safe Practices for Crane Operations;

    b) Safe Practices for Electrical Testing

    c) Safe Practices for Fork Lift Truck Operations

A copy of the Safety Rules and each such manual will be provided to the Union.

The Union will actively encourage employees to observe the safety rules, practices and procedures outlined in the documents referenced above, which may be amended, cancelled, and/or added to by the Company. The Company will advise the Union of any changes prior to issuing them to employees.

17. The wearing of Company-approved safety toe protection is mandatory for employees whose regular work assignment is in an area designated as a toe protection area. For employees in such designated areas who have completed one hundred and twenty (120) worked days with the Company, the Company will, effective on and after June 1, 20XX, pay $50.00 once per calendar year toward the cost of safety shoes approved by the Company. For employees who have not completed one hundred and twenty (120) worked days with the Company, the Company will reimburse employees $50.00 after the completion of one hundred and twenty (120) worked days. (The present subsidy of $30.00 will apply until May 31, 20XX). Payroll deduction will be available to employees requiring approved safety shoes.

18. Company-approved safety glasses will be required to be worn by all employees who work in or enter any area designated as an eye protection area. The Company's responsibility under this program will be to:

a) designate the type and style of safety frames and lenses;

b) designate the opticians authorized to dispense prescription safety frames and lenses;

c) provide at no employee cost (other than prescription and fitting costs), through designated opticians, one (1) pair of safety frames and lenses for employees requiring prescription glasses and who completed one hundred and twenty (120) worked days with the Company;

d) employees who have not completed one hundred and twenty (120) worked days with the Company and who purchase approved prescription safety glasses through designated opticians, will be reimbursed the cost of the glasses following completion of one hundred and twenty (120) worked days;

e) provide "Plano" safety glasses for employees not requiring prescription glasses not more frequently than once (1) every two (2) years;

f) provide visitors' safety glasses for employees and visitors entering an eye protection area who do not normally work in such an area;

g) request the Workers' Compensation Board to replace safety glasses broken or damaged as a result of work-related activity;

h) make payroll deduction available to employees requiring approved safety glasses;

The employee's responsibility under this program will be to:

a) provide a prescription from an ophthalmologist or optometrist;

b) pay for any fitting charge levied by the optician;

c) pay for lost, damaged, or replaced prescription safety glasses;

d) pay for "Plano" safety glasses that have been lost, broken, or damaged within two (2) years of issue, other than those damaged or broken as a result of work-related activity.

19. At the request of either party a meeting will be held at a mutually convenient time for the purpose of discussing matters related to the safety and health of employees. The party making a request for a meeting will supply to the other, at least three (3) working days in advance of the proposed meeting,

a list of topics to be discussed. Each party will send to the meeting not more than four (4) representatives.

20. It is agreed that no matter respecting the safety and health of employees, or this Appendix, nor any differences arising thereunder, shall be subject to grievance or arbitration.

REVIEW QUESTIONS

1. What is the general purpose of this Agreement?

2. Which employees are excluded from coverage?

3. What protection are employees given from discrimination by employer and union?

4. What undertakings about lockouts and strikes are contained in the Agreement?

5. What arrangements are agreed with regard to union activity on company premises and during company time?

6. What undertaking does the union give with regard to output and company property?

7. What "rights" are specifically reserved for management in this Agreement?

8. What does the Agreement provide with regard to the employer's provision of work?

9. Explain and discuss the measures contained in Appendix D of the Agreement for the safety and health of employees.

10. What has been agreed with regard to hours of work and overtime?

11. What are the holidays provided? When would an employee not qualify for payment for any of these holidays?

12. How are vacations with pay determined?

13. What wages are to be paid? How can an employee ensure that he or she is in the right job classification?

14. What is the shift bonus? Why is it provided?

15. How is employee seniority determined? What purposes is it used for?

16. When does an employee lose his seniority? What happens during sickness and layoffs?

17. What is a "probationary employee"? What are his rights?

18. How is a grievance defined in this Agreement?

19. What is the grievance procedure?

20. What company grievances are permitted?

21. What can happen if an employee feels that he or she has been unjustly discharged or suspended?

22. What provision is made with regard to union stewards and their work on behalf of the union?

23. Is the union free to post notices in the plant?

24. Explain the provision for bereavement pay.

25. What happens if an employee is called for jury duty?

26. What information is to be supplied by the company to the union?

27. When may an employee receive a leave of absence? What conditions apply to such leaves? How is seniority affected?

28. What provision is made with regard to maternity leave?

29. How is a ``transfer" defined in the Agreement? What provisions apply with regard to pay?

30. What provision is made for the checkoff of union dues?

PART I: CASE STUDIES

GIBSON PRODUCTS (CANADA) LTD

Allegation of Employer Interference Prior to a Representation Vote

In a decision dated September 21, the provincial Labour Relations Board found that no less than thirty-five per cent of the employees of Gibson Products (Canada) Ltd. in the voting constituency were members of the union, and accordingly directed the taking of a representation vote which was held on October 5. The union filed a section 79 complaint on September 30, alleging violation of sections 3, 56, 58 and 70(2) of the Labour Relations Act and at the same time asked the Board to certify it without a vote pursuant to section 7a of the Act because, it claimed, the effect of the alleged unfair labour practices committed by the employer was to make it unlikely that the true wishes of the employees would be ascertained by a secret ballot vote. In the face of these charges having been filed by the union on September 30, the Board directed that the boxes be sealed pending a determination in this matter. The vote, therefore, has already been taken but the ballot box has been sealed.

A group of employees who have not heretofore been made a party to the certification application sought to intervene in these proceedings. Their intervention was challenged by the trade union. The Board is of the view that the filing of a request under section 7a of the Act constitutes a new point of departure in the certification process. It is a point at which employees not previously involved in the proceedings are entitled to intervene and be heard. Accordingly, the Board ruled at the hearing that the employees were entitled to intervene, to be made a party for the duration of the process and to make their representations. The Board cautioned the intervening employees, however, that its determination of the Section 79 matter would be based upon an objective assessment of all evidence before it relating to the alleged misconduct of the respondent employer, and not simply upon the claims of individual employees that they had not been unduly influenced. Such claims, following upon the alleged intimidation, coercion or undue influence, are of little probative value. Where there is clear evidence of intimidation or threats, it is of little consequence if one or more employees testify that they were not intimidated. Indeed, the Board must recognize that this testimony itself may be influenced by or be the product of the employer's coercive conduct.

The alleged misconduct in the instant case occurred in the period September 20-September 30, the period following the Board's decision directing the taking of a representation vote. During this period the Vice-President and General Manager of the company wrote four letters to the employees and made two speeches to the employee body during working hours with respect to the upcoming vote. The employees were a "captive audience" for the two speeches. The initial task which confronts the Board is to decide if the written and verbal comments of Mr. Winters, the Vice-President and General Manager, constitute "coercion, intimidation, threats, promises or undue influence" within the meaning of Section 56 of the Act or if his comments are within the bounds of freedom of expression which is protected by Section 56 of the Act.

Section 56 of the Act reads:

> No employer or employers' organization and no person acting on behalf of an employer or an employers' organization shall participate in or interfere with the formation, selection or administration of a trade union or the representation of employees by a trade union or contribute financial or other support to a trade union, but nothing in this section shall be deemed to deprive an employer of his freedom to express his views so long as he does not use coercion, intimidation, threats, promises or undue influence.

The line which separates freedom of expression from undue influence or the other prohibitions found in Section 56 of the Act is a thin one which must be drawn having regard to the facts of the particular case. There are, however, certain broad indicia which have been well set out in the Dylex case (supra) at paragraph 19:

> In seeking to establish where the line lies the Board starts with the presumption that employees recognize that employers generally are not in favour of having to deal with employees through a trade union, and that therefore it ought not to surprise them when their employer indicates that he would prefer if they voted against a trade union. Following from this the Board takes the view that an invitation to employees from their employer to vote against a trade union, in the absence of any surrounding facts or circumstances which would cause the employees to place undue emphasis on such statements, does not constitute undue influence within the meaning of section 56. (See: Playtex Limited, 73 CLLC 16,086, 1972, OLRB Rep. Dec. 1027). On the other hand, however, the Board is also cognizant that an employee may be peculiarly vulnerable to employer influences. This point is clearly brought out in the decision of the Canada Labour Relations Board in the Taggart Service Limited case (1964) CLLR Transfer Binder '64-'66, 16,015, at page 13,055; 64(3) CLLC 16,015,

the following excerpt from which was cited with approval by this Board in the leading case of Bell & Howell Ltd., (1968) OLRB Rep. Oct. 695 at p.706:

"An employer may express his views and give facts in appropriate manner and circumstances on the issues involved in representation proceedings insofar as these directly affect him and has the right to make appropriate reply to propaganda directed against him in relation thereto. However, he should bear in mind in so doing the force and weight which such expressions of views may have upon the minds of his employees and which derive from the nature and extent of his authority as employer over his employees with respect to their wages, working conditions and continuity of employment. He should take care that such expressions of views do not constitute and may not be reasonably construed by his employees to be an attempt by means of intimidation, threats, or other means of coercion to interfere with their freedom to join a trade union of their choice or to otherwise select a bargaining agent of their own choice.''

The employer established his position of dominance and set the theme for his subsequent comments in the first letter to the employee body, dated September 20, where he stated:

Your best interests lie with the company.... The company pays your wages and provides you with your benefit programs......

The underlying thrust of the employer's message is brought home to the employees in the letter of September 28:

...You must always consider the possibility of a financially crippling strike. Strikes are not a pleasant subject to consider, but they are a fact of life in unionized locations. We all know that where there are unions there are strikes and strikes are costly. Costly to the company in terms of loss of business and possibly customers, and costly to you, the employee, in terms of lost wages which can never be regained.

Certainly you have a keen interest in both regards since a loss of customers affects your job security, and a loss of wages would affect your financial security.

Keep working toward job security. Don't place a "third party'' between yourself and the customer. Avoid this possibility and vote "no'' on October 5.

The employer's theme can be summarized as follows: Strikes are a "fact of life"; strikes mean loss of business and possibly customers; "customers affect your job security"; "don't place a third party between yourself and the customers"; avoid this possibility and vote "No". This theme which was followed by Mr. Winters throughout his remarks was made particularly relevant to the employees of Gibson by the clear message that in order to "maintain" their present level of benefits in negotiation with the company, the employees would have to resort to a strike.

> All of these benefits are and have been yours without the necessity of your paying costly dues, for these are benefits provided by your company.
>
> As stated before, your benefits will become negotiable if the union wins the election. The outcome of any negotiations is difficult to predict; however, it is a fact that other locations which are presently represented by unions do not have benefit programs which are as comprehensive as the one which you NOW enjoy.
>
> Consider your alternative carefully. Ensure that you maintain the present level of benefits for yourself and your family. Vote: No Union.

This threat is repeated by Mr. Winters in his "captive audience" speech of September 22 in which he reviewed in minute detail a manual of employee benefits which had been given to the employees on that same day and concluded as follows:

> I would like to remind you that the manual is good only so long as there is no union. The minute the union comes in, this book becomes void and each item becomes negotiable. And these are items the company will take a strike on.

The threat was again delivered to the employees in the "captive audience" speech of September 28:

> ...and negotiations often go on for many months and could end up in a strike ...
>
> We start bargaining as though we had no wage structure and as though the benefits did not exist. There is no law that says that we have to agree to a single particular demand made by the union.

The employer has drawn a direct relationship between strikes, customers and job security and has put his employees on notice that they will have to strike in order to "maintain" the existing level of benefits if they choose the trade union as their bargaining agent. In his speech on September 30, Mr. Winters returned to the theme of job security and implicitly threatened his employees in the following terms:

> As matters now stand – you have a job and steady employment here at Gibson. Naturally we hope things get even better. It can be better if you can get this union matter behind us and settle down to the business all of us are supposed to be here for.

The union has asked the Board to apply section 7a of the Act and certify it without regard to the vote which was conducted on October 5. Section 7a of the Act provides:

> Where an employer or employers' organization contravenes this Act so that the true wishes of the employees of the employer or of a member of the employers' organization are not likely to be ascertained, and, in the opinion of the Board, a trade union has membership support adequate for the purposes of collective bargaining in a bargaining unit found by the Board pursuant to section 6 to be appropriate for collective bargaining, the Board may, on the application of the trade union, certify the employees in the bargaining unit.

There are three conditions which must exist before the Board may exercise its discretion under Section 7a of the Act. These are:

1) The employer has contravened the Act.

2) The contravention has resulted in a situation where the true wishes of the employees are not likely to be ascertained.

3) The trade union has membership support adequate for the purpose of collective bargaining.

The Board must now turn its attention to the question of whether the trade union has membership support adequate for the purposes of collective bargaining. A remedial authority similar to that now found in Section 7a has been part of the Act for some years. Section 7(4), the immediate predecessor to section 7a, provided:

> If the Board is satisfied that more that 50 per cent of the employees in the bargaining unit are members of the trade union and that the true wishes of the employees are not likely to be disclosed by a representation vote, the Board may certify the trade union as a bargaining agent without taking a representation vote.

Section 7(4) could not be invoked unless the union had filed membership evidence on behalf of at least fifty per cent of the employees in the bargaining unit and the true wishes of the employees were not likely to be ascertained. In introducing Section 7a, the legislature deleted both the requirement for majority support and the reference to the representation vote, and added the requirement that the alleged employer misconduct must amount to a violation of the Act. While in the opinion of the Board there must be membership support adequate for collective bargaining, there need be no specific percentage or majority. Indeed, since the Board must be satisfied that the true wishes of the employees are unlikely to be ascertained, it may be very difficult to find untainted evidence as to the union's support. In such circumstances the Board may have to rely heavily on the membership cards filed with the Board as required by the Act since those cards represent a voluntary and unequivocal expression of support for the union and for collective bargaining.

In this case the Board has before it signed evidence of membership submitted on behalf of more than 50% of the employees in the bargaining unit. This evidence, in the form of combination applications for membership and receipts acknowledging the required $1 payment, was submitted prior to the unlawful interference by the employer. The Board also has before it two statements dated October 13, some eight days after the taking of the vote, which bear signatures of 41 of the 62 bargaining unit employees. The preamble to these statements reads as follows:

Messrs. Carrie and O'Dea
Barristers and Solicitors
555 Talbot Street
St. Thomas, Ontario
N5P 1C5

The undersigned hereby retain you to act as our solicitors and authorize you to appear on our behalf before the Labour Relations Board on October 20th, and there to make the following representations:

a) The results of a vote taken on the premises of Gibson Products (Canada) Ltd. on October 5th, to establish the International Union of Electrical, Radio and Machine Workers as our bargaining agent should stand.

b) We were not unduly influenced as a result of discussions with and letters received from management of Gibson Products (Canada) Ltd. concerning the application of the Union, nor were we in any way threatened, coerced or intimidated by management or anybody on its behalf.

c) The interests of the undersigned will not be best represented by the applicant Union.

The undersigned undertake to pay the fees and expenses of our solicitors properly incurred in carrying out the above instructions.

Sixteen of the thirty-three bargaining unit employees who had signed membership cards in support of the union and who had paid the required $1 subsequently signed the above statement in opposition to the union.

DOMINION STORES

Application for Certification — Employee Status of Bakery Store Managers Questioned – Report of the Labour Relations Board

1. An Application for certification on behalf of all bakery store managers of the respondent at its retail stores in Sault Ste. Marie was filed by the applicant. A dispute arose at the hearing as to the status of the bakery store managers as employees under the Labour Relations Act and accordingly the Board appointed a Labour Relations Officer to inquire into the duties and responsibilities of those in the classification of bakery manager. The Board has now reviewed the report of the Labour Relations Officer and the representations of the respondent thereof.

2. Section 1(3)(b) of the Act states:

1. (3) Subject to Section 80, for the purposes of this Act, no person shall be deemed to be an employee, (b) who, in the opinion of the Board, exercises managerial functions or is employed in a confidential capacity in matters relating to labour relations.

3. The effective operation of the system of labour relations which presently exists in this jurisdiction is based on an underlying recognition of the inherent difference between employer and employees and a need for an arm's length relationship between the employer, as embodied by those who exercise managerial functions or are employed in a confidential capacity in matters relating to labour relations, and the employees. The purpose of Section 1(3)(b) of the Act is to ensure that persons who in the opinion of the Board exercise managerial functions or are employed in a confidential capacity do not find themselves faced with a conflict of interest because of their inclusion within a bargaining unit of other employees. Persons who exercise such function are deemed not to be employees pursuant to Section 1(3)(b) of the Act and as a result are denied access to the collective bargaining process. In view of this remedial aspect, the onus is placed on the party seeking to exclude a person from the operation of the Act to satisfy the Board of the exercise of managerial functions.

4. The Board has seen fit to exclude as managerial, not only persons who make independent decisions with respect to policy and the running of an organization but also, having regard to the underlying purpose of the section, persons who can materially affect the terms and conditions of employment of other employees. The evidence is clear that Mr. Geddes, the bakery manager examined in the instant case, does not become involved in policy or independent decision-making as it relates to the management of the respondent company or the operation of the bakery. The bakery managers do not become

involved in decisions with respect to budgeting, capital outlay or the future development of the respondent company. With respect to the bakery, the products produced, the ingredients and baking formulas and the prices charged are all determined by head office as is the "person-hour structure" which sets out the number of man-hours which the company will permit in a department. The "person-hour structure" relates to the sales volume of the department. The store hours are also determined by head office. The bakery manager does not have a power of independent decision-making with respect to the operation of the baker. All matters of consequence are predetermined by the company head office.

5. There are eight persons assigned to the bakery department "managed" by Mr. Geddes. They include persons in the classification of baker, counter girl, wrapper and decorator. Mr. Geddes testified that he supervises, instructs and assigns work to these persons. The Board accepts this evidence but has taken particular note of the fact that the head office supplies the formulas and the variety book and as a result must conclude that the supervision and instruction are somewhat circumscribed. The Board would point out, however, that it does not exclude a person from the operation of the Act on the basis of supervisory function, circumscribed or otherwise, as borne out by the traditional inclusion within the bargaining unit of the "lead hand" and by the "white collar" cases. The Board must determine if the supervisory duties in combination with other responsibilities enable a person, either directly or by means of "effective recommendation", to affect the terms and conditions of employment of other employees. (See McIntyre Porcupine Mines Limited case (1975) OLRB Rep. Apr. 261 at page297). The Board has examined the evidence and has concluded that the bakery managers do not exercise managerial functions within the meaning of Section 1(3)(b) of the Act.

Authority of Bakery Managers

6. The persons employed in the bakery department are covered by a subsisting collective agreement which sets out the terms and conditions of employment including wage, benefits, holidays with pay, vacations, seniority and grievance procedures. The bakery managers do not participate in the negotiations nor are they involved in the grievance procedure. The bakery managers can grant short periods of time off but all leaves of absence are processed through the regional personnel office. The bakery managers set the work schedules but these are subject to the ``person-hour structure'' which also determines the complement and indirectly occasions the lay-off of employees. Mr. Geddes stated that he makes the lay-off decision but also submitted:

> If the person has the least seniority and doesn't present a problem I may have
> to deal through the union or the store manager, to find out whether I can do it
> or not.

Although Mr. Geddes testified that he has the authority to assign overtime, and has done so, he acknowledged that he had been told by the store manager at different times that no one was to authorize overtime. Mr. Geddes does not assign vacation times nor does he make any written assessment of the employees in the bakery department.

7. Although Mr. Geddes testified that he has the authority to hire employees and gave as an example the hiring of Richard Boucher, he admitted that if the store manager had disagreed with the placing of Mr. Boucher on payroll he would not have been hired. Furthermore, Mr. Bruno Temeline, the store manager who was called by the respondent company to give evidence, testified that the store manager makes the decision as to who will or will not be hired. Mr. Geddes admitted that the placement of someone to work behind the bakery counter is determined by the union seniority list. Mr. Geddes testified that he has the authority to discipline other employees. It would appear that the discipline imposed by Mr. Geddes has been primarily restricted to verbal warnings although the evidence establishes that on one occasion he terminated an employee. Mr. Geddes testified that he reported this action to the store manager not to gain final authority but to inform him. This testimony is inconsistent with the circumscribed authority of Mr. Geddes in all other areas as brought out in evidence. It can perhaps be explained, however, by the fact that the store manager has the opportunity to overrule or affirm actions taken by department managers (some of whom are in the bargaining unit) at the first step of the grievance procedure. Step one of the grievance procedure as set out in the collective agreement between the parties provides that:

> The employee concerned and a Union Steward or Union Representative may
> within five (5) working days of the alleged occurrence said to have caused the
> grievance, take the matter up with the Store Manager who shall give his
> answer within three (3) working days. The Store Manager and a Union
> Steward will confirm in writing that a Step One meeting had taken place,
> showing on a form to be supplied by the company, store, date, grievor's name,
> and indicate that a verbal Step One meeting had been held. This form will be
> signed by the Store Manager and the Grievor. If the grievance has not been sat-
> isfactorily settled, then ...

No Managerial Function

8. The bakery managers do not exercise duties and responsibilities which enable them to materially affect the terms and conditions of employment of other employees of the respondent so as to create a conflict of interest if they were to be given access to the collective bargaining process. The responsibilities of the bakery managers can be likened to those of the ``lead hand'' in the industrial setting and as such the Board is not prepared to find on the basis of their duties and responsibilities as of the date of this application, that the bakery managers exercise managerial functions within the meaning of Section 1(3)(b) of the Act.

9. The Board finds that all employees of the respondent in its stores at Sault Ste. Marie, Ontario, save and except store managers, assistant managers, persons above the rank of assistant manager, district office staff, persons employed for not more than 24 hours per week, persons employed during the school vacation period and persons covered by a subsisting collective agreement between the applicant and respondent, constitute a tag end unit of employees of the respondent appropriate for collective bargaining.

10. The Board is satisfied on the basis of all the evidence before it that more than 55 per cent of the employees of the respondent in the bargaining unit at the time the application was made, were members of the applicant on April 6, 1976, the terminal date fixed for this application and the date which the Board determines under Section 92(2)(j) of The Labour Relations Act, to be the time for the purpose of ascertaining membership under Section 7(1) of the said Act.

11. A certificate will be issued to the applicant.

Dissent

N.B. SATTERFIELD, Member: I would dismiss the application for certification of bakery store managers of the respondent at its retail stores in Sault Ste. Marie because they exercise managerial functions within the meaning of Section 1(3)(b) of the Act. This conclusion is based on the following facts and arguments derived from examination of the evidence in the report of the Labour Relations Officer.

1. The Bakery Store Managers regularly supervise the bakery employees in the following matters:

a) assigns daily duties;

b) evaluates the quality of employees' performance in these duties;

c) instructs them;

d) hires new employees;

e) assures they follow established time recording procedures and attend at their jobs for the required time each day;

f) grants permission for requested time off up to one day;

g) assigns and authorizes overtime;

i) schedules the days and hours of work of the employees.

The testimony of William Geddes is that he supervises in the above manner eight employees in four classifications. By his own words, he is supervising "All the time I'm there...". His performance of work covered by the subsisting collective agreement is limited to filling in for his employees on their jobs. The Bakery Store Managers get much of their authority and supervision from "...Bakery Supervision in Head Office" (Toronto), and the balance from their Store Managers. The Bakery in a store is separated from the rest of the store and is a self-contained unit. Therefore, both sources of supervision available to the Bakery Store Managers may be said to be remote and indirect, rather than immediate and direct. Given the nature of the supervision which they exercise and the sources of their own supervision, they can hardly be held to be ...

> ...merely a conduit carrying orders or instructions from management to the employees...

in the words of the Board in the Falconbridge Nickel Mines Limited case (1966) OLRB Rep. 379. That decision in referring to positions in dispute re their managerial nature states in part as follows:

> ...if a person is primarily engaged in supervision and direction of other employees and has effective control over their employment relationship, even though the person occasionally performs work similar to the rank and file employees... to relieve an employee during occasional periods of absence ... such occasional work in no way derogates from his prime function as a person employed in a managerial capacity.

The Bakery Store Managers are "primarily engaged in the supervision and direction of other employees". The two stores with bakery units employ 14 full-time and 7 part-time employees. Mr. Geddes' evidence is that he does not spend more than 50% of his time doing work of a non-supervisory nature. If the Managers were not spending the rest of their time supervising, it would not make sense to have them there. The nature of their supervisory responsibilities and the physical and organizational environment in which they must exercise it puts them in a conflict position with their employees in their charge. Therefore the decisions they make do materially affect the conditions of employment of other employees.

2. In addition to managerial responsibilities associated directly with the supervision of other employees, the Managers perform other tasks ordinarily associated with managerial responsibility such as: ordering all supplies for the bakery without having to seek prior approval or direction; assuring that the required mix of product is produced; the correct product formula is used; and the proper manning levels are maintained according to the level of output and the man-hour structure (i.e., budget). Mr. Geddes has a key to the store and is free to enter it at any time, as distinct from having the key so that he can share in the opening and closing of the store as is the case with non-managerial employees.

3. The Bakery Managers are also distinguished from the employees whom they supervise in respect to certain working conditions. They are paid a regular salary; and are not deducted pay for time off; and are not paid overtime; schedule their own hours; and only notify the Store Manager if taking time off.

Responsibility of Bakery Managers

4. I disagree with the conclusions reached in the majority decision at paragraph 4 that "All matters of consequence are predetermined by the company head office", and at paragraph 8 that "the responsibilities of the baker managers can be likened to those of the 'lead hand' in the industrial setting". It is quite clear that these managers have their responsibilities circumscribed by procedures laid down from head office in respect to budgeting, pricing, man-hour structures, store hours, formulas and variety books; from district personnel office in respect to leaves of absence; and by the subsisting collective agreement in respect to wages, overtime, discipline and transfers from part-time to regular employment.

However, as earlier stated in paragraph 1, much of their own supervision is from the remoteness of head office which, coupled with separateness of their units in the stores and the limited form of supervision received from the Store Managers, means someone with more authority than that usually associated with a "lead hand" must be responsible to assure that all of the policies and procedures are properly applied at the local level. In fact, Mr. Geddes supervises a lead hand who is responsible to him for the night shift operation. The Store Managers are clearly not responsible for the bakery units in respect to particular head office procedures such as budgets, man-hour structures, formulas and variety books and they exercise no authority over the ordering of supplies. If the Bakery Store Managers were to be determined as non-managerial within the meaning of Section 1(3)(b) of the Act, it would mean the Store Managers and Assistant Store Managers, in the two stores having bakery units, alone would hold managerial responsibility. These two stores have a total of 191 full-time and 119 part-time employees. By the sheer size of the work force alone, it would impose an unreasonable expectation for a Manager and Assistant Manager in one store and a Manager in the other to provide the only "non-bargaining unit" supervision, notwithstanding the fact that the store Department Managers are included in the existing unit. Furthermore, the Store Managers themselves have their responsibilities circumscribed in an almost identical manner to the Bakery Store Managers. If it is held that such limiting of supervisory function places those jobs within the Act, this conjures the absurd situation of the stores in questions being supervised from district or head office.

I endorse the representations of counsel for the respondent in that "... the evidence as a whole demonstrates that the Bakery Managers exercise discretionary powers which exclude them from the Act". On page 4 of counsel's written representations starting in the second paragraph, counsel sums up the totality of the situation as being that, in addition to the specific indicators of managerial status,

> They are responsible to the Company for the operation of an entire enterprise — the Bakery unit. It is an operation which, to a significant extent, operates independently of the main store. There is no interchange of employees between that Department and the rest of the store. The Bakery area is isolated from the store, and the employees enter "through a door which separates it from the main store". All the necessary equipment is in the Bakery area. A separate budget is established for that Department. It is the responsibility of the Bakery Manager to see to it that the budget is adhered to and that the Company's profit margin is maintained. He does this by exercising his own judgment and is not given "any direction in operating the bakery by the Store Manager". Most of the directions he receives from senior management appear to come straight from Head Office rather than from the Store Manager. This is true of such important matters as the type of product, prices, man-hour structure, and operating hours.

> The Bakery Manager is in charge of the operation of the Company's Bakery unit. To the extent that managerial responsibilities are needed, Mr. Loucks and Mr. Geddes exercise them. They make decisions crucial to the successful and profitable operation of the Company's bakery business. Their responsibility to the Company inherently places them in a conflict position with other employees.

LAKE SHORE MILLS INC.

Contracting Out — Work of Watchmen Assigned to Private Firm — Application of Control and Organization Tests

The grievance was filed by the general chairman of the union and alleges that the company violated the collective agreement by assigning certain watchman's duties to personnel supplied by Allen International Security Services Limited ("Allen"). It is the position of the union that this assignment does not represent a genuine contracting out of the watchman's functions but that the individuals who perform these duties are, in fact, employees of the company.

The collective agreement contains the following provisions:

ARTICLE 1 — BARGAINING UNIT

1.1 The provisions of this Agreement shall apply to all employees in positions listed in Article 4, and to employees who are assigned to positions similar in kind or class to those listed in Article 4 which might be created during the term of this Agreement.

ARTICLE 2 — UNION RECOGNITION

2.1 The Company recognizes the Union as the sole and exclusive bargaining agent of employees in positions listed in Article 4 and employees who are assigned to positions similar in kind or class to those listed in Article 4 which might be created during the term of this Agreement.

Included in art. 4 is the classification of Watchman.

The company operates a grain elevator and is engaged in receiving, storing and transporting grain. Watchman's duties were performed by members of the bargaining unit. One employee was on duty at a time from 5:00 p.m. to 1:00 a.m., Monday to Friday, and from 8:00 a.m. to midnight on Saturdays, Sundays and holidays. The watchman's hours differed from those of the remaining employees who regularly worked from 8:00 a.m. to 5:00 p.m., Monday to Friday. There was, however, some overlap due to the fact that these employees were frequently required to work overtime in order to unload vessels.

The prime function of the watchman was fire detection and prevention, as the dust produced by grain handling creates a substantial risk of fire. The watchman was also required to check for vandalism, trespassers or problems with company equipment and machinery. In addition, the watchman performed certain cleaning functions, as well as a number of miscellaneous duties, such as snow shovelling and answering the telephone in the office.

At the commencement of his shift, an employee occupying the classification of Watchman was required to report to the office of Ross Davidson, the operations manager. At that point, either Mr. Davidson or Joe Hampton, the foreman, provided the watchman with any specific instructions there might have been relating to the shift. When not performing other duties, the watchman returned to Mr. Davidson's office. It was there that the watchman was required to answer the telephone and relay to management any messages in relation to matters such as the docking of a vessel or anything of an emergency nature which arose during the shift. On occasion, the watchman was also required to monitor the use of the telephone by crew members of docked vessels to ensure that all long-distance calls were placed collect.

The watchman was provided with a detex clock and was required to make rounds on the company premises where he would ``clock in'' at various predetermined stations. The clock produced a tape-recording of the time at which the watchman clocked in and, apart from providing the company with verification that the watchman performed his duties, the tape was required by the company for insurance purposes. At the conclusion of his shift, the watchman left messages for management as to any significant events which had taken place during the shift.

Ross Davidson began to consider the possibility of contracting out the watchman's work and decided to request an estimate from Allen of the cost of providing security services. Allen prepared a confidential security proposal for the company's facility. Mr. Davidson testified that the proposal revealed that there would be substantial cost saving to the company and, on the basis of the proposal, a decision was made to contract out the watchman's work.

By letter dated December 13, 20XX, the union was advised of the company's intention to retain the services of a private security firm and to eliminate the position of watchman. This letter provides as follows:

REGISTERED

December 13, 20XX.

Mr. D. J. Scott
Union Chairman

Dear Sir:

Please be advised that the position of Watchman is to be eliminated effective December 31, 20XX.

Anticipated reduction of available grain business for next year makes it more essential that our costs be reduced, wherever possible.

Necessary security functions will be performed by a Private Security firm.

No layoff is anticipated, at this time. The employees now performing watching duties will be employed in the normal operation of the Elevator for the winter shipping season.

Yours truly,

LAKE SHORE MILLS INC.

"W. R. Davidson"

W. R. Davidson
Operations Manager

Mr. Davidson confirmed that no lay-off resulted from the company's decision to contract out the watchman's work. He acknowledged, however, that by retaining the services of Allen, two jobs were lost to the bargaining unit.

With the exception of cleaning duties, the personnel provided by Allen performed essentially the same functions as those previously performed by members of the bargaining unit occupying the classification of Watchman.

The contract provides that Allens shall furnish the company,

> ... with Security Personnel at location or locations from such starting dates and times and during such hours with special equipment, such as radios, patrol cars, watch clocks, etc. as ALLEN and Client shall mutually agree upon in writing. Uniformed Security Personnel shall be equipped with ALLEN uniforms.

Mr. Davidson testified that, whereas the company was previously obliged to replace a bargaining unit employee occupying the classification of Watchman who became ill and that the company might have incurred overtime costs, Allens now assumes responsibility for assigning personnel. In the event that a security guard is sick, a replacement is provided at no additional cost.

Security guards assigned to the company are paid bi-weekly by Allen and Allen is also responsible for payroll deductions, workers' compensation remittances and for providing comprehensive general liability insurance.

In addition to the items referred to, the contract between the company and Allen also contains the following:

Employees

> The Parties intend that an independent contractor relationship will be created by this contract. ALLEN shall not be considered to be an agent or an employee of Client for any purpose. Security Personnel of ALLEN are not entitled to any of the benefits that Client provides for Client's employees. Security Personnel are employees of Allen and Allen will pay all wages and other payroll related

costs of Security Personnel. Allen will exercise complete control over the conduct, duties and all other matters concerning Security Personnel.

Supervision and Quality Assurance

Allen shall be responsible for the direct supervision of all Security Personnel through designated representatives, who will be available at reasonable times to consult with client.

Service

The services to be rendered under this Agreement by Allen shall be in conformity with operating procedures mutually agreed upon by Client and Allen. If, at the request of Client, Security Personnel are assigned duties other than those agreed to by Allen, Client shall assume complete responsibility for and all liability arising therefrom. Allen will remove from service as soon as a qualified replacement is available any Security Personnel who, in Client's opinion, are not qualified to perform the work assigned.

Mr. Allen testified that he screens and selects the security guards personally. Guards are trained for approximately five hours at the branch office, with the training consisting of a lecture and a film. In this case, the initial orientation to the company premises was provided by Joe Hampton who gave a tour of the operation to the Allen supervisor responsible for the location and to the two security guards who were to begin work at the facility. Mr. Allen testified that replacement personnel have been trained by the Allen security guard on site or the responsible supervisor. In addition, on-the-job training of 8 or 16 hours has been provided by Allen.

When an Allen security guard reports to the company premises, he is required to check in with another member of the Allen staff stationed elsewhere. The security guard reports to Mr. Davidson's office as was previously the case with bargaining unit members and, at this juncture, last minute instructions with respect to the shift may be provided by Mr. Davidson or Mr. Hampton. Although Mr. Davidson suggested that he would relay certain instructions to an Allen supervisor rather than to the security guard directly, Mr. Allen testified that Mr. Davidson is free to give instructions to the guards personally and that if these involve a permanent change in procedure, the post orders would be amended accordingly.

Allen security guards conduct rounds and, again with the exception of cleaning duties, their tasks are virtually identical to those previously performed by bargaining unit watchmen. The security guards, however, do prepare logs and reports with respect to their shifts, as well as incident reports in the event that anything significant occurs on the shift. This procedure was not previously followed by members of the bargaining unit but is apparently standard procedure for Allen personnel and Mr. Davidson acknowledged that he agreed to the preparation of these documents. The originals of the documents are left on Mr. Davidson's desk at the end of each shift. At the conclusion of the shift, the security guard is again required to contact the Allen staff member elsewhere.

Mr. Allen testified that "Allen" assumes responsibility for the supervision of its security guards and that this is accomplished primarily by way of spot checks and the roving supervisor responsible for the company location, endeavours to visit each client's premises once a week.

Allen supplies to its security guards a uniform and safety shoes. Allen also furnishes the report forms and logs which the guards are required to complete. The company provides the detex clocks and keys, a hard hat, flashlight and dust mask, if requested.

The issue then is whether, in the circumstances described, the company has effected a genuine contracting out of the watchman's duties or whether the relationship between the company and the security guards supplied by Allen is truly one of employer and employee. In this case, the collective agreement contains no prohibition against contracting out and, as a consequence, it was not suggested that the company was without authority to contract out the work in issue.

Union Argument

The Union argued this arrangement does not constitute a genuine contracting out of the watchman's functions but that the individuals who perform these duties are in fact employees of the company. With the exception of the cleaning duties, the individuals perform essentially the same functions as those previously performed by members of the bargaining unit occupying the classification of watchman. Further, these individuals are performing these duties under the control of the company.

In support of its position, the Union referred the arbitration board to the following decisions to support its position.

In Norton Co. of Canada Ltd., Hamilton and The United Steelworkers 4 L.A.C., p. 1454, in addressing the factor of control the Board commented as follows:

> In determining whether the contract amounted to one for services, as distinct from a contract of service, some assistance can be derived from the Law of Master and Servant. It is stated in Diamond's "The Law of Master and Servant", Second Edition, at Page 1, that

"The relation of master and servant exists between two persons where, by Agreement between them, express or implied, the one is under the control of the other.

A person is under the control of another as he is bound to obey the orders of that other not only as to the work which he shall execute, but also as to the details of the work and the manner of its execution.''

At Page 5 it is stated that

"The question of whether a person is under the control of another is a question of fact. Control may exist between two persons although the one

1. did not appoint the other;

2. does not pay the remuneration;

3. has no power to dismiss; and

4. has not the exclusive control.''

Further, the board noted the following:

> To weigh the significance of control, arbitrators have assessed the degree of the party-employer's right to direct the person's job performance appropriate to the nature of the particular job and the person's skill. In many awards, the party-employer did not choose the person, did not pay him directly and did not purport to discipline him on the spot. Nevertheless, arbitrators defined the person as an employee if he performed the job with the party-employer's materials on the party-employer's premises with the party-employer exercising to a substantial degree the right to direct the job performance.

The Union argued that the individuals were within the control and direction of the company and that the grievance should, therefore, be upheld.

Company Argument

The Company argued that, under the collective agreement, there was no restriction on its right to subcontract. Mr. Davidson testified that there was substantial cost saving and therefore the decision was made to contract out the work.

Security guards are paid by Allen and Allen is also responsible for payroll deductions, workers' compensation remittances and for providing general liability insurance. Previously, when a watchman became ill, the company had to provide a replacement, which might have involved overtime pay.

Allen assumes responsibility for assigning personnel and, in the event of illness, provides a replacement at no additional cost.

Allen screens, selects, trains, and supervises these individuals. They are not employees of the Company and do not have the same relationship to the Company as employees of the Company.

Counsel for the Company, also made reference to the decision of the board in Re Social Planning Council of Metropolitan Toronto and C.U.P.E., Local 1777 (1980), 28 L.A.C. (2d) 134 (Knopf). The board specified the following criteria to be the most important in determining whether certain project employees were actually employees of the party-employer:

1. Control over the selection of employees.

2. Control over the method and performance of the work.

3. Control over the decision whether money should be paid for wages or other expenditures.

4. Control over the length and duration of the performance of job functions.

5. Whether the work performed was part of or integral to that of the alleged employer.

6. Who benefited from the work performed.

Clearly these individuals are not controlled by the company. For all of these reasons, the grievance should be dismissed.

ADAMS INDUSTRIES LTD.

Language Interpretation — Payment for Time Spent on Union Activities

Background

Adams Industries Ltd. ran its manufacturing operations on a three-shift basis. Shifts were scheduled on a rotating basis _ that is, the first week a group of employees would work days, the second week afternoons, and the third week, nights.

From time to time, as required by the collective agreement or for other reasons, the company scheduled meetings with the Union. Under the provisions of the collective agreement, certain Union representatives had the right to attend these meetings. Managers and senior supervisors of the company normally worked days. As a result the company was inclined to schedule meetings with the Union during the day shift when its managers and senior supervisors were at work. Those Union representatives who were scheduled to work during the hours of the meeting and who had the right to attend these meetings would normally leave their assigned work with permission, attend the meeting and, when the meeting was finished, return to work. As provided by the collective agreement, these Union representatives would be paid by the company for the time spent at these meetings.

On occasion, those Union representatives who were scheduled in the second or third shift would come into the plant for the period of time required to attend a meeting which was scheduled in the day shift. When the meeting was finished they would leave the plant and return to whatever they were doing during this period which was outside their working hours.

To some degree the company established a practice of paying such people for the time they had spent at these Union meetings. For example, if a Union representative was scheduled in a given week to work on the 3-11 shift and if he worked the 3-11 shift for eight hours each day, he would receive 40 hours' pay for it. In the event the company called a meeting with the Union at 10:00 a.m., when he was on the 3-11 shift and the meeting lasted for one hour, he would receive one hour's pay for this meeting and therefore at the end of the week he would be paid for 40 hours' work plus one hour for the Union meeting for a total of 41 hours' pay for a 40-hour week.

The pertinent clauses of the collective agreement are as follows:

> "7.01 The Union acknowledges that committee men and Union officers have duties to perform on behalf of the company, and that such persons will not leave their regular duties without arranging the matter with their foreman, or immediate supervisor, and when resuming their regular

duties, they will report to their foreman or supervisor and will give reasonable explanation which may be requested with respect to their absence.''

"7.02 It is clearly understood that committee men will not absent themselves from their regular duties unreasonably in order to deal with grievances of employees or with other Union business and that in accordance with this understanding the company will compensate such employees for the time spent in negotiating with the company, in handling grievances of employees and attending meetings of the Union committee with the management, at their average hourly earnings for piece work employees, and at their hourly rate for day work employees.

It is understood that the time paid by the company to such employees for negotiations shall be limited to an aggregate of two hundred (200) hours.''

In the recent negotiations, the company placed a demand to modify the agreement to provide that Union representatives would be paid under these provisions only for time spent attending such meetings with the company during their assigned working hours. The Union rejected the demand and the agreement was renewed with no changes in these clauses.

Immediately after signing the agreement the company notified the Union that the Company would pay Union representatives for the time spent in meeting with the company only when the Union representative leaves his scheduled work in order to attend the meeting and in proportion to the time spent.

Subsequently the Union filed the following grievance:

"The company have notified us that we will not be paid for time spent in meetings with the company unless time is lost during the shift the meeting is held on. We have previously been paid for time spent in all meetings with the company."

Union Argument

The Union argued that clauses 7.01 and 7.02 are clear and unambiguous. The clauses state that in accordance with the understanding the company will compensate such employees. The understanding is that committee men will not absent themselves from regular duties unreasonably in order to deal with grievances of employees or with other union business. In return for this understanding the company agreed to certain compensation.

Clause 7.01 further underlines the responsibility of committee men and Union officers; mainly that they will not leave their regular duties without making prior arrangements with their foreman or immediate supervisor and that they will report on their return to work and will give reasonable explanation which may be requested with respect to their absence.

In clause 7.02 it is clearly stated that the Union has an obligation to the company and the company has an obligation to the Union. What are these obligations?

The Union argued that it is clearly understood that committee men will not absent themselves from their regular duties unreasonably in order to deal with grievances of employees.

First there is not any argument on the first part as the Union clearly upheld their part of the bargain and did not absent themselves unreasonably at any time.

The second part does not spell out any time limits, exceptions or any reasons for not compensating the Union representatives for handling grievances or attending meetings of the Union committee with management. The only exception is made and clearly spelt out when negotiations take over 200 hours. This exception was negotiated into the collective agreement after the original clauses 7.01 and 7.02 were negotiated. This is the only way any change should be made in the collective agreement. This the company tried to do regarding clauses 7.01 and 7.02 during the last negotiations but they were not successful in changing these clauses.

If committee men should only be compensated for time lost during their shift, surely the agreement would have said this, but instead it clearly says for time spent in order to deal with grievances of employees or with other Union business.

It would seem very strange for the company to have compensated Union committee men for so many years in this manner unless it was originally agreed that it was only fair to compensate in this manner for time spent. It would appear that only with many changes in management personnel has there been any change in the company's thinking on this matter.

Article 7.01 states that committee men have many duties to perform on behalf of the company. Surely the company does not wish or expect committee men to perform these duties without compensation.

Company Argument

The company argued that the meaning of the clause was clear and unambiguous. Under the terms of the agreement and the Ontario Labour Relations Act, the arbitrator has the right to interpret the collective agreement. However, he can only consider past practice when the meaning of the language in the agreement is ambiguous. In this case there is no ambiguity in the language. Therefore, the arbitrator does not have the right to consider past practice.

The facts are that a number of years ago the company agreed to put into the collective agreement clauses 7.01 and 7.02, and they were subsequently amended to provide the 200-hour limitation. The company administered the clauses as written and in the same manner as its present practice. There was no objection from the Union. With certain changes in management personnel, in the recent past, an unfortunate practice did develop. The company decided to correct this situation, and return to the proper meaning of the clause with its previous practice. It decided, rather than unilaterally change the practice, to wait for negotiation and discuss the matter with the Union. However, the Union refused to agree to the company's plan. As a result the agreement was renewed with no change in these clauses, and the company advised the Union that it was going to make the change.

Clause 7.01 concedes that Union representatives have duties to perform on behalf of the company and they will not leave their regular duties without arranging the matter with their foreman, and when resuming their regular duties they will report to their foreman and will give reasonable explanation which may be requested with respect to their absence.

Clause 7.02 is dealing with the situation referred to in clause 7.01 and states that Union representatives will not absent themselves from their regular duties unreasonably and in accordance with this understanding, the company will compensate such employees for time spent in negotiating with the company, in handling of grievances and attending meetings with management.

The company is agreeing to compensate such employees. Such employees are those who have not absented themselves unreasonably from their regular duties. One who qualifies therefore is one who absents himself from his regular duties reasonably for these purposes. The only ones who can do this are those who are otherwise scheduled to work at the time. Therefore if a meeting is held on the day shift, an employee on the day shift may qualify for payment. An employee on the afternoon shift does not absent himself from his regular duties either reasonably or unreasonably and therefore does not bring himself within the meaning of clause 7.02 which provides for payment. Therefore he is not entitled to payment.

RONALD FIELDS
Policy Grievance — Seniority

Background

Due to lack of orders at Fairfield Controls Ltd., there was a shortage of work in the light assembly department. As a result, the company found it necessary to reduce the number of employees in the department until the level of orders increased and the amount of work available rose accordingly.

Article 14 — Seniority, included a provision that when it was necessary to reduce the number of employees in a department because of lack of work, the junior employees will be transferred from the department first, provided the remaining employees can do the work available.

A grievance was submitted by one of the persons transferred, Ronald Fields, which stated in effect that he had more seniority than one of the employees retained in the department and claimed that he was capable of performing the work that that employee was doing.

Ronald Fields' grievance was processed to the first step and received a negative answer from the supervisor _ namely, that he was not qualified to do the work being done by the employee grieved against. Subsequently Ronald Fields' grievance was processed into the second step and again received a negative answer from the superintendent _ namely, that he was not qualified to do the work being done by the person he had grieved against. The company heard nothing more of the grievance which was considered to have been dropped.

If the Union was not satisfied with the company's answer at the second step, it could process the grievance to the third step but only within a period of ten calendar days after the second step answer. However, the Union did not do this.

The Union then submitted a policy grievance under the provisions of clause 6.10 which was worded as follows:

"Non-application of Article 14 — re departmental seniority. That all people affected because of the company's action be compensated for all monies lost and that they be returned to their old jobs."

The company responded by letter to the Union as follows:

"The subject matter referred to in the Union's alleged policy grievance is not properly the subject of a Union policy grievance but is the subject of an individual grievance. The subject matter has already been dealt with and as a result is considered to have been settled or abandoned. As a result the Union's

346

alleged policy grievance under the provisions of the collective agreement is not subject to arbitration.''

The applicable provisions of the collective agreement are as follows:

6.01 It is the mutual desire of the parties hereto that complaints from the employees shall be adjusted as quickly as possible, and it is generally understood that an employee shall not file a grievance until he has first given his supervisor an opportunity of adjusting his complaint.

6.02 The complaint shall be taken up as a grievance only within six months of the event giving rise to the complaint.

6.03 Step No. 1 — Between the Employee, his Steward, and his Supervisor.

An employee with a grievance may discuss the matter with his steward who may present the grievance in writing, signed by the employee, to the supervisor, setting forth the Article of the Agreement which he alleges has been violated. The grievance will be signed by the supervisor indicating the time and the date of receipt by him. The supervisor shall give an answer in writing to the steward within two working days.

6.04 Step No. 2 — Between the Employee, the Chief Steward, and the General Superintendent or his nominee.

If settlement of the grievance has not been reached under Step No. 1, then this step shall commence within four working days following receipt by the steward of the answer in Step No. 1. The General Superintendent or his nominee shall give an answer in writing to the Chief Steward within three working days of receiving the grievance.

6.05 Step No. 3 — Between the Employee, the Union, and the Supervisor, Industrial Relations or his nominee.

If a settlement of the grievance has not been reached under Step No. 2 then this step shall commence within ten calendar days following receipt by the Chief Steward of the answer in Step No. 2. The Supervisor, Industrial Relations or his nominee shall arrange a meeting within one week of receiving the grievance and shall give an answer in writing to the Union within not more than five working days following such meeting. The Union will be given a minimum of forty-eight hours' notice prior to such meeting. Union representatives at the third step of the grievance procedure may consist of the President of the Local, the Chief Steward, and the Steward representing the grievor, and one Union representative who is not an employee of the Company, and any employee possessing factual knowledge bearing on the matter in dispute. The Union may appoint an alternate to act in place of any of the foregoing employees, when such employee is unavailable at the time of a third step grievance hearing.

6.06 A grievance which is not processed within the time limits set out in this Article, or which is not posted to arbitration, within thirty calendar days after the answer has been given under Step 3 hereof, shall be deemed to have been settled or abandoned.

6.10 It is recognized that the Union shall have the right to take up a policy grievance with the Company relative to the violation, misinterpretation, or non-application of any provision of this Agreement. The grievance shall first be presented in writing to the Company and a meeting will be held within one week between the Union and the Company. The Company shall answer the grievance within one week of such meeting.

Article 7 — ARBITRATION

7.01 A grievance which is not disposed of under the provisions of Article 6, which arises from the interpretation, application, administration of alleged violation of any provision of this Agreement, including any question as to whether a matter is arbitrable, may be referred by letter to arbitration within 30 calendar days from the date of the receipt of the third step answer.

7.02 Within seven days of the notice of desire to arbitrate, each of the parties shall notify the other of the name of its appointee to an Arbitration Board. The two appointees so selected shall, within seven days of the appointment of the second of them, appoint a third person who shall be the chairman. If the two appointees fail to agree upon a chairman within this time, the appointment shall be made by the Minister of Labour for the Province of Ontario upon the request of either party.

7.03 The unanimous or majority decision of the Board of Arbitration shall with respect to matters coming within the jurisdiction of such Board pursuant to the provisions of the Agreement, be final and binding on both parties.

Company Argument

In arbitration, the company argued that the matter in question appears to be a policy grievance but it is in fact the individual grievance of Ronald Fields which had already been processed through the first and second steps of the grievance procedure and then dropped.

It was submitted by the company that clause 6.06 applies which says in part: "A grievance which is not processed within the time limits . ... shall be deemed to have been settled or abandoned."

Clause 6.05 requires that the grievance be processed into the third step within ten calendar days after the answer has been given by the company in the second step. The union failed in this instance to process the grievance within the 10 calendar days and accordingly the grievance of Ronald Fields must be deemed to have been settled or abandoned under the provisions of clause 6.06 referred to above.

The company argued that surely it was not the intention of the parties that when an individual grievance had been settled under the grievance procedure that the Union was not bound by it and at all times had the right to raise the matter again as a policy grievance. In order for any such construction to be put onto clause 6.10 it would be necessary to read into it the words "notwithstanding that the matter had been settled or abandoned under the grievance procedure". To find such meaning in the clause would be manifestly absurd because it was clear that the parties were aware that the settlement and disposal of grievances was a highly desirable objective of their agreement and this was clearly provided in clauses 6.01 and 6.06.

The company argued the case against the policy grievance because the grievor was aware of the rights, did in fact grieve, and his grievance was settled. Whether it was settled by the Union or by the employee himself is immaterial to the decision. The settlement itself is the vital factor in precluding the Union from now bringing the matter forth as a policy grievance.

Union Argument

The Union argued that the grievance submitted by the Union to the Company was in fact a grievance — an alleged violation of the collective agreement. The Union has the right to file a grievance including one that alleges violation of the agreement. The company refuses to process it under the grievance procedure. Therefore, the Union has no alternative but to submit it to arbitration and the arbitrator was bound to make a decision on it.

Under the grievance procedure it is self-evident that an employee has the right to file a grievance. Under clause 6.10 it is clear the Union has the right to file a grievance. There is no restrictions on this right. If it was intended to have restrictions on this right the company would have written such restrictions into the agreement. This the company did not do. The company is asking the arbitration board to imagine that there are restrictions in clause 6.10 which do not in fact exist. The company in effect is asking the arbitration board to amend the agreement but the arbitration board does not have this power. The wording of the clause is clear. The arbitration board must interpret the words of the agreement as written. Clause 6.10 says the Union has the right to file a grievance. It did so. It has been properly processed to arbitration and the arbitration board must deal with it.

The Union grievance deals with the application of seniority in situations such as transfers of employees from one department to another of the firm due to work shortage. Although it includes the transfer of Ronald Fields from the department, it is nevertheless dealing with the question of the overall application of seniority in this kind of situation, and is properly before the arbitration board.

AMALGAMATED BEER DISTRIBUTORS LTD.

Policy Grievance — Management Rights — Drinking and Rules

Background

The Union filed a policy grievance which read as follows:

> The Company has improperly, unreasonably and inconsistent with the current Collective Agreement imposed a company policy in respect to the consumption of alcohol during an employee's work day (lunch break).

> The union requests that the Company immediately withdraw this policy and abide by the Collective Agreement.

Attached to the grievance was a notice to all hourly employees under signature of Mr. R. J. Jalabowski, the president and general manager of the employer.

It declared that as of April 1, this year, the following policy became effective:

> The consumption of alcoholic beverages by any employee during any part of their shift may result in immediate dismissal.

By way of explanation the following comment was also made:

> Specifically, no alcoholic beverage may be consumed at any time during your shift including rest periods (coffee breaks), lunch or dinner breaks.

In this place, there were three components to the work-force. Some were involved in bottle sorting, some in the warehouse, and some in the transportation of beer and/or empty bottles to and from breweries, customers and the warehouse. There were also helpers who worked with the drivers and on occasion worked as drivers. The employees working in the bottle-sorting area or in the warehouse were not involved in driving motor vehicles on the public highways but some of them might be involved in the operation of fork-lift trucks, and other similar vehicles within the warehouse.

The lunch or dinner breaks were unpaid.

The total workforce was approximately 200 and there were 50 or 60 drivers in the transport division. The drivers operated tractor/trailers and there were also approximately 30 helpers who could be required to drive.

Within the warehouse, there were approximately 35 employees who used fork-lift vehicles or some similar type of power transportation.

There were approximately 70 employees in various categories who worked in the bottle-sorting area and those employees could be called upon to work on power equipment. As there was moving equipment in that area, all employees had to be extremely alert.

There was an absolute bar to the consumption of any alcoholic beverages within the lands and premises of the employer and this rule had not been contested by the union.

The drivers of the employer generally operated only within the bounds of the perimeter highway and were required, on many occasions, to drive through residential areas.

A group of documents were entered as exhibits. Exhibit 3 was an employee bulletin, issued nine years ago, and the relevant portion of same read as follows:

> 1. The consumption of any alcoholic beverage or non-prescribed mind expanding drugs while on duty is strictly prohibited. "On Duty" is defined to include the entire shift of an employee, from the time he reports for work until he completes his shift as signified by his time card.

Exhibit 4 was another employee bulletin dated November 2, eight years ago, and the relevant portions read as follows:

> The consumption of any alcoholic beverage or non-prescribed mind-expanding drugs while on duty is strictly prohibited. "On Duty" is defined to include the entire shift of an employee, from the time he reports for work until he completes his shift as signified by his time card.

Exhibit 5 was a notice to all employees dated June 8, six years ago, and the relevant portions reads as follows:

> The consumption of any alcoholic beverage or non-prescribed mind-expanding drugs while on duty is strictly prohibited. "On Duty" is defined to include the time for which an employee receives compensation.

Exhibit 6 was a notice to all drivers and helpers dated October 27, four years ago, and reads as follows:

> When you are finished work bring your vehicle back to the warehouse and punch out before you sit in a bar and start drinking.

Exhibit 7 is a notice to all employees dated August 31, of last year, and the relevant portion reads as follows:

> The consumption of alcoholic beverages while on shift is expressly forbidden and any violation of this policy is a dismissable offence.

Union Argument

The Union counsel did not dispute that the employer had the right to promulgate a prohibition against drinking during working hours and/or within the confines of the employer's premises. He stated that the employer did not have any right to direct what the employees did or did not do during their unpaid lunch or dinner breaks if taken away from the premises.

He pointed out that the parties had already mutually agreed that impairment due to the influence of alcohol or non-prescribed drugs was undesirable. Article 8.04 of the collective agreement addressed the issue as follows:

> 8.04 Due to the mutual concern of the parties to this agreement, with respect to the safety and welfare of the employees, it is understood and agreed that employees shall not report for work or work while in an unfit condition due to the influence of alcohol or non-prescribed drugs.
>
> It is understood that any violation of the above understandings will result in disciplinary action.
>
> 5.03 Seniority shall be considered broken by virtue of the following reasons:
>
> . . . .
>
> (b) If an employee is discharged for cause not reversed by the grievance procedure.

The Union counsel defined the issue as follows: ``Can the Company unilaterally impose a rule that affects an employee, when that employee leaves the premises during an unpaid lunch break.''

He pointed out that there was no objection to the drinking prohibitions during the course of paid labour, nor to the necessity of employees coming to and remaining at work in a fit condition.

He submitted that the reasons given in evidence by the employer for the rule were not reasonable. He summarized the employer's reasons as follows:

1. The employer was concerned that if an employee left the plant he/she would not have just one beer, but might have three or four and that the employer had no control over this.

2. If there was drinking during the lunch hour, then neither the rule nor art. 8.04 could be easily enforced.

3. That the employer had an image problem with respect to employees drinking excessively.

He submitted that the employer could not dictate off-premises behaviour unless it could demonstrate a tangible effect on the employer. He stated that the only issue that the employer could and should be concerned with was conduct while an employee was on duty. If there was an abuse, then the employer had the right to act under the collective agreement.

He argued by analogy that an employer, if this rule stood up, could violate an employee's civil liberties. He pointed out that one or two drinks did not necessarily mean impairment, and that there was no prohibition against driving unless one was impaired. He felt that the employer was going beyond the law which affects all citizens.

With respect to drivers/helpers, he stated that the obligation was on the drivers not to drive while impaired. In his opinion, the employer must demonstrate that there was a problem with drinking drivers, and that the employer had not satisfied that onus. He submitted that similar prohibitions did not apply to bus drivers or people involved in other like work.

In summary he stated that the parties had, in the collective agreement, agreed to a standard as set forth in art. 8.04, i.e., they were not to ``report for work or work while in an unfit condition''. He stated that in the union's view the employer could not go beyond this provision.

Company Argument

The Company counsel took the view that the employer had a high profile in the community and was subject to extraordinary scrutiny because it was involved in the brewery business. He reviewed the dangers which could ensue if a large trailer load was involved in an accident in any neighbourhood, but especially in a residential area where children might be injured. He stated that the employer would be in an extremely difficult position if, in any hearing, someone was able to come forward and say that the employee was observed drinking prior to the accident and that there was no company rule against drinking. He asked the board to note that the employer, if it relied on the new rule to impose discipline, would still have to prove just cause.

Counsel said that if someone absolutely had to rush out at lunch time to have a drink, then that individual had a problem with alcohol. He asked the board to note three reasons why the rule was reasonable. These were as follows:

1. The enforcement as to the quantity of drinking was practically impossible and it was more realistic to say that there would be no drinking during the working hours.

2. He said that the issue of safety had not been contested by the union and that we also had to consider the effects of a breach of safety on any ``non-drinking employees''.

3. He submitted that the issue of the image of a purveyor or a supplier of alcoholic beverages was self-evident.

He asked the board to consider that the rule against consuming alcohol had been in force, in one form or another, for 10 years and had never been grieved. He noted that as early as 1981 (ex. 3), the consumption of alcohol while on duty was strictly prohibited. He noted that "on duty" at that time was defined to include the entire shift of an employee, from the time he reports for work until he completed his shift as signified by his time-card. In his view the policy statement of April 1, this year, simply clarified the rule. He also said that art. 8.04 had been there since the inception of the collective agreement.

He stated that we had to consider the perception of society towards drinking. He disputed that there had to be an incident first before the employer might be involved or that its image could be detrimentally affected.

In conclusion, counsel summarized the employer's position as being: "That the rule was completely reasonable in that it was reasonable, was necessary, was in the best interest of the Employer and the employees, and did not deprive any employee of any substantive right and was clear and unequivocal."

CIVIC GENERAL HOSPITAL
Admissibility of Performance Evaluation in a Discipline Case

Grievance

The grievance, on behalf of Donna Kivachik, alleged that "The letter of termination effective April 16, this year, is a contravention of the terms and conditions of the Collective Agreement". The relief sought is that the grievor be reinstated without loss of benefits, wages and seniority and the letter of termination be withdrawn.

Articles of Collective Agreement

The pertinent articles of the collective agreement are herein set forth:

ARTICLE 11: SHOP STEWARDS

11.03 The employee or the Local Union shall have the right at time to have the assistance of a C.U.P.E. representative.

ARTICLE 12: GRIEVANCE PROCEDURE

12.02 Settling of Disputes and Grievances

Step 1

a) An employee who believes that she has a problem arising out of the interpretation, application or alleged violation of this Collective Agreement shall first discuss the matter with her immediate supervisor within seven (7) days of the date she first became aware of, or reasonably should have become aware of, the occurrence. "Immediate Supervisor" means that person from whom an employee normally receives her work assignments. The employee shall have the right to be accompanied by a Shop Steward or Local Union Officer while discussing the matter with her immediate supervisor. A sincere attempt shall be made by both parties through discussion to resolve the problem at that level. The immediate supervisor shall advise the employee of her decision within seven (7) days of the date the matter was first discussed.

ARTICLE 35: DISCIPLINE & TERMINATION

35.01 Written disciplinary notice shall be given to employees for poor conduct or unsatisfactory job performance.

a) This does not prevent immediate dismissal for just cause, subject to the grievance procedure.

b) Copies of all disciplinary notices shall be forwarded to the Union. Employees shall be given the opportunity to sign disciplinary notices as having been read.

Admissibility of Evaluations

At the outset of the hearing, having been made aware that the employer proposed to introduce performance evaluations of the grievor in evidence, counsel for the union objected to the introduction of such evidence. It being apparent, from the submissions of counsel, that the issue is complex and of considerable significance, the board decided that it would reserve its ruling on the objection and permit the introduction of the evidence on the understanding that the board's eventual ruling might render the evidence inadmissible.

The Union Argument

The evaluations are not relevant and not admissible because they do not constitute discipline and are therefore not grievable. The evaluations of the grievor's performance could be characterized as negative in comment, but there is nothing in the evaluations suggesting that they are disciplinary or warning that some further action will result if there is not improvement. Furthermore, the evaluations were obviously not considered by the employer to be disciplinary because the employer did not, as required under Article 35.01, and as it did in other disciplinary situations, forward copies to the union.

There was no suggestion in any documentation, relating to the suspension and termination, that the employer had taken into account the performance evaluations. They have done so, at the hearing, simply to "build their case". This board ought not to consider the evaluations other than, perhaps, the most recent evaluation if it can be reasonably construed as giving notice of a particular standard expected of the grievor which she failed to achieve and is therefore being disciplined for. The most recent evaluation was August 15, of last year, which preceded the termination by eight months. The previous evaluations were on August 19 and May 31, two years ago, and on November 8, three years ago, all of which are stale. Furthermore, the evaluations do not, with very few exceptions, refer to specific situations or examples and would be almost impossible, in a grievance setting, to respond to.

Employer Argument

There is, in the collective agreement, no restricted definition of "record" or what constitutes discipline. A performance evaluation is disciplinary in nature, is communicated to the employee and is therefore relevant and admissible. When an employee is spoken to about her performance, and receives and acknowledges a performance evaluation, that evaluation becomes part of her record. There is nothing in the collective agreement to prevent employees grieving their performance evaluations.

The evaluation serves to present the full picture with respect to an employee's job performance including the standards expected of her and the improvement, or lack thereof, in attaining those standards. The evaluations led, in part, to the discipline of the grievor, and are related to the discipline.

This board should admit the evaluations as being part of the performance record of the grievor and attach such weight as the board deems appropriate.

MUNICIPAL GENERAL HOSPITAL

Call-in — Work Assignment — Nurses Required to Perform Only Tasks They Would Normally Perform

The nurses' association brings a policy grievance and group grievance alleging a violation of the collective agreement, arising from the hospital's rule requiring nurses to work four full hours on each occasion they are called in to work outside their regularly scheduled working tours. By way of relief, the association seeks a declaration of such violation and an order requiring the hospital to cease this practice.

The parties filed an agreed statement of fact pertinent to both the grievances which reads as follows:

Agreed Statement of Fact

1. Prior to the implementation of this collective agreement, Operating Room Registered Nurses were placed on standby while outside their regularly scheduled hours, and as required, were called in. They were paid at the appropriate rate (1 1/2 their regular hourly rate) for all such hours worked.

2. Article 14.07 of the collective agreement provides for a standby arrangement and Article 14.06 provides for a call-in arrangement, which includes a minimum guarantee of four hours pay at time and one half the regular hourly rate on a call-in.

3. On or about September 27, 20XX, the Employer implemented a new rule regarding Operating Room Nurses and call-in. The rule was articulated as follows:

   "When called back (when on standby) and finished work in O.R., and discharged the patient, notify supervisor of time you arrived. If 4 hours have not elapsed, she will assign other nursing tasks."

4. No discussions were held between the Hospital and the Association prior to the implementation of the rule described in paragraph 3 above.

5. On October 5, a policy grievance was filed challenging the practice described in paragraph 3 above.

6. On or about October 17, the grievors, Young and Webber, were called in to the Operating Room outside their regularly scheduled working hours. The grievors attended to duties in the Operating Room from approximately 2120 hours to 2350 hours. From approximately 2350 hours to 0120 hours, the grievors were assigned work in the Emergency Department. Their assigned duties at that time included, among other duties, scrubbing stretchers in the Emergency Department.

7. Both grievors are experienced and qualified to work in the Emergency Department. However, neither of the grievors regularly works in the Emergency Department.

8. The application of the rule as outlined in paragraph 3 above can and does result in Operating Room Nurses being assigned to nursing duties outside the Operating Room. None of the O.R. Nurses regularly work outside the Operating Room, but may be assigned to other areas when not required in the O.R.

9. Operating Room nursing duties include recovery room nursing duties.

10. Records kept by the Hospital over the period September 10, to November 3, indicate the following:

    (a) A nurse will be on standby for a period usually ranging from one to three consecutive days. A nurse may on occasion be on standby for a longer period of consecutive days.

    (b) The incidence of call-in, 2 nurses per call-in, was approximately as follows:

April	—	6 call-ins
May	—	10 call-ins
June	—	7 call-ins
July	—	13 call-ins
August	—	9 call-ins
September	—	10 call-ins

    Total = 55 or approximately 9.16/month

    (c) During the period April to September there have been approximately five instances of more than one call-in on a single day. (Of the total figure of 55 call-ins, on five of the 50 days of call-in, there were two call-ins and in some, both individuals on call-in worked for the entire standby assignment.)

11. The arrangement with respect to call-ins is that a nurse receives time and a half her regular salary or the equivalent in time off.

12. An O.R. nurse who is called-in and works a minimum of 2 hours is given a paid half-hour meal break.

13. The regular duties of an O.R. nurse include cleaning stretchers and the regular duties of an emergency department nurse also include cleaning stretchers (normally on nights for emergency).

A further point was added that overtime is first assigned to operating-room nurses who are on stand-by duty.

Union Argument

The association contended that the hospital's rule is contrary to the provisions of art. 14.06 of the collective agreement and furthermore that the rule is unreasonable and therefore in contravention of art. B of the local appendices. On the first branch of its argument, the association contended that the employer's rule constitutes a unilateral amendment to art. 14.06 to the effect that a nurse on call-in shall be required to perform nursing duties other than those he or she regularly or normally performs and other than those which precipitated the call-in.

Furthermore, the association pointed out that art. 14.06 provides a minimum guarantee of four hours' pay at premium rates irrespective of the number of hours worked on the call-in, whereas the hospital's rule provides a minimum guarantee of four hours' work at premium rates of pay. In this regard, the association claimed that the rule undermined the purpose and effect of the minimum guarantee.

On the other branch of its argument, the association claimed that the employer's rule was unreasonable in that it fails to achieve adequate proportionality between the objective sought of efficient deployment of nursing personnel for dollars spent and the means used to accomplish this objective. The association pointed out that this hospital has a small pool of O.R. nurses to cover considerable stand-by, call-in and overtime requirements in addition to the regularly scheduled shifts. As such, since the number of call-ins during a period of stand-by cannot be ascertained, the association characterized as unreasonable the employer's requirement that the nurses work during the entire four-hour period rather than be allowed to rest until required for O.R. nursing duties on the next call, because it needlessly exhausts the O.R. nursing personnel. Such a rule would thereby threaten safety because the nurses may not be alert or careful in attending to their demanding O.R. duties required subsequently. The association pointed out that from the patient's viewpoint, the nurse who is rested and alert for his or her duties is to be preferred.

While the association concedes that the grievance does not allege violation of art. 18.06 requiring preliminary discussion of a new rule with the association, but the failure of the hospital to so discuss its rule indicates that it failed to consider the interests of the employees as well as its own interest in promulgating the rules.

Employer Argument

The hospital argued that the management rights provisions authorized it to assign nurses to any duties within their classification which they are qualified to perform in any area of the hospital, in the interest of efficient operation and high standards of service. The hospital claimed that the evidence demonstrated that the duties to which the nurses were assigned on October 17, 19XX, fell within their classification as graduate or registered nurses and were tasks which the nurses were qualified to perform. It was common ground that the nurses in question although regularly assigned to O.R. duty, could be assigned to other areas when not required in the O.R. The hospital characterized the association's position as an attempt to rewrite the collective agreement so as to prevent transfers to other departments on a call-in. The hospital contended that art. 14.06 did not guarantee that the nurses would not be working for the full four-hour period and in the interest of efficient allocation of nursing personnel and high standards of service to patients it was best to deploy the nurses at nursing tasks which need to be performed, once called in, for the entire four-hour period. Furthermore, the hospital could not understand how the rule could be unreasonable since it was not requiring anything different of the nurses on call-in than during their regular tour when they are no longer required in the O.R. or recovery rooms. The hospital pointed out that it was not requiring the nurses to stay beyond the minimum guaranteed pay period except when their assignments in O.R. extend beyond this period. In summary, the hospital contended that the association had failed to establish any specific limitation on its prerogative to assign nurses to any duties within their classification which they are qualified to perform and had failed to establish that the rule was either unreasonable or inconsistent with the provisions of the collective agreement.

The provisions of the collective agreement pertaining to this dispute are the following:

Article 14 — Premium Payment

14.06   Where a nurse has completed her regularly scheduled tour and left the Hospital and is called in to work outside her regularly scheduled working hours, she shall receive time and one-half her regular straight time hourly rate for all hours worked with a minimum guarantee of four (4) hours' pay at time and one-half her regular straight time hourly rate except to the extent that such four (4) hour period overlaps or extends into her regularly scheduled shift. In such a case, she will receive time and one-half her regular straight time hourly rate for actual hours worked up to the commencement of her regular shift.

Article 18 — Miscellaneous

18.06 Prior to effecting any change in rules or policies which affect nurses covered by this Agreement, the Hospital will discuss the changes with the Association and provide copies to the Association.

. . . . .

LOCAL APPENDIX

Article B — Management Functions

B-1 The Association recognizes that the management of the Hospital and the direction of the working forces are fixed in the Hospital and shall remain solely with the Hospital except as specifically limited by the provisions of this Agreement and, without restricting the generality of the foregoing, the Association acknowledges that it is the exclusive function of the Hospital to:

. . . . .

c) determine, in the interest of efficient operation and high standards of service, job rating and classification, the hours of work, work assignments, methods of doing the work and the working establishment for the service;

. . . . .

e) make and enforce and alter from time to time reasonable rules and regulations to be observed by the nurses provided that such rules and regulations shall not be inconsistent with the provisions of the Agreement.

B-2 These rights shall not be exercised in a manner inconsistent with the provisions of this Agreement.

WILLIAM DANBROOK

Discharge — Previous Disciplinary Record — Significance of Last Incident

Background

The facts leading up to the grievance are as follows: The grievor William Danbrook was employed continuously by the company for twenty-five years until the date of his discharge on May 30th, last year. After nine years of employment, he was elected as Union Steward for the department and, three years later, was elected as Union Chief Steward for the zone of the plant in which he worked.

On May 29th, last year, he was absent from work. The next day, May 30th, he reported for work at 7:45 a.m., without having in the meantime notified the company of his absence the day before. He was subsequently interviewed by two company officials to whom he explained that he was absent the day before because of illness which had prevented him from notifying the company.

Subsequently that day he received notice of discharge which read as follows: "Following review of your recent unreported absence, and your record of continuous violations of company rules, you are hereby advised that you are dismissed from employment effective immediately. Your separation papers and wages will be mailed to you under separate cover."

The grievor then filed this grievance:

> "I contend that I have been discharged without just cause. I am requesting that I be reinstated immediately with full compensation for lost earnings."

Applicable provisions of the collective agreement are as follows:

2. The union acknowledges that it is the exclusive function of the company to

a) maintain order and efficiency;

b) suspend or otherwise discipline employees provided that a claim that an employee has been discharged or otherwise disciplined without just cause may be made the subject of a grievance and dealt with in accordance with the grievance procedures;

c) make and enforce reasonable rules and regulations relating to discipline, safety and general conduct of the employees.

3. The company agrees that these functions will be exercised in a manner consistent with the terms of this agreement.

Rule No. 9 states that an employee should notify by telephone to the Guard's office of inability to report for work as scheduled providing satisfactory reasons before the beginning of the scheduled shift.

Note that the notice of dismissal contains two reasons for the company's action in discharging the grievor:

1. The unreported absence of the grievor on May 29th, last year, and

2. The grievor's record of continuous violation of company rules.

On June 6th, pursuant to the provisions of the Collective Agreement, a meeting was held between the company and the Union, at which the grievor was present when his grievance was discussed and the union was given a partial listing of the grievor's previous violations of the company rules.

On June 8th, last year, the Company wrote to the Union Business Agent as follows: "A claim by Mr. Danbrook that he was discharged without just cause on May 30th, was heard in accordance with Clause 16.01 of the Collective Agreement, on June 6th. At the meeting convened to discuss the matter, the union was advised that the grievor had been dismissed from employment because of his unreported absence and because of his record of continuous violations of company rules. Also at this meeting, the Union was given a partial listing of such violations. A more complete listing of Mr. Danbrook's disciplinary record over the previous three years, is summarized as follows:

1. November 28th — Absent from work station — Warning.

2. March 19th — Absent from work station — Further Warning.

3. April 15th — Absenteeism — Further Warning.

4. May 29th — Absenteeism without proper notification — Warned that 'further infractions of the plant rules will result in further disciplinary action which may include discharge.'

5. September 11th — Excessive lateness and absenteeism and failure to notify company when absent — Suspension of three days.

6. July 15th — Disregard of Safety Rules — Further Warning.

7. October 3rd — Restricting Output — Further Warning.

8. October 6th — Absent without prompt notification — Warned that 'any further breach of company rules and regulations could result in a more severe penalty, including discharge.'

9. October 27th — Absent from work station — Further Warning.

10. April 29th — Washing up before quitting time — Further Warning.

11. April 6th — Absent from work station — Further Warning.

12. April 19th — Restricting Output — Further Warning.

13. May 3rd — Careless workmanship and absent from work station. Suspension of five days, and warned that 'any further breach of company rules and regulations will result in a more severe form of disciplinary action.'

It is noted that the investigation of the grievance has shown that Mr. Danbrook has not denied that he failed to notify the company concerning his absence from work on May 29th last year, and it is therefore concluded that Plant Rule No. 9 was in fact violated.

It is further concluded that the penalties imposed as a result of his prior record of continuous violations of company rules and regulations have not had any constructive influence on him. In the light of the facts concerning the company's action, including those facts set out above, the grievance contending that the discharge was without just cause, is denied."

The company's answer to the grievance was not acceptable to the Union and as a result the grievance was processed to arbitration.

Union Argument

At the arbitration hearing, the Union contended that the company had gone to great lengths to compile and build up a record of the unsatisfactory conduct of the grievor in order to justify its dismissal of the grievor for his failure to notify the company of his absence on May 29th last year. The Union suggested that unless the final incident giving rise to the grievor's discharge, being his unexplained absence on May 29th, could be found to be in itself just cause for the grievor's dismissal, the company then had no right to justify his dismissal on the basis of his previous record of offences.

The grievor testified that on Monday, May 28th, he worked his regular shift though he was not feeling very well. This being the first day that he was wearing his new prescription bifocals, he attributed his condition to this circumstance and felt that he would shortly adjust to the new optical conditions. When he retired that night, he still did not feel very well, but managed to go to sleep. He awoke between 5 a.m. and 6 a.m., with severe cramps coupled with diarrhea which got progressively worse involving numerous trips to the bathroom. He finally fell asleep between 11 a.m. and 12 noon, and did not wake until between 3:30 p.m. and 4 p.m. He then consumed some hot milk and cheese in an effort to alleviate his dysentery, took a bath, and between the hours of 6:30 and 6:45, left his apartment to see a doctor.

He first called at the offices of a Dr. Cheung, who was his regular medical advisor, found no one in the doctor's office, and inquiring nearby, was advised by a woman that the doctor no longer held office hours at night because he had had a heart attack. He thereupon boarded a bus, and went to the office of a second doctor, Dr. Allen, which was approximately five blocks away from the office of Dr. Cheung, and was the nearest doctor's office to that point. Dr. Allen examined the grievor, and gave him certain tablets to take to correct his condition.

The next morning, while still feeling unwell, he reported for work at the company's premises at approximately 7:45 a.m., and changed into his working clothes. He then found that his blue attendance card was not in the rack provided for that purpose, asked a clerk why this was so, and at this moment, at approximately 8:05, his foreman arrived in the office, and told him not to bother about his card, but to change into his street clothes, and report to the Employment Office for an interview. The grievor did so and then had the interview previously described. In the interview the grievor was asked his reason for not reporting to work on May 29th, last year, and for not phoning in his reasons for his absence, and the grievor explained that due to his illness, described above, he had not been able to get to a phone, and that no one came to his door that day to whom he could convey a message.

The grievor testified that the lived alone, in an apartment, and that he had no telephone in his apartment, and the nearest telephone was a public telephone approximately a block from his apartment at the intersection of Newington and Rainham Streets. At the interview, above referred to, the grievor was asked: "If you were so sick that you could not get to the telephone, how is it that you are at work today?", to which the grievor replied, "I'm still shaky, but I felt that I should come to work. I am willing to submit myself to an examination by the company doctor, to verify my statements."

Company Argument

The company introduced in evidence as Exhibit 5, a map showing the relative locations of the grievor's residence, the company's premises, the two doctors' offices, and the guards' office of the company. It, and the evidence adduced, indicated that the route taken by the grievor on proceeding at approximately 6:30 p.m., on May 29th, last year, to Dr. Allen's office, passed right by the public telephone, referred to by the grievor in his evidence and right by the company premises and only a block from the guards' office, where as directed by Company Rule No. 9, he should have notified the company of his absence.

The grievor, in this connection, explained his failure either to telephone the company when passing the public telephone booth or to stop by the company offices by stating that on a previous occasion when he had been absent from work, he did telephone an explanation at about noon on the day of his absence but was subsequently disciplined by receiving a written warning for neglecting to follow Plant Rule No. 9 which warning advised him that a further infraction of the plant rules would result in further disciplinary action which might include discharge. This warning, and others, were filed together as Exhibit No. 2, and this warning referred to an offence listed as No. 9 in the letter to the Union, dated June 8th, last year, reproduced above.

Evidence was also adduced that the reason for Rule No. 9 was so that the Company could properly schedule the next day's operations. Consequently, the grievor explained, that he did not telephone after 6 p.m. to notify the company of his absence that day because he had been disciplined for not phoning to the company on a previous occasion before noon and also because he did not feel that such notification would be of any use, inasmuch as he hoped to be, and subsequently was, at work the following day.

Two points therefore emerge from this evidence, for the Board's consideration, namely the genuineness and severity of the grievor's illness on May 29th, and the reasonableness of his explanation for his failure to telephone or otherwise notify the company of his absence.

Concerning the first point the Board was urged in the light of the grievor's past record to consider with suspicion the grievor's allegation that he was ill at all, or the alternative, that he was so ill that he could not, in some way, notify the company of his absence, or induce someone else to do so for him. The Board has before it certain corroborative evidence, namely a copy of a doctor's certificate dated June 7th, last year, purporting to be signed by R. C. Allen, M.D., at his address, 327 George Street, as follows: "To Whom It May Concern: This is to certify that I attended Mr. William Danbrook, 27 Riley Row, on May 29th. He had acute entero colitis."

FRED CUMMINGS
Physical Contact — Threatening of Management Personnel

Background

Company and Union representatives agreed on the following:

On March 4, this year,, shortly after 1 p.m., just outside the Crossway's Tavern, four company management employees and four company employees who were members of the bargaining unit represented by the union, were involved in a physical scuffle. This had been preceded by a verbal exchange between some of the parties some 10 to 15 minutes previously while they were all in the tavern. As a result, the four Union represented employees were not allowed to return to work on their next shift. Subsequently the four were advised of their discharge.

They then grieved that they had been discharged without just cause.

The company's answer did not change the discharge and subsequently the Union processed the grievance to arbitration.

At the arbitration hearing, the grievors all testified that there had been trouble at the plant that morning with regard to the matter of raises for certain employees. There had been heated discussion between management and the Union personnel regarding certain management decisions, particularly the policy adopted in giving these raises. Cummings was one of the stewards involved in these discussions. Shortly after these discussions had ended, Cummings requested permission of his supervisor, Walker to leave work that day. He stated that he was upset because of the lack of sleep due to a sick child and the event of the morning had aggravated his condition. Out of concern for the safety of himself and others, permission was granted. He went to the Union Hall where he met the four other grievors. They stated that they played shuffleboard until 11:15 or 11:30 a.m. when they left to have lunch at the tavern as it was one of the places where they could play bank board shuffleboard. They denied they went to the Crossway's Tavern because they were aware that some of the management personnel would also be there for lunch.

At the hotel, the grievors got a table near the shuffleboard, ordered beer and went to the counter to buy a sandwich. Later, according to his statement, Cummings went back to the counter to buy another sandwich. Between his two trips to the counter, four management employees arrived for lunch and seated themselves some distance away from the grievors. Cummings left the lunch counter and went over to the booth where the management people were seated. They were Richards, department manager, scheduling; Miner, department manager, stock cutting; Johnston, time study engineer; and Monroe, safety and security manager. Cummings addressed Richardson as follows:

"Hi creep! Where's my f__ telegram?" Cummings stated that he thought Richardson would understand this statement as a private joke. However, Richardson apparently didn't agree. Further discussion between Cummings and the group became an argument between Richardson, Miner and Cummings. Shortly after the argument began, the three other grievors moved from the table where they had been sitting, to a table close to the argument. Nothing was said between them and the management group. However, shortly after they moved, Johnston, the time study engineer, went over to their table and had a conversation with them unrelated to the argument. Eventually the bar manager came and told Cummings to sit down and lower his voice. he apparently sat down but continued to argue. The argument centred around the method of scheduling the work in the plant which Cummings claimed cut his incentive earnings. The argument continued until the bar manager asked Cummings to leave. Cummings requested the bar manager to ask the people in the booth to leave as well, but he refused. Cummings then left.

The management group discussed calling the police for protection because of Cummings' attitude, but decided against it. Both groups got up to leave. The management group moved toward the door. Johnston left the Union group to join them. Johnston said that at that time he did not anticipate any further trouble.

As they walked out, Johnston first, followed by Richardson, Miner, and Monroe, they were followed by three of the grievors. One of the grievors, Dalton, testified that a scuffle ensued when Scott, one of the grievors, apparently tripped over the doorstep and fell forward brushing against Richardson, the department manager scheduling. Immediately afterwards, Miner, the department manager, stock cutting, seized Scott and pushed him up against the outer wall of the building. According to his statement, Cummings, who had been waiting outside for transportation, saw what was happening. Anticipating an assault on Scott's person, he ran over and threw himself between Miner and Scott and in the process attempted to forestall Richardson from attacking Scott.

On the other hand, Richardson and Miner stated that it was Scott who seized Richardson and held him up against the wall as Cummings who had been standing beside a parked car just outside, came towards the group as they were leaving the tavern. Each of them felt Scott was trying to set up Richardson for an assault by Cummings.

The conflicts of evidence became even more pronounced as each of the witnesses gave his version of the events which apparently resulted in each being struck once or twice, not clearly by whom. There was considerable punching and shoving, resulting among other things in Richardson being struck several times, his glasses being knocked off, and a cut opened on his nose.

The bar manager stated that he came out and interpreted the situation as wrestling around in a half-hearted manner between Cummings and Richardson. He said that he told them to stop and take the company's business back to the company. Cummings continued to swear at Richardson and threaten some future action. Monroe stayed behind after Richardson, Miner, and Johnston left and discussed the matter with the grievors without further incident.

Later the grievors were advised not to report for work on their next shift and subsequently were discharged.

Company Argument

The company argued that the actions of the grievors were such that they were directly related to the company, involving altercations between the grievors and the management personnel in regard to company business. Therefore discharge was warranted for protection of other employees, the company and the proper carrying on of its business.

Cummings initiated the action that led to the argument and to the scuffle. If he had had cause for a grievance, he should have used the grievance procedure.

His actions and the actions of the others were a verbal and physical assault on management representatives and, further, in regard to matters relating to management.

There is no need to, and management cannot tolerate such action, and it is essential that the arbitration board uphold the discharge.

Union Argument

The union argued that under all of the circumstances of the case the incident was not sufficiently serious to warrant discharge. The misconduct must be viewed in relation to the nature of the employment, the persons, and the situation involved, all within the context of the material facts. All of the grievors had good work records. Cummings is considered by management to be a skilled competent employee with only a minor reprimand on his record. The others have no disciplinary records. The conduct of the grievors did not harm the reputation of the company. The action of the grievors was not such as to seriously impair employer-employee relationships. None of the grievors was under the direct supervision of the management personnel involved.

The incident could not be considered a serious assault upon the various persons concerned and was quickly and easily broken up. This was an isolated instance with no recurrence of any kind. While the argument was initiated

EASTERN UTILITY COMPANY

Discharge — Off Duty Conduct — Vandalism and Damage to Public Property

Background

The employer and the union agreed on the following statement of fact.

The grievors were classified as linemen and were sent on a special assignment in April, 20XX, in the Pembroke Sound area approximately 60 miles from their home location. The assignment involved working on a project to upgrade customer service in rural areas. When in Pembroke Sound, the grievors' travelling and living expenses were paid by the employer. During the night of April 26 - 27, the grievors caused damage to a Police cruiser by kicking one of its doors, kicking in the trunk, and twisting and bending signal lights. The cruiser was parked behind other cars on a service station lot on one of the principal streets in Pembroke Sound.

At the time in question, the grievors were off duty and were not wearing any uniform clothing supplied by the employer that would identify them with the employer, nor were they operating any vehicles owned by the company. As a result of the incident, the grievors were arrested, taken into custody by the Pembroke Sound police, and charged with criminal offences. The grievors were scheduled to report for work on the morning of April 27 but did not do so as they were in police custody from the time they were arrested until 1:30 p.m. on April 27.

Later in the afternoon of April 27, the grievors were suspended by a company official pending further investigation of the incident. Following a meeting on May 1 between management and the grievors at which the grievors admitted responsibility for the incident, the grievors were suspended for five working days.

The incident received news coverage by radio, television, and newspaper over about a 100-mile radius. However, the name of the employer was not mentioned. Several charges were laid against the grievors which were subsequently dropped after the grievors paid for the damage to the police cruiser. After the suspensions, the employees were reassigned to the project on which they had been working at the time of the incident.

Employer Argument

The employer acknowledged the general rule of arbitration that an employee's life is his own and that what he or she does away from work is his or her own business and is no affair of the employer.

However, the employer also pointed out that a number of exceptions have developed to this general rule.

There are two cases that set out the questions that determine this type of issue. The first is Huron Steel Products Co. Ltd. and U.A.W. Local 195 (1964) 15 L.A.C. 288 (Reville). The following statement from that case is often cited:

> It has been held in many arbitration cases that under normal circumstances an employer is only properly concerned with an employee's due and faithful observance of his duties on his job. However, no hard and fast rule can be laid down, and in each case the determination of three questions of fact will determine the issue. These are:
>
> 1. Was the employee's conduct sufficiently injurious to the interests of the employer?
>
> 2. Did the employee act in a manner incompatible with the due and faithful discharge of his duty?
>
> 3. Did the employee do anything prejudicial or likely to be prejudicial to the reputation of the employer?
>
> If one or more of the above questions must be answered in the affirmative on all the evidence, then the company is properly concerned with the employee's conduct regardless of whether it occurred on or off the company property or in or out of working hours, and depending on the gravity of that conduct, the company will be justified in taking appropriate disciplinary action.

The second case of relevance is Re Millhaven Fibres Ltd., Millhaven Works, and Oil, Chemical and Atomic Workers Int'l Union, Local 9-670 (1967), IA Union Management Arbitration Cases 328 (Anderson), quoted in the Re Air Canada Int'l Association of Machinists, Lodge 148 (1973), 5 L.A.C. (2d) (Andrews). In the Millhaven Fibres case, the arbitrator said:

> ... if the discharge is to be sustained on the basis of a justifiable reason arising out of conduct away from the place of work, there is an onus on the Company to show that:
>
> 1. the conduct of the grievor harms the Company's reputation or product
>
> 2. the grievor's behaviour renders the employee unable to perform his duties satisfactorily
>
> 3. the grievor's behaviour leads to refusal, reluctance or inability of the other employees to work with him.

4. the grievor has been guilty of a serious breach of the Criminal Code and thus rendering his conduct injurious to the general reputation of the Company and its employees.

5. places difficulty in the way of the Company properly carrying out its functions of efficiently managing its Works and efficiently directing its working forces.

In Air Canada, the Arbitrator added that with respect to the factors set out in Millhaven Fibres: "It is my interpretation that it is not necessary for a company to show that all five criteria in the Millhaven Fibres case have followed on the employee's conduct; rather, any one of the consequences named may warrant discipline."

The Counsel for the Eastern Utility Company particularly stressed the first criterion, namely, that the grievor's conduct may harm the company's reputation or product. He stated that this depends very much on the type of company and its place in the commercial world but in this case the company affected is a major public utility with a high public profile. Therefore, its reputation must always be of great concern to it. Accordingly, the employer is entitled to take very seriously any employee conduct that would damage that reputation. While it was true the grievors were not on duty on a company project, their living expenses were being paid by the company, and in a large sense they represented the company.

The employer argued that the fact the employee was not particularly connected with his employer by the news media did not prevent the employer from being associated with the employee as a result of other particular facts of the case, including the serious and flagrant nature of the offence and the widespread publicity surrounding it.

Union Argument

The union argued that none of the criteria set out in the Millhaven Fibres case and outlined above had been met in this case. There was no contention or evidence that the grievors had acted in a manner incompatible with the discharge of their duty to the company; that their behaviour had rendered them unable to perform their duties satisfactorily; that their behaviour would lead to refusal or reluctance or inability of other employees to work with them; or that their conduct had placed any difficulty in the way of the company properly carrying out its functions of efficiently carrying out its works and efficiently directing its working forces. Thus the case comes down to the single question of whether the grievors' behaviour had harmed the company's reputation or was otherwise injurious to the interests of the employer.

CANADIAN AMALGAMATED TRUCK LINES

Criminal Charges Laid Against Grievor — Whether Indefinite Suspension Proper

Background

The Grievance, dated May of last year, reads as follows: "I grieve that the suspension I received on April 27, 20XX, was without just cause and that the penalty is too severe. I claim lost pay and benefits from the date of April 27."

On April 27, 20XX, the grievor received a letter notifying him of his suspension. The substance of that letter is as follows:

> You were picked up by the City Police on April 27, and charged with possession of stolen goods from Canadian Amalgamated Truck Lines Limited.

> Therefore, you are suspended (without pay) from Canadian Amalgamated Truck Lines Limited.
> This suspension will remain in effect until your case is heard in court and if found guilty, your employment will be terminated with Canadian Amalgamated Truck Lines Limited.

On June 9, the grievor received another letter, as follows:

> On May 31, you were found guilty as charged on April 27. This became known to me on June 8.
> As per the letter sent to you by registered mail on April 28 (dated April 27), you are terminated from Canadian Amalgamated Truck Lines Limited.

The union and the employer agreed that the subject matter of the arbitration was the suspension not the discharge of the grievor. There was no dispute between the parties with regard to the facts. The grievor had been employed by the company for twelve years. At all material times he worked as a city driver. His duties involved his transporting goods from the company terminal to various customers in the city and from customers in the city to the terminal. City drivers are alone in their trucks and there is no direct supervision by anyone from the Company.

On or about April 27, the grievor was arrested by the City Police and charged with theft of over $200. The items allegedly stolen by the grievor were sets of socket wrenches which were to be delivered to one of the company's customers in the city. Some other employees of the company, all of whom were employed as dockmen, were also arrested and charged with possession of stolen property.

On April 27, the company was informed by City Police that the grievor had been arrested and charged with theft of the goods in question, and had confessed to the theft. The company had not initiated the police investigation.

On May 31, the grievor pleaded guilty to theft over $200 and was convicted. He was sentenced to one day in jail and a fine of $500.

Evidence was also given about other jobs available in the Bargaining Unit which showed that the employees worked with no or very little supervision. All highway and city drivers work with no direct supervision while they drive and employees on the dock are not closely supervised at all. Both drivers and dockmen have access to goods transported in the course of its business as a common carrier. Both drivers and dockmen are directly entrusted with the safe carriage of goods.

Union Argument

The union argued that the company had a duty, under the circumstances, to offer alternate employment to the grievor during the period of his suspension from his regular job as a city driver. And that this duty had been neglected. The union argued furthermore that the company had acknowledged in its evidence that it had not considered alternate employment for the grievor during the period between his arrest and trial.

Company Argument

The company was aware at the time of the suspension that the grievor had been arrested for theft of property carried by the company and had confessed to that theft. It was also aware the grievor's job would place him in constant contact with goods carried by the company and that there would be no effective way of supervising him while he was driving. This knowledge must also be considered in light of the company's concern about thefts and its relation to its customers. The evidence before the Board was that the company's city operations had experienced losses from theft of between $5,000 and $10,000 per year. There was also evidence that the customer who was the intended recipient of the stolen goods had lost about $1,000 worth of goods carried by the company in the past year and that the customer was fed up and was threatening to transfer his business to another carrier.

The company also showed that is operations were such that there were no bargaining unit jobs in which the employee could be closely supervised or in which he would not be in contact with a customer's goods.

For all of these reasons, the company argued that the Arbitration Board should dismiss the grievance.

TOWN PLAZA HOTEL

Discharge — Theft — Minimal Value

The grievor, Mrs. Elisabeth Meyers, was discharged from her employment as a cook on July 10, for alleged theft. She filed a grievance claiming unjust dismissal which was then processed to arbitration.

Facts

The grievor was 54 years old, had six years of service and a good record.

The essential facts are not in dispute. On Friday, July 4, 20XX, the grievor was working as a Cook III. At the close of her shift, at approximately 4:00 p.m., she was observed by the food service supervisor, Ms. Karen Schaefer, near the back of the kitchen searching through boxes on a garbage wagon. The grievor approached Ms. Schaefer and told her she needed empty boxes to help a friend who was moving. Shortly after this, Ms. Schaefer noticed the grievor pacing in front of the garbage wagon. The grievor then took a sweater she was carrying under her arm and reached behind a doorway into an adjacent store-room. She appeared to drop her sweater and then extracted a box from the store-room. Ms. Schaefer approached the grievor and removed the sweater from the box. Upon doing so she found in the box three wrapped pairs of muffins and one individually wrapped muffin, two pieces of cheese souffle and a piece of bavarian meat loaf. The items were wrapped in a saran wrap type material.

Ms. Schaefer asked the grievor if she had paid for the food products. The grievor responded by naming specific employees from whom she said she had purchased the muffins and souffle. She told Ms. Schaefer she had not paid for the bavarian meat loaf because it was for her dog and was to be thrown out in any event. Ms. Schaefer said (referring to the bavarian meat loaf) "Elisabeth, this is stealing". The grievor replied "I know". Ms. Schaefer said she would have to investigate the matter and that she would get back to the grievor. Ms. Schaefer confiscated the box and food items and the grievor left the hotel premises.

Ms. Schaefer then contacted the employees from whom the grievor said she had purchased the items. She determined that the grievor had not purchased the muffins or souffle as alleged by the grievor. Ms. Schaefer then contacted the director of dietary services, Mrs. Lydia Greco. Mrs. Greco has direct responsibility for all food production services at the hotel including the supervision and discipline of staff. Mrs. Greco contacted the grievor by telephone at home and told her that the matter was under investigation and the grievor was not to report to work until further notice.

Mrs. Greco testified that during her telephone conversation with the grievor, the grievor reiterated that she had paid for the muffins and souffle but not for the meat loaf because it was going to be thrown out. She again asserted that she was taking the meat loaf home for her dog. Mrs. Greco said that the grievor was very agitated and upset on the telephone. The grievor pleaded with Mrs. Greco to forgive her and said she was very sorry. She asked Mrs. Greco not to take the matter further with administration. Mrs. Greco told the grievor that she would get back to her the following Monday or Tuesday after she had completed her investigation and after she had discussed the matter with hotel administration.

In her own testimony, the grievor quite adamantly denied that she told Mrs. Greco on the telephone that she had paid for the food items. She did, however, acknowledge that she was crying and upset and that she had pleaded for another chance. The grievor said she was under the impression she was probably going to be fired as a result of her conduct.

On Monday, July 7, 20XX, the grievor endeavoured to see the assistant executive director, employee relations, Mr. John Kasik. Mr. Kasik was away for that day. She was waiting for him in his office when he arrived at work on July 8. Mr. Kasik had not yet been briefed by Mrs. Greco concerning the events of the prior week. He agreed to speak with her. He testified that Mrs. Meyers was very upset and that her comments were disjointed and close to incoherent. He testified she told him she was in a lot of trouble. She said "It was the diet that had done it to her — it had driven her crazy". She produced a photocopy of a diet from a tabloid newspaper and explained to Mr. Kasik that she was on a salt-free diet and, as a result, she had a craving for salt. He testified she said she took the food items because they contained an excess amount of salt. Mr. Kasik quickly determined that the matter should more properly be handled by the grievor's department head and referred her to Mrs. Greco.

The grievor's recollection of her conversation with Mr. Kasik differed quite materially. She said she showed him the newspaper diet only to establish that her diet was salt-free. She said her diet only allowed her to eat vegetables and salad. She testified she showed Mr. Kasik the diet in order to establish that she was not taking the food for herself but rather for her dog. The grievor testified that she did not recall telling Mr. Kasik that she had a craving for salt.

When the grievor left Mr. Kasik's office, she went to see Mrs. Greco. Mrs. Greco testified that the grievor showed her a copy of a diet extracted from a newspaper. The grievor told her she was on a low salt diet and, accordingly, it left her with a craving for salt. Mrs. Greco said the grievor told her the reason she took the muffins and meat loaf was because of the salt content. She said the grievor confirmed that the meat loaf was going to be thrown out anyway. Mrs. Greco disagreed and told the grievor that the department would find a use for it.

The hotel made its decision to dismiss the grievor on approximately July 10, after reviewing the facts of the case. On July 10, Mr. Kasik and Mrs. Greco met with the grievor, her husband and union representatives. Mr. Kasik reviewed the facts leading up to the meeting including the various versions of events given by the grievor. According to Mr. Kasik, during the meeting the grievor told him that she had taken all the food products for her dog. She maintained that the food had no value because it was going to be thrown out in any event. She acknowledged that she had not paid for the souffle, meat loaf or six of the muffins. She said that she had paid for one muffin.

In her testimony before this board, the grievor said that her recollection of the meeting on July 10 was unclear. She testified that she had taken valium prior to the meeting to calm her nerves and, as a result, did not recall much of the discussion.

Company Argument

Mr. Kasik outlined the reasons for the termination. Those reasons included the fact that the grievor had committed what the hotel considered a serious offence, i.e., alleged theft; that the grievor had acted in what appeared to be a premeditated manner; that the grievor held a position of trust in that she had access to departmental property and, on occasion, cash; that the grievor had lied to her supervisor on several occasions in endeavouring to cover up her involvement and that the grievor had breached departmental policy on the purchase of food products.

Employee Argument

At this arbitration hearing, the grievor testified she took the food for her dog. She maintained that the food items were of no value because they were to be discarded. She said she had been advised earlier in the day on July 7, to gar-burate the souffle. She testified the meat loaf had already been reheated one time and she did not think it was safe for reuse. She testified that during the day of July 7, she had removed the muffins from a warmer and that, as they appeared "squashed and crumbled" she thought they would be discarded. During the day she removed these food items to the storage room where she placed them in the box. She denied wrapping the muffins in pairs in saran wrap.

She did acknowledge that she told Ms. Schaefer that she had paid for the food product when confronted by Ms. Schaefer in the kitchen. She said she was frightened at the time. She testified she was aware she could not take food home and was also aware of a hotel policy to the effect that employees could not purchase food at the hotel for home consumption. She testified at the time Ms. Schaefer approached her, she "felt trapped". The grievor said she did not recall telling either Mr. Kasik or Mrs. Greco in the meetings of July 8th that her diet had created a craving for salt.

UNIVERSITY HOSPITAL

Incompetence — Discharge and Discipline — Long Standing Poor Performance of Employee Tolerated by Employer

Background

The grievor was notified on March 17, 20XX, that he would be dismissed effective September 19. The reason for the dismissal can be summarized as poor work performance with no realistic expectation that the employee would improve to a level acceptable to the employer.

The grievor was hired seven years earlier, and has worked continuously as a storekeeper since that time.

While the dismissal, if upheld, would not take place until September 19, the parties agreed that the grievance was properly before the arbitrator having jurisdiction to rule on the merits of the grievance as though the grievor had actually been terminated on the day of notification, March 17.

The notification of termination from the grievor's manager follows:

> As you know, the Hospital has been concerned about your poor work performance for some time and I have reaffirmed this concern on numerous occasions. I have stressed the need for improvement in your work performance to the level acceptable for the department.
>
> You have been given numerous opportunities to improve. The last time, you were given a 45 day period in which you were told significant improvement in your performance was required or your employment would be terminated. Although there was some improvement, your work performance is still at a level unacceptable for the department.
>
> As it appears that you are unable to achieve the level of performance required for the department, and there is no indication that further retraining or time on the job would improve your performance, we have no alternative but to terminate your employment.
>
> The Hospital is giving you six (6) months notice of termination. If you are not successful in obtaining alternate employment, you will be terminated effective Friday, September 19, 20XX, at 1630 hours.

The grievance dated March 26, 20XX reads:

> The Employer has violated the collective agreement, Article #7 — Grievance and Arbitration Procedure and any other related clauses with a letter of intent to terminate me without just cause to take effect Friday, September 19, 20XX, at 1630 hours.

I request that the letter of intent to terminate me be withdrawn and destroyed from my record and that I be fully compensated with full redress of any loss of wages, benefits and opportunities as of September 19, 20XX, at 1630 hours.

Pertinent sections of the collective agreement follow:

ARTICLE 7 — GRIEVANCE AND ARBITRATION PROCEDURE

7.06 A claim by an employee who has completed his probationary period that he has been unjustly discharged or suspended shall be treated as a grievance if a written statement of such grievance is lodged by the employee with the hospital at Step. No. 3 within seven (7) calendar days after the date the discharge or suspension is effected. Such special grievance may be settled under the Grievance or Arbitration Procedure by:

  a) confirming the Hospital's action in dismissing the employee, or

  b) reinstating the employee with or without full compensation for the time lost; or

  c) by any other arrangement which may be deemed just and equitable.

  Wherever the Hospital deems it necessary to suspend or discharge an employee, the Hospital shall notify the Union of such suspension or discharge in writing. The Hospital agrees that it will not suspend, discharge, or otherwise discipline an employee who has completed his probationary period, without just cause.

. . . . .

7.12 The Arbitration Board shall not be authorized to make any decision inconsistent with the provisions of this Agreement, nor to alter, modify, add to or amend any part of this Agreement.

The storekeeper *job description* reads:

Position: STOREKEEPER

Reports to:
Manager — Material Distribution

Qualifications:
Secondary School Graduation Diploma or an equivalent combination of education and experience. Previous distribution experience would be an asset.

Conditions of Employment:
Must be physically able to perform the essential duties of the job.

Job Summary:

Under the direct supervision of the Manager – Material Distribution, performs all duties related to the Materials Distribution function.

Major Duties:

1. Maintains a perpetual inventory control.

2. Performs shipping and receiving functions.

3. Operates printing press, copier, and other related equipment, and performs limited maintenance on them.

4. Processes purchase orders and invoices (Kardex — pricing) and follows up as required.

5. Distributes all supplies as per authorized requisition forms.

6. Maintains work area.

7. Performs I.V. Solution Top Up on a daily basis.

8. Assists in the physical inventories as required.

9. Performs any other related duties as required.

Employer Argument

The employer's case was presented through the evidence of one witness, the grievor's manager. The union did not cross-examine the employer's witness and elected not to call on the grievor.

The uncontested evidence of the employer is that while the grievor had been on substantially the same job for some seven years and though his performance had not deteriorated over that period of time, he had been unsatisfactory over his term of employment and was currently unsatisfactory. Further, there was no reason to think that sufficient improvement would be forthcoming to warrant his continued employment.

The employer counselled the grievor numerous times over the period of his employment but concrete action was not taken until September 4, of the previous year, when a meeting was held with the grievor, union representatives and management representatives in attendance. This meeting was called by the union. The employer outlined the areas of dissatisfaction which resulted in inadequate service by the department and in concern by the grievor's fellow employees that the workload was not being properly shared. The efficiency of the department was impaired because the grievor could not be trusted to carry out certain assignments on time and with accuracy. The meeting terminated with a three-point programme in place:

1. the grievor would identify those parts of his job where he felt he would benefit from retraining;

2. the grievor's job performance would be evaluated over a period of 45 days with feedback sessions every two weeks; and

3. a formal evaluation would be conducted at the end of the 45 days.

The grievor was given the opportunity to state his retraining needs but did not indicate any requirements. An informal interim performance evaluation was conducted on September 20th and discussed with the grievor. Several areas of concern were expressed by the grievor's manager. Feedback sessions were held with a union representative present. Management expressed continuing dissatisfaction but the grievor appeared to believe that he was doing an effective job.

The formal 45-day evaluation was conducted on November 7, and was reviewed with the grievor and a union representative on November 12th. The summary of the evaluation showed continuing concern in the areas of work performance, judgment and initiative.

A meeting was held on November 14th including several union representatives, management representatives and the grievor. It was decided to give the grievor another 45 working days to see if he could improve, this time assigning a fellow employee/union representative to act as a working "buddy" for 20 of those days. One reason for this additional trial period and the employment of the "buddy" system was because the union said that there was a personality conflict between the grievor and the manager.

Performance problems continued and the evaluation of January 31, 19XX, indicated substantial dissatisfaction and it was noted that, while there was no doubt the grievor was trying, the improvement was not significant enough to meet the standards of the department.

The employer considered other work for the grievor but did not find a suitable opening anywhere in the hospital. The grievor received his notice of termination March 17, 20XX.

Union Argument

The union urged that the grievor should be retained on the job because of the several years he had performed the same function without discipline as well as because the employer failed to set out reasonable and clear standards of performance expectations. Further, it was alleged that the employer had released the grievor because he was not as good as other employees rather than because he was not performing the job satisfactorily.

KEITH ROWAN

Seniority — Bumping — Reasonable Evidence — Similarity of Skills

Background

Due to lack of work, Keith Rowan, a sheet metal worker in Department 21, was given notice of layoff.

The company had a plant-wide seniority system in its collective agreement with the Union which provided basically that an employee who was otherwise about to be laid off was entitled to take the job of another employee in the company with less seniority whose job he could perform. Rowan asked for and was given an up-to-date copy of the plant-wide seniority list and decided to claim the job of Murray Northrup, a welder-fitter in Department 14, who had slightly less seniority than him. He was interviewed for the job by the foreman, Mr. Irwin, who after the interview informed Rowan he was not qualified for the job. Rowan decided to file a grievance claiming Northrup's job. The grievance was heard and subsequently denied by the company. The Union decided to process it to arbitration.

The grievance read as follows:

> "I contend I am being laid off contrary to the seniority provisions of the collective agreement. I contend I can perform the work of M. Northrup who is being retained by the company and has less seniority than I. I am requesting a five-day trial period as provided for by clause 1205 D(ii) to prove that I can perform this work."

The applicable provisions of the collective agreement are as follows:

> 1205 Layoffs or transfers due to lack of work will be governed by the following provisions:

> D(ii). Following the application of the procedure under section 1205 D(i) an employee who is about to be laid off (without prejudice to his right of grievance under such section) will be transferred to a job held by an employee with less seniority or an open job on a trial basis where the company has reasonable evidence either that the employee has transferable skills which would enable him to meet the normal requirements of the work of such job within a maximum period of five working days (which may be extended by agreement) or that having previously worked on such job (or on a job requiring similar skills) he could so perform it within such period. The employee so transferred will be acquainted through demonstration and information with the normal duties of the work. Should the employee upon being so transferred be unable to meet

such requirements during the minimum period of five working days (or as extended by agreement) or should it become so apparent in a lesser time than the five-day period, he will be eligible for one further transfer to a lesser skilled job held by an employee with less seniority or an open job which he can perform without trial as otherwise provided in this clause.

Union Argument

For the Union, the grievor testified that he had been instructed to see Mr. Irwin, Foreman of Department 14, to see if he could bump Northrup, who was classified as welder-fitter, job code Number 56. It was stated his job included the following functions:

a) arc welding,

b) gas cut to layout (up to 4" plate)

c) all position pipe welding

The grievor stated Irwin showed him the welding work and asked him if he could do the job. He replied yes. Irwin asked if he had any pipe-welding tests and the grievor produced two certificates — one from the Ministry of Labour for welding metallic arc in flat positions and secondly, a certificate from the Canadian Welding Bureau for welding on flat, horizontal and vertical positions up to three quarters of an inch.

Irwin asked if he had a test of six-inch pipe all-position welding. When the grievor said he did not, Irwin told him he was not qualified for the job.

The grievor then asked for a test by the Welding Inspector. Irwin replied the Welding Inspector was out and could not give him a test. The grievor stated he told Irwin he could do the all-position pipe-welding. He stated for a period of time he worked in Department 32 where he did gas cutting and in Department 34 where he did gas cutting on plates of up to one-inch thickness. In Department 32 he was gas cutting to layout.

He admitted that in October of the previous year he had failed a test in gas cutting of two-inch steel because he was not familiar with the tips and the percentage of air and oxygen to use, and that he had no further experience in gas cutting.

He also admitted that he had never done all-position pipe welding although he had read about it.

With respect to the cutting, he said that work was not demonstrated to him and that if he had a half hour he could do it and certainly could do it within five days.

Mr. Northrup gave evidence and stated he started to work with the company as a welder as had the grievor. He stated between then and now, he and the grievor had been transferred to various departments and in each case had done the same work.

He expressed the opinion the grievor could do the work required and was a better than average welder.

He stated that when he was given a gas cutting test, he passed it and that he had been told about the proper mix before he tried the test. Northrup stated he was trained on all-position welding and had failed his first two tests and received training between each test. The training consisted of practices.

Northrup expressed the opinion the grievor would require training on all-position welding.

Mr. Davey gave evidence and stated he bumped into the same department a year earlier. He stated before he took his all-position pipe welding test, he practised on pipe for two or three hours; took a test, and failed it. He again practised for two or three hours, and passed his test.

He expressed the opinion that a good welder could do all-position pipe welding.

Evidence was also given that a number of employees who came into this department passed the test on their first day.

For the grievor, Mr. Rowan, the Union representative, argued the grievor's record showed many transfers and that other employees with similar records had been taken onto this job in this department. He argued that Rowan's experience as a welder entitled him to a test on all-position pipe welding.

He further argued that this section of the agreement provided for demonstration and information with respect to normal duties of the work and if this were given to the grievor he would be able to do the work without training.

Section 1205 D(ii) provides for the transfer of an employee who is about to be laid off ``where the company has reasonable evidence of transferable skills which could enable him to meet the normal requirements of the work of such job within a maximum period of five working days.''

The Union argues the company did have such reasonable evidence and as a result the grievor is entitled to such a trial.

Company Argument

The Company called no evidence.

For the company, Mr. Nelson argued that the grievor failed to show he had the necessary skills to do the job or that he had worked on the job.

He pointed out that qualification for all-position pipe welding was a requirement of the job and that even Northrup in his evidence stated the grievor would require training for this work.

He also pointed out that the grievor had failed the year before on a gas cutting test and that the grievor admitted he had no further knowledge of or qualification for the work since that test was given.

He argued the section of the agreement relied upon by the grievor does not require the company to train an employee for the job.

GEORGE ROBBINS

Seniority — Bumping — Suitability of Evidence — Concern about Safety Hazards

Background

On November 7th, 20XX, George Robbins was advised by his foreman that there was no more work available for him in his present job and as a result he was being declared surplus. The company had a departmental and plant-wide seniority system. Under its provisions an employee like Robbins who was surplus in his job could bump another employee in his department who had less seniority and whose job he could do, and failing that could bump any other employee in the plant who had less seniority and whose job he could do.

Robbins apparently recognized there was no one in his department with less seniority whose job he could do and indicated he wanted to exercise his plant-wide bumping rights. He was therefore sent to the personnel department and after a examination of seniority lists and some discussion, was advised that there was no one in the plant with less seniority whose job he could do and as a result was given written notice as required by the collective agreement that he would be laid off in seven days.

After further examination of the seniority lists, Robbins decided to file the following grievance:

> "I contend I am being laid off out of seniority as I contend I can do the work of John Mills, Maintenance Department, and under the provisions of Clause 1205 D(ii), claim a five-day trial period."

The grievor Robbins had a seniority date about eighteen months earlier than the one for the person whose job he claimed, John Mills.

Robbins, immediately prior to his layoff, was classified under Job Code 121-1, Painter Brush and Spray 1st Class. Mills, whose job he claimed, was classified under Job Code 122 — Painter Maintenance. The rate of pay for the job Robbins performed was 6 cents per hour higher than that of the job held by Mills.

The job description of the two jobs are as follows:

Job Code 121-1 Painter — Brush and Spray, 1st Class

Occupational duties:

Experienced brush and spray painter on products requiring a slow finish. Match colours and prepare metal for painting. Sand, fill, mask in, and polish when necessary. Be familiar with the consistency of paints under various conditions. Work from paint specifications. Apply paints such as dulux, duco (baking and air dry) lacquer, enamel, etc., with a smooth even coating to avoid runs and orange peel effect. May do some flowing and dipping of parts. Clean and adjust own equipment. Minimum supervision. Work on products such as metal cabinets, shelving panels, etc.

Job Code 122 — Painter Maintenance

Occupational duties:

Mix up standard paints and varnishes, etc. for all maintenance painting. Paint windows, doors, partitions, walls, pipes, etc., with brushes or spraying equipment. Work from ladders or scaffolding. May be required to perform other duties as per foreman's instructions.

The applicable provisions of the collective agreement are as follows:

1205 Layoffs or transfers due to lack of work will be governed by the following provisions:

D(ii). Following the application of the procedures under 1205 D(i), an employee who is about to be laid off will be transferred to a job held by an employee with less seniority, or an open job, on a trial basis where the company has reasonable evidence, either that the employee has transferable skills which would enable him to meet the normal requirements of the work of such job within a maximum period of five working days (which may be extended by agreement) or that having previously worked on such job (or on a job requiring similar skills) he could so perform it within such period. The employee so transferred will be acquainted through demonstration and information with the normal duties of the work. Should the employee upon being so transferred be unable to meet such requirements during the maximum period of five working days (or as extended by agreement) or should it become so apparent in a lesser time than the five- day period, he will be eligible for one further transfer to a lesser skilled job held by an employee without trial as otherwise provided in this clause. In laying off an employee because such a lesser skilled job is not available, the provisions with respect to notice of layoff will not apply.

Subject to filing the grievance, Robbins was interviewed by the maintenance foreman who has responsibility for the job claimed, Mr. Dickson, but the decision was made that he was not entitled to a trial period under the provisions of the agreement and as a result he was laid off as scheduled and the grievance was taken to arbitration.

Union Argument

At the arbitration hearing, Mr. Robbins gave evidence and stated that he had worked on a variety of jobs including Bench Hand, Painter-Brush and Spray, for some four months, machine work, as well as Storekeeper and various other jobs in the plant.

He stated that prior to coming to the company he had worked with a painting contractor, painting houses, and had to work off scaffolds and had mixed paint.

He was not interviewed in connection with Mills' job before filing the grievance, but after he did file it, he had an interview with Mr. Dickson, the maintenance foreman.

He said Dickson told him that to qualify for the job he would have to use a pneumatic breaker, chip paint, glaze windows, and various other types of work that were done by Mills.

He said he would be required to work from a bosun's chair (a bosun's chair is a device which is attached to a series of ropes that can be slung across various high bays of the plant; the occupant sits in the chair and is propelled to the appropriate location to do the required work) and showed him some broken windows in one of the buildings some 65 feet up and said if he did get the job, his first assignment would be to replace those broken windows.

He admitted that he had never worked from a swinging scaffold but said that he could. He also admitted he was not an experienced glazier but stated he had done glazing for himself. He told Dickson that he could do the work required of him.

On behalf of the Union, James Morley gave evidence. He stated he had worked for many years in the maintenance department in which Mills was now working. He said he was experienced in the rigging of bosun's chairs and that during the period he was there this work had always been given to the machine movers. He said anyone could learn the job of rigging a bosun's chair in an hour and a half.

On this evidence the Union argued there could be no doubt that Robbins had all of the qualifications required for the painting work involved in the job of painter maintenance. Further, that the other duties according to the occupational duties filed, were to perform other duties as instructed by the foreman and these duties consisted of glazing and general labour work only.

The Union further argued the grievor had had a variety of jobs in the plant, that he undoubtedly had, to the knowledge of the company, transferable skills which would enable him to meet the normal requirements of the work of the job claimed in accordance with the provisions of clause 1205 D(ii) of the collective agreement and he was therefore to have the opportunity of proving he could perform this work during the five-day period provided for in this section.

Company Argument

Mr. Dickson, foreman of the maintenance department, gave evidence.

He said there were thirteen employees in his group including a bricklayer, two machine movers, two painters, a truck driver, a storekeeper, two elevator operators, a group leader and a cement finisher. He said they maintain machines, replace floors, paint, and glaze windows as required, in all the buildings, and on occasion they have to uncover water lines and dig foundation bases. He said some of the work was heavy work such as that of using concrete breakers, and that this could continue for days.

He said that over the last five months prior to December 20XX he went over the company records and a breakdown of Mill's work showed that he spent 21% of his time painting, 16% glazing, 13% machine moving, and 50% general labour. He said at times it was necessary for the painter to work on a bosun's chair and on a swing scaffold and on such occasions two painters worked together.

For the company Mr. Allen, company counsel, agreed the whole question before the Board was whether, on the evidence, Mr. Robbins was entitled to the trial period as provided for in clause 1205 D(ii).

He pointed out the period was a trial period, not a training period, and the question was whether Mr. Robbins had knowledge and experience sufficient to enable him to do the job without training.

He admitted Robbins had the necessary painting qualifications to perform the basic duties of a painter-maintenance.

He argued the company had no evidence the grievor could work from scaffolding or from a bosun's chair, and argued that the foreman had made an assessment of the work to be done and the ability of the grievor to do the heavy tasks involved, and that his assessment was correct.

He agreed Robbins was a capable employee in his own classification.

RUSSELL COLEMAN

Seniority — Bumping — Evidence — Test — Similarity and Difference of Jobs

Background

Russell Coleman was employed as shipper in the assembly department of the switchgear division. He was hired by the company on April 8th, 20XX. As a result of the application of the plant-wide seniority provisions of the collective agreement with the Union, he was dispatched from his job by another employee whose job had been eliminated as a result of a work shortage in another department of the company.

His foreman, Mr. Randall, reviewed his own departmental seniority list, and then discussed the matter with the company's personnel department. The conclusion was there was no job held by a person with less seniority that Coleman could perform and as a result he was given notice of layoff.

Subsequently Coleman filed the following grievance:

> "I contend I am being laid off in violation of the collective agreement as H. Schultz has less seniority and is being retained on a job that I can perform. Under the provisions of clause 1205 D(ii), I claim a five-day trial on the job held by H. Schultz, seniority date June 20th, 20XX."

Schultz was employed as a storekeeper in the same department in which Coleman was employed.

He was subsequently formally interviewed for the job by his foreman Mr. Randall. The company considered he was not qualified for the job and as a result his grievance was denied and he was laid off.

The Union subsequently decided to process the grievance to arbitration.

Applicable provisions of the collective agreement:

> 1205 Layoffs or transfers due to lack of work will be governed by the following provisions:
>
> D(ii) Following the application of the procedure under section 1205 D(i) an employee who is about to be laid off (without prejudice to his right of grievance under such section) will be transferred to a job held by an employee with less seniority or an open job on a trial basis where the company has reasonable evidence either that the employee has transferable skills which would enable him to meet the normal requirements of the work of such job within a maximum period of five working days (which may be extended by agreement) or that having previously worked on such job (or on a job requiring similar skills) he could so per-

form it within such period. The employee so transferred will be acquainted through demonstration and information with the normal duties of the work. Should the employee upon being so transferred be unable to meet such requirements during the maximum period of five working days (or as extended by agreement) or should it become apparent in a lesser time than the five-day period, he will be eligible for one further transfer to a lesser skilled job held by an employee with less seniority or an open job which he can perform without trial as otherwise provided in this clause. In laying off an employee because such a lesser skilled job is not available the provisions of section 1205 C shall not apply.

Union Argument

The evidence in support of the grievance brought by the Union was basically the evidence of the grievor himself. He claimed he was qualified to do Schultz's job because he was familiar with the material handled in that storeroom through his work as a shipper in that department and because he was previously a storekeeper in another department.

He claimed that because he was a storekeeper he was familiar with the duties of a storekeeper and could perform these duties. He said the difference between one storekeeping job and another was primarily the material in the storeroom. Therefore, he was familiar with the storekeeper's job. He stated in his duties as a shipper, he had to go to the storeroom every day for material although he admitted he had been inside the storeroom on only very few occasions. Under cross-examination, he admitted that in his previous job as storekeeper, the stores contained only 400–500 items and that storeroom was much smaller than the storeroom in the job claimed.

Company Argument

The company called the grievor's foreman, Mr. Stephen Randall to give evidence. Mr. Randall stated the job of storekeeper which the grievor claimed was far more complicated and required far greater knowledge than the job of storekeeper which the grievor had previously held. In addition they were different in that the stores included a different range of material and different forms than required in the previous storekeeper job held by the grievor. He stated there was some 4,500 items kept in the storeroom claimed and there were some 12 forms that had to be used in connection with the storeroom. This was a storeroom from which the manufacturing process in the department was supplied.

It was far different from the storeroom the grievor was accustomed to in the other division. His evidence stated that as shipper he would only become familiar with some 25% of the parts he would be required to know as store-keeper in the department. The storekeeper would also be required to be famil-iar with the location of the parts in the storeroom and he stated it would take some considerable time for the grievor to familiarize himself with the loca-tion of the parts in the storeroom. He stated that in his judgment it would take the grievor at least 4 to 6 weeks to learn the job Schultz was doing.

He stated that, after the grievor filed his grievance, he decided to arrange a formal interview for the job claimed in order to be entirely fair to the griev-or and in order to appear to be fair in case the grievance went to arbitration. He stated in the interview he asked the grievor a number of questions and that while he answered some correctly, he was quite hazy in answer to other ques-tions, and there were a number of others where the grievor had no basis for an answer at all. He stated he asked the grievor questions in regard to the job to establish whether or not the grievor was familiar with it. He was complete-ly unfamiliar with quite a number of parts and he acknowledged he was not familiar with quite a number of the forms in the job.

DAVID SHEPHERD

Seniority — Job Posting — Lines of Progression —Language

Background

Labour grades in the company are classified in numerical order. The higher ranking the job, the higher its numerical designation. The labour grades come from a company-wide job evaluation system. The value of each of the jobs in the company is ranked relative to each other. Those that are considered to have the same value are assigned to the same labour grade regardless of the department in which they are located or the type of work being performed. The work in one department with, for example, a labour grade 13 value, might be entirely different from the work in another department which also has a labour grade 13 value. The skills are different but the value of the jobs is considered to be the same.

The lowest labour grade in the company is labour grade 1 and the highest is labour grade 15. There is a differential of 10 cents per hour per labour grade — that is, labour grade 2 is paid 10 cents per hour more than labour grade 1, and so on.

In the metal perforating department the lowest job is labour grade 6 and the highest is labour grade 14. In the clean, heat-treat and coating department, the lowest is labour grade 2 and the highest is labour grade 10. In the shipping department the lowest is labour grade 2 and the highest is labour grade 9.

On October 15th, 20XX, the company posted a vacant job of labour grade 6 in the metal perforating department. No employee in the department bid for the job. Mr. Shepherd, with seniority of September 10th, five years earlier, who was a labour grade 7 in the clean, heat-treat and coating department, and Mr. Weber, with seniority of August 20th, also five years earlier, who was a labour grade 3 in the shipping department, both applied for the job. The company awarded the job to Mr. Weber, whereupon Mr. Shepherd filed the following grievance.

> "I applied for and under the provisions of the seniority article am entitled to the job in labour grade 6 in the metal perforating department posted on October 15th, 20XX. I have more plant-wide seniority than Mr. Weber who was awarded the job and I also have the ability to perform the work of the job posted. I request that I be assigned to the above job."

The company refused to grant the grievance. As a result, the Union processed it to arbitration.

The applicable provisions of the collective agreement are as follows:

6.07 Job vacancies shall be posted on plant bulletin boards for 2 working days. Employees may apply for jobs which constitute an opportunity for promotion. The job will be offered to the employee with the most seniority who applies for the job unless a junior employee who applies for the job is more qualified.

Company Argument

In arbitration, the company argued that Weber was assigned to the job because it was a promotion for him. His previous job was in labour grade 3 in the shipping department and the job vacancy was in labour grade 6 in the metal perforating department. It is clearly a promotion to go from labour grade 3 to labour grade 6. The grievor Shepherd was in labour grade 7 in the clean, heat-treat and coating department and applied for a job in labour grade 6 in the metal perforating department. This was clearly not a promotion for him and as a result he was not entitled to the job under the provisions of the collective agreement.

The company stated it was prepared to concede that one employee was as qualified to do the job as the other. The company further argued that Weber was effectively at the bottom of the training progression in the shipping department. While the training he had received in shipping was lost to the company, he had in fact received very little training and therefore there was very little loss. In effect, he would receive training in the perforating instead of shipping, in order to be promoted, and would be promoted in perforating instead of in shipping.

The grievor Shepherd, in the clean, heat-treat and coating department, had received sufficient training to advance to labour grade 7 which was well up the line of promotion in that department.

The company argued to transfer him from labour grade 7 in the clean, heat-treat and coating department to labour grade 6 in the metal perforating department would mean that in future it was wasting all of the training he had received in order to be promoted to labour grade 7 in clean, heat-treat and coating. To reassign him to the other department would require starting the training cycle for him all over again.

The company stated that, in the previous agreement, there had been no job posting provision. The Union placed a demand for such a provision and argued it was necessary in order to give Union employees proper consideration for promotion, which they felt they had not previously been receiving. In the negotiations there has been much discussion back and forth on the problem and many counter-proposals were exchanged between the company and the Union.

Finally, the company made a proposal which the Union accepted, which is the clause in the present agreement. The company stated the intent of the clause was that the company would post job vacancies and those employees for whom the job would be a promotion could apply for it, and the company would make its selection under the provisions of that clause. For Shepherd to go from labour grade 7 to labour grade 6 was clearly not a promotion. As a result, he could not bring himself within the meaning of the clause and was not therefore entitled to the job under the provision.

Union Argument

The Union argued first that, while neither of the employees was qualified for the job because neither of the employees had worked in the area, they were equally qualified. Therefore, the senior employee was entitled to the job. The Union conceded the company would have to train somebody for the job, and therefore the Union argued the company should train the senior employee for the job. The Union argued the grievor was in the clean, heat-treat and coating department on labour grade 7. The department's progression only went to labour grade 10. In the metal perforating department the progression went to labour grade 14. Therefore, the grievor, to go from labour grade 7 in the clean, heat-treat and coating department to labour grade 6 in the metal perforating department, was in fact an opportunity for promotion because he could go to labour grade 14.

In addition, the Union argued that in this particular case the employees in the clean, heat-treat and coating department who held the jobs with the higher labour grades than the job held by the grievor, were only slightly older than the grievor and were in the judgment of the grievor and the Union the kind of people who were healthy and would live for a long time and who would stay with the company until retirement. Therefore probably the grievor would never receive a promotion as long as he stayed in the clean, heat-treat and coating department.

On the other hand, the employees in the metal perforating department were all relatively young and would probably have a fairly high turnover rate. In addition, the metal perforating department was expanding rapidly while the clean, heat-treat and coating department was having no expansion. As a result an employee in metal perforating was much more likely to be promoted than a person in clean, heat-treat and coating. The Union argued therefore that for Shepherd to go from labour grade 7 in clean, heat-treat and coating to labour grade 6 in metal perforating was first of all an opportunity for promotion as provided in the agreement and also on a logical, practical basis was a much greater opportunity for promotion than the opportunity he had in his present department.

COUNTY GENERAL HOSPITAL
Job Posting — Interpersonal Skills — Requirement of Job Posting

Background

This grievance arises out of the filling of a posted job vacancy for "two part-time Registered Nurses for Cat Scan". The grievor had more seniority than one of the successful applicants, Mrs. Jean Grady, and claims she was qualified for the job and that, under the terms of the collective agreement, the job should have been awarded to the grievor. The posting read as follows:

A vacancy exists in the Department of Radiology for:

2 (two) part-time Registered Nurses for Cat Scan

Requirements

5 years nursing experience at R.N. level

Able to perform all general nursing duties as required.

Prior working experience in a Radiology Department (C.T.) an asset.

Will be responsible for the administering of I.V., contrast, etc.

Will liaise with nursing staff from other hospitals concerning transfer of patients.

Job sharing.

Please apply to the Personnel Office *before* December 27, 20XX.

The relevant article of the collective agreement is art. 10:05(c) which reads:

> Nurses shall be selected for positions under either 10:05(a) or (b) on the basis of their skills, ability, experience and qualifications. Where these factors are relatively equal amongst the nurses considered, seniority shall govern providing the successful applicant, if any, is qualified to perform the available work within an appropriate familiarization period. Where seniority governs, the most senior applicant from the bargaining unit in which the vacancy arose, if any, shall be selected. Where the applicant has been selected in accordance with this Article and it is subsequently determined that she cannot satisfactorily perform the job to which she was promoted, the Hospital will attempt, during the first thirty (30) days from the date on which the nurse was first assigned to the vacancy, to return her to her former job, and the filling of the subsequent vacancies will likewise be reversed.

Selection Process

Twenty-six employees responded to the posting. The format of individual responses varied between a written note or a request for transfer form in accordance with art. 10:05(b) to submission of a personal resume. The grievor, by covering letter of December 22, 20XX, forwarded a resume of her qualifications and experience. Dr. Deacon, chairman of the department of radiology and Mr. Ray Travis, chief technologist of the department, concluded that it would be unwieldy to interview all 26 applicants and in order to assess all applicants on a consistent basis then requested the personnel department to contact those applicants who had not submitted resumes and request same. Deacon and Travis then reviewed the applications and resumes, to "weed out those we felt were not suitable candidates".

It was Dr. Deacon's evidence that the "weeding out" process was conducted in accordance with certain criteria. He stated that all criteria had not been spelled out in the job posting in order to avoid having applicants being led to what they might consider a desired response and crafting their response accordingly. Dr. Deacon stated "we wanted to know why they wanted to change jobs. It was a very important point." He enumerated the criteria as:

1. Ability to start I.V. lines.

2. Skills in handling medical emergencies — although he pointed out that the frequency of reaction to intravenous injection was in the order of 1 to 40,000, and so the weighing of this factor was very low.

3. Interpersonal skills were identified as probably the "most important thing we were looking for". He elaborated that the psychological preparation of the patient was very important in explaining the nature of equipment, the process and the necessity for the patient to be very still. He stated that they were looking for someone with "a pleasing, effervescent personality who could work well with the radiologist and technical staff and complement the personality of the chief technologist. It was also pointed out that the acquisition of the CAT Scan equipment had been exclusively the result of community financial support and it was expected that there would be a large number of visitors and therefore an "out-going personality" was desirable in receiving these visitors and explaining the nature of the work.

4. Administrative skills required in organizing the flow of patients and in responsibility for inventory control. It was pointed out that the job had limited supervision and the successful applicant should be a self-starter and have a genuine interest in the particular job and not merely an interest based on such things as achieving more desirable working conditions.

Employer Argument

The employer argued the job had been posted as required by the collective agreement. It had invited resumes from all applicants and had reviewed the resumes using certain criteria to establish which applicants would be interviewed.

The grievor admittedly had more seniority than the person selected for the job. However, under the provisions of Clause 10:05(c), the grievor is entitled to the job only if she is relatively equal in regard to skill, ability, experience and qualifications.

The initial review of the twenty-six applicants was conducted solely on the applications and resumes submitted by the individual employees, and on this basis the number of applicants under consideration was reduced to eight.

The grievor was not included in this group because Dr. Deacon did not see things in the resume which were as good as others in respect to personal skills and being a self starter. While recognizing the most important of the criteria was nursing skills, that had to be coupled with patient contacts, and while the grievor's resume indicated she had played the church organ, that would not be an activity involving people contact. Grady's resume indicated she had held the position of municipal deputy reeve and had taught nurses indicating a superior people involvement.

In addition, each of the eight was accorded a 15-20 minute interview by Dr. Deacon and Mr. Travis. They were asked questions to which they separately ascribed a numerical score. After a comparison of the numerical rankings, they identified the two present incumbents as the ones to be selected. Later Dr. Deacon talked to people at the hospital and was told the two selected were excellent candidates.

The person selected was clearly properly placed in the job under the terms of the collective agreement and the grievance should be denied.

Union Argument

There is an obligation on the employer to administer the posting and selection process in a fair and reasonable manner. It is self evident that, in order to discharge this obligation, all applicants must have an equal opportunity to put forward their qualifications and to have these judged fairly against the same standards.

The grievor was not made aware in the posting itself that interpersonal skills were "probably the most important thing" and while those interviewed were asked questions to bring out their interpersonal skills, no such opportunity was awarded the grievor.

None of the applicants had previous experience in a radiology department which the posting had indicated would be "an asset".

Both the grievor and the incumbent possess the required nursing qualifications. Both have considerable and varied nursing experience in this hospital.

The evidence establishes them both to meet the qualifications specifically set out in the posting except for prior experience in a radiology department which no applicant had.

In their various assignments, both would have used and demonstrated with patients and their families the type of communications skills required in the job in question. Evidence regarding playing a church organ or acting as a municipal reeve is not relevant to the job in question.

For all of these reasons there is no basis to support the employer's position of placing Mrs. Grady on the job.

Both are qualified for the job and, under the terms of the collective agreement, the grievor, who is the most senior of the two, is entitled to the job and the arbitration board should award the job to the grievor, Mrs. Cusick.

STEEP ROCKS COUNTY SCHOOL BOARD

Seniority — Bumping — Retention of Redundant Teachers

Background

A grievance was filed by a Teachers' Association on behalf of one of its members, Clara Cavendish, claiming improper layoff by the Steep Rocks County School Board in violation of the collective agreement. This was the result of a decision by the Board to terminate the teaching contract of the grievor effective August 31 as a result of staff redundancy.

Certain underlying facts were agreed upon by the parties to the dispute. The grievor was first employed by the Board two years ago and during the current school year she was employed as a primary teacher in Memorial School. Her qualifications under Program 2 of the Qualifications Evaluation Council of the Province was level A1 based on a B.A. degree from McMaster University and a teacher's certificate in Manitoba.

The position of the Teachers' Association is that the Board's decision to terminate the grievor's contract due to redundancy is in violation of the collective agreement between the Board and the Association. In the Association's view, the person whose contract should have been terminated is a Serena Shaw, a primary teacher in Centennial School. Serena Shaw's employment with the Board commenced with the current school year last September. Her qualification is also level A1 based on a Bachelor of Arts Degree and a Bachelor of Education degree, both from Lakehead University.

It was agreed that the question before the Arbitration Board was whether the contract of Serena Shaw or the contract of Clara Cavendish should be terminated.

The evidence established that because of financial pressure and declining student population, a reduction in the number of teaching contracts would be required and that a careful examination had been carried out to determine where the cutbacks should be made. The full teaching complement of Centennial School is four persons. It already has split classes with two grades being taught together and it would not be practical to reduce the teaching complement any further. In addition, there has been a fairly high rate of turnover in the staff of Centennial which has resulted in some dissatisfaction in the community. As the staff is now working well together and achieving community acceptance, it was desired to maintain the stability within that School.

The decision was made that the teaching position to be eliminated would have to come from Memorial School which is the largest school in the system, employing some seventeen teachers. The grievor was the most junior teacher in that school and the Board decided that it was her teaching position that was to be cut. The Teachers' Association did not dispute that, with respect to the staff of Memorial School, the grievor was the member of the staff who should first be declared redundant.

The collective agreement deals with staff redundancy in Article 4:01, as follows:

> "Staff redundancy will be according to Board Policy Statement No. 9." This Policy statement was approved and adopted by the Board on October 26 of last year.

This was the sole contractual reference to staff redundancy and to the rights and obligations of the parties in situations of staff redundancy.

The applicable provisions of Policy Statement No. 9 previously referred to read as follows:

Staff Redundancy

1. In the event that there are not enough teaching positions for the number of teachers presently under contract, teachers wholly or partly redundant to a school are identified by the Board on the basis of the following consideration and criteria:

    (a) Length of teaching experience

        i) with the Steep Rocks County School Board and its predecessor Boards

        ii) in the province

    (b) Qualifications

    (c) Characteristics of Position(s) with regard to subject and/or level.

2. The Board will make every possible effort to maintain said teacher(s) on staff within the system if there is a position available and if in the opinion of the Board the teacher(s) is suited to that position.

Union Argument

Counsel for the Teachers' Association argued that the language of the policy statement placed on the School Board two basic obligations. First, within a school there are three specific criteria that must be met by the Board in identifying a redundancy. The first paragraph of the policy statement deals specifically with the situation in a particular school, the second paragraph in the policy statement, dealing with the Board's obligation within the entire system applies. He argued that the only rational implication to be drawn from the second paragraph is that the teacher identified in Paragraph 1 has the right to have the Board try to keep him or her in the system. If, in the system, there exists another position for which the teacher would be suitable, he or she is to be placed in that position.

In determining whether or not a position is available under the language of Paragraph 2, consideration must be given to the obvious intent of the paragraph in an industrial relations context. It was argued that the language of Paragraph 2 was very similar to the language found in industrial relations contracts that tended to give rise to bumping situations. It was Counsel's position that the only meaning that could rationally be ascribed to Paragraph 2 is that it puts into the collective agreement the concept of seniority preference, including the whole concept of bumping rights. An available position would then be any position in which the incumbent was junior to the redundant teacher.

Employer Argument

Counsel for the School Board argued that within the policy language, the concept of redundancy is already identified solely with a particular school and a particular teacher becomes redundant in relation to that teacher's school under Paragraph 1. Paragraph 2 then constitutes a very strong best efforts clause imposing on the Board the obligation to employ the teacher elsewhere within the system if there is a position available.

The Counsel for the School Board then argued that the Board is not required to make a position available in the event that teachers with less seniority are employed within the system. And that a redundant teacher has a claim only on teaching positions that become available through natural processes of attrition or through expansion of the overall system.

It was however the Association's position that the Board, rather than terminating the grievor's contract, should have terminated Serena Shaw's contract. Clara Cavendish, the grievor, should then have been moved to Centennial School by reason of the fact that her qualifications were equivalent to those of Serena Shaw, and that she had an additional year's teaching experience.

PART J: TRUE STORIES

Negotiations for a Collective Agreement

The following three case studies (Beatty Manufacturing, Purity Products, and Rusco Industries and Kozik Manufacturing) are true stories of actual negotiations. They demonstrate different approaches taken by employers and unions to negotiations and the consequences of having different people, different attitudes, and different circumstances involved.

The case studies also demonstrate that, while each involves a history of negotiations between the employer and the union, the process is complicated. This is because many different negotiations are taking place at the same time: between the industrial relations consultant and the general manager; between the general manager and the owner; and between the consultant and the owner. Also, the union representative is negotiating with the union committee, and the members of the union negotiating committee are negotiating with each other. Also, the union representatives and the union negotiating committee are negotiating with the members of the union. They have to establish what the union members will agree to, and convince the union members that the best settlement the union representatives can get, is attractive enough for the union members to approve when they vote on the settlement.

BEATTY MANUFACTURING

Non-Union Company Unionized

An outline of events from certification to a collective agreement between the company and the union describing some company reactions to unionization and some reasons why employees value unions.

It includes some description of a series of negotiation meetings, with changing positions of both company and union, resulting in a settlement leaving the company with the right to manage the business, providing employees reasonable wages and benefits and the union with the provisions it needs.

The Characters Involved

President of Company	- referred to as the client
Chairman of The Board of Company	- who is Chief Executive Officer owner often called the Boss
Consultant	- who speaks for the company
Union Representative	- who speaks for the union

Case Outline

Brief General Background

Meeting With The President - 1

      The Consultant Meets The President
      Company History and Background To The Situation
      Some Reactions To Unionization

Meeting With The Owner - 1

      "The Union Is Not Going To Tell Him How To Run His Business"

Meeting With The President - 2

      The Consultant Decides To Tell The Union It Is Not Needed

Informal Communication With The Union Representative

      "They Want To Walk Tall - Not Be Snivelling Bootlickers"

Meeting With The President - 3

      It Is Agreed To Commence Negotiations

Negotiation Meeting - 1

      Union Demands And Company's Opening Comments

408

Brief General Background

There had been three newspaper stories the previous month about small companies in which a Union had obtained the right to represent the employees concerned. The companies were all reasonably local, within a 100 mile range. In each case, the company had been started some years ago by a person, who had worked long and hard to build a successful business that was now a reasonably significant local employer. In each case, on hearing that his employees had joined the Union, the owner simply announced that he was closing the plant, going out of business, and retiring. The result was, of course, that somebody who had cared enough to build a business had given up his business, the Union had gained bargaining rights in a company that did not exist, and employees who used to have jobs, no longer had them.

Meeting With The President - 1

The Consultant Meets The President

The consultant was on his way to lunch with a prospective client. It had been arranged by a phone call from the client and not much information had been offered. However, it was clear it was a company that had not previously had a Union, whose employees had now decided to become unionized.

The restaurant was not pretentious, but quiet and conducive to good private conversation. After being seated, the consultant and his client briefly exchanged pleasantries. This initial exchange made them both think that perhaps they were the kind of people who might be able to work together.

The client volunteered that he had checked with the consultant's previous employer, who had listened briefly to his problems and, in response to a question, suggested perhaps this consultant could be of help to him, and that it might be worth talking to him. The consultant's previous employer had also suggested that even though the businesses were somewhat different and the geography of their locations was somewhat different, there seemed to be enough similarity that the consultant could make a worthwhile contribution towards solving his problems. In any event, it might be worth a conversation. The client also stressed that the previous employer had spoken well of the consultant.

The client stated he was aware that the consultant was new in the consulting business and asked politely how he liked it and how well he was doing. The consultant stated that business was reasonable, but he needed more clients. However, he was planning to be selective regarding the clients that he accepted. He stated there are companies around who are successful financially, but who take advantage of their employees at every opportunity, paying the least they can get away with, and treat their employees like a commodity. He said he was recently approached by a company who stated their plan was to open a plant in a low wage area, pay as little as they could, delay improvement as long as possible, then close the plant and move on to another low wage area. He told them that he did not want their business.

He hoped to work with clients who try to hire good employees and try to treat them reasonably, based on the economics of business, of course — and hoped, through a combination of good management and other factors, to be successful in this approach, which he believed was not only more ethical, but also more sensible. He also stated that he enjoyed being a consultant. When he was an employee, previously, he was conscious that the boss may not always be right, but the boss is always the boss. He always tried to do a good job and believed he had never compromised himself. However, the manner of dealing with the union and with negotiations is important and the boss did not necessarily have the knowledge or background or experience to appreciate such things. He was, and intended to continued to be, straightforward with his clients and expected the clients to receive his views in that sense and to respond accordingly.

The client offered the information that he was the President of the company and ran the company. However, he went on, and smiled in very clear communication, that the owner was the Chairman and Chief Executive Officer of the company, and therefore also his boss. He thought it judicious that the first meeting should be over lunch in this restaurant and off company premises so no one would know of the conversation at the time.

Company History and Background to the Situation

The reason the president had called the consultant was that 100% of the employees had signed Union Cards and the company had to decide how to respond. By way of background, he explained that the owner had a lot of experience in the business. The owner had seen how the business operates and how the business was run with a previous employer, and decided he could do it better. He quit, got a glorified garage to work in, and became his own salesman, engineer, then production manager. He got some business and hired some employees. He tried to hire good ones, trained them, and tried to treat them well. He tried to build them up, not knock them down. With his maximum effort, the business grew slowly but steadily. In due course, he had to get larger and better premises and, of course, steadily hire more and more good employees who he also trained and treated well. He tried to let his employees get some satisfaction from their work. The company has also stayed abreast of the competitive situation, regularly looking at what other employers pay, their fringe benefits, statutory holidays, vacations, and so on. The company has tried to keep up to date and honestly thinks it is up-to-date.

The business has not grown fantastically fast or on a straight line curve, but generally steadily, recognizing the ups and downs of the economy and the business. When business turned down, they tried to avoid layoffs, although this was not always possible. The employees seemed to realize the company had tried to avoid layoffs.

As any company gets bigger it gets less personal. The owner is conscious of it. When time permits, the owner and the president get out to the plant and talk to people. When they have time they go out to see what is going on. They make sure the employees know them and they know the employees. They thought it was all working pretty well. The owner has been away a lot, talking with customers and others. He also had been away a lot. This is the busiest period the company has ever had. Everybody is going at maximum to keep up and get the work done. Now, in this very busy period, they have become unionized.

Some Reaction to Unionization

On the day the formal notification was received, the president waited until the end of the day, and when the office was almost empty, went into the owner's office and told him the employees had unionized. The boss's first reaction was to tell them to go away — he hasn't time — the company is too busy — but he realized he couldn't do that. The next reaction was, Why? The president told the owner he didn't know either. He didn't think there was any reason for it. The owner said "It is a fact, we have to deal with it!" And then, after a pause, he said he was busy and had a dinner meeting. He suggested they both think about it overnight and talk sensibly about it in the morning.

In the morning the owner had those newspaper clippings on his desk — the ones about those companies that got unionized, then shut down and the owner retired. He said maybe they're the smart guys. A person spends half his life building a business, creating jobs for people, thinking he is accomplishing something. He said nobody appreciates anything any more. He didn't need the money, and since the president owned part of the company, he was O.K. too. Maybe they should simply close down, auction off the machines and equipment, sell the plant, and tell the employees that, since they think they are so poorly treated here that they had to join a Union, they can go and find somewhere else where they'll be treated better. Why not retire, or go on a world cruise or something. No Union was going to tell the boss how to run his business.

The President ended his account by acknowledging the company's lack of knowledge and experience regarding unions, and said the company wanted to make use of the consultant's knowledge and experience.

An Understanding Begins

"Sounds like it could be interesting and good for everybody to help save your business for you and at the same time save the jobs for the employees", the consultant responded. If they were so unhappy, he wondered, why hadn't they already quit and gone somewhere better? He said that if he were to get involved, he would bargain hard but bargain fair. He would give his recommendations honestly and, based on past experience, most of the time they would be good. If he, the consultant, wasn't prepared to follow instructions, the client would know about it and that would be the end of it.

The client responded, "You are saying that if you've had enough of me, if you don't like what I want to do, you are just going to tell me so, and that's the end of it?

Does that work both ways? "Absolutely", the consultant replied. "We are going to get along fine", the client responded, with a big smile.

Meeting With The Owner - 1

The Union is Not Going To Tell Him How To Run His Business

The next session was with the owner and founder of the company, in his office. It was small and functional, no pretense — desk, plastic laminate top, and chair, three extra chairs, the walls covered in charts and diagrams. The owner was polite and courteous, and indicated management had had some conversations about the union and promptly stated that he wished the Union would go away. The union sure wasn't going to tell him how to run his business. He built the business, gave the employees jobs, and trained them — their job security depended on him! They were well paid, with good benefits. His company almost never had layoffs. As for the future, their job security depended on him, not on the union. If he couldn't get business, they wouldn't have jobs. They had as much security as he had. He could close the place down if he wanted to. "If that's the way they feel about it" the owner finished, "they can quit and do whatever they want to do, and see if they're any better off than they are now. After they find somewhere else to work, they'll realize how well off they were."

The silence was broken when the consultant asked why the owner hadn't closed down and retired last year. The answer was that he liked what he was doing. He had plans and dreams, and didn't want to hurt those people who worked there. Then this! They weren't going to tell him how to run his business, he repeated.

The consultant was told that wages and benefits were as good as or better than competitors' or anyone else's around the area. The company couldn't pay what the automotive or basic steel industries do, but neither could their competitors.

The consultant continued, "I don't understand why you are going to give up what you want to do. Can your employees complain if they want to complain?"

"Of course."

"Do you discipline or discharge employees without just cause?"

"Of course not."

"Do you want to lay off your senior employees and keep your junior employees if your senior employees can do the work?"

"Of course not, we start training employees the day they are hired. The more training they have, the more valuable they are to the company. I don't want to lay them off if there is any reasonable way to avoid it."

"All these statements and policies, are they written down anywhere?"

"No."

"If the things you said were written down, along with your practices on vacations, holidays and overtime payment, would you sign an agreement saying that?"

"I just want them to go away", the owner said. "If they won't go away, I suppose there is not much harm in writing it down. They aren't going to tell me how to run my business. The Union wouldn't sign anything like that." The consultant said he wouldn't agree to anything without approval, but would go away and do some work, and see what happened.

Meeting With The President - 2
The Consultant Decides To Tell The Union It Is Not Needed

Back in the President's office, the consultant made the comment that it would sound strange if everything the owner had said was true. Why was there a Union? The President agreed. One thing he forgot to mention previously — which probable didn't make any difference — was that when they were very busy, a man came in looking for temporary work. He was hired because he had the skills they needed. He was from that plant down the street — said he retired early. About the only significant comment he made — and many people heard him — was, "I'm sure glad we don't have a Union in here!"

The consultant said that he thought he would check out the Union Representative, the union employee who had organized the company's employees and would now negotiate for them, and perhaps see if he could have a private chat with him to try to find out what was going on. He would tell the union representative that the employees don't need a Union, and that he should spend his time on somebody who does need a Union.

Informal Communication With The Union Representative
They Want to Walk Tall - Not Be Snivelling Bootlickers

The consultant called the Union Representative, indicating that there was a possibility he would be involved with his new bargaining unit and that he used to have the occasional private conversation with another representative of his Union. That person used to explain himself by saying, ""Let's have a conversation that didn't happen!" The Union Representative answered that he was busy Friday morning, but might have some time on Friday afternoon. If so, he would be in the bar at that hotel near the plant between 3:00 and 3:30, before a dinner meeting.

On Friday afternoon they met in the hotel bar. They exchanged a polite, friendly greeting. The Union Representative said he liked and understood the expression "A conversation that didn't happen". He had done some checking and decided it was safe to listen, and volunteered that he had been told that the consultant bargained hard, but bargained fair.

The consultant said, "You guys bargain hard, too. You seem to find employees who need help and do your best to help them, and usually you make some progress."

The consultant said he did not understand this situation. He had had a session with the top people where he had asked some pretty blunt questions and seemed to get some pretty straightforward answers. "We both know why people join Unions, but they don't apply here. Wages and benefits are as good as in unionized plants. In a growing company like this, they have more job security than most places, and when the occasional layoff has occurred, the company has applied seniority. The company values the training they have provided and doesn't want to lose it. There isn't any discipline problem and they don't want to punish the employees. Employees get fair treatment and can talk to the top people anytime. Management tries to build people up — not knock them down. They want the employees to have job satisfaction and a sense of accomplishment."

He continued, "You've heard about those other companies where other Unions organized and the company just shut down. You are asking for another one here. It could very easily be that, as a result of your actions, there will be no company, no jobs, and a bunch of people saying they will never have another job as good as the one they had — and it'll all be your fault. I think you should go away and leave them alone, and everybody will be happy."

The Union Representative answered, "I have listened, now you listen. They don't want to have to rely on trust. The owner can die, management can change or the company can be sold. They don't want to be snivelling boot-lickers, to bow and bend and scrape or be in fear of the company. They want to do their jobs and be proud of their work. They are willing to follow orders, but not to be subservient. They know there is a boss — he can do his work and they will do theirs. Somebody owns the plant, but he doesn't own the employees. They are willing to show proper respect, but they also want respect for what they do and for what they are. They have their dignity and they want to walk tall like real men and women.

"They recognize the company has rights and will respect them, but they want the company to realize employees have rights too and they want the company to respect the employee's rights. They think the Union helps. If they want our help, we will help them. I will go away when they want me to go away. The company says they treat people properly, let them write it down in a union contract and show the people conditions won't change without their agreement." There was a long pause while they looked at each other.

The consultant answered, "If I represent the company, I will bargain with you; bargain fair, but bargain hard."

The Union Representative responded that he would too, and hoped that the company realized that they know how to deal with people who don't.

Meeting With The President - 3

It Is Agreed To Commence Negotiations

The consultant reported back to the President about his conversation with the Union Representative, and summarized what was said. He stated that he didn't think the union would go away, and he recommended they negotiate, see how they make out, and decide what to do from there. It was agreed to proceed.

Negotiation Meeting - 1

Company Opening Comments and Union Demands

At the opening negotiation meeting, appropriate introductions were made and pleasantries exchanged between the three Union representatives on the one hand, and the Plant Manager and the Consultant, on the other . When everybody had taken their places at the table, the consultant opened the meeting by stating that he felt he should formally advise them that he had agreed to represent the company and was the company spokesman. He proposed to explore with the Union, the possibility of making an agreement that he could recommend to the company. He stated his assessment of the situation: that it was a good company that had hired good employees, paid good wages and benefits, trained them well, and treated them well. He also made it clear that if this were not the situation, he was prepared to be convinced that he was in error and perhaps changes should be made. He underlined that his function was to see if it was practical to reach an agreement that he could recommend to management.

The consultant went on to say that the owner had given the impression that he was a reasonable man, but that he also made it clear that if the company was going to continue, it would continue the way he wanted it. The consultant also quoted the owner as saying, "If somebody can run it better than I can, I will hire him as manager and let him run it."

The consultant told the Union Representative the owner had said that people should realize that, if he could no longer enjoy running the company, he was prepared to close the plant, auction off the equipment, sell the real estate, and spend the rest of his time doing other things that he wanted to do. In the meantime, the company was willing to listen, consult and discuss, and give proper consideration to any proposals put forward.

The Union then submitted their demands and the consultant and the plant manager scanned them quickly. The consultant stated the company would read the demands carefully, pay close attention to the Union justification, give each item proper consideration, and respond. However, after a quick scan of the demands, he said it was only fair to tell them that his first reaction was that they were going to have to do a lot of changing before any agreement could be reached. He said he thought that if he took these demands to the owner it would be a very short conversation — probably a dozen well-chosen words which, to say the least, would be negative — extremely negative. He said he would see them next week.

Union Demands

The Union demands are specified at the end of this case. They are set out as Articles in a proposed Agreement. The Articles that were subsequently agreed to with the Company are also shown, side by side, for purposes of comparison.

Meeting With The President - 4

The Company Approach To Negotiations

The next session was with the President. The consultant stated that he had received the union demands and had given the union a quick reaction — very negative — and gave a summary of what was said, along with a copy of the Union demands. After a brief pause, he commented that the Union had asked for everything anybody had ever asked for anywhere, plus a few new things nobody had ever thought of before. Next week he would give the union time to explain and justify their demands, get their arguments, and listen for problems. He would take a position on each item; with few exceptions, his response would be negative, and he would give reasons for it. He would listen to the union arguments in support of their demands, and suggested that later the company should agree to some of them. However, generally he would try to convince the union to agree with the company. In doing so, he would try to convince the union representatives that the company was going to resist strongly on some items and let the union representatives indicate the items about which they felt most strongly.

In doing this, he and they would explore possibilities of settlement on the various items and also on the overall package. He would convey to the Union that the company could make some concessions, but let the union know they couldn't have everything they were asking for. Also, while recognizing the union's ability to strike, he would remind them that they have to consider the company's ability and will to resist.

Negotiation Meeting - 2

Both Sides Talk Tough - But Agree To Meet Again

At the beginning, the parties exchange pleasantries. The company representatives stated the Union's demands had been reviewed and they were prepared to listen to what the Union had to say. They proposed to listen to the Union's justification and reasons and also suggested that some items should be put aside for detailed discussions at a later time.

The discussion proceeded with the Union arguing and trying to justify their position. On almost every item, they had to admit their justification was based on experience somewhere else, and in almost every case they were forced to admit that there was no such problem in this relationship. The company listened closely to the Union's arguments and made careful notes. It was agreed to set aside certain items for later discussion — seniority and statutory holidays. Otherwise, the company rejected each item the Union had proposed and gave reasons for it — most often, that the Union showed no problems in this relationship to justify their demands and that their arguments were based on experience somewhere else that did not apply in this situation.

Frustration showed as the Union representative leaned back in his chair and complained that so far the company had agreed to nothing and asked when the company was going to begin to negotiate. The company response was that they <u>were</u> negotiating, and the Union knew it. The Union had told the company what the Union wanted, but they had not convinced the company. The company had said "no" and had given their reasons for it. If they wanted to get closer to an agreement, the Union should drop some of their demands.

Again, the Union frustration showed. The Union Representatives stressed that these demands were important to the Union members. If the demands weren't taken seriously, the company might be heading for a strike.

The consultant responded that the company wanted an agreement, and hoped the Union did too. The Union would have to get realistic or they might have to strike. On the other hand, it could be that they would end up with no bargaining unit, and the employees would end up with no jobs. The consultant reiterated that the owner was a man who would not tolerate interference in running the business. The consultant had told the owner the Union would get realistic eventually. He didn't want to give the owner a detailed report on the Union position at that time. He would not report to the owner on this meeting; he was concerned about what the owner might do.

The consultant asked the union representatives to give some thought to those articles set aside and suggested the parties try to discuss and problem-solve them at the next meeting. He would try to have some submissions to give to them. They adjourned until the following week.

As they were getting up from the table, standing and sorting papers and so on, the consultant spoke to the Union spokesman, saying that the meeting was over, but that he wanted to provide some informal communication which might be enlightening. He hadn't seen the owner that morning, and had found out he was spending the day in his office with a real estate person — a specialist in selling islands in the Bahamas, where there was good fishing, good weather, and no income tax. He said he hoped the Union would look at those items set aside and see about making some progress at the next meeting. He would see if he could make some submissions to them.

Meeting With The President - 5

Plans To Work Toward An Agreement

Later the consultant reported to the President and provided a brief summary of the meeting. The Union had threatened them; it was time to get serious. There could be a strike. The consultant reported that he had told the Union that they had better get serious too, because they could end up with no jobs and no bargaining unit, and that they had better modify their position before that happened. The Union had been appropriately serious and impressed with his comments. The consultant said he would draft some submissions for approval and plan for a serious discussion on selected items to convey to the union the company's willingness to make some progress.

Negotiation Meeting -3

Discussion Toward An Agreement

At the opening of the next meeting, the consultant stated that the company had submissions to give to the Union on the balance of the Union demands. However, he would keep them until the end of the discussion. He went on to say that the company recognizes that in a settlement there may have to be some monetary changes made: for example, in wages. However, the submissions from the company listed present wages and other items (for example, vacations), and specified present conditions. This was not necessarily to be interpreted that there could not be changes in reaching a settlement. The submissions were proposed language for an agreement. The company was prepared to listen to the Union's suggestions for changes.

However, the company felt that, in general terms, for what the Union needs and can reasonably expect, it would be impractical to bargain every sentence.

The company and union representatives then proceeded to discuss the items that were set aside for further detailed discussion. This turned into a thoughtful, rational, logical discussion. Full notes were taken on the Union's position, and it appeared that the Union was taking careful notes on what the company said.

The Union made it clear that it was necessary that the company accept a seniority system and the company acknowledged it would accept the concept. It was agreed seniority had to be defined and the company insisted there be a probationary period for new employees.

It was agreed that the union needed seniority information. The company agreed to provide seniority lists, post them on bulletin boards, and update them regularly.

The company stressed the importance of minimizing disruption due to seniority by localizing the application. The union emphasized the importance of the layoff of the junior employees first, and a seniority application from one area to another. The company responded that this had to be restricted by a delay provision. They discussed the idea of two sections, with transfer from one to the other, only for persons with at least 15 months seniority.

The company stressed that it must be able to retain employees with the required skills and ability and have the right to have temporary layoffs out of seniority. It was agreed that it was necessary to agree on rules regarding accumulation and maintenance of seniority under different situations. After more general discussion, the company agreed to draft a proposal for discussion.

It was agreed that the company would pay for certain specified holidays and it was necessary to define the applicable rate of pay. The company stated the necessity of an employee working the day before and the day after, with special provisions regarding layoff and illness. The union specified the importance of premium pay for the time worked on a holiday. The company said it would draft a proposal. The union stated they were not agreeing to anything yet, but would consider the company proposal.

At the end of this discussion it was agreed that they adjourn until the following week. The company gave the Union the submissions they referred to earlier, asked the Union to give them careful consideration, and commented that some union positions had been included in the company submissions.

Negotiation Meeting - 4

More Discussions Toward An Agreement

The Union said that they wanted to talk about the Statutory Holiday provisions. At the moment they were not talking about the number of holidays, since that was a monetary item, and monetary items would be discussed later. They had, they said, strong objections to the company requirement that an employee had to work a full shift the day before and the day after the holiday in order to qualify for payment for the holiday. There is agreement to pay for the holiday and a person should be paid for it. The agreement provides payment for a day not worked, therefore the company should make the payment for the holiday, without placing conditions on it.

The company disagreed emphatically. They did agree that the employee could have the day off with pay, provided he met certain conditions. The cost of a holiday is not only the cost of 8 hours pay, the lost production for the 8 hours means fewer hours of production over which the company can spread overhead. However, if the employee misses the shift before the holiday, the company loses another 8 hours production. The company is willing to pay the 8 hours and lose 8 hours production, but is not prepared to lose more production and therefore insists on the requirement to work the full shift the day before and the day after the holiday.

The Union stated they did not agree. The company should pay 8 hours but, even if it did agree with the company, there are many reasonable situations in which an employee should not have to work the full shift — for example, when an employee is unavoidably late.

The company answered that the employee is paid for 8 hours not worked under the specified conditions. If he fails to meet them, he does not get the payment. The Union responded that they could not agree to that and suggested talking about it later.

The Union next raised the issue of seniority. They said that the general concept the company had set out was acceptable. The company would lay off the junior employees first, when the remaining employees had the required skill and ability; but when a senior employee is laid off first, the union said it would be necessary to deal with the claim of the senior employee that he could do the work of the junior.

The company interjected that they could not keep people who can't do the work, and lay off those who can do it.

The Union continued that the problem, from their perspective, was that the company would decide who would be laid off, and employees would have no immediate recourse, even if they had higher seniority and were able to do a junior employee's work. The Union admitted that if the employee doesn't agree with the layoff decision, he could grieve, but as they both knew, that can mean he would get a decision months later. That wasn't good enough. They suggested the company give him a trial and see if he can do the job.

The company responded that when the company knows the employee can't do the job, giving a trial is just a waste of time and money. The company doesn't like laying off people. To provide a trial period at the time of layoff gives the employee an incentive to claim a trial on a job he knows he cannot do, in order to delay his layoff. The result would be to increase the company's costs. The Union suggested talking about this item later too. After some more discussion, it was agreed to adjourn.

The consultant said he would give serious consideration to everything the Union had said, and suggested the Union do the same thing with regard to what the company had said. He proposed that, at the next meeting, the parties make a serious effort to resolve all outstanding matters.

The Union responded that they were always prepared to review and reconsider, and would do so, but the company would have to do some reconsidering if they expected to get a settlement.

The Union again expressed very strong views on the items set aside for detailed discussion, which the company rebutted emphatically. Again, both sides took very careful notes. The Union commented that maybe at that stage the best they could do was to agree to disagree. The company agreed. The two sides exchanged a few general comments on the balance of the items in dispute — certainly not agreement — but nothing to indicate strong disagreement. They adjourned.

Meeting With The President - 6

The President Authorizes Some Concessions To The Union

The consultant told the president, "We haven't talked money, but otherwise things are coming along. We are getting most of what we want. Even on statutory holidays and seniority. However, we do have some problems.

"I can argue as long as he can, but that does not mean a settlement. They feel strongly and they have some good arguments about the statutory holiday pay problem. If a person is 15 minutes late because of a flat tire, slow traffic, or a sick child the day before the holiday, it's not reasonable that he lose his holiday pay. I am on the union's side of the argument."

"Regarding a trial period — if a person who can do a job, or thinks he can do a job, or his fellow workers think he can do a job, gets laid off because the company won't give him a trial, nobody will think that is fair. We create that attitude and then what happens to employee relations?"

The President responded, "They have some good arguments, but at the time of layoff is when the company can least afford to give a trial. Everyone will want a trial. It would delay the layoff. The company delays layoffs as long as it can, and only has layoffs when it doesn't have work. If they want a trial, they should request it when the work is needed instead of when we can least afford to provide a trial. It's a problem. Find a solution, but look after what's important to the company."

Negotiation Meeting - 5

Progress Towards An Agreement

At the next meeting the consultant opened with a brief presentation — a very serious presentation — reminding the Union representatives that at the previous meeting, the parties had agreed to explore the possibility of settlement. The company, of course, could not do this by itself. It needed a two-way negotiating session. In any event, the company had given the Union submissions on all outstanding articles and, generally speaking, expected that these were acceptable to the Union. The company recognized that in the previous meeting the Union had highlighted major concerns in detailed discussion on certain selected items, without reaching an agreement on those items.

The consultant proposed that, subject to agreement on the whole, everything else be considered resolved, based on the company submissions, and that they spend their time on the two items set aside for detailed discussion, and on wages and monetary matters. The consultant continued, saying that in the past it had been company policy to treat its employees well, to regularly review wages, working conditions and other matters, and to keep up to the ever changing times and conditions. The company thought it had had good relations with its employees and believed this was partly because of their regular review. It had been some time since the company had made changes in these conditions. The process had been delayed by the disruption caused by the Union and the bargaining process, but the company planned to continue the practices, and thought it was time to get on with these things.

The consultant admitted he might be trying to move faster than was wise. However, one reason for this was that the boss was getting impatient; he wanted to know whether he should continue to plan to run his business or whether he should recognize that the time had come to get on with some of the other desires in his life.

The Union responded by saying that, in general terms, they agreed that the proposals the company had made could perhaps be considered or construed to meet the minimum needs of the Union. The Union's attitude could be influenced by the company's approach to what it would call the more important outstanding items, but stated emphatically that there had to be a lot of effort put into the other outstanding items — and, of course, concessions in the monetary area.

The company responded that the union had what it needed for settlement; both the employees and the Union and could sign an agreement and be proud of it after the resolution of these items. Based on these understandings and assumptions, the company was prepared to make offers and an agreement could be signed on this basis.

If the Union was still concerned with hypothetical problems, they should collect data on these problems during the life of the agreement. If they were not resolved, they can be raised in the next negotiations.

Negotiation Meeting - 6

Settling Remaining Differences

The Union was very serious and stated their position very clearly. They felt it was essential to deal with the statutory holiday and seniority problems which were discussed and set aside — and, of course, all monetary items — in order to reach a settlement. Although they were not entirely happy with a lot of other things, they were willing to state that, provided these items were resolved satisfactorily, the company's position as stated was acceptable on all other outstanding items.

The company responded that it was very concerned at all the things the Union stated still had to be resolved. However, it was encouraged to hear the Union was prepared to accept the company's position on the other matters. Therefore, based on that Union statement, the company was prepared to make an offer to settle all outstanding matters.

The consultant stated to the Union that both parties realize negotiations can drag on for weeks and months longer, and either party may consider they are taking significant risks to try to speed things up. However, the company's owner was rather impatient to decide whether he should be trying to run his business, or whether he should be planning other aspects of his life. This could affect his tolerance for prolonged negotiations. Therefore, the consultant was going to act faster than he otherwise might.

Regarding statutory holidays — the company was not impressed with the Union's argument, but was impressed with the Union's concern. To deal with that concern, the company was prepared, to add the words "And has not reported more than one hour after his starting time" to the provision requiring employees to work a full scheduled shift the day before and the day after the statutory holiday.

Regarding the Union's problem on seniority, the company was not impressed and did not propose to deal with the Union's problem. The Union should withdraw the proposal.

Further to the company's on-going review of wages and other conditions, the company was satisfied to include a provision for 4 weeks vacation, and proposed 4 weeks vacation after fifteen years. This review also concluded that there was no justification for other changes in the monetary package other than wages, and the company was taking a rather firm position on this matter.

On wages, it had been some time since the employees had received their last wage increase, partly because of the Union certification and negotiations. As a result of this review, the company was prepared to pay a general wage increase, effective on the date of agreement, of 1%. On a longer term basis, the company expected the rate of increase in the cost of living was going to slow down or flatten out. The company was also very concerned with the state of the economy, and with the price level for its own products. However, in spite of all of these concerns, the company was prepared to offer a two-year agreement, effective the date of signing, and on the anniversary date, provide a $1/2$% wage increase.

After a long pause, the Union responded that they were not pleased with the company's offer. However, they were pleased the company had finally made an offer and proposed they take some time by themselves to give proper consideration to the company offer before responding to it.

After the adjournment, the Union came back and stated that they had already given the company all their arguments. So, instead of arguing further, they would make a statement of their position regarding the first year. 1% was not enough. In the second year, the company must give consideration to the cost of living; $1/2$% alone was not good enough. Also something had to be done to solve the seniority problem. They would leave the company to consider its next position.

The Union returned when the company told them it was ready. The company stated that the Union was overly concerned about seniority. However, the company would give them a letter — not part of the agreement and not automatically renewed in the next negotiations — saying the employee has the right at any time during the life of the agreement to apply in writing for training on a variety of jobs, up to a total of three. The company would endeavour to provide such training when the work was required and when it was practical to train. In effect, this meant the company was offering training on request at a time when work was available and it is practical to train, as opposed to a training period at the time of layoff. If an employee didn't want training when it was practical for the company, he would not be entitled to training at the time of layoff.

However, in addition, in the second year after the cost of living has increased by $1/2$%, the company was prepared to pay further wage increases of 1% after each additional 1% increase in the cost of living, as measured by the Consumer Price Index (National), limited to a maximum of 2% increase in the second year. This provision would be effective in the second year after the cost of living has increased by $1/2$% in the second year. Regarding wages in the second year, the company was still prepared to offer $1/2$% as stated.

There was a long silence on both sides. The Union broke the silence by asking what about the first year. A long pause ensued, then the company said if it would mean getting a settlement, they would offer a 2% wage increase in the first year, instead of only 1%.

"That," said the consultant, "is our offer. It's now your job to accept or reject"

The Union representative looked at the two other members of his committee and asked for a few minutes to consult with them. A little later, the committee returned and told the company it was agreed. When it was written up, they would sign and were confident the membership would vote to accept it. Everyone shook hands and left the room.

Summary Report to the Owner

The Company Can Still Run Its Business

In a summary report to the owner, the consultant reminded him of previous conversations and stated that the agreement contained provisions which the Union needed for its operation, but these would not interfere at all with the operation of the business. The agreement also provided in written form the practices which the owner said he had been following and planned to continue to follow. These were amended somewhat in a manner to which he had had no objection. Provisions had been generally updated to provide wages and benefits which were consistent with company practices. "It also leaves the company with the ability to operate the business in the way you want to, and the way you say you have to, and still allow you to treat your employees the way you have been treating them and the way you want to treat them."

However, the consultant reminded the owner that the Union would be watching during the agreement for problems and that they would have to be resolved in the next negotiations.

"I guess you will be too busy running your business to do all that fishing in the Bahamas!" the consultant joked.

The owner was silent for a moment, then replied, "At this stage I am not really sure which I would rather do — maybe I need two years to decide!"

Casual Meeting With Union Representative

Some Comments On The Settlement, Union Organizing and Negotiations

The consultant was leaving the hotel, when he was seen by the Union representative, who said "Join me for a drink. I'm glad you arrived, so you can pay!" After a polite exchange he concluded, "We both bargained hard and fair. You gave me what I need. The Union has its protection. The agreement is reasonable; it provides decent wages and benefits. Nobody got hurt. The owner can't complain very much. He can run his business. We don't want to interfere with that when he does it so well. But, we will be watching for two years."

The consultant responded, "That's fine by the company. It's your job to be watching. They will make sure you don't find anything to worry about."

"I know you are wondering how the plant got unionized", the Union representative said. "One of our members took early retirement from another company, but still wanted to work. Your company was busy and needed help so they hired him. All he did was tell people he sure hoped they didn't get a Union. You said management was so busy they didn't take time to maintain communications with the employees. The employees began to feel insecure with the changed climate and decided to protect themselves and joined the Union. I hope the plant stays and I hope the jobs stay with it. Do you think he would have closed the plant?"

"He was seriously considering the option, and looked happy with that real estate woman. I wasn't bargaining when I told you that I stayed away from him so I wouldn't have to tell him how tough your position was that day. I was afraid that could have made the difference.

"For your information, when I asked him if he would be too busy running his business to go fishing in the Bahamas, he half smiled and said, maybe he needs two years to decide! I'm not sure what his answer means."

FOR DISCUSSION OR ASSIGNMENT

The company considered itself a good employer and wanted to continue to be a good employer. It intended to retain its right to run the business, and was willing to write its practices into a collective agreement.

1. Do you agree with this approach? What alternatives would you suggest?

2. Why do you think the various employers reacted to the newspaper clippings the way that they did?

3. Is it significant that, in each case, it was a small company which had operated without a Union until that time.

4. How would you react in such a situation? Why?

5. Comment on the consultant's attitude in selecting clients, and towards maintaining his relationship with the client.

6. The owner is concerned that the Union is going to try to tell him how to run his business. This is stated emphatically to the Union with the statement that the company considers itself a good employer and plans to continue to be a good employer. What messages do you think the company is conveying to the Union? Do you agree? Why?

7. The consultant tells the Union representative that these employees don't need a union. The Union representative disagrees, with reasons. State your views on the conflicting statements.

8. "The conversation that did not happen." How can the strangers agree to such a conversation? What would be the consequences of exposing such a conversation?

9. The consultant explained to the Union that his function was to find if it was practical to reach an agreement with the Union. What was he trying to convey to the Union? How might the Union react?

10. The consultant was emphatically negative to the Union demands, gave the Union little opportunity to discuss the company submissions, established the problem areas and concentrated the discussion on these areas. What do you think he is doing? Do you agree with the approach?

11. Speculate on the consultant's informal communication about the Bahamas, the possibility of a strike and the possibility that there might be no jobs.

12. Comment on the company approach — If all other company positions were acceptable, the company was willing to deal with the agreed-upon problem areas, and they had better reach agreement quickly or it might be too late.

Appendix: Comparison of Union Demands With Settlement Provisions

ORIGINAL UNION DEMANDS

Article 1
Purpose

.01 The general purpose of this Agreement is to provide orderly collective bargaining relations between the Employer and its employees represented by the Union; to provide for the prompt and fair disposition of grievances; and to provide mutually satisfactory working conditions, hours of work, and rates of pay, with due regard to the efficiency of the operations, quality and quantity of production, and the safety and health of the employees.

Article 2
Recognition & Scope

.01 This Agreement will apply to all hourly rated employees of the Employer at its plants situated in the City of _____ , save and except foremen, persons above these ranks, office clerical, technical and sales staff.

.02 The Employer recognizes the Union as the sole and exclusive collective bargaining agent for all employees of the employer in the bargaining unit as defined above.

.03 The Employer agrees that those employees as defined in (article 2.01) not in the bargaining unit, will not perform any work which is recognized as the work of the bargaining unit.

ACTUAL COLLECTIVE AGREEMENT

Article 1
Purpose

The general purpose of this Agreement between the Company and the Union is to establish and maintain orderly collective bargaining relations, to provide a procedure for dealing with grievances, and to set forth formally, the rates of pay, hours of work and other working conditions that have been agreed upon.

Article 2
Recognition & Scope

2.01 The Company recognizes the Union as the collective bargaining agency for all employees of its Plant located at _____ , save and except the foremen, persons above the rank of foreman, office and sales staff and students hired on a co-operative basis with a school or university programme.

.04 The Employer agrees that, students and persons employed for not more than twenty four (24) hours per week, will not be employed in bargaining unit work, if members of the regular bargaining unit are laid off. The Employer agrees that in recognition of the above, there will be no more than 10 such persons employed at any one time.

.05 The Employer agrees that in the event of relocation of all or part of its business from its current locations, within a 100 km radius, to recognize the Union its members and this agreement at the new location.

Article 3
Promotion of Mutual Interests

.01 In the interest of promoting harmonious relations, the Employer agrees to give to all present and future employees a copy of this agreement.

.02 The Employer further agrees to allow the Unit Chairperson the privilege of a ten (10) minute discussion during working hours with all new employees of the bargaining unit. The purpose of discussion will be to introduce the new employee to the Collective Agreement and the Union.

Article 4
Union Security

.01 All present and future employees, as a condition of employment, shall become and remain members of the Union.

Article 3
Promotion of Mutual Interests

3.01 In the interests of promoting understanding of the Agreement, the Company will supply present and future employees with a copy of this Agreement.

Article 4
Union Security

4.01 All present and future employees, as a condition of employment, shall become and remain members of the Union.

.02 Dues are defined for the purpose of this clause as the regular Union dues and initiation fees as prescribed by the Constitution of the Union.

.03 (a) The Company will, upon completion of an authorization card, signed by an employee covered by Clause 4.01 of this agreement, deduct from the pay cheque for the second pay period of each month, the regular monthly dues of such employees, and remit monies to the Financial Secretary of the Local No. ___ of the National Union by the tenth (10th) of the following month for which the dues were deducted.

(b) Initiation fees shall be taken off after the employee has completed the probationary period and shall be taken off on a different pay period than the dues deduction period, immediately after an employee has completed his probationary period.

(c) The Company will, at the time of making each remittance, supply a list of the names of each employee from whose pay deductions have been made and the amount deducted for the month including the name and status of any employee from whom the Company has made no deductions. This list will also indicate any employee whose employment is terminated, transferred out of the Bargaining Unit or who has died.

4.02 Dues are defined for the purpose of this clause as the regular Union dues and initiation fees as prescribed by the Constitution of the Union.

4.03 (a) The Company will, upon completion of an authorization card, signed by an employee covered by Clause 4.01 of this agreement, deduct from the pay cheque for the second pay period of each month, the regular monthly dues of such employees, and remit monies to the Financial Secretary of the Local No. ___ of the National Union by the tenth (10th) of the following month for which the dues were deducted.

(b) Initiation fees shall be taken off after the employee has completed the probationary period and shall be taken off on a different pay period than the dues deduction period, immediately after an employee has completed his probationary period.

(c) The Company will, at the time of making each remittance, supply a list of the names of each employee from whose pay deductions have been made and the amount deducted for the month including the name and status of any employee from whom the Company has made no deductions. This list will also indicate any employee whose employment is terminated, transferred out of the Bargaining Unit or who has died.

.04 The Company agrees to supply the National Representative with a list of all employees' names, addresses, postal codes and telephone numbers upon ratification of the Agreement. The Company further agrees to provide the Financial Secretary of Local ___ with a quarterly list of any changed addresses and postal codes along with names, addresses, postal codes and telephone numbers of new employees hired.

.05 No deductions shall be made from the pay of any employee covered by Clause 4.01 of the Agreement, in any month, where such employee has worked less than a total of forty (40) hours.

.06 Paid vacation days and paid holidays will be considered as days worked. The Company agrees to include on an employee T-4 slip for income tax purpose, the total Union dues paid for the year excluding any initiation fees.

.07 The Union agrees to keep the company harmless from any claims against it by an employee, which may arise out of deductions made in accordance with this article.

Article 5
No Discrimination

The Company and the Union agree there shall be no discrimination, interference, restriction or coercion exercised or practised with respect to any employee by reason of age, marital status, sex, race, creed, colour, national origin, political or religious

4.04 The Company agrees to supply the National Representative with a list of all employees' names, addresses, postal codes and telephone numbers upon ratification of the Agreement. The Company further agrees to provide the Financial Secretary of Local ___ with a quarterly list of any changed addresses and postal codes along with names, addresses, postal codes and telephone numbers of new employees hired.

4.05 No deductions shall be made from the pay of any employee covered by Clause 4.01 of the Agreement, in any month, where such employee has worked less than a total of forty (40) hours.

4.06 Paid vacation days and paid holidays will be considered as days worked. The Company agrees to include on an employee T-4 slip for income tax purpose, the total Union dues paid for the year excluding any initiation fees.

4.07 The Union agrees to keep the company harmless from any claims against it by an employee, which may arise out of deductions made in accordance with this article.

Article 5
No Discrimination

The Company and the Union agree there shall be no discrimination, interference, restriction or coercion exercised or practised with respect to any employee by reason of age, marital status, sex, race, creed, colour, national origin, political or religious affiliations, disability, sexual orientation nor by reason of union membership or activity.

affiliations, disability, sexual orientation nor by reason of union membership or activity.

Article 6
Management Rights

Article 6
Management Rights

The Union acknowledges that it is the exclusive function of the Company:

6.01 It is recognized that management of the plant and direction of the working force are fixed exclusively in the Company, which maintains all rights and responsibilities of management not specifically modified by this Agreement.

(a) to maintain order, discipline, and efficiency;

(b) to hire, retire, classify, direct, transfer, promote, demote, lay off, discipline, suspend or discharge employees, provided that a claim of discriminatory promotion, demotion or transfer, or a claim that an employee has been discharged, suspended, or disciplined without cause may be the subject of a grievance, and dealt with hereinafter provided;

The exercise of such rights shall include but not be limited to:

(a) The right to hire, assign, increase and/or decrease the working forces, promote, demote, transfer and make temporary lay-offs for lack of business or material.

(c) generally to manage the industrial enterprise and without restricting the generality of the foregoing, to determine the number and location of plants, the products to be manufactured or handled, methods of manufacturing, schedules of production, kinds and locations of machines, tools and equipment to be used, processes of manufacturing and assembling, the engineering and designing of its products, and the control of materials and parts to be incorporated in the products manufactured or handled, save only where such rights and obligations are explicitly abridged or amended by

(b) The determination of: the number and location of plants, the products to be manufactured, the methods of manufacturing, schedules of production, kinds and locations of machines and tools to be used, processes of manufacturing and assembling, the engineering and design of its products, and the control of materials and parts to be incorporated in the products produced.

(c) The making and enforcement of rules and regulations, not inconsistent with this Agreement, relating to discipline, safety and general conduct of employees, and to suspend and discharge or otherwise discipline employees for just cause.

the express terms of the collective agreement.

(d) to make, alter and enforce rules and regulations to be observed by employees, provided such rules and regulations are not inconsistent with the terms of this agreement.

6.02 To enable the Company to keep its products abreast of scientific advancement the Company may from time to time, without reference to seniority hereinafter set forth, hire, teach, transfer or assign duties to technically trained men and technical students and deal with them as it deems advisable. This practice, however, shall not adversely affect the employees in the bargaining unit.

6.03 The Company agrees that these functions will be exercised in a manner not inconsistent with the terms of this Agreement.

6.04 Claims of discriminatory upgrading, demotion or transfer, or a claim that an employee has been suspended or discharged without just cause may be made the subject of a grievance and dealt with as provided in the Agreement.

Article 7
Strikes and Lockouts

.01 The parties hereto agree that there shall be no strikes, work stoppages or lockouts during the life of this agreement.

Article 7
Strikes and Lockouts

7.01 During the term of this Agreement, the Company agrees that there shall be no lockout and the Union agrees that there shall be no slowdown, strike, or other work stoppage or interference with work.

7.02 The Union agrees that unless duly authorized:

(a) Union meetings will not be held on Company premises.

(b) No employee or Union official will solicit membership in the Union, collect dues, or engage in any Union activity on Company time, during his working hours, or the working hours of any employee, except as provided for in this Agreement.

7.03 The union agrees that, in recognition of the fact that efficient and economic production is in the interest of both parties, it will promote amongst its members good workmanship and regular attendance. It is further agreed by the Union that the employees will at all times protect the property of the Company against damage by themselves or others.

Article 8
Union Representation

.01 The Company acknowledges the right of the Union to elect a Plant Committee which shall be composed of three (3) Committeepersons, one of which will be the Plant Chairperson who shall be assigned to the day shift. In addition the Company will recognize up to eight (8) stewards.

The Committeeperson and Plant Chairperson and stewards at the time of their election must have been employees of the Company with seniority of one (1) year or more.

The duty of the Committeepersons, or Plant Chairperson shall be to represent the employee(s) in the processing of grievances or complaints as outlined in the Grievance Procedure, and deal with matters

Article 8
Stewards

8.01 The Company acknowledges the right of the Union to appoint or elect a Steward to assist employees in presenting their grievances, for each of the following sections of the Shop (one of these Stewards may be designated as "Chief Steward"):

1) Feeder Maintenance Section.

2) Paint and Assembly Section.

8.02 An employee will not be eligible to serve as a Steward or as a member of any Union Committee until he has established seniority with the Company.

8.03 The Union acknowledges that Stewards, as well as other members of the Union Committees and Union Officers, will continued relating to the administration of the collective Agreement.

.02 The Union will inform the Company, in writing, of the names of the committeepersons, and Plant Chairperson and any subsequent change in the names of the Committeepersons and Plant Chairperson, and the Company will not be required to recognize the Committeeperson, Steward(s) and Plan Chairperson until such notification from the Union has been received.

.03 The Committeeperson, the Plant Chairperson and/or grievor shall report to and obtain permission from their supervisor or his representative, whenever it becomes necessary to leave their work, for the purpose of processing grievances, as outlined in the Grievance Procedure. Such permission may be granted when, in the opinion of the Company, the production of the work area/or plant is not unduly affected; the Committeeperson, the Plant Chairperson and/or grievor shall report back to their supervisor, or his representative at the time they return to work.

.04 Company approved time off work by the Committeeperson, or the Plant Chairperson or the grievor, processing in-plant grievances or complaints only, will be paid by the Company at their normal hourly rate. It is agreed by the union that only such time as is reasonably necessary will be consumed by such to perform their regular duties on behalf of the Company and that such persons will not leave their regular duties without first having received permission from their supervisor. Any Union representative who is privileged by the Agreement to take up Union business in a Section other than his own will first report to the foreman of that Section.

8.04 A Steward may assist in the presentation of grievances in the Section which he represents, with the exception that when a steward is absent from the Section, the Chief Steward may assist in presenting grievances for that Section.

8.05 The Company will pay for 50 per cent of time lost on grievance handling with the Company supervision to a maximum of $1^1/_2$ hours' pay in any one week to the Department Steward and the President of the Union Local (when the latter is acting as a member of the Grievance Committee). In addition, the Chief Steward will be compensated on the same basis as the above to a maximum of $2^1/_2$ hours' pay in any one week.

persons during working hours in order to attend to in-plant Union business. The Union recognizes that cases may occur where the Company may need a reasonable period of time to provide a replacement. He will advise his supervisor of his destination and general nature of his business and the time anticipated to transact such business.

.05 The Committeepersons together with the Plant Chairperson shall form the Plant Committee for the purpose of meeting with the management for the administration of this Collective Agreement.

.06 The Union will be allowed to post, on a bulletin board, provided by the Company, notices regarding meetings and matters pertaining only to the Union. Before posting, all such notices must be approved by the Plant Manager or his representative.

.07 The President of the Local Union and/or National Representative, will be entitled to be present at meetings with Company.

.09 The Employer agrees to retain Union representatives defined in this article above, in the event of lay offs or cutbacks in employment, provided they are willing and able of performing the normal requirements of the remaining work.

Article 9
Grievance Procedure

.01 It is the Mutual desire of the parties hereto that any complaint or cause for dissatisfaction arising between an employee and the Company with respect to the application, interpretation or alleged violation of this agreement, shall be adjusted as quickly as possible.

Step 1

The employee accompanied by a steward, will verbally submit his grievance to his immediate supervisor or his representative, within five (5) working days from the date of the alleged violation of the agreement, or from the date the alleged violation of the agreement became known to the grievor. The supervisor shall render a verbal decision within five (5) working days following this meeting.

Step 2

Failing an answer from his supervisor, or a satisfactory settlement as in Step 1, within five (5) working days, the aggrieved employee, accompanied by a steward, shall meet with his immediate supervisor, or his representative. At this time, the grievance must be submitted to the Company in writing. A decision in writing, will be rendered by his immediate supervisor, or his representative, within five (5) working days following this meeting.

Article 9
Grievance

9.01 A grievance is defined to be any question between the Company and one or more of the employees, as to the application, interpretation or violation of the terms of this Agreement, or any matter involving hours or working conditions covered by this Agreement, or if it is claimed that discriminatory practices are being performed or that an employee is not being paid the proper rate within the rate range of his classification.

9.02 A grievance must be filed within 30 days from the date of the occurrence which gave rise to the grievance except grievances alleging violation of Section 11.03(a) or (b) of Article 11 which must be filed within 7 days of the date of the alleged improper transfer or layoff or thirty (30) calendar days from the date when an employee commences work who has allegedly been improperly hired in place of the grievor. If such a grievance is sustain, liability on the part of the Company will be limited to a maximum of seven (7) calendar days immediately preceding the date on which the grievance is lodged.

The following is the procedure for adjusting grievances:

a) It is recognized that when an employee has a just or reasonable complaint, his immediate supervisor should be informed as quickly as

Step 3

Failing an answer from his supervisor, or a satisfactory settlement as in Step 2, within five (5) working days, or such time mutually agreed to, the aggrieved employee with the Plant Chairperson shall refer the grievance, in writing, to the plant manager, or his representative. At this meeting the Union or the Company may request the presence of a staff representative of the Union. The plant manager, or his representative, shall render his decision, in writing, to the employee, within ten (10) working days from the date the grievance was submitted to him in writing.

.02 Policy or group grievance initiated by the Company or by the Union will be originated at the third (3rd) step of the grievance procedure.

.03 Grievance dealing with discharge or suspension shall commence with third (3rd) step of the grievance.

.04 The time limits foreseen at the various steps of the grievance procedure may be extended by mutual consent, in writing, by both parties.

.05 Failing a satisfactory settlement, as in Step Three (3), the grievance may be submitted to arbitration.

possible and that an employee should not consider that he has a grievance until his immediate supervisor has had an opportunity of adjusting the complaint.

b) If after complying with Section 9.02(a) above, and failing reasonable satisfaction, an employee with a grievance may take the matter to the Union Steward of his Section, and the Union Steward, with the employee, may present the grievance in writing to the foreman. A grievance must be signed by the employee concerned. The foreman shall give a reply within three full working days.

c) If the foreman's disposition of the grievance is unsatisfactory, his section Union Steward may confer with the Chief Steward and if the latter decides to take up the grievance with the Plant Manager or his designated alternate he shall do so in writing, within three working days after the receipt of the foreman's answer. The Plant Manager or his designated alternate shall give a reply within three full working days.

d) If the disposition of the grievance by the Plant Manager or his designated alternate is unsatisfactory, the grievance may then be referred to the Union Grievance Committee, made up of three members who shall be employees of the Company, and such committee may take the grievance within three working days after the receipt of the Plant Manager's answer or his designated alternate's, and a meeting will then be held within 10 full working days. At this stage, the Union Grievance Committee may be assisted by a duly authorized official of the Union, and any employee possessed of factual knowledge touching on this matter. A reply shall be given within ten full working days.

9.03 Grievances not filed within the time limits of three days as shown in Sections (c) and (d) hereof shall be considered settled or disposed of.

9.04 (a) If a grievance has not been settled under the procedure set forth in Section 9.02 and it is alleged that such a grievance involves misinterpretation or violation of this Agreement, such alleged misinterpretation or violation may be referred to arbitration if it is so requested within thirty (30) days after the final answer is given, as in Section 9.02 of this Article.

b) When a grievance is posted for arbitration, it shall state the Article and Section of this Agreement, which have allegedly been breached.

Article 10
Arbitration

.01 It shall be the responsibility of the party desiring arbitration to so inform the other party, in writing, within thirty (30) working days after the plant manager, or his representative, failed to render a decision, or

Article 10
Arbitration

10.01 It shall be the responsibility of the party desiring arbitration to so inform the other party, in writing, within thirty (30) working days after the plant manager, or his representative, failed to render a decision, or satisfactory settlement as provided in Step 3 of the grievance procedure.

.02 A notice of intent to arbitrate, with a sole arbitrator shall contain a list of three (3) arbitrators for consideration. Within ten (10) working days from the receipt of the list of recommended arbitrators, the other party will either accept one (1) arbitrator from the list, or submit a list of three (3) arbitrators to the aggrieved party for consideration. If no single arbitrator can be agreed on from this list within ten (10) working days, either party may request the Ontario Minister of Labour to name an arbitrator.

.03 The sole arbitrator will set a date for the hearing, within reasonable time delays, to permit both parties to present their case, and will render a decision, as soon as possible, after the completion of hearing all evidence.

.04 The decision of the sole arbitrator shall be binding and final upon both parties. The sole arbitrator shall be restricted in his award to the provisions of the collective agreement, and shall not in his award add to, delete from, or otherwise alter or amend any provisions of the agreement.

.05 Each party will equally bear the fees and expenses of the sole arbitrator.

.06 Any extension of the time limits may be made by either party by mutual consent, in writing; or by the sole arbitrator, who will advise the parties in writing.

satisfactory settlement as provided in Step 3 of the grievance procedure.

10.02 A notice of intent to arbitrate, with a sole arbitrator shall contain a list of three (3) arbitrators for consideration. Within ten (10) working days from the receipt of the list of recommended arbitrators, the other party will either accept one (1) arbitrator from the list, or submit a list of three (3) arbitrators to the aggrieved party for consideration. If no single arbitrator can be agreed on from this list within ten (10) working days, either party may request the Ontario Minister of Labour to name an arbitrator.

10.03 The sole arbitrator will set a date for the hearing, within reasonable time delays, to permit both parties to present their case, and will render a decision, as soon as possible, after the completion of hearing all evidence.

10.04 The decision of the sole arbitrator shall be binding and final upon both parties. The sole arbitrator shall be restricted in his award to the provisions of the collective agreement, and shall not in his award add to, delete from, or otherwise alter or amend any provisions of the agreement.

10.05 Each party will equally bear the fees and expenses of the sole arbitrator.

10.06 Any extension of the time limits may be made by either party by mutual consent, in writing; or by the sole arbitrator, who will advise the parties in writing.

Article 11
Probationary Period

.01 New hires shall be considered probationary until they have completed a total of a sixty (60) calendar day period, after which they shall become regular employees as defined in clauses and their seniority rating shall date back to their date of employment.

Article 12
Seniority

.01 The fundamental rules respecting seniority are designed to give employees an equitable measure of security based on length of service with the company.

.02 Seniority will be established and maintained for all employees in the bargaining unit on a plant-wide basis.

.03 All employees' names will appear on a seniority list as of their date of hire, and be revised every three months and posted on plant notice boards. A copy of such list will be given to the Unit Chairperson of the Committee.

.04 Employees will be regarded as probationary employees for the first sixty (60) calendar days of their employment. Seniority will start from the first date of hire and their name will appear on the Seniority List in order of the respective date of hire.

.05 In the event more than one employee is hired on the same date, the Company will randomly assign

Article 11
Probationary Period

11.01 New hires shall be considered probationary until they have completed a total of a sixty (60) calendar day period, after which they shall become regular employees as defined in clauses and their seniority rating shall date back to their date of employment.

Article 12
Seniority

12.01 The seniority of each employee covered by this Agreement shall be established after a period of probation of 60 worked days, and shall then count from the date of employment with the Company.

12.02 a)Plant-wide and Section seniority lists shall be established and compiled by the Company and posted on bulletin boards in the Plant. The lists shall be fully revised by the Company at least once every six months. Copies of the seniority lists shall be supplied to the Union.

b) The plant seniority list shall be made up in the following sections:

1) Feeder Maintenance Section
2) Paint and Assembly Section

c) An employee's name shall be included on both Plant-wide and Sectional seniority lists when he has completed 15 months' service with the Company. Prior to the completion of 15 months' service with the each employee with a seniority code number, this number will be used in determining each employee's seniority standing. i.e. lowest seniority code number will be highest seniority standing on such date.

Loss of Seniority

Seniority rights shall cease for any of the following reasons:

1) If an employee voluntary quits the employ of the Company.

2) If an employee is discharged for just cause and such employee is not reinstated pursuant to the provisions of the grievance procedure.

3) If an employee overstays a leave of absence or remains away from work without permission for a period of more than five (5) consecutive working days, the employee shall be subject to discipline up to and including discharge, unless the employee has a justifiable reason for such absence.

4) If an employee fails to report for work in accordance with a notice of recall, or within seven (7) working days after registered mailing date of such notice, which ever is later, unless a satisfactory reason is given.

5) If laid off, an employee will be retained on the seniority list for a period of thirty-six (36) months or for a period of time equal to their accumulated seniority at date or lay-off whichever is greater.

6) If an employee is transferred to a position outside the bargaining unit.

Company, his name shall be included on the Sectional seniority list only.

12.03 a) Seniority will be the major factor governing lay-offs and transfers due to lack of work, subject to the provisions that employees with higher seniority have the necessary skill and ability to perform the normal requirements of the work available.

b) Subject to the provisions of Section 12.03(a) hereof, employees who are laid off shall be recalled in reverse order to that in which they were laid off, subject to their ability to perform the work required. A laid-off employee must advise the Company of his intention to return within 3 working days and must report for work within 7 days from the day such registered letter is mailed, except in the case of verified illness.

c) When a reduction in working force is necessary, all probationary employees will be laid off first provided that the retained employees have the necessary skills and ability to perform the work available.

d) The provisions of this Article will not apply in cases where there is a temporary shortage of work and the Company may then lay off an employee up to a total of 15 working days in each calendar year without regard to the seniority provisions of this Agreement. In calculating the 15 working days above, a lay-off for the second half of a shift

Layoffs and Recalls

.01(a) The Company will give at least seven (7) days notice to employees and the Union of any contemplated layoffs.

.02(b) Whenever it becomes necessary to decrease the working force, probationary employees will be the first laid off, if further layoffs are necessary, employees with the least amount of seniority shall be laid off, provided those remaining employees with more seniority are able and willing to do the work available. In the event of such a layoff all employees will be given five (5) working days notice of the layoff.

.03(c) In the event of a dispute regarding an employee's ability to perform the available work, such employee will be given a five (5) working day trial for the purpose of determining their ability.

.04(d) Employees who have been laid off in accordance with the above provisions will be returned to work in line of seniority in which they were laid off provided they are able and willing to do the work available.

.05(e) The Company will provide the Chairperson of the Union Plant Committee with a list of employees to be laid off or recalled, also any cancellation of such notices.

.06(f) The Company agrees to retain Union representatives at work during the layoffs or cut in employment provided they are willing and able to perform the remaining work.

or portion thereof will be deemed half a day, and shall be counted against the 15 working days.

Time lost for the following causes will not be subject to the seniority provisions of the Agreement. Neither will it be counted in the 15 day exception referred to herein:

i) Time lost by an employee during the annual vacation shutdown as a result of such employee's vacation entitlement being less than the shutdown period.

ii) Time lost by an employee due expressly to a shutdown caused by fire, lightning, flood, tempest or due to circumstances beyond the Company's reasonable control, causing damage to the Plant, or part of its equipment.

e) An employee who is about to be laid off under the provisions of the Article will be given at least 5 working days' notice of such layoff. This shall not apply to a layoff under the provisions of Section 12.03(d), but in such case as much notice as possible will be given.

12.04 An employee shall maintain and accumulate his seniority under the following conditions:

a) During a layoff not to exceed twelve months.

b) During absence due to illness not to exceed fifty-two consecutive weeks.

c) During leave of absence granted by the Company in writing.

Wage Administration and Rate Protection

An employee who is upgraded shall have his/her wages adjusted on the date of such assignment.

An employee who is moved by the Company to a lower paying job shall maintain his/her rate of pay in effect at the time of such move for the life of the agreement. This rate protection will not apply to an employee moved from a temporary assignment, or to an employee who refuses to return to his/her formerly held job from which they were moved.

Job Posting

1) If a permanent job vacancy exists, or new job classifications are created such openings shall be posted on the bulletin board for a period of five (5) work days, during which time, employees may make application for such job vacancy.

2) Employees shall be permitted to bid for a higher classification, except that the successful regular employee shall be entitled to only one such transfer once every six (6) month period as a result of obtaining such job transfer by job posting.

3) Employees bidding for a permanent job vacancy, under this article shall be considered, by the Company, on the following factors, at the time of job postings:

a) length of seniority
b) qualifications, ability, skill

12.05 Seniority shall be maintained only as follows:

a) During absence due to illness not to exceed fifty-two consecutive weeks for which the Company may require written verification.

b) During a period of layoff in excess of twelve months but not in excess of twenty-four months.

12.06 An employee shall lose his seniority under the following conditions:

a) If an employee leaves the employ of the Company.

b) If an employee is discharged for just cause, and such discharge is not reversed through the grievance procedure provided herein.

c) If a person fails after a layoff to return to work within seven days after the Company gives such person notice of recall by registered mail to his latest known address.

d) If a person fails to notify the Company of his intention to return to work within three working days following the date on which he is recalled under Section 12.03(b).

e) If an employee overstays a leave of absence without the written permission of the Company; except where he overstays such leave due to illness verified by a doctor's certificate when required by the Company or other cause, verified in writing, which is in the opinion of the Company beyond the control of the employee.

The posting will include a full description of the job duties and qualifications along with the respective rate of pay.

f) If an employee is laid off for twenty-four consecutive months.

12.07 Notwithstanding his position on the seniority list, a Section Steward who has at least one (1) year's service will be retained in his department provided there is work available for him which he is qualified to perform in accordance with the provisions of Section 12.03(a). Subject to the same conditions, the Local President will be retained within the bargaining unit.

12.08 An employee with seniority who has been absent from work due to illness or accident and, when medically cleared to return to work, is unable in the opinion of the Company to perform the requirements of the job performed by him immediately prior to such illness or accident, may be eligible for an open job provided he has the skill and ability to perform such open job.

Article 13
Temporary Transfer

.01 An employee temporarily assigned, at the direction of the Company, to a classification other than his regular base hourly rate of pay or the classification rate of the job to which he is transferred, whichever is higher.

.02 A transfer shall be considered temporary provided it does not exceed ten (10) working days, and during this period, will not be subject to the seniority provisions of this agreement. If such transfer exceeds

Article 13
Temporary Transfer

this period, it will be declared as a permanent vacancy and posted for job bidding.

.03 Vacant jobs created as a result of illness, injury or occupational accident or illness, or leave of absence shall not be posted as permanent vacancies and may be filled at the discretion of the Company on a temporary basis for the duration of the illness, injury, occupational accident or illness, or leave of absence.

Article 14
Hours of Work

The Union proposes a discussion, at the bargaining table, prior to the formulation and submission of a proposal in this area.

Article 14
Hours of Work

14.01 The normal hours of work shall be 40 hours per week consisting of five eight-hour shifts Monday to Friday inclusive. This is not to be read or construed as a guarantee to provide work for any period whatsoever.

14.02 Hours of work in excess of 8 hours per day, Monday to Friday, inclusive, and hours of work on Saturday and Sunday, will be treated as overtime hours and will be paid for at a premium rate as provided under Section 14.03(b) below, except that when employees change shifts at their own request, they shall not be entitled to such premium rate by reason of the fact that they have worked two eight-hour shifts in the 24-hour day.

14.03 a) In computing daily overtime hours, a day shall be the twenty-four hour period following the regular starting time of the shift on which the employee is working.

b) Overtime hours worked will be paid for at a premium rate calculated on the basis of one and one-half times an employee's hourly wage rate except in the case of Sunday, in which case the overtime hours worked will be paid for at a premium rate calculated on the basis of two times an employee's hourly wage rate.

14.04 As far as possible, overtime hours worked will be equally distributed amongst the employees. Each employee is expected to co-operate with the Company in the performance of such work and the Company agrees to accept reasonable grounds for the employee declining to perform such work.

14.05 For the purpose of calculating payment for time worked under this Article 14 and under Article 15, time worked on a scheduled shift commencing prior to 10:00 p.m. shall be treated as if worked on the calendar day on which such shift commences. Time worked on a scheduled shift commencing at or after 10:00 p.m. shall be treated as work performed on the immediately following calendar day.

Article 15
Overtime

As above

Article 16
Shift Premiums

As above

Article 16
Shift Premiums

16.01 When employees are engaged on a regularly scheduled

shift commencing before 6:00 a.m. or after 12:00 noon, they shall be paid a bonus of sixty (60) cents per hour for all regularly scheduled shift hours worked. There shall be no shift bonus worked. There shall be no shift bonus allowed for hours paid at overtime premium rates.

Article 17
Paid Holidays

.01 The Company agrees to pay an employee, as provided below, for the following specified holidays without requiring an employee to render service:

New Year's Day
Heritage Day or the 3rd Monday in February
Good Friday
Victoria Day
Canada Day
Civic Holiday
Labour Day
Thanksgiving Day
Christmas Day
December 26th
Plus three (3) PPH Days

.02 In order to be paid for a Specified Holiday an employee must work on his normal scheduled shift prior to the holiday and on his normally scheduled shift after the holiday.

Note: In addition an employee must be on the payroll of the employer for at least fifteen (15) days (calendar) in order to receive pay for such holidays.

Article 17
Specified Holidays

17.01 During the term of this Collective Agreement, the Company agrees to pay an employee, as provided under Section 17.03 below, for the following specified holidays without requiring an employee to render service:

New Year's Day	Labour Day
Good Friday	Thanksgiving Day
Victoria Day	Christmas Day
Dominion Day	

The last half of his regular shift immediately prior to each of Christmas and New Year's Day up to a maximum of four (4) hours.

Three additional days to be observed each year in December, as agreed.

17.02 An employee shall qualify for payment of the aforementioned holidays subject to the following conditions:

a) If he works his full shift on the work day immediately preceding and immediately following a holiday referred to in Section 17.01 and has not reported for work more than one

.03 The following will be exercised by the Company, if a paid holiday falls within an employee's annual vacation: an employee will be allocated an extra day in his vacation, or at a later date.

.04 Employees eligible for payment their applicable base hourly rate, multiplied by eight (8) hours, or twelve (12) hours, dependent on working schedules.

.05 If any of the paid holidays listed in clause 17.01 falls on a Saturday or a Sunday (and has not been replaced by another day, by statute or decree), such holiday will be observed either on the previous Friday or the following Monday.

Note: The Union will enter a proposal respecting application of (.05) for those working 12 hour shifts, after discussion at the bargaining table.

(1) hour after his scheduled starting time.

b) If he has worked one or more full scheduled shifts in the pay period in which a holiday fell and is prevented from complying with the provisions of 17.02(a) absence or illness verified by a doctor(s), when required by the Company.

c) If he has worked one or more full scheduled shifts in the ten (10) normally scheduled working days immediately preceding or immediately following the Christmas Holiday period and is prevented from complying with the provisions of 17.02(a) above, as a result of a lay-off, leave of absence, or illness verified by a doctor(s) when required by the Company.

d) If, in the opinion of the Company, he is prevented from complying with the provisions of Sections 17.02(a), (b) or (c) due to circumstances beyond his reasonable control.

17.03 The specified holiday pay as referred to in this Article will be calculated on the basis of the employee's hourly wage rate multiplied by the number of hours in the employee's standard work day.

17.04 An employee required to work on the day on which the specified holiday is observed as referred to in 17.01 will receive overtime pay as shown in Article 14, in addition to the specified holiday pay.

Article 18
Vacations

.01 Vacations with pay will be granted to all employees on the payroll of the company on the basis of their length of service with the Company as defined in Article of the Collective Agreement.

.02 The Company reserves the right to spread vacations over the vacation season, or in the alternative, to close the plant for an interval not to exceed two weeks during the period July 1st to August 31st. Preference of time at which employees wish to take their vacation will be given consideration, but the Company shall have the final decision. The Company will set the vacation period by not later than February 1st of the current year.

.03 Employees shall be paid vacation pay immediately prior to the taking of their respective vacation.

Note: Vacations to be discussed
re   - calculation period
       - entitlements
       - level of payment

Article 18
Vacation With Pay

18.01 Annual vacations will be paid on the following basis:

i) Three weeks after 5 years' continuous service if completed by December 31st.

ii) Two weeks after 1 year's continuous service if completed by July 31st.

18.02 Vacations will be scheduled by the Company and shall be completed within the calendar year. It is not permissible to postpone the vacation period or any part thereof from one year to another.

18.03 The allowance for each week of vacation will be determined by multiplying the employee's hourly wage rate by the number of hours in the employee's regular weekly schedule. This will not include hours for which overtime premium is paid.

a) An employee with less than 12 months' continuous service will be paid a vacation allowance calculated on the basis of four per cent (4%) of the employee's earnings during the period from the employee's date of hiring to July 31st.

b) An employee who has been laid off, or an employee who's had leave for a period in excess of 60 working days during the vacation year (August 1st to July 31st) will be paid vacation pay to an amount of

4% or 6%, whichever is applicable, of his gross earnings during the year.

18.04 a) An employee with less than 12 months' continuous service with the Company, whose service is discontinued, will be paid four per cent (4%) of the employee's earnings.

b) An employee with more than 12 months' continuous service with the Company, whose service is discontinued, will be paid two per cent (2%) for each week of vacation entitlement.

Article 19
Occupational Accidents or Illness

.01 When an employee suffers an occupational accident during his working hours, and requires treatment from a doctor or hospital, such employee will be paid his base hourly rate for the balance of his shift.

.02 In the event an employee becomes physically handicapped and is unable to continue their job, exception will be made in favour of such employee on the following basis.

.03 If a job vacancy occurs, which an incapacitated employee can perform, they will be placed on such job.

.04 A Doctor's certification of disability by the employee's own doctor, must be submitted.

.05 An employee placed on a job because of a disability will have

Article 19
Occupational Accidents or Illness

19.01 When an employee suffers an occupational accident during his working hours, and requires treatment from a doctor or hospital, such employee will be paid his base hourly rate for the balance of his shift.

19.02 In the event an employee becomes physically handicapped and is unable to continue their job, exception will be made in favour of such employee on the following basis.

19.03 If a job vacancy occurs, which an incapacitated employee can perform, they will be placed on such job.

19.04 A Doctor's certification of disability by the employee's own doctor must be submitted.

19.05 An employee placed on a job because of a disability will have that disability reviewed at least annually.

.06 The Company will review all the circumstances with the Union Committee before exercising this provision. All exceptions to the seniority provisions of the Collective Agreement must be mutually agreed to by the parties.

Article 20
Leave of Absence

.01 Upon application and one (1) week's notice, except in cases of emergency, leaves of absence will be granted employees without loss of seniority. Leaves of absence must be signed by the Company and a copy given to the Shop Committee.

.02 Any employee of the Company elected or appointed to a full-time position in the Local Union or National Union, will be granted a leave of absence by the Company. Such leaves will remain in effect until notice to cancel such leave is given by the Union.

.03 The Company will grant a leave of absence with pay to members of the Union to attend Union business outside the plant and will bill the Union monthly for reimbursement.

that disability reviewed at least annually.

19.06 The Company will review circumstances with the Union Committee before exercising this provision. All exceptions to the seniority provisions of the Collective Agreement must be mutually agreed to by the parties.

Article 20
Leave of Absence

20.01 The Company may grant leave of absence without pay for personal reasons, and such leave will not be unreasonably withheld.

20.02 Upon written request by the Union, and if reasonable notice is given, the Company will grant leave of absence without pay of up to two (2) employees for one day per month. The aggregate total of days not to exceed twelve (12) days per year, for the purpose of carrying out business for the Union.

20.03 The Union may appoint or elect an employee(s) to attend a convention or conference and such employee(s) will be granted leave of absence without pay by the Company if reasonable notice is given. The employee will maintain and accumulate seniority during such leave of absence.

The following conditions apply:

a) each leave must not exceed 7 days.

b) no more than 3 leaves will be granted to an individual employee in any one year.

c) not more than 2 employees will be granted leave at any one time.

d) no more than 25 days total leave of absence will be granted in any one year.

Time spent by an employee on negotiation preparations and processes, or while attending a hearing of a Board of Arbitration in connection with a dispute or grievance involving the parties to this Agreement, shall not be subject to (a), (b) and (d) above.

The Union agrees that, except for leaves for negotiation purposes, the Company may withhold leaves requested and ask the Union to substitute other employees if the number of leaves requested in respect of any job or section interferes with the operating requirements of the Company.

20.04 Subject to the following conditions the company will grant leave of absence without pay to a pregnant employee at her request:

a) The employee must have completed her probationary period.

b) Medical certificate(s) attesting to the employee's condition will be supplied on Company request.

c) Leave of absence will normally be granted for a period of three (3) months prior to confinement and two (2) months following confinement except the Company may require leave of absence to be of longer duration if her physical condition is considered to be a hazard to herself or her fellow employees or is interfering with her ability to perform her job.

20.05 The Company will not unreasonably refuse to grant leave of absence to an employee for personal reasons.

Article 21
Public Office Leave of Absence

An employee with seniority, elected or appointed to an essential full-time Federal, Provincial, or Local public office, may make written application for a leave of absence for the period of his/her first term of active service in such public office. If such leave is granted, additional leaves of absences for service in such office may be granted at the option of Management upon written application by the employee.

Any employee granted such leave of absence shall be entitled to reinstatement at the then current rate of pay, to such work as he/she may be entitled on the basis of the seniority provisions of this agreement. Seniority and pension rights will continue to accumulate during the period of such leave of absence.

The employee's request for leave of absence may also include the necessary time to campaign for such office.

Article 21
Public Office Leave of Absence

An employee with seniority, elected or appointed to an essential full-time Federal, Provincial, or Local public office, may make written application for a leave of absence for the period of his/her first term of active service in such public office. If such leave is granted, additional leaves of absences for service in such office may be granted at the option of Management upon written application by the employee.

Any employee granted such leave of absence shall be entitled to reinstatement at the then current rate of pay, to such work as he/she may be entitled on the basis of the seniority provisions of this agreement. Seniority and pension rights will continue to accumulate during the period of such leave of absence.

The employee's request for leave of absence may also include the necessary time to campaign for such office.

Article 22
Bereavement Pay

.01 Subject to the following regulations, the Company will make payment of wages to an employee who is absent solely due to death in his/her immediate family.

a) such employee must have completed sixty (60) days.

b) such employee except for the death and funeral would otherwise be at work.

.02 Members of the employee's immediate family are defined for the purpose of this agreement as:

a) spouse, son, daughter, father, mother and
b) brother, sister, father-in-law, and mother-in-law
c) grandfather, grandmother, grandson, granddaughter, brother-in-law, sister-in-law.

.03 An employee will receive payment for time lost from his/her regularly scheduled hours on the following basis:

a) payment will be made on the basis of the employee's hourly wage rate for the employee's regularly scheduled shift up to eight (8) hours per day, exclusive of overtime and other forms of premium pay.

b) payment will be made for up to five (5) days absence in the case of the death of a member of the employee's immediate family as defined in 22.02(a) and in such case,

Article 22
Bereavement Pay

22.01 Subject to the following regulations, the Company will make payment of wages to an employee who is absent solely due to death in his/her immediate family.

a) such employee must have completed sixty (60) days.

b) such employee except for the death and funeral would otherwise be at work.

22.02 Members of the employee's immediate family are defined for the purpose of this agreement as:

a) spouse, son, daughter, father, mother and
b) brother, sister, father-in-law, and mother-in-law
c) grandfather, grandmother, grandson, granddaughter, brother-in-law, sister-in-law.

22.03 An employee will receive payment for time lost from his/her regularly scheduled hours on the following basis:

a) payment will be made on the basis of the employee's hourly wage rate for the employee's regularly scheduled shift up to eight (8) hours per day, exclusive of overtime and other forms of premium pay.

b) payment will be made for up to five (5) days absence in the case of the death of a member of the employee's immediate family as defined in 22.02(a) and in such case, the time to be paid for may be any five (5) consecutive working days from the day of death through the second day after the funeral, inclusive.

c) payment will be made for up to three (3) days absence in the case of the death of a member of the employee's immediate family as defined in 22.02(b) and in such case, the time to be paid for may be any three (3) consecutive working days from the day of death through the day after the funeral, inclusive.

d) payment will be made for one (1) day's absence, to attend the funeral, in the case of the death of a member of the employee's immediate family as defined in 22.02(c).

.04 An employee will not be eligible to receive payments under this agreement for any period in which he/she is receiving other payments in the form of vacation pay, specified holiday pay, disability benefit, or Workers' Compensation.

Article 23
Jury Duty

.01 An employee who is called for jury service shall be excused from work for the days on which he/she serves, and shall receive, for each day of jury service, on which he/she, otherwise would have worked, the difference between his base hourly rate, and the payment he receives for jury service. The employee will present proof of service and the amount of pay received therefore.

the time to be paid for may be any five (5) consecutive working days from the day of death through the second day after the funeral, inclusive.

c) payment will be made for up to three (3) days absence in the case of the death of a member of the employee's immediate family as defined in 22.02(b) and in such case, the time to be paid for may be any three (3) consecutive working days from the day of death through the day after the funeral, inclusive.

d) payment will be made for one (1) day's absence, to attend the funeral, in the case of the death of a member of the employee's immediate family as defined in 22.02(c).

22.04 An employee will not be eligible to receive payments under this agreement for any period in which he/she is receiving other payments in the form of vacation pay, specified holiday pay, disability benefit, or Workers' Compensation.

Article 23
Jury Duty

23.01 An employee who is called for jury service shall be excused from work for the days on which he/she serves, and shall receive, for each day of jury service, on which he/she, otherwise would have worked, the difference between his base hourly rate, and the payment he receives for jury service. The employee will present proof of service and the amount of pay received therefore.

Article 24
Reporting-in Pay

.01 An employee who has not been notified in advance "not to report for work", and who reports for his regular scheduled shift, will be paid for a minimum of four (4) hours, at his base hourly rate, or six (6) hours dependent on work schedule.

.02 The obligation on the Company will not prevail if no work is available because of:

a) Conditions beyond the control of the Company.

b) If the employee has not kept the Company informed of his current address and a listed or unlisted telephone number.

Article 24
Reporting for Work

24.01 An employee who reports for work at the normal starting time of his shift shall be given four hours' work and will be paid his regular hourly rate. If work is not available, he will be paid for four hours at his regular hourly rate.

24.02 Section 24.01 will not apply under the following conditions:

a) Where the employee has been informed a minimum of six hours in advance of his regular starting time that he is not to report for work.

b) Where the interruption of work is due to power failure, fire, lightning, flood, tempest, or any other condition of any kind whatsoever beyond the control of the Company.

c) Where the employee is not willing to perform alternate work of a reasonable nature.

d) Where the employee fails to keep the Company informed of his latest address and telephone number.

Article 25
Call Back Pay

.01 An employee who has completed his full daily or weekly shifts, and who has left the plant and is called back to perform additional or emergency work, will be paid for the time actually worked at the applicable overtime rate. Employees

Article 25
Call Back Pay

25.01 An employee who has completed his full daily or weekly shifts, and who has left the plant and is called back to perform additional or emergency work, will be paid for the time actually worked at the applicable overtime rate. Employees called back under this clause will be guaranteed a minimum of three (3) hours of work at the appropriate overtime rate.

Article 26
Job Classification & Wage Rates

.01 The hourly wage rate for the job classifications covered in this agreement, are outlined in Schedule "A" of this agreement and by reference herein are made part of this agreement.

called back under this clause will be guaranteed a minimum of three (3) hours of work at the appropriate overtime rate.

Article 26
Wages

26.01 The regular hourly rates set out in Appendix A shall remain in effect for the duration of this Agreement.

26.02 a) The Company shall have the right to establish and implement new job classifications and hourly rates not covered by this Agreement. Such new job classification(s) and hourly rates shall have provisional status for a period of 90 working days.

b) Following the 90 working day provisional period, the Union shall be advised of the finalized regular hourly rate.

c) An employee who receives such regular hourly rate for such job classification, or the Union, may lodge a grievance under Section __ of this Agreement within fifteen days of the effective date applicable under Section 26.02(b).

d) In any arbitration of such a grievance, the Arbitrator shall be limited to determining whether or not the new rate is in proper relationship to existing undisputed rates established for job classifications covered by this Agreement.

Article 27
Technological Change

Technological change means the introduction by the company of equipment, work methods, organization, processes or operations different in nature or type or quantity from that previously utilized by the Company or any modifications to present equipment, work methods, organization, processes or operations.

Advance Notice

The Company will notify the union of any technological change prior to the time of final decisions, but in any case not less than 160 days prior to the implementation of such change.

Such notice shall be given in writing and shall contain pertinent data including:

(i) the nature of change,

(ii) the approximate date of which the company proposes to effect change,

(iii) the approximate number, type and location of employees likely to be affected by the change,

(iv) the effects the change may be expected to have on employee's working conditions and terms of employment,

(v) all other pertinent data relating to the anticipated effects on employees including the change in skills.

Article 27
Technological Change

27.01 This Article shall have application when the Company introduces machinery or equipment, including new devices to existing machinery or equipment, and such introduction has the initial result of:

i) displacing an employee, or

ii) changing the immediate job of an employee by establishing a different labour grade.

Where an employee(s) is affected as set out in either (i) or (ii) above, the Company will notify the Union as far in advance as practicable and, upon request, the Company will arrange a meeting with the Union for the purpose of discussing the effects on the employment status of such employees in applying this Article.

27.02 The Company will provide a training period of up to twenty (20) working days (which may be extended by agreement) on a new or changed job created as a result of technological change as defined under Section 27.01 to an employee with seniority who is thereby displaced. An employee will be selected for a training period on the basis of seniority provided the Company has reasonable evidence in its records or as furnished by the employee or the Union that the employee has transferable skills

The Company will also update the information provided, on a continuous basis, as soon as new developments arise or modifications are made.

Consultation Committee

Within sixty (60) days of the signing of this Agreement the parties will establish a joint Union/Management Technological Change Committee at each location covered by this Collective Agreement.

These Committees will be comprised of three (3) representatives of the Union and will meet and hold constructive and meaningful consultations in an effort to reach agreement on solutions to the problems arising from any intended technological change, on measures to be taken by the Company to protect employees from any adverse effects and on measures to ensure that technological change improves working conditions and job design and provides new opportunities for employees.

The Committee will meet quarterly or at the request of either party and when notice is given of a technological change.

Protection-Job Security & Income Protection

During the term of this Collective Agreement, no member of the bargaining unit shall be laid off or suffer a reduction in wages as either the direct and indirect result of technological change.

which would enable him to meet the normal requirements of the job within a maximum period of twenty (20) working days. If the new or changed job thus created is classified in an occupational classification with a lower labour grade than the classification to which the employee was assigned before the new equipment was introduced, the employee may elect to be placed in accordance with Section 16.02.

A displaced employee unable to qualify for a training period as provided herein will be subject to the provisions of Article 12 in locating another job. Further, an employee selected for training hereunder but unable to meet the normal requirements of the work of such job during the maximum period of twenty (20) working days will be subject to the provisions of Article 12 in locating another job.

27.03 An employee with seniority whose job is directly eliminated by the introduction of a robot or the introduction of an automated manufacturing machine and who as a consequence, is transferred to a lower hourly rated job shall retain his former hourly rate for up to twenty-six (26) weeks from the date his job was eliminated.

The term "robot" means a programmable multifunction manipulator designed to move materials, parts, tools, or specialized devices through variable programmed

Protection of Bargaining Unit Work

No job currently performed by a bargaining unit member will be reclassified as a non-bargaining unit job or transferred to non-bargaining unit personal as either a direct or indirect result of technological change.

No job function, duties or responsibilities currently performed by a bargaining unit member will be reclassified as non-bargaining unit functions, duties or responsibilities or be performed by or temporarily as either a direct or indirect result of technological change without the written mutual agreement of the parties.

Article 28
Duration of Agreement

The Agreement shall be effective from the ___ day of the _____ , 20__ to and including the _____ of _____ , 20__ . Either party shall be entitled to give notice in writing to the other party as provided in the Labour Relations Act of its desire to bargain with a view to the renewal of the expiring Collective Agreement at any time with a period of ninety (90) days before the expiry date of this agreement. Following such notice to bargain the parties shall meet within fifteen (15) days of notice or within such further period as the parties mutually agree upon.

It is agreed that during the course of bargaining, it shall be open to the parties to agree in writing to

motions for the performance of a variety of tasks.

The term "automated manufacturing" means a device for doing production work which has programmable controllers (PC), computer numerical controls (CNC), or direct numerical controls (DNC).

Article 28
Duration and Termination

28.01 This Agreement shall remain in effect from the ____ day of ____ , 20__ and unless either party gives to the other party written notice of termination or of its desire to modify the Agreement, then it shall continue for such period as the parties agree upon.

Notice that modifications are required or that either party intends to terminate the Agreement may only be given within a period of ninety (90) to seventy (70) days prior to the expiration date of this Agreement.

28.02 Negotiations shall begin within fifteen (15) working days following notification as provided in extend this agreement beyond the expiry date of ___ day of ___, 20__, for any stated period acceptable to the parties and in accordance with the Labour Relations Act.

If negotiations for renewal of this Agreement should extend beyond the expiry date, it is agreed that the negotiated wages of the agreement will be retroactive to the termination date of the previous Agreement, regardless of the date the Agreement is executed.

It is understood that, during any negotiations following upon notice of termination or notice or amendment, either party may bring forward counter proposals arising out of related to the original proposals.

The Union reserves the right to add to, or modify these proposals during negotiations.

Provided that for purposes of all notices under this article, notice in writing shall be deemed to have been received by the party to whom it is sent upon the mailing of such notice by registered mail addressed to the current address of the other party.

the preceding Section 28.01, or within any extension mutually agreed to by the parties.

SIGNED by the parties hereto on the ___ day of _____ , 20__ , at the City of _____ .

Progression Step Rates, effective _____ , 20XX_ .

LABOUR GRADE	START RATE	JOB RATE
1	$13.973	$14.597
2	14.061	14.690
3	14.450	15.099
4	14.527	15.181
5	14.668	15.329
6	14.799	15.467
7	14.799	15.641
8	14.799	15.865
9	14.819	16.196
10	15.129	16.570
11	15.795	17.302
12	16.204	17.748
13	18.164	19.759

PURITY PRODUCTS

Management action, perceived as unreasonable, resulted in a long, nasty strike.

In a legal strike, employees were invited to cross picket line - New employees hired - Picket line violence erupts - Effect on community - Problem for police - High cost to company employees and union - Ultimately a settlement.

Perhaps actions and consequences could have been avoided through better negotiations.

Background

The company is located in a small city about 100 miles (160 km) from a major city. It is a regional commercial and industrial centre of about 90,000 people and is considered by its residents to be a very pleasant place to live.

The two largest employers are unionized and, for bargaining purposes, are considered part of the automotive industry, with wages at a correspondingly high level. The next largest employer is considered part of the textile industry and pays wages exceptionally high for that industry and reasonably close to the national average. The remaining employers are smaller, paying a range of wage levels generally lower than those of the three large employers, and many of their employees are represented by a variety of unions.

The city is generally considered to have a good labour relations climate, and normally, as labour collective agreements expire, they are renegotiated successfully without strikes and with varying amounts of public attention. Over the years, on occasion, strikes have occurred at the larger plants. In most of these cases, the union announced the strike, operations ceased, and the gates were locked by the company. Picket lines were set up and maintained. Those employees not represented by the union crossed the picket line, generally without incident, except for the usual harassment. Strikers were disciplined and well-organized. Although hundreds of strikers were involved, usually law and order was readily maintained with only a single police officer at the gate.

Negotiations Commence

The company, which employed about 200, was wholly owned by an international company and manufactured hospital supplies. Average wages in the company were about $2.00 above the minimum wage, and there was a modest but reasonable benefit package. The work would commonly be considered unskilled to, at most, semi-skilled, and was light, clean, and performed in a clean, well-lighted, well-ventilated plant.

The collective agreement was due to expire May 29. The union asked for a wage increase of $1.00 in the first year and 80¢ in the second year. In due course, the company offered 20¢ over two years and later, after six meetings, the company increased its offer to 40¢ over two years. Then there was an impasse. The union called a membership meeting, and the membership voted to strike if necessary. The company sent a letter to the employees at their home addresses saying the company had "weathered strikes of up to nine months' duration against such worthy opponents as the Teamsters," and that strike replacements would be hired if a strike was called.

The Strike Commences

The union called a strike. The company announced it would continue to operate and invited employees to cross the picket line and report for work. Some employees did go to work — they were met with harassment by a large group of picketers. Law and order was maintained by police. The company obtained only very limited production. Replacement workers were hired in a nearby city and school buses were used to take them across the picket line. The yellow school buses, each protected with wire mesh, infuriated the strikers. They tried to stop the buses, but the buses proceeded through the picket line. The police were involved to maintain law and order and to protect people's rights.

Violence Erupts

Most of the strikers were women; some were earning a second income for their families, some were working to support themselves, and some were supporting both themselves and their children. The sight of the big yellow buses relentlessly forcing their way through the picket line carrying strike breakers to take their jobs caused very emotional reactions. Rocks, bricks, cans, bottles and a torrent of abuse greeted the buses every morning coming in, and every afternoon going out. One woman commented, "The sight of those damn yellow school buses loaded with scabs made me want to push the buses over." She was still angry a year later. Another said, "Some days I felt like crying. It wasn't that the girls were violent — it was what the company did to make them violent."

The Plant Manager reacted too. One day while he was watching, a rock smashed through a bus windshield, the only window not protected by iron mesh. He entered the bus, looked at the young women he had hired, listened to the jeers of the strikers outside, and thought to himself, "if you want to fight, we'll fight."

And so it went on for several months. Windows were smashed. Cars were kicked, dented and rocked. Car aerials were bent and snapped off. The plant's garbage disposal unit was set on fire. Stones and rocks were thrown at police and firefighters; shots were fired from a passing car. Strikers claimed that the police helped the scabs. The company complained that the police helped the strikers. Police complained of being bitten and jabbed with hairpins and more. A supervisor's house was sprayed with paint. Some cars were spray painted, and heavy oil, as thick as tar, was poured on other cars.

Reactions

It was a small city. People were friendly and knew each other. Many people knew personally some of the people involved in the strike and many knew some of the people on the police force. People would drive past the plant and gaze in wonder at the seething mass of literally hundreds of employees, strikers and police.

The police also were union members. The city and citizens depend on the police to maintain law and order in the city. Their ability to do so depends to some degree on the image the police build and maintain and the perception of the police amongst the citizens. In this case, a significant percentage of citizens were union members and their families.

The Strike Continues

The company's original token offer had been 20¢ over two years, and before the strike, had increased the offer to 40¢.

After the long summer, the company thought about 60 people were ready to cross the picket line and return to work. It was believed these people had turned against the union because they could see the company was not backing down. The company had withdrawn its last offer. The summer was over, and the weather was getting chilly. The company sent another letter directly to the workers offering 45¢ over two years. The letter attacked the union leaders and blamed them for the strike.

The union called a meeting and accused the company of trying to bypass the union, of trying to avoid bargaining with the union. The employees voted not to go back to work because the company could then disregard the union. Effectively they would lose their union, their long bitter strike would have failed, and their efforts and sacrifices would have been wasted. The company letter and its offer failed to cause the strikers to go back to work.

The Strike Ends

Shortly thereafter, a meeting was arranged by a mediator between the company and the union. The strike was finally settled in October. The union did win a better contract for its members. They received 50¢ over two years as well as improved sickness and accident benefits, an improved drug plan, improved group insurance, and a new 10 minute break in the afternoon.

And there was the summer without work.

Company Reflections

The strike cost the company $300,000 directly. This is what was spent on guards, legal fees, buses for strike breakers, and repairs. Another $800,000 was lost in sales, some of it permanently, to other companies. The company had been badly in the red when the strike began.

The Plant Manager was 37, aggressive, and he enjoys the challenge of coming to a plant and "turning it around." When he arrived that year in April, the plant had been losing money for 10 months. It lost $200,000 in April, $90,000 in May, and $50,000 in June. If it had not been for the strike, it would have been profitable in August.

The Plant Manager blamed lack of communication for much of the labour management difficulties. The plant had had four general managers within a few years. Workers complained they never knew how the company was doing and, when they were told before the strike the company was losing money, they did not believe it. "If you communicate with people, you don't have any problems," the Plant Manager said. "The company in the past has laid people off and did not say why they were laying them off." He did not blame the employees for the ugliness of the strike; he blamed the union.

The canteen workers are shunned by most workers because they came in during the strike. There was one male worker who came in during the strike who was also greeted with cold stares by the union workers. Some of the office staff who are not unionized do not talk to workers who abused them during the strike.

FOR DISCUSSION OR ASSIGNMENT

1. Should the Company and the Union, through good skilful bargaining, have been able to reach the same settlement without a strike?

2. Compare this strike to the concept of disciplined, well-organized strikes.

3. The Company's letter to the employees stating that it had weathered strikes against worthy opponents, the invitation to cross the picket lines, and the yellow school buses - what was the cause of the violence?

4. If the Company succeeds in getting its production, what happens to the employees' jobs? What happens to the Union? What do the employees and the Union perceive as the issues in the strike?

5. What is the role of the police? How will this duty affect the police in carrying out other duties in the city? Will it affect the attitude of citizens toward the police? Will it affect the ability of the police to perform other functions?

6. After the strike, what attitudes would you expect from strikers and non-strikers towards each other and towards the company? Would such attitudes affect production and profits?

RUSCO INDUSTRIES AND KOZIK MANUFACTURING
Different approaches to labour negotiations

Background

Rusco Industries is an old family-owned company, well known for its ability to engineer and manufacture complex machines and equipment which generally were sold to other manufacturers. Part of the company's competitive advantage was the family's reputation for skill, competence, and other abilities. This reputation was apparent to the employees, who had confidence in the management. In the past, when layoffs had seemed imminent, the owners would disappear for a few days and return with a sales order to avert the crisis. The company is located in a town which was close to a medium-sized manufacturing city. A significant proportion of the plants in the city could be classified as heavy industry.

In the process of growth, the company separated a portion of its business into the Tool and Gauge Division, and located it in a separate building across the street.

General trading conditions and price competition, largely from foreign competitors with lower wage costs, hurt the company's ability to compete. The employees chose to become represented by a major union and the union gained some improvements for the employees. Eventually the company was sold to a conglomerate. After a few years, the new owner sold the business to a second conglomerate which hoped to use the excess capacity to expand its ability to produce earth-moving equipment. However, the market forecast for earth-moving equipment turned out to be overly optimistic. The decision was made to hire new managers to run the business. Part of the problem was that for some years so much time and effort had been spent in buying and selling the business, not enough attention had been given to managing it.

New Management

A decision was made to hire a general manager and a director of personnel. The conglomerate asked Brian Walker to be the Director of Personnel. He had what they considered to be a good and appropriate business education and excellent labour relations experience in highly unionized situations in companies with similar operations. He was agreeable to doing the work required, but was not willing to become an employee of the company.

For the position of General Manager, the conglomerate hired a person named Walter Kozik, who was an excellent engineer, very customer-oriented, and had the type of good general management experience which made him extremely well qualified for the job. He was made Vice President and General Manager.

The two were asked to meet and decide if they wanted to work together. They did meet and learned they were very compatible, with similar and complementary attitudes, objectives and goals. With mutual agreement, Kozik, the Vice President and General Manager, recommended that the company offer a six-month consulting contract to Walker to review, improve and reorganize the personnel function and carry out other responsibilities as agreed. This agreement was accepted and was implemented by the company.

Kozik, the new Vice President and General Manager, started on a program of reducing costs to improve the company's competitive position, with more aggressive marketing to increase sales volume. He also started a search for a new product for the company.

Walker, the Director of Personnel, started his duties by trying to encourage free and open discussion of his assignment with the personnel staff and inviting their participation in obtaining the desired results. He was delighted with their positive response and scheduled individual meetings with each to obtain their recommendations. Nearly all of their recommendations were accepted and each agreed to implement the accepted recommendations. It was obvious that in the past they had been frustrated because their recommendations had not been seriously considered.

Labour Relations Problems

Over a period of time, Walker learned more about the operation and the nature of the work force, and his study of the collective agreement was helped by the necessity of applying it to the various problems that arose. It was apparent that the agreement was poorly written and in places the meaning was not clear. This, combined with the frequent changes in ownership and the resultant changes in management, put management at a disadvantage. When the meaning of the agreement was not clear, the union invariably offered their interpretation based on their knowledge of the intent of the negotiators. They would also point out that there was no current manager who had worked for the company at the time the agreement was negotiated and, as a result, the company should accept the union's argument. When the company disagreed, based on the language of the agreement, the union often responded that they did not have these problems in the past because previous management was reasonable.

It was also apparent that, after all the changes in ownership and management, the union was perceived as the one constant factor, whereas management was considered temporary and transient.

With the lack of growth and some layoff of lower-seniority employees, the average age and the average seniority of the group was higher than might have been expected. People were very concerned with the importance of the application of seniority.

Because of their length of service, nearly all employees were entitled to three weeks' vacation with a significant proportion entitled to four and five weeks' vacation. While the company did not resent providing the vacations that had been agreed upon, there was the problem of getting work done while people were away. In this case, the problem was greater because the agreement gave the employees the right to take their vacations during July and August, and most employees did so.

While the company had a pension plan, providing a pension at age 65, over the years negotiation pressures had tended to put increased labour cost into wage increases rather than into the pension plan. As a result, pension benefits were less attractive than those in some other companies. This agreement did not provide for mandatory retirement at 65. The practice had developed that people at age 65 did not retire but kept on working and also received their pension. These people regarded the pension simply as increased income.

Before the end of the six-month contract, and of course long before union negotiations were due, Walker discussed these negotiation problems and others at length with the Vice President. They agreed some difficult decisions would be required — the problems were complex and should receive full consideration. They needed to decide what was necessary, what objectives were attainable, and what difficulties would be encountered.

As the end of the six-month contract approached, Kozik asked Walker to negotiate the agreement when the time came. Walker said he considered it an interesting challenge that he would be pleased to accept.

The other duties were successfully completed, and with mutual respect, there was an amicable parting.

One Year Later

The next meeting of Kozik and Walker was nearly a year later. Ownership had changed again. A foreign multi-national organization had decided to buy the company, but did not want the tool and gauge division. As part of the arrangement, Kozik signed a one-year contract maintaining his title as Vice President and General Manager. He also obtained ownership, financed with a bank loan, of the Tool and Gauge Division. The now-separate division was renamed Kozik Manufacturing. As part of the arrangement, Kozik had agreed to stay off the premises of the new company during normal working hours, defined as 8 to 5. He advised Walker that, at his insistence, the representatives of the new owners had listened to his views on the union situation. These views were a reflection of their previous conversations. He had tried to impress on the new owners' representatives that the problems were complex and needed careful analysis, and that because of his skills, knowledge, and experience, Walker should be consulted. They contacted head office but were instructed to use a lawyer and not to consider using Walker. Kozik's recommendation was rejected. He said he felt the rejection of his recommendation left him free to request Walker's services for his own company, and this was readily agreed. He contacted Walker and suggested they both give the matter some consideration before discussing it.

One Week Later

Kozik and Walker met again the following week. Walker said that major revisions to the agreement were needed, for Kozik Industries, and that, making financial assumptions which he thought were valid, cost increases should be kept low. However, with the union's history of success, the employees' loyalty to the union and their attitude that ownership and management was transient, the chances of success without a major strike were very poor. Walker recommended that the negotiating strategy should be to fight hard to keep costs under control, but to stop short of provoking a strike. As to the other revisions needed, the underlying issues had not yet caused the end of the world, and probably would not before the end of the next agreement.

Kozik thought the assessment and recommendation sounded good and stated he wanted to hear more about it before telling him about developments in Rusco Industries. The new owners of Rusco had engaged a lawyer. It was agreed that his reputation was good and his views in some ways were similar to Walker's and Kozik's. The lawyer felt that major changes were necessary, and it would take a four-month strike to achieve the desired result. The company agreed, and the lawyer was instructed to proceed.

Walker commented, "Maybe with their money and perspective it makes sense. I can understand the need for a long strike, but I don't understand how he can specify four months. If he's wrong, I wonder what they will do if it goes past four months. However, that's their problem.

"We will be watching them, they will be watching us, and the two unions that used to be one union will be watching each other. Rusco is big and we are small. It would be easy to follow them, but we could easily follow them into a strike that I don't think you want or can afford.

"I don't think it is likely that the union will give in easily, but we want to avoid the situation where Rusco gets changes they want that we don't get, simply because we did not ask for them. It is certainly not accepted practice to raise additional demands partway through negotiations. If the union settled and we made new demands, they might use that as a reason for a strike to show their members and both companies that they won't be pushed around."

"Let's submit our demands at our first meeting and delay the meeting until after Rusco has submitted their demands. Once they are submitted, they are general information. Somehow we can get a copy, and delay finalizing our opening position until we know theirs. In the meantime, let's plan our negotiations as though Rusco did not exist."

Agreement on Targets

After much consideration, it was agreed that the first target for Kozik Manufacturing had to be to avoid a strike and accept only small cost increases. It would be desirable to radically revise the provisions and wording of the agreement. However, the agreement had been around for years and, if necessary, could be left largely unchanged until the next set of negotiations. Similarly, the many smaller problems that had occurred and any anticipated problems could, if necessary, be left for the duration of another agreement.

It was agreed that it was essential to deal with certain problems. The matter of long-service employees' right to take many weeks of vacation during July and August was an important problem. This could make it impossible for the company to obtain, or complete on schedule, important orders. The application of seniority on layoff needed to be improved. Problems of disagreement over skills required to claim other jobs had to be reduced. The arguments, trial periods and disagreement on results and performance during the trial period with the resulting production, quality and cost problems needed to be reduced. The problem of retirement-age employees collecting pensions while continuing to work had to be faced. There was also agreement the company should try to obtain all the improvements obtained in negotiations by the other company, Rusco.

Kozik and Walker decided to have their items prepared with the heading "Selected Items for Negotiations" to give to the union at the proper time and to await further developments.

Kozik Manufacturing's Negotiations Begin

Within the time provided, a letter was received from the union advising of their intention to amend and renew the collective agreement. A little checking established that Rusco had received a similar letter and had agreed to meet with the Union on a certain day. Walker and the union agreed to have their first meeting several days later.

After the first Union meeting with the other company, Rusco, a copy of the Rusco company proposals was obtained and examined. In a many-page document, the company demanded that the union agree to changing almost every clause in the agreement to the advantage of the company.

Still skeptical of the other company's chances but wanting to be in a position to take advantage of any success Rusco might obtain, Walker had the papers copied with Kozik Industries' name at the top of the page and placed in a folder labelled "Company Proposals". The group of items considered essential was listed on a separate page with the company name and the heading, "Selected Items for Negotiations" and placed in a folder marked accordingly.

First Kozik Negotiation Meeting

Walker, the Kozik company spokesman, took both folders to the first negotiation meeting and placed them on the table in front of him.

The representatives of both sides readily agreed they all knew each other from the time when they previously worked for another company. Walker quickly stated, "In the past there was one company, now there are two. In the past there was one union; now there are two. In the past there was one negotiation; now there are two. We negotiate, they negotiate. What happens in one place does not necessarily happen in the other place. The time of settlement is not necessarily the same, the terms of settlement are not necessarily the same, and the decision regarding the matter of a strike is not necessarily the same."

He went on and said, "They are a small operation of a big company, while we are the only operation of a small company. Do they have lots of money? How will they spend it? Who knows? We are a small company trying to survive and grow. Who makes their decisions and what their objectives are, who knows? In this company we make the decisions and, good or bad, we will be rewarded or pay for them."

He hoped that the union realized, "If the other union obtains something, it does not mean this union will obtain it. If the other union chooses to strike, it doesn't mean this union has to strike. If it should happen the other union has a strike and does obtain their objectives (and this is not to be interpreted as a threat), it does not mean the same thing will happen here. You might find after a long strike, this company might have ceased to exist and you would have nobody with whom to settle the strike."

The union representative responded he was pleased to hear the comment was not to be interpreted as a threat. "However, the company has to remember that any settlement has to be ratified by the membership. For years the members on this side of the street received the same treatment as those on the other side of the street. What will make the membership on this side of the street accept something different to those on the other side of the street, and how can the union agree to something on this side of the street and refuse to agree to the same thing on the other side of the street? In any event, we have the union's demands for you." He handed them across the table. It was quickly acknowledged they were the same as the ones presented to the other company.

The company referred to the large file labelled "Company Proposals" but did not give them to the union, and then from the other file read the title, "Selected Items for Negotiations." A copy of the second document was distributed to each person. The company explained them briefly and asked the union to give consideration to them for discussion at a further meeting. At the end of this short discussion, the company opened the large file marked "Company Proposals" and distributed a copy to each person.

In response to a union question, the company readily agreed they were the same as the other company's demands and added the company wanted to be in a position to insist the union make the same concessions to the little company as they did to the big company across the street. The union said they would contact the company to schedule the next meeting.

Rusco Negotiation Meetings

A meeting was held at the large company, Rusco. The union strongly rejected the company demands for major revisions and the company strongly restated its position.

Another meeting was held at the large company. Again the union rejected the company demands and again the company strongly restated its position.

Kozik Negotiation Meetings

The union contacted the small company, Kozik, and scheduled a meeting. The union wanted to hear about the selected items. The company explained at length the nature of its concerns and the reasons for them. There was some discussion of possible solutions. It was logical and rational but there was no agreement. The union proposed adjournment and they agreed to another meeting.

There was another meeting, and more discussion, but nothing was agreed.

Rusco Negotiations

More meetings at the larger company resulted in no progress. The meetings were becoming emotional and bitter.

The union for the large company had a membership meeting. The members authorized the negotiating committee to call a strike if necessary.

There was another meeting with the large company, but no progress was made.

The union called another membership meeting. The membership decided that, unless there was a settlement, to call a strike after two weeks. The company was so advised.

Kozik Negotiations

A meeting was arranged at the smaller company. The union wanted to talk about the selected items and stated they wanted to explore possible settlement. After discussion, it was agreed that in future an employee reaching normal retirement age of 65 would not be eligible for a pension until retirement and by the end of the agreement, those over 65 who had not yet retired, would no longer receive pension income until they did retire.

After more discussion, it was agreed that employees would take no more than two weeks' vacation during July and August unless the company was satisfied that this could be done without inconveniencing production.

After still more discussion, it was agreed that there were four types of machines. In a layoff situation, an employee could use his seniority to take the job of an employee with less seniority on the same type of machine on which he worked. He could similarly use his seniority on other groups of machines where the company was satisfied he had demonstrated his ability to do the work. In cases where he claimed he could do the work on other machines, but there was not sufficient evidence, he could request the opportunity to demonstrate his skills at a time convenient to the company. Such opportunity would not be unreasonably refused.

Regarding wages, recognizing the company's uncertain future and the concern with its ability to compete, a two-year agreement was reached, providing below-average wage increases. All other company and union demands were withdrawn.

The union quickly called a membership meeting and the settlement was approved by the members. An agreement was signed without a strike.

Rusco Negotiations

After allowing time for word to get around that the Kozik employees had settled, the union arranged a meeting at the larger company. The company remained adamant. The union called a strike as scheduled. It dragged on. After four months, nothing happened. After five months, the company asked for a meeting. After discussion, the company dropped all its demands and the union dropped all demands other than wages; they reached a two-year agreement granting above-average wage increases. The membership approved the settlement and the strike ended.

FOR DISCUSSION OR ASSIGNMENT

1. Analyze the different approaches and decisions that were taken by the two companies and the two unions. Were the circumstances the same? How did each of the negotiations affect the other?

2. The proper recommendation would be to radically revise the collective agreement to correct the problems. Because of the strong possibility of a strike, its cost and consequences, the recommendation was to control the cost increase, avoid a strike and strive for as much improvement as possible. Analyze the recommendation.

3. The Union was perceived as the unchanging stability and management as temporary and transient. Discuss.

4. The Collective Agreement was poorly worded and the meaning was not clear. Through the changes in ownership and management, the Union remained constant. Invariably the Union offered their interpretation, which would support their position, based on stated knowledge of the intent of the negotiators. Comment on these statements.

5. How will the negotiations described in each case affect future negotiations?

Employee Involvement and Participation

The following two cases (Central Manufacturing Company and Western Manufacturing) are illustrations of problem-solving through employee participation. Each case involves a situation of common interest to both employee and employer

Employees were given full information and were permitted and encouraged to contribute and did in fact contribute to solutions which benefited both employee and employer. As well as communicating full information, the employer listened and reacted positively to the employees' suggestions and other contributions. In one case, employees recognized that if the firm did not get a particular purchase order, there could be job losses as well as lost profits for the company. In the second case, the employees recognized that poor safety practices did result in injury to fellow employees. In both cases, employees recognized that common interest and solutions would benefit both employer and employees.

Employee involvement and participation can result in greater employer respect for the employees as a result of recognition of the employees' contributions. As well as obtaining recognition, the employee obtains dignity, satisfaction, self-respect, fulfilment, and self-worth.

Employees expect the union, through negotiations with the employer, to maintain its historical functions of (a) protecting the employees from adverse company actions, (b) obtaining a proper share of company revenues through increases in wages and benefits, and (c) retaining job security for the employees.

The company can also use the employees' faith and trust in the union to facilitate and build co-operation between the employees and the company. This can improve the overall performance of the company and thereby increase the net income of the company. This income can in turn be allocated by the company not only to increase shareholder profits but also to help maintain and improve the financial well-being of its employees.

The first case study illustrates the importance of the attitude of the owner of a successful small business and how this attitude needs to be influenced by the manager and industrial relations consultant to promote a settlement. The second case study illustrates the influence of the decision of the employer to wait for the union to call a strike and then to encourage union members to keep on working and then hire more employees. The union perceives this as a threat to the existence of the union, and employees perceive it as a threat to their jobs. These circumstances result in the described actions by the parties.

In the third case, one employer and one union have existed together through a long relationship. They are divided into two employers and two unions, at the divided location, attempting to renegotiate from identical labour relations agreements. Between the two companies, the ownership is different, the management situation is different, the financial strength is different, the approach to negotiations is different and the results are different.

Together, these case histories illustrate the importance of considering many factors before and during negotiations and how negotiation results can be affected by the attitudes and perceptions of all the people who are involved, as well as the financial strengths of the parties.

CENTRAL MANUFACTURING COMPANY
Unionized employees' reaction to factual communication

Background

The company is owned by a reasonably large conglomerate. Historically, it had been mainly a manufacturer of industrial machines and had good engineering skills, knowledge and capability, and with a good reputation for quality. It had gradually lost a large part of this business, as had its competitors, to foreign competition. It gradually evolved so that much of the work is now custom machining and fitting work which the company obtains from other companies through a process of competitive bidding.

The Vice President and General Manager is relatively new on the job. Hired from outside, he is an excellent engineer with the type of good management experience which makes him eminently qualified for the job. The Director of Personnel is also relatively new but with a good educational background, and amongst other things has had excellent labour relations experience in highly unionized companies with similar operations.

The Problem

The company is facing a layoff situation. It has quoted on a number of possible jobs on different products with little success. The equipment is sufficient for the work, and the employees have the necessary skills. They can easily meet the required quality standards and they can meet the delivery dates, but the company's costs are too high.

The company has been losing money. Under the current management, losses have been gradually but steadily reduced. The failure to get orders would reverse this trend. In recent years, the company has gradually stopped quoting on one product after another — in effect admitting on product after product that it could no longer compete profitably. Profits are the reason for being in business, and without profits there would not be jobs.

The management had analyzed many possible new products and areas of business with some limited success, but not nearly enough. The analysis was extended into a re-examination of former products. They nearly always reached the same conclusion. They were losing orders to competition mostly because their costs (and therefore their prices) were too high.

Analysis

The Vice President and General Manager commented, "Maybe it is simply that we used to get eight hours work for eight hours pay and we don't any longer. A major part of the work involves watching the machine run to ensure

480

it is performing properly. The operators can even drink their coffee or socialize to some degree while the machine is running. On some products, to take the order is to lose money, but to not take the order means to lose money because it doesn't pay the overhead." He referred to a product they had previously made called a Mine Hoist (an elevating device for raising and lowering material in a mine.)

Production people have been told and told but nothing happens. The cost of the product has to be reduced in order to meet price competition and make a profit. There must be profits or there won't be a company. It's the orders that provide the jobs and the job security. All these old orders for Mine Hoists on which the company lost money are the same. We know it and the records show it. The jobs took too many hours, resulting in the costs being too high."

The Personnel Director commented that the facts seemed clear. "The people doing the work are intelligent and sensible people who know their jobs. Instead of telling them again, let's give them the facts so they can understand them. Let them figure it out, draw their own conclusions, and see what the reaction there will be." It was agreed.

The attached notice was prepared and made available to the employees. All the records were made available.

NOTICE TO ALL EMPLOYEES

It must be apparent to employees in the heavy machining and fitting areas that work for these areas is in short supply. The Company has been trying to get work for these areas but to date without enough success.

Negotiations are presently in progress for an order for a Mine Hoist. The price the customer is prepared to pay for the Mine Hoist is $600,000.00, but this price, based on past experience, will not provide any profit and will perhaps result in a loss.

The labour required to build this Mine Hoist is about 15,000 hours which is equal to a year's work for seven and a half men. Over the last year, for cost reasons the Company has refused to quote on five Mine Hoists. If these orders had been obtained they would have provided work for about 37 men for a whole year. Instead these orders went to European competition.

If the time spent on doing the work was reduced by 10 per cent it would provide $20,000.00 profit on the order. In this case, the Company's profit on the order would go to reduce the overall Company loss.

You are asked to give serious consideration to the following.

	LOST TIME
If an employee starts his machine 5 minutes after the start of his shift	5 minutes
If an employee stops his machine 5 minutes before lunch break	5 minutes
If an employee starts his machine 5 minutes after the end of his lunch break	5 minutes
If an employee stops his machine 5 minutes before the end of his shift	5 minutes
If an employee stops his machine for 15 minutes for coffee in the morning	15 minutes
If an employee stops his machine for 15 minutes for coffee in the afternoon	15 minutes
TOTAL	50 minutes

An eight hour day is 480 minutes. Fifty minutes is about 10 per cent of the working day. If an employee has been doing the above and would now stop, the Company could get back into the Mine Hoist business and, based on last year, provide 37 to 38 jobs that would otherwise not exist.

Each person knows where time is wasted. In the interest of your own job security, cut down your lost time and encourage others to do the same. Have coffee if you wish but drink it while you are working or while your machine is running.

Get your machine started on time and running — and work to the end of your shift.

Do everything possible to cut down time lost during the day.

It is your job — It is your job security — Look after your own interest — Build your own job security.

Employee Response

Shortly thereafter, a small delegation including a union steward asked to see the Vice President and General Manager. After asking questions and examining cost information, they asked the company to accept a Mine Hoist order at the available price and guaranteed production cost requirements would be met. The company did. The cost requirements were met. The company was back in the Mine Hoist business — at a profit. And job security was improved.

FOR DISCUSSION OR ASSIGNMENT

1. Production people have been told and told, but nothing happens. The cost of the product has to be reduced in order to meet price competition.

2. Give them the facts so they can understand them. Let them figure it out.
   Why did nothing happen under 1) above?
   Why was the reaction different under 2) above?

3. What problems and attitudes seem apparent?

4. How do you suggest dealing with these problems and attitudes?

WESTERN MANUFACTURING
Involvement and improved safety performance

Background

The Western Manufacturing company employed about 1300 people, of whom about 900 were unionized, in four separate plants located in four different municipalities, up to 100 miles from head office. Each of the plants was represented by a different union.

The Human Resources Manager, who reported to the Executive Vice-President, had been working for the company only a short time. When hired, it was made clear to John Willis that the company's first concern in the human resources area was labour relations, and he was selected primarily because of his experience and skills in that area. It was anticipated that about half his time would be spent on labour relations and the other half on his other responsibilities.

Previously employed in the human resources department of a much larger company, Willis had acquired some knowledge of most of the other human resources functions, including safety. His previous employer had had a safety program, providing some contact with the safety people. Although he was personally concerned, Willis had had no responsibility in the safety area in his previous job.

Very shortly after Willis joined the company, negotiations commenced with the company's largest and most militant union, creating a difficult and busy period.

Willis had to assess the situation in the industry, in the area, and in the company, make recommendations to top management, struggle to get them approved, and then avoid a strike by negotiating a settlement with the union on terms acceptable to the company.

During the negotiation period, other areas of responsibility did not receive proper attention. He was instructed to leave these other matters until after negotiations. However, once a settlement was reached and he began to review the monthly safety and accident reports, he became concerned with the particularly high accident frequency in Plant #4.

Safety Concerns

After the settlement was made with the Union, the top priority problem in the company became marketing and sales promotion, and this kept top management fully occupied. Not involved in these problems, the Human Resources Manager decided to use his freedom to work on the safety and accident area. Accidents are costly for the company and therefore properly a financial

484

concern. However, there are also other consequences like human pain and anguish, as well as arms, legs, and fingers which need fixing, and even worse injuries which perhaps cannot be fixed at all. He had strong feelings about these aspects as well as the financial concerns, believing that when people go to work to make a living, they should complete their day's work without personal injury.

Analysis

The initial analysis showed that safety performance in three of the plants, while not good enough, was at least reasonable. The accident frequency in each of these three plants was significantly less than the average of the plants owned by other companies considered to be a proper comparison.

The fourth plant was the problem. Ranked in a comparison of thirty-three plants, accident frequency per hour worked was greater than all except two. It was number thirty-one out of thirty-three.

All of the company's plants had similar safety programs, with safety committees consisting of management and union employee representatives, regular meetings and safety inspections and analysis of possible hazardous conditions. The company was receptive to complaints or suggestions from anyone. There was a detailed analysis of every accident with action required, hopefully to ensure the accident wouldn't happen again.

In three plants, the system seemed to be working, but results in the fourth plant were not acceptable.

The Problem Plant

In the fourth plant, the regular safety inspections seemed to show that the plant, work stations, machines, equipment and working procedures were all safe, and there was no criticism or disagreement from the union employee representative.

The files contained the two previous annual reports to the President, which acknowledged the very unsatisfactory performance and admitted an inability to make recommendations to solve the problem. The reports were signed by both the manufacturing and the human resources representatives.

An analysis of the report on each individual accident showed that almost invariably, the cause of the accident was the person involved. There was no apparent pattern to the accidents related to such things as supervisor, area, time, day or shift.

Raising the problem with the Executive Vice President, the Human Resources Manager was told bluntly that the strike had been averted and the Executive Vice President had no more time for human resource problems. Furthermore, the Human Resources Manager was paid not to raise problems for discussion, but to recommend solutions and, after approval, to implement the decisions effectively.

Special Safety Meeting

Wanting to solve the safety problem and not knowing how, the Human Resources Manager called a special safety meeting at Plant #4 and told the safety committee that he was frustrated and discouraged. All the information available had been reviewed and all the plants had the same safety programs. Three plants had good results — never good enough, of course, but much better than average. The results in Plant #4 were terrible. All the information indicated that the accidents were the operators' fault. He was concerned, but they were not his arms and legs. He said he cared, and the company cared. "You represent the Union and the Members. You say you look after their interests — do the employee representatives care about the members' arms and legs? What are you going to do about the safety of the Union members?"

There was a long silence. Finally the senior employee union representative spoke. He said he was almost speechless at the company's statements. "This company has always said the company managed and the employees did what they were told. When the employees spoke, nothing ever happened. It seemed a waste of time talking. Now there is a problem that the company doesn't know how to solve, and it becomes an employee problem" After a long pause, he said the employees would respond to the company at the next meeting.

Union Action

A Union Bulletin was distributed to the membership the next morning. It stated that the company had given the union employees responsibility for the safety program and there would be a special union meeting Friday evening to permit membership involvement in solving the problem. The Bulletin ended with large print "BE THERE — IT'S YOUR ARMS AND LEGS".

At the membership meeting, the union representatives reported on the union meeting with the Human Resources Manager and, while explaining the problem to the employees, reported that the company wanted to prevent accidents and had not been successful. The company and the union representatives agreed that the plant was safe — the machines, the work stations, the methods were safe — and that the cause of the accidents was the employees. They quoted the company, "They're your arms and legs — you solve the problem!" The Union reminded people of the common complaint that the company doesn't listen. Now the company would have to listen. There was a very lively discussion and it was generally agreed — "Watch yourself and watch your buddy!"

Next Safety Meeting

At the meeting with Willis, the union employee representatives stated they had agreed on the following:

1) A draw prize to be donated by the company at the end of each month. The only people eligible for the prize would be those in each department which had no lost-time accidents in the month. They had voted that the prize would be a 9 x 12 carpet of the winner's choice.

2) A safety sign showing accidents by department for the month to be placed in the middle of the walkway inside the plant door.

3) A union representative to be paid by the company for a half hour at the beginning of each shift to talk safety to the employees coming to work.

4) Billboard-type signs at specified locations in the plant, displaying this slogan: "Look after your own arms and legs and win a carpet by looking after your buddy's arms and legs!"

5) The company to post on the bulletin board details of the contest with a copy mailed to each employee's home.

6) At the end of each month, the company to post the name of the prize winner and the departments with the names eligible for the prize, and also the departments with names not eligible for the prize and not included in the draw.

7) The company to send a copy to each employee's home.

Immediately the company representatives agreed to all union requests.

The union representatives expressed both delight and amazement that the company agreed to adopt their recommendations — and so quickly.

Results

All of this was done.

Quickly the plant conversations became "arms and legs" and a little later "carpets", and then, "My wife wants a carpet", and then "My relatives want carpets", and "carpets make wonderful gifts", and "free carpets".

Safety performance improved — first a little, and then more and more. Within a year, on the industry ranking of lost-time accidents, the plant's previous ranking of 31 out of 33 had improved to second best out of 33.

Management Reaction

The Executive Vice President had been away on a number of trips and had been busy on other matters. One day he called the Human Resources Manager to his office. Safety reports were on his desk. He said he was pleased with the results and asked for an explanation, which was provided in detail.

The Executive Vice President spoke slowly. "You did not follow procedures. You did not make recommendations and get approval and we didn't really manage. We let them get involved and they got the results we could not get ourselves. They solved our problem because we let them do it."

After a long pause he said, "At my next meeting with the managers, I want to discuss more application of the concept of <u>involvement</u> — less management and more involvement."

FOR DISCUSSION OR ASSIGNMENT

1. What is your reaction to the Executive Vice President's comment at the end?

2. How would you improve on the company approach to the problem?

3. Would you use this approach on other problems?

4. Would you anticipate adverse reactions? If so, what type of reactions?

5. After an employee involvement program is successfully implemented, how would you get it stopped?

6. A company owner and president said the employee involvement program in his company is so successful, he feels he has lost the ability to manage his own company, but said he doesn't care because the employees are doing a better job than he could. Comment.

PART K: INDUSTRIAL RELATIONS GLOSSARY

Accreditation: the process whereby an employers' organization is certified as the bargaining agent for a unit of employers.

Affiliation: link between two or more labour organizations, whereby each retains a high degree of autonomy, subject to the limits imposed by their affiliation agreement (e.g. between a labour union and the CLC).

American Federation of Labour: the AFL is a U.S. central labour organization, having, as affiliated members, craft or horizontal type labour unions.

Arbitration: use of an outside third party, called an arbitrator, to investigate a dispute between the employer and the union and impose a settlement. Sometimes, a three-person arbitration board, rather than a single arbitrator, is used.

Bargaining agent: the union that is recognized as the exclusive representative, for collective bargaining purposes, of a group of workers. In the case of a group of employers, it is the employers' association.

Bargaining unit: the group of employees in a firm, plant, or industry that has been recognized by the employer and certified by a labour relations board as appropriate for collective bargaining purposes.

Blue-collar workers: term used to describe plant workers (production and maintenance) as compared with office workers (white-collar).

Boycott: organized refusal of union employees, families, friends, and others to buy the products of a company whose employees are on strike, in an effort to reduce sales and exert economic pressure on the employer.

Bumping: displacement of employees from their jobs by more senior employees when a firm needs to lay off or dismiss workers.

Business agent: full-time paid employee of a union local whose duties involve handling grievances, helping to enforce the collective agreement, assist with organizing, etc.

Canada Labour Code: federal labour statute that applies to employers and employees in industries falling under federal jurisdiction.

Canada Labour Relations Board: group of persons, consisting of a chairperson, at least one vice chairperson, and not less than four and not more than eight members, appointed under the industrial relations section of the Canada Labour Code. The Board's powers and duties include the determination of appropriate bargaining units, the certification or decertification of trade unions, decisions as to unfair labour policies, failure to bargain in good faith, etc.

Canadian Labour Congress: the CLC is the central labour organization in Canada with the largest number of affiliated union members. It was formed in 1956 from the merger of the Trades and Labour Congress and the Canadian Congress of Labour.

Certification: procedure whereby a labour union obtains a certificate from the Labour Relations Board declaring that the union is the exclusive bargaining agent for a defined group of employees in a bargaining unit that the Board considers appropriate for collective bargaining. This follows proof of majority support for the union among eligible employees in the bargaining unit.

Checkoff: clause in a collective agreement that directs the employer to deduct union dues and remit these funds to the union concerned.

Closed shop: union security clause that requires all persons to be union members in good standing before they may be hired. Usual only in the construction and longshoring industry.

COLA clause: a cost-of-living allowance, included as part of a collective agreement, that provides for the agreed wage to be adjusted upwards to offset increases in the cost of living during the life of the agreement.

Collective agreement: a written agreement between an employer and the union representing its employees, valid for a period of from one to three years, covering rates of pay, hours of work, conditions of employment, etc.

Collective bargaining: term used to describe the negotiations that take place between a labour union, collectively representing the employees of a plant or industry, and the employer or employers' association, in drawing up a mutually acceptable labour-management agreement.

Competition Act: a federal statute that makes illegal various activities, such as price-fixing and bid-rigging, that reduce the amount of competition among business firms in Canada, to the detriment of the public, and establishes an agency to conduct investigations and lay criminal charges.

Conciliation: use of an outside third party, called a conciliator, to assist a company and the union representing its employees to come to a mutually satisfactory collective agreement. Unlike arbitration, no settlement can be imposed. The labour dispute is hopefully resolved by compromise or voluntary agreement. Conciliation is required under the Labour Relations Act before a legal strike or lockout may be declared.

Confederation of National Trade Unions: The CNTU is the second largest central labour organization in Canada, with its base in Quebec. Its name, in French, is the Confederation des Syndicats Nationaux, or CSN.

Congress of Industrial Organizations: the CIO is a U.S. central labour organization established in 1937 by a number of industrial-type unions that had broken away from the AFL in 1932 to set up a Committee for Industrial Organization, the CIO's predecessor.

Contracting out: the use by an employer of outside persons, on a contract basis, to do work formerly performed by the employer's own work force.

Cooling-off period: time period required by a Labour Relations Act, following unsuccessful conciliation attempts, before a strike or lockout may be declared.

Cost of living: the amount of money required to pay for food, shelter, transportation and other basic necessities. Usually, attention is paid to changes in the cost of living, as indicated by Statistics Canada's Consumer Price Index (CPI).

Craft: manual occupation, such as plumbing, carpentry, and electrical that requires a high level of skill and prior training, often in the form of an "apprenticeship".

Craft union: a labour organization representing workers practising the same craft or "trade". However, many craft unions now include workers practising skills not closely related to the originally designated craft.

Decertification: process whereby a union is legally deprived of its official bargaining rights for a group of employees.

Directly chartered local union: local labour unions which have been organized by, and received their charter, directly from the Canadian Labour Congress.

Discipline: a system of punishment (including verbal and written warnings, suspension, and discharge) for breaches of company rules and regulations by employees.

Dues shop: also called "agency shop", this type of union security clause gives an employee the option of being a union member or not but requires all eligible employees to pay union dues.

Employee association: association of workers in a particular plant or industry that has not been certified under the Labour Relations Act as the official bargaining agent for these employees. The association may nevertheless be recognized by the employer as the spokesperson for its employees.

Employers' association: an organization representing employers in a particular industry that engages in one or more activities: bargaining with labour unions, co-ordinating the collective bargaining activities of its members, education, and lobbying.

Employee involvement: a work climate in which employees, at all levels, can achieve individual goals and work satisfaction by directing their energies and talents toward clearly defined company goals.

Employment insurance (EI): federal program that provides cash benefits for a given period of time to unemployed persons. To be eligible, a person must have contributed to the fund for a specified number of weeks. Also, there is a waiting period before the cash benefits are available immediately.

Equal pay: principle that wage rates should be based upon the job, rather than upon the sex, nationality, race, colour, etc. of the employee that performs it. Also, that workers should receive the same rate of pay for work of equal value.

Fair representation: duty of a union or an employers' association to represent fairly the interests of each member of its organization in its dealings with the other party.

Featherbedding: employee practice of restricting output to create the need for more workers than are really required.

Fair employment practice: practice of employers (and unions) of offering workers equal employment (and membership) opportunities regardless of their sex, nationality, race, colour, etc.

Federal jurisdiction: authority of federal government over employers and employees in any enterprise of a national, interprovincial, or international nature such as banking, broadcasting, and air transportation.

Federation of Labour: group of labour unions in one or more industries, within a district, province, or country, allied together. The CLC is an example of a national federation.

Final offer selection: form of arbitration whereby, after a period of unsuccessful union-company negotiations, each side puts forward its final offer and the arbitrator or arbitration board chooses one or other of them, without modification.

Foreperson: supervisory employee, usually considered to be part of management. Also called "supervisor".

Fringe benefits: items such as paid vacations, pensions, health care, and bonuses that are paid to an employee above and beyond the regular rate of pay.

General strike: cessation of work by all workers in a particular geographical area, perhaps as a form of political, as well as economic protest.

General union: a labour organization whose membership is not confined to workers in one type of skilled occupation or to one type of industry.

Grievance: an alleged violation of a collective agreement, or, of traditional work practices, filed usually by an employee, but sometimes by the union or by the company.

Grievance procedure: the steps by which a dispute between an employer and an employee or between an employer and the union during the life of a collective agreement may be amicably settled.

Grievance rate: number of grievances filed in relation to the number of union members in a company.

Grievor: the person (employee, company, or union) filing a grievance.

Hiring hall: hall or office, run by a union or jointly by union and employer, used to direct workers to jobs or to hire them on the spot, subject to prior union membership.

Illegal strike: a strike by the employees in a bargaining unit that contravenes the terms of the Labour Relations Act — for example, a strike called by the union before fulfilment of the conciliation procedure or when certification proceedings are still under way, or even during the life of a collective agreement, because of a dispute over interpretation of the collective agreement in force.

Independent local organization: local labour unions not formally connected or affiliated with any other labour organization.

Industrial democracy: term that refers to the degree in which the rank and file employees, or their elected representatives, are allowed to participate in management decision-making.

Industrial harmony: situation in which management and employees co-operate willingly in the pursuit of a company's commercial objectives and in which a high level of employee satisfaction exists.

Industrial union: a labour organization whose members usually, but not always, include most of the workers eligible for union membership in a particular company or industry, irrespective of the type of work performed.

Industrial relations: a broad term that refers usually to relations between the employer and the union representing its employees.

Injunction: court order forbidding the named persons from carrying on a particular activity.

Interests dispute: a dispute that may arise between a company and a union as to the terms of a new collective agreement that is being negotiated or with regard to the revision of an agreement that has just expired.

International Confederation of Free Trade Unions (ICFTU): an international trade union body, established in 1949, consisting of many national labour organizations such as the Canadian Labour Congress, together representing most union members in the non-communist countries.

International Labour Office: the secretariat of the International Labour Organization, responsible for administering and co-ordinating ILO activities.

International Labour Organization (ILO): an international body representing labour, management, and government which, since 1946, has been a specialized agency of the United Nations. It sets minimum international labour standards called ``conventions'' and invites member countries to ratify them. It also disseminates labour information to workers of all countries.

International union: a labour union with branches and members, in both the United States and Canada, but which has its head office in the U.S.

Job description: a written description of a particular job, including the tasks involved, responsibility, its relation to other jobs, qualifications required, etc.

Job enrichment: attempt to make jobs more interesting and less monotonous for the individual worker by means of job enlargement, etc.

Job security: extent to which a worker has steady employment because of the nature of the good or service produced, special skills, knowledge, employer's attitude, etc.

Jurisdictional dispute: conflict between two or more labour unions as to whose members have the right to perform certain types of work.

Jurisdictional strike: strike by members of a union to protest the performance of work in the same plant by members of another union.

Labour Canada: federal government department with responsibility for administering the Canada Labour Code and providing information on labour-related issues. The goals of the department are (a) to promote stable industrial relations in Canada, (b) to establish appropriate labour standards, and (c) to ensure occupational health and safety in industries within the federal jurisdiction. Also the department tries to promote labour-management co-operation throughout Canada, and to co-ordinate Canada's efforts to help improve labour conditions throughout the world.

Labour College of Canada: bilingual institution of higher education for trade union members, operated jointly by the Canadian Labour Congress, McGill University, and the Université de Montréal. Its purpose is to provide a training ground for Canada's future trade union leaders.

Labour Council: organization established by a labour federation in a particular town or city, by charter of the CLC, to which the locals of many labour unions in that area are affiliated. It is financed by a per capita tax on affiliated unions.

Labour Federation: organization established in each province, by charter of the CLC, to represent organized labour at the provincial level. Each member union retains its own autonomy yet co-operates to achieve common goals.

Labour force: all persons 15 years of age and over who are either employed, temporarily idle, or unemployed but seeking employment.

Labour law: that area of the law that deals with all matters involving employer-employee relationships and company-union relationships, including collective agreements, employment practices, wrongful dismissal, etc.

Labour organization: a broad term that includes not only various types of labour unions and other employee associations, but also various regional and central labour bodies such as the CLC.

Labour Relations Board: group of persons, provided for under the Labour Relations Act, with responsibility for determining bargaining units, certifying trade unions, ensuring that dispute-settling provisions are included in collective agreements, and investigating allegations of bad faith in collective bargaining.

Labour turnover: rate at which workers change employment — usually calculated by taking the number of employees leaving a plant or industry during a given period of time and dividing this figure by the average number of employees in the plant or industry during the same period, and expressing it as a percentage.

Labour union: an association of workers, practising a similar trade or employed in the same company or industry. Also called a trade union.

Lay-off: temporary, prolonged, or final withdrawal by employer of employee's job because of lack of work.

Local: basic unit of a labour union, formed in a particular plant or locality.

Lockout: temporary refusal of a company to continue providing work for its employees which may also involve the temporary closing of the employer's establishment. Its purpose is to put pressure on union members to agree to the employer's offer with regard to wages, working conditions, etc.

Maintenance of membership: union security clause that requires existing union members to maintain their union membership but gives new employees the option of joining the union or not.

Management rights: these are rights traditionally reserved to management that are not subject to collective bargaining — for example, production planning.

Mediation: use of an outside third party to assist a company and the union to reach an agreement by peaceful persuasion. Unlike conciliation (a similar process but one that is required by law before a strike or lockout may be declared), mediation is a voluntary process. Unlike arbitration, no settlement can be imposed.

National union: labour union whose head office, locals, and membership are all within Canada.

Off-shift premium: extra pay for working at unusual times during the day and on weekends.

Organized labour: all labour unions and other employee organizations whose purpose is the protection of worker interests.

Organizer: person employed on a full-time, permanent basis by many large labour unions to plan, organize, and carry out membership recruitment campaigns at plants that are not yet unionized.

Organizing: term used to describe the process of recruiting new union members.

Organizing committee: group of persons consisting of union representatives, including the organizer, if any, and volunteers willing to devote the time and effort necessary to contact employees, present the union's case for unionization, and sign up new union members.

Pattern bargaining: collective bargaining tactic whereby a union first obtains a generous settlement from one employer and then uses it as a bargaining chip to secure a similar settlement from other employers in the industry.

Picket line: groups of striking workers, usually carrying signs, stationed at the entrance and exits of a struck plant.

Picketing: stationing of union members at entrances and exits of a struck plant to publicize union demands, discourage replacement workers from moving in and out, and to hamper the delivery of materials and parts into the plant and the shipment of finished goods from it.

Profit-sharing: arrangement whereby employees receive a set percentage of the employer's net profit, in addition to their regular wages. This may be in cash, in company shares, or as a deferred payment.

Quality circle: a group of production workers who volunteer to meet on a regular basis, usually with management encouragement and assistance, to discuss and suggest improvements in production methods, quality control, job enrichment, etc.

Raiding: a union's attempt to increase its membership by persuading members of another union to leave that union and join it.

Rand Formula: compromise arrangement, suggested by Ivan C. Rand former Chief Justice of the Supreme Court of Canada, that employees be given the choice of joining a union or not but be required, whatever the choice, to pay the normal union dues.

Rank and file: name given to union members with no special status (i.e. not union officers or shop stewards).

Ratification: process of having a proposed new collective agreement approved by the union members, as well as by the employer or employers' association.

Recognition: employer's acceptance of a labour union as the exclusive bargaining agent for its employees.

Representation vote: a vote conducted by the Labour Relations Board in which the employees in a bargaining unit indicate, by secret ballot, whether or not they wish to be represented, or continue to be represented, by a labour union.

Residual rights: all rights belonging to management not specifically mentioned in a collective agreement.

Retroactive payment: in the case of a grievance, payment to an employee who has won a claim about rates of pay for time worked in the past, to compensate for past underpayment.

Rights dispute: a labour disagreement between a union and a company with regard to the interpretation or application of one or more clauses of the collective agreement currently in force.

Right-to-work: right of an employee to work in a company without being forced to join a union.

Scab: derogatory term used by union members to refer to workers currently employed who disregard a strike call and to persons hired as replacements for striking workers.

Scanlon Plan: a plan developed by Joseph Scanlon, one-time research director of the United Steelworkers, to encourage greater worker productivity by sharing the savings achieved, between the company and the employees involved.

Secondary boycott: refusal to buy or handle goods of employers not directly involved in a labour dispute, but who are supplying parts, materials, etc. to the firm subject to a primary boycott.

Seniority: an employee's standing in a company, based on length of service. Usually employees with the least seniority are the first to be laid off or dismissed because of lack of work. Those with the greatest amount of seniority usually have greater job security, vacation entitlement, promotion opportunities, etc. Sometimes, depending on the employer, merit may be given equal or greater emphasis.

Severance pay: lump-sum payment made to an employee for whom the company no longer has a job.

Shift: scheduled daily work period for a group of employees (e.g. 9 a.m. to 4 p.m., 4 p.m. to midnight, and midnight to 8 a.m.).

Shift differential: extra pay for working on late shifts (i.e. other than the day shift).

Shop committee: group of workers elected by fellow-employees to act as their representative in grievance and other labour matters.

Shop steward: union member elected by workers in a particular shop or department of a firm to act as their union representative in that area. The shop steward's functions may include receiving, investigating, and attempting to resolve complaints and grievances, disseminating union information, announcing meetings, recruiting new members, and collecting union dues (if not deducted at source by the employer and remitted to the union).

Sit-down strike: a form of industrial action whereby employees stop work and sit down in the plant, thereby bringing production to a halt.

Slowdown: a form of industrial action whereby employees exert pressure on an employer by slowing down the rate of work and therefore productivity.

Speed-up: union term that refers to the employer practice of speeding up production without an offsetting increase in worker pay.

Split-shift: requiring an employee to spread his or her working hours over two different shifts in order to meet peak production needs.

Stretch-out: union term that refers to the employer practice of requiring a worker to assume extra duties, without extra pay.

Strike: temporary refusal of the employees to continue working for the employer, so as to exert pressure in contract negotiations or as a protest against unreasonable working conditions, etc.

Strikebreakers: term variously used to refer to: (a) persons who continue to work during a strike even though their fellow union members are refusing to work, (b) persons hired as replacement workers, and (c) persons hired by an employer to assist in breaking a strike.

Strike benefits: a small regular payment made by the union from its strike fund to striking workers, perhaps conditional on picket duty performance. In some cases, food rather than money is distributed.

Strike fund: funds held by the union to help cover such expenditures during a strike as strike pay, publicity, legal fees, etc. The money for such a fund may be collected from union members while still employed, as a regular monthly assessment, additional to the union dues. The fund may also be augmented during a strike, by donations from other unions.

Strike notice: formal written notice by a group of workers, or their union, to the employer that the employees will cease work on a certain date.

Strike vote: a vote conducted among the workers in a bargaining unit to determine whether the union should call a strike.

Sweat-shop: plant in which the conditions of employment, including pay, health, and safety, are sub-standard.

Sweetheart contract: derogatory term used to describe a contract made between an employer and a union, that grants generous terms and conditions of employment, designed to keep out another labour union.

Sympathy strike: a strike by employees in one plant to express sympathy or "solidarity" with striking workers in another plant.

Technological unemployment: unemployment resulting from the introduction in a plant of more labour-saving equipment.

Trade union: an association of workers, practising a similar trade or employed in the same company or industry. Also called a labour union.

Unemployed: persons without work, but who are available and seeking work.

Unfair labour practice: action by employer or union that contravenes the principle of "bargaining in good faith" — for example, dismissing an employee, perhaps on some false pretext, for attempting to form or join a union.

Union dues: regular monthly payments by union members to help finance the activities of their union.

Union organizer: person hired by the union on a full-time basis to plan and execute a union membership recruitment campaign. Term sometimes also used to refer to volunteer recruiters.

Union security: clause inserted in a collective agreement to protect the interest of the labour union, covering the collection of union dues and requirement of union membership for continued employment. There are several different types of union security clause: union shop, closed shop, dues (or agency) shop, maintenance of membership, and voluntary checkoff.

Union shop: union security clause, used in many collective agreements, that makes union membership and the compulsory collection of union dues a condition of employment.

Union trusteeship: situation in which a union head office suspends the operations of a union local and takes over its administration and assets. Such an action is provided for in the constitution of many national and international unions to counter mismanagement, corruption, etc. at the local level.

Unjust dismissal: dismissal of an employee in a manner that is arbitrary and unfair, and that contravenes the Labour Relations Act or the collective agreement.

Unlawful lockout: lockout of its employees by an employer that contravenes the Labour Relations Act and lays the employer open to charges and possible fines and/or periods of imprisonment.

Unlawful strike: strike by union members that contravenes the Labour Relations Act and lays the union and its members open to charges and possible fines and/or periods of imprisonment.

Voluntary checkoff: a union security clause whereby an employee is not required to join the union but can request that the employer collect union dues from his or her pay and remit them to the union.

Voluntary recognition: an employer agrees in writing to recognize a labour union as the exclusive bargaining agent for a group of its employees, without resorting to the formal certification procedure.

Wage and price controls: controls imposed by the government, through a specially-established review or control body, on increases in wages and prices, as part of an anti-inflation program.

Wage differentials: difference in wage rates between one job and another because of the nature of these jobs, location, skills involved, educational requirements, stress, responsibilities, etc.

Wage parity: the principle of equality of wages for workers in the same occupation but in different geographical areas. Also, for workers in the same sector, but in different occupations.

Walkout: situation when employees spontaneously, but in a co-ordinated fashion, put down their tools, usually at the beginning of a strike, and walk out of the plant.

Wildcat strike: a spontaneous, usually short-lived work stoppage by union members that is not authorized by the union concerned.

Work sharing: plan that involves the sharing of available work among all the employees on a reduced hourly basis, when planned output declines, rather than laying off some employees. Since 1982, under the federal government's Work Sharing Program, employees on reduced time have their pay supplemented by unemployment insurance benefits. Under the same program (which is administered by Human Resources Development Canada (HRDC)), appropriate vocational training is provided to workers affected by the work sharing program, to improve their chances of alternative employment.

Work to rule: a form of industrial action whereby the employees slow down production by observing all the rules and regulations relating to the job that are normally ignored.

Work stoppage: general term used, particularly in statistical documents, to refer to strikes and lockouts, without assigning responsibility for the breakdown in labour-management relations.

Worker participation: involvement of employees, either directly or indirectly (through elected representatives), in management decision-making. This can vary, in effect, from mere communication of information from management to the workers, to consultation before making decisions, or even to co-determination where workers share jointly in management decision-making.

Workers' Compensation: provincial system of compensation, funded by employers but administered by a provincially-appointed Board, for injuries sustained by workers during the course of their employment.

Working conditions: factors involved in an employee's job environment, including hours of work, rate of pay, safety, health, paid holidays and vacation, rest periods, shift work and promotion possibilities.

Works Council: a plant level committee of workers, or workers and management, that reviews and makes recommendations to management on employee rights and employee welfare in the organization. A form of industrial democracy found in Britain and other West European countries.

PART L: SUMMARY OF ONTARIO'S LABOUR RELATIONS ACT, 1995

1. **Definition** of various terms used in the Act (e.g. bargaining unit, collective agreement).

2. **Purposes** of the Act (e.g. to promote the expeditious resolution of workplace disputes).

PURPOSES AND APPLICATION OF ACT

3. **Non-application** — i.e. persons to whom the Act does not apply (e.g. a domestic employed in a private home).

4. Certain **Crown agencies** are bound by the Act.

FREEDOMS

5. **Freedom** of an **employee** to join a trade union, etc.

6. **Freedom** of an **employer** to join an employers' organization, etc.

ESTABLISHMENT OF BARGAINING RIGHTS BY CERTIFICATION

7. **Application for certification** — how a trade union applies for certification as a bargaining agent.

8. **Voting constituency for representation vote** — Labour Relations Board determines who is included in bargaining unit and, if 40% or more appear to be members of the union, provides for a secret representation vote.

9. **Board to determine appropriateness of bargaining units,** including craft units, etc.

10. **Certification after representation vote** if more than 50% of the ballots cast are in favour of the union; no certification if 50% or less; one-year bar before reapplying.

11. **New representation vote where Act contravened** by employer, etc. and vote does not represent the wishes of employees, etc.

12. **Certification of Councils of trade unions**

13. **Right of access** — the Board may order an employer to permit the representative of a trade union to have access to property on which employees reside for the purpose of attempting to persuade the employees to join a trade union.

14. **Security guards** — special provisions apply to guards who monitor other employees or who protect the property of an employer. Mixed bargaining units permitted, unless employer objects.

15. **Union not to be certified** — if an employer or employers' organization has participated in its formation or administration or contributed financial or other support to it or if it discriminates against any person because of any ground of discrimination prohibited by the Human Rights Code or the Canadian Charter of Rights and Freedoms.

NEGOTIATION OF COLLECTIVE AGREEMENTS

16. **Notice of desire to bargain** — written notice to employer by trade union, following certification, or voluntary recognition, of desire to bargain with a view to making a collective agreement.

17. **Obligation of parties to bargain in good faith,** 15 days from the giving of the notice, or later by agreement.

18. **Appointment of conciliation officer** by Minister, upon request by either party, to confer with the parties and endeavour to effect a collective agreement.

19. **Appointment of mediator:** the Minister may, upon written request of the parties, appoint a mediator selected by them jointly instead of appointing a conciliation board, or to replace a conciliation officer.

20. **Duties of a conciliation officer:** to confer with the parties and endeavour to effect a collective agreement, reporting the result to the Minister within 14 days of the appointment, or longer by agreement.

21. **Conciliation board:** this may be set up (with a member from each party who then jointly recommend a third person as chair) if the conciliation officer is unable to effect a collective agreement within the time allowed.

22. **Persons prohibited** from acting as members of a conciliation board: those with any pecuniary interest in the matters coming before it or those who, within the previous six months had acted as solicitor, counsel, or agent of either party.

23. **Notice to parties** by the Minister of appointments to a conciliation board.

24. **Replacement of vacancies** in a conciliation board: appointment of new members by the Minister after consultation with the party whose views are represented by that person.

25. **Terms of reference** of a conciliation board: delivery by the Minister to the chair of the board of a statement of the matters referred to it.

26. **Oath of office** by members of a conciliation board before entering upon their duties.

27. **Duties of conciliation board:** to endeavour to effect agreement between the parties on the matters referred to it.

28. **Procedure:** a conciliation board shall determine its own procedure. **Evidence:** the board shall give full opportunity to the parties to present their evidence and make their submissions.

29. **Sittings of conciliation board:** the chair, in consultation with the other members, is to fix the time and place of the sittings.

30. **The Minister of Labour to be informed** of first sitting: the chair is to notify the Minister in writing once the first sitting has been held.

31. **Quorum of conciliation board:** the chair and one other member, or the other two members with the chair's written consent; reasonable notice to be given to the absent member.

32. **Casting vote** by chair, if disagreement.

33. **Powers of conciliation board:** to summon and enforce the attendance of witnesses, etc.; to administer oaths, etc.; to enter premises; to authorize others to enter premises, etc.

34. **When report to be made** to Minister: findings and recommendations within 30 days after the first sitting; however, the period may be extended.

35. **Duty of mediator:** if appointed, he or she will confer with the parties and endeavour to effect a collective agreement; has all the powers of a conciliation board.

36. **Failure** of conciliation officer **to report** within the time provided does not invalidate the proceedings of the conciliation officer.

37. **Industrial inquiry commission:** the Minister may establish such a commission to inquire into and report to the Minister on any industrial matter or dispute that the Minister considers advisable.

38. **Appointment of special officer:** such a person may be appointed by the Minister at any time during the operation of a collective agreement if the Minister considers that it will promote more harmonious industrial relations between the parties. Such a person will confer with the parties and assist them in an examination and discussion of their current relationship or the resolution of anticipated bargaining problems. The officer must report to the Minister within 30 days of his or her appointment.

39. **Disputes advisory committee:** appointment by Minister, composed of one or more representatives of employers and one or more representatives of employees, at any time during the course of bargaining, either before or after the commencement of a strike or lockout, where it appears to the Minister that the normal conciliation and mediation procedures have been exhausted, to confer with, advise and assist the bargaining parties.

40. **Voluntary arbitration:** by irrevocable agreement in writing by the parties, at any time following the giving of notice of desire to bargain, to settle all matters remaining in dispute by an arbitrator or board of arbitration.

41. **Employee ratification vote** may be ordered by the Minister at any time after the commencement of a strike or lockout, if considered in the public interest, to accept or reject the last offer of the employer.

42. **Vote on employer's offer**: an employer has the right to request, before or after commencement of a strike or lockout, that a vote of the employees be taken to accept or reject the employer's last offer to the trade union.

43. **First agreement arbitration:** where the parties are unable to effect a first collective agreement and the Minister does not intend to appoint a conciliation board or such a board's report has been released, either party may apply to the Labour Relations Board to direct the settlement of a first collective agreement by arbitration.The Board will approve such a request if the process of collective bargaining has been unsuccessful because of various specified circumstances (e.g. the refusal of the employer to recognize the bargaining authority of the trade union). Private arbitration, by agreement of both parties, may be permitted instead of a Board-appointed arbitration board.

44. **Mandatory ratification vote** by employees in the bargaining unit is required for a collective agreement to come into effect, unless the agreement is one that is imposed by order of the Board or settled by arbitration.

CONTENTS OF COLLECTIVE AGREEMENTS

45. (1) **Recognition** of the trade union as the exclusive bargaining agent of the employees in the bargaining unit.
    (2) **Recognition** of accredited employer's organization, where appropriate.

46. Provision against **strikes** and **lockouts** during term of the agreement.

47. (1) Deduction and remittance to trade union of **union dues.**
    (2) **Definition** of union dues.

48. (1) Provision for final and binding settlement by **arbitration,** without stoppage of work, of all differences between the parties relating to the agreement.
    (2) **Deemed arbitration provision** if no provision contained in the agreement.
    (3) Where arbitration provision **inadequate,** Board may modify.
    (4) **Appointment** of arbitrator **by Minister** where parties fail to do so.
    (5) Appointment of **settlement officer.**
    (6) **Payment** of arbitrators.
    (7) Arbitrator's **decision** required within 30 days.
    (8) **Arbitration board** to give **decision** within 60 days.
    (9) Possible **time extension** for decision.
    (10) Provision for **oral decision.**
    (11) Minister's power to **make orders** re delays, etc.
    (12) **Powers** of arbitrators, chair of arbitration boards, and arbitration boards.
    (13) **Restriction** re **interim orders.**
    (14) Power re **mediation.**
    (15) **Enforcement power** of arbitrator or chair of arbitration board.
    (16) **Extension of time** re steps in grievance procedure.
    (17) **Substitution of penalty** by arbitrator, etc. in discipline cases.
    (18) **Legally binding nature** of decision of arbitrator or arbitration board upon the parties, etc.
    (19) **Enforcement** of arbitration decisions, in same way as a judgment or order of the Ontario Court (General Division).
    (20) The **Arbitration Act, 1991,** not applicable to arbitrations under collective agreements.

49. (1) Provision for **referral of grievances** to a **single arbitrator** for settlement despite the arbitration provision in a collective agreement or deemed to be included.
    (2) and (3) Request for **references.**
    (4) and (5) **Minister to appoint** arbitrator.
    (6) Provision for appointment of a **settlement officer** to act prior to arbitrator's hearing.
    (7) **Powers** and **duties** of **arbitrator.**
    (8) **Oral decisions.**
    (9) **Payment** of arbitrator.
    (10) **Approval** of arbitrators, etc.

50. (1) Provision for a single **mediator-arbitrator** to resolve grievances.
    (2) **Prerequisite** — agreement by parties upon nature of any issues in dispute.
    (3) **Appointment** of mediator-arbitrator by Minister.

(4) **Proceedings** to begin within 30 days of appointment.

(5) **Joint request** for starting date.

(6) The mediator-arbitrator to endeavour to assist the parties to settle the grievance by **mediation.**

(7) If mediation fails, grievance to be settled by **arbitration.**

(8) Limitation of **evidence,** etc.

(9) **Decision** within 5 days of completion of proceedings.

(10) **Application** of decision.

51. (1) **Permissive provisions:**

    (a) for requiring membership in the trade union and payment of union dues as a condition of employment.

    (b) for permitting an employee, representing the union, to attend to trade union business, during working hours.

    (c) for permitting the trade union use of the employer's premises without payment therefor.

(2) Where **non-member** of the **trade union** cannot be required to be discharged from employment.

(3) **Unlawful activity** by employee against the trade union.

(4) **Compulsory union membership** only allowed in first agreement if 55% or more employees were members when the agreement was entered into. Exceptions.

(5) Continuation of permissive provisions during bargaining for renewal of the collective agreement.

(6) Continuation of permissive provisions if business sold.

52. Employee who objects, on **religious grounds,** to joining the trade union or paying union dues may donate the amount to an agreed charity.

OPERATION OF COLLECTIVE AGREEMENTS

53. **Agreement invalid if employers participated** in its formation or administration or contributed financial support to the trade union.

54. A collective agreement must not discriminate against any person if the **discrimination** is contrary to the **Human Rights Code** or the **Canadian Charter of Rights and Freedoms.**

55. **Only one collective agreement** permitted between a trade union and an employer.

56. **Binding effect** of collective agreements on employers, trade unions and employees.

57. **Binding effect** of collective agreements on members of employers' organizations. Duty to disclose.

58. (1) **Minimum one year term** for collective agreements.
    (2) Parties may **extend term** for up to one year while they are bargaining for a renewal.
    (3) and (4) A collective agreement may not be **terminated early** without consent of the Labour Relations Board.
    (5) Provision for **revision,** of any section of a collective agreement by mutual consent of the parties.

59. Notice of **desire to bargain** for a new collective agreement may be given by either party to the other, within 90 days before agreement ceases to operate.

60. Application of sections 17 to 36.

61. Requirements for **dissolution** of a council of certified trade unions.

TERMINATION OF BARGAINING RIGHTS

62. **Replacement** of one trade union by another, following certification.

63. (1) **Failure** of trade union **to make a collective agreement** within one year after its certification.
    (2) **Time restrictions** as to when an employee can apply to the Board that the trade union no longer represents the employees in the bargaining unit.
    (3) **Notice to employer** and to trade union.
    (4) **Evidence** of the wishes of the employees.
    (5) If 40% or more of the employees appear to have expressed a wish not to be represented by the trade union, provision for a **representation vote** among the employees in the bargaining unit.
    (6) **Number of employees** wishing not to be represented by the union.
    (7) **Number of employees** in the bargaining unit.
    (8) **No hearing** by Board required.
    (9) **Timing of vote** — within 5 business days after day on which the application is filed with the Board.
    (10) Provision for **secret representation vote.**
    (11) Sealing of **ballot box,** etc.
    (12) **Subsequent hearing** by Board, if necessary.
    (13) **Exception.**
    (14) Declaration of **termination** if more than 50% of the votes are against the trade union.
    (15) **Dismissal of application,** if 50% or less of the votes are against the trade union.
    (16) Dismissal of application, if **misconduct** by employer.

(17) Declaration of termination if trade union no longer wishes to represent the employees (called **abandonment**).

(18) **Declaration** by Board, automatically terminates a collective agreement.

64. (1) Termination where trade union has obtained a certificate by **fraud.**

(2) Non-application.

(3) Termination if **decertification** obtained by **fraud** and restoration of
previous trade union as bargaining agent.

(4) Non-application.

65. (1) Termination if trade union **fails to give employer written notice,**
within 60 days following certification, of its desire to bargain with a
view to making a collective agreement or if it fails to give notice to
bargain for a renewal of a collective agreement within the 90-day
period before the agreement ceases to operate.

66. Termination of bargaining rights after **voluntary recognition**, upon application by employee or trade union, during first year, on grounds of non-
representation at time of voluntary recognition.

TIMELINESS OF REPRESENTATION APPLICATIONS

67. (1) and (2) Application for certification or termination after **conciliation.**

(3) Application for certification or termination during a **lawful strike.**

SUCCESSOR RIGHTS

68. Board may declare that, by reason of a merger or amalgamation or a transfer of jurisdiction, a trade union **has** or **has not** acquired the rights,
privileges and duties under the Act, of its predecessor.

69. (1) **Definitions.**

(2) **Successor employer,** until the Board otherwise declares, is bound by
the collective agreement that already exists.

(3) same.

(4), (5) and (6) **Powers of Board.**

(7) **Notice to bargain.**

(8) Powers of Board before disposing of application.

(9) Where employer **not required to bargain.**

(10) Effect of **notice of declaration.**

(11) **Successor municipalities.**

(12) Power of Board to determine **whether a business has been sold.**

(13) **Duty of respondents.**

UNFAIR PRACTICES

70. **Employers,** etc., not to interfere with unions.

71. **Unions** not to interfere with employers' organizations.

72. **Employers** not to interfere with **employees' rights.**

73. (1) **Employers** not to interfere with **bargaining rights.**
    (2) **Trade unions** not to interfere with **bargaining rights.**

74. **Duty of fair representation** by a trade union of all employees in the bargaining unit.

75. **Duty of fair selection, referral,** etc. of persons to employment by a trade union.

76. No **intimidation** or **coercion** permitted by a trade union, employers, etc. with regard to union membership or other employee rights.

77. No authorization to **persuade** an employee, during working hours, to join or not join a trade union.

78. **Strike-breaking,** and strike-related misconduct **prohibited.**

79. (1) **No strikes** or **lockouts** permitted while collective agreement is in operation.
    (2) If no agreement, a **conciliation officer** or **mediator** must first make his or her report, and a time delay has elapsed.
    (3) **Mandatory strike vote** — "If a collective agreement is or has been in operation, no employee shall strike unless a strike vote is taken 30 days or less before the collective agreement expires or at any time after the agreement expires and more than 50 per cent of those voting vote in favour of a strike."
    (4) "**If no collective agreement** has been in operation, no employee shall strike unless a strike vote is taken on or after the day on which a conciliation officer is appointed and more than 50 per cent of those voting vote in favour of a strike."
    (5) **Construction industry** exempt from (3) and (4) above.
    (6) "No employee shall threaten an unlawful strike and no employer shall threaten an unlawful lock-out of an employee."
    (7) Strike or ratification vote to be **secret.**
    (8) All employees in a bargaining unit have the **right to vote.**
    (9) All those entitled to vote must be given the **opportunity to vote.**

80. (1) Employee is entitled to be **reinstated** after a lawful strike.
    (2) **Exceptions:** (a) no work of same or similar nature; (b) suspension of employer's operations.

81. **Unlawful strikes** prohibited.

LOCALS UNDER TRUSTEESHIP

INFORMATION

ENFORCEMENT

CONSTRUCTION INDUSTRY

PROVINCE-WIDE BARGAINING

INDEX